BEYOND BROADCASTING:
INTO THE CABLE AGE

TIMOTHY HOLLINS

BEYOND BROADCASTING: INTO THE CABLE AGE

Published for the Broadcasting Research Unit by
BFI Publishing
127 Charing Cross Road
London WC2H 0EA

First published 1984

Cover design by John Gibbs

British Library Cataloguing in Publication Data

Hollins, Timothy
Beyond broadcasting.
1. Cable television – Economic aspects
I. Title
384.55'563   HE8700.7.C6
ISBN 0-85170-148-5

Printed in England by Total Graphics Ltd., London

Contents

PREFACE ix

INTRODUCTION 1

PART ONE: THE CABLE DEBATE
1. What is cable? 9
2. Cable in the telecommunications context 20

PART TWO: CABLE IN BRITAIN –
        THE HISTORICAL AND POLITICAL BACKGROUND
3. Origins and development 35
4. The political debate 51

PART THREE: THE CANADIAN EXPERIENCE
5. Canada's cultural dilemma 83
6. Into the third phase 95

PART FOUR: THE UNITED STATES
7. The coming of cable 113
8. Cable systems – boom or bust 125
9. National basic services 144
10. Pay and pay-per-view 177
11. The local element 198
12. Enhanced and business uses 215
13. Cable and the American consumer 239
14. Cable and programme production 251
15. Cable, broadcasting and the cinema 261

PART FIVE: BRITISH PLANS AND PROSPECTS
16. The regulatory environment 275
17. Cable systems – plans and prospects 292
18. Cable services 308
19. The consequences for broadcasting 335
20. The cinema, film and production industries 346

CONCLUSION: INTO THE CABLE AGE 355

APPENDICES 363

INDEX 371

The Broadcasting Research Unit is an independent research body jointly funded by the BBC, the BFI, the Markle Foundation of New York and the IBA.

Acknowledgments

In the course of this study I have talked with many people in the United States, Canada and Britain. I should like to thank all who have given so freely of their time and knowledge in what is, after all, a highly commercial business.

Several organisations and individuals have allowed me to quote or make use of their own research. I am expecially grateful the Eurodata Foundation, the Paul Kagan organisation, Donaldson Lufkin and Jenrette, David Londoner of Wertheim Inc., the National Cable Television Association of America and Ralph Negrine.

Throughout my research I have had the invaluable assistance of the BFI Information Division and of my colleagues in the Broadcasting Research Unit, particularly Michael Tracey, Kirstie Laird and Olivia Stewart. I should also like to thank Tony Harwood, Richard Hoggart, John Howkins and especially Janet Morgan for reading and commenting on part or all of the typescript. Geoffrey Nowell-Smith has similarly shown himself to be editorially unflappable and ever helpful.

My deepest thanks must go to those who have provided essential moral support and kept me sane in an extremely hectic eighteen months. Jim Ballantyne, Jacqui Bedford, Sue Duncan, Catherine Ellen, Virginia Hennessy, Joan Ingram, David Morrison, Olivia Stewart and Kirstie Laird were all in this way instrumental in the book's completion. Above all I have had the constant encouragement and support of my family – my mother and father and my brother, Christopher, who has borne the brunt. Without them this book would be neither finished nor begun.

Preface

The issue of cable has enormous technical, economic, political and social complexities and implications. Yet so far there have been few attempts to present the debate in manageable and comprehensible terms for the interested layman. Nor, where there has been public discussion, has it gone much beyond futuristic and semi-utopian speculations on the one hand and Cassandra-like prophesies of doom on the other.

The Broadcasting Research Unit is giving high priority to assisting public discussion on cable and the other new technologies. In January 1984 we published the *Report of the Working Party on New Technologies*. We are now pleased to be able to publish a further major contribution, *Beyond Broadcasting: Into the Cable Age* by Timothy Hollins, prepared during his time as a Research Fellow with the BRU.

His book contains a vast amount of information on the technology, history, political background and practical implications of cable, as well as on developments in Canada and the United States and current plans and prospects in Britain. It is not a BRU position paper but is published as an aid to the necessary ensuing discussion. As such, it should be of value and interest not only to those who are closely involved in the cable revolution, but also, and more importantly, to all of us who are about to experience it.

RICHARD HOGGART
Chairman, BRU Panel

LIST OF ABBREVIATIONS

ABC   American Broadcasting Company
ACARD   Advisory Council for Applied Research and Development
ACSN   Appalachian Community Service Network
ACTT   Association of Cinematograph, Television and Allied Technicians
AFD   Associated Film Distributors
AGB   Audits of Great Britain
ATC   American Television and Communications
AT&T   American Telegraph and Telephone
BARB   Broadcasters' Audience Research Bureau
BBFC   British Board of Film Censors
BBG   Board of Broadcast Governors
BET   Black Entertainment Television
BT   British Telecom
CATV   Community Antenna Television
CBC   Canadian Broadcasting Corporation
CBN   Christian Broadcast Network
CBS   Columbia Broadcasting System
CHN   Cable Health Network
CNN   Cable News Network
CPRS   Central Policy Review Staff
CRTC   Canadian Radio-Television Commission (now Radio-Television and Telecommunications Commission)
CSL   Cable Sport and Leisure
C-Span   Cable Satellite Public Affairs Network
CTA   Cable Television Association (of Great Britain)
DBS   Direct Broadcasting by Satellite
DTS   Digital Termination Service
ECS   European Communications Satellite
EFT   Electronic Funds Transfer
ELRA   East Lansing Research Associates
ERG   Electronic Rentals Group
ESPN   Entertainment and Sports Programming Network
FCC   Federal Communications Commission
FNN   Financial News Network
HBO   Home Box Office
HTN   Home Theatre Network
IBA   Independent Broadcasting Authority
IPA   Institute of Practitioners in Advertising
IT   Information Technology
ITAP   Information Technology Advisory Panel
ITCA   Independent Television Companies' Association
ITV   Independent Television

KTVU   call sign of one American independent TV station
MATV   Master Antenna Television
MCA   Music Corporation of America
MDS   Multipoint Distribution Service
MPEAA   Motion Picture Exporters' Association of America
MSN   Modern Satellite Network
MSO   Multiple System Operator
MTV   Music Television
NBC   National Broadcasting Company
NCTA   National Cable Television Association (of America)
NERA   National Economic Research Associates
NTSC   National Television Standards Committee
OfTel   Office of Telecommunications
PABX   Private Automatic Branch Exchange
PAL   Phase Alternating Linear
PBS   Public Broadcasting Service
POEU   Post Office Engineering Union
PTL   Praise The Lord
PTT   Postal Telegraph and Telecommunications
RCA   Radio Corporation of America
RFP   Request For Proposals
SATV   Satellite Television
SBS   Satellite Business Systems
SIN   Spanish International Network
SMATV   Satellite Master Antenna Television
SNC   Satellite News Channel
SPN   Satellite Program Network
STV   Subscription Television
TBS   Turner Broadcasting System
TCI   TeleCommunications Inc.
TEG   Television Entertainment Group
TMC   The Movie Channel
TVEC   French Canadian regional pay-TV service
TVRO   Television Receive Only
TVS   TV South
UCP   United Cable Programmes
UHF   Ultra High Frequency
VCR   Video Cassette Recorder
VHF   Very High Frequency
WGN   ⎫
WOR   ⎬ Call signs of the three American superstations
WTBS   ⎭
ZDF   Zweites deutsches Fernsehen (West German second television channel)

INTRODUCTION:
The Cable Age

Rarely can an issue of such potentially far-reaching consequences for the nature of society, culture, politics and the economy have burst upon us with the rapidity which cable appears to have done. Before February 1982 few people in Britain had any inkling that cable was more than just another name for a telegram or a piece of wire. Now many believe that it will be the vanguard of a technological revolution, the nervous system of an information-centred society and a means by which the old limitations in the radio spectrum will be overcome, allowing a tremendous expansion in our communications capability. Television, for many their most important window on the world, is seen as becoming also a vital means of communicating with that world. Others are less enthusiastic; to them cable, particularly privately financed as the present government intends and with relatively light regulatory controls, could turn out to be a Gordian knot which, if mismanaged in its unravelling, will destroy rather than create jobs, give little stimulus to our electronics industries, quickly become technically outmoded, pull down all that is good in our present broadcasting system and prove culturally damaging and socially divisive.

Cable is a prosaic and earthbound word. But what it is concerned with is the electronic lifeblood of the modern world – information and communications. Indeed, rather like 'the press' the very lack of descriptiveness as to what it can do is an indication of its vast range of applications and of its potentially far-reaching impact. As Lord Whitelaw has said, this new technology could lead to 'the development of an infrastructure which will pave the way to the world of the future in which business and work may be undertaken in new and very different ways' (Parliamentary Debates (House of Lords), July 1983, col. 654). The idea that cable systems could form the nervous system of a new information-based society has undoubtedly been central to recent ministerial thinking about cable in Britain and, as we shall see later, primarily responsible for the present initiative.

Not surprisingly, however, it has been cable's capacity to increase the number of television channels available to the ordinary consumer which has most caught the public's attention and imagination, particularly since it is that part of the cable revolution which is most actively being promoted and developed in the United States and which has been most publicised here. As with cable itself opinions as to the future of broadcasting in a cabled world, and one in which video recorders and satellites also play their part, are sharply polarised. To many these new technologies promise to open new horizons in broadcasting, to extend our individual freedom of choice and to release the creative talents in our society from the constraints imposed by the existing regulatory structure of television. Cable, in this view, will allow the communication of visual information at a more personal level than hitherto, making possible a much greater degree of audience involvement in the programmes received. New outlets will give an opportunity for quite different types of programme, including truly local community television, and will permit greater specialisation of content so that minority interests will be served much more fully than before. The result will be a service which meets the needs of all and from which all will gain, an opinion which marries happily with those as to cable's economic benefits.

On the other side is the view that additional television channels will fatally fragment the audience and lead to an inevitable decline in programme standards. Competition both for audiences and for programmes will increase while the amount of money each television organisation has to spend on programming will fall. Foreign imported material and foreign influences upon home-produced programmes will swamp our broadcast cultural identity and true originality and creativity will be lost. An increase in the number of channels will thus paradoxically weaken the domestic programme production sector and result in reduced rather than greater programme choice.

Although cable's development is frequently justified in terms of its cultural benefits – choice, individual freedom, minority and community interests, etc. – few would deny that the primary motor forces behind the present activity, not just in Britain but in most developed nations, have been economic, technological and political. It is not surprising therefore, in a country where broadcasting has always been discussed in terms of cultural objectives and where broadcasting policy has been determined with such considerations uppermost, that a debate in which very different criteria are applied should be so vehemently contested. Britain is justly proud of its traditions of public service broadcasting which, despite undeniable faults and weaknesses, has produced a remarkable record of widely varied and high-quality programming.

Nevertheless, changes to the structure and philosophy of broadcasting seem now as inevitable as technological change itself, and whether public service broadcasting as we know it – the result of a sixty-year evolution – can survive seems increasingly uncertain. Our existing broadcasting institutions, despite everything still redolent of middle-class liberal democratic values, were born in a paternalistic age wedded to the ideals of duty and service. The BBC in its early Reithian years demonstrated this very clearly with its acknowledged sense of mission, its decidedly didactic commitment to educating the audience upwards to higher forms of culture and its belief in rationalism as the attainable and perfecting agent in democracy. Yet these years did see established the fundamentals of public service broadcasting, in particular a commitment to quality, to providing the same level of service to the entire country irrespective of geographical location or social and economic circumstance and to presenting issues impartially and in a balanced manner. During the late 50s and 60s the new competition from commercial television actually strengthened the public service concept as the BBC came to appreciate that true service meant breaking out from its essentially narrow and pyramidal view of culture and applying the principle of excellence to all the diverse cultural forms within society, from sport and light entertainment to current affairs and drama, in order to create a rounded broadcast menu. In this way the preferences of the audience, evident through its exercise of choice between channels, became a major factor in programming policy. Meanwhile, the limited character of the new competition made possible two financial precepts generally regarded as central to public service broadcasting – the notion firstly that no two broadcasting organisations should compete for the same source of revenue and secondly that, even within commercial television, the making of programmes should not be directly related to the revenues that can be raised from them. By these means the competitiveness of the duopoly has been held within certain limits, with each organisation seeking a wide audience but without sinking to the tactic of lowest common denominator programming. The result has been a compromise between the more traditional values of service, reflected in the BBC/IBA commitment to universality of reach and wide diversity of programming, and the recognition of the legitimate expectations and demands of the audience. It is this synthesis of service and satisfaction, of tempered competition, which has shaped the character of British broadcasting since the mid-50s.

Now cable, privately financed and operated and market led, promises to take the process yet one stage further, greatly increasing the number of competitors and outlets, significantly reducing the regulatory rules of the game, turning the relationship of producer and consumer more nearly into one of direct commercial transaction and relating the worth of a programme much more directly to the audience it attracts and revenue it earns. Behind these practical changes lie three major shifts in broadcasting philosophy: firstly, an implicit rejection of the notion of universality of service and an acceptance of different geographical and social circumstances as a factor in what each person will be able to receive; secondly, a belief in the capacity of the market to determine consumer demand more accurately than the programme planners of the BBC and IBA; and thirdly, a confidence in the market's ability, through the new outlet of cable, to reflect the plurality of our society – the enormous diversity of opinions, interests and cultures – more fully than the existing regulated and physically restricted system. If these beliefs prove justified, then public service broadcasting may turn out to have been no more than a cultural and institutional red herring in the search for a communications structure which will truly meet the needs and reflect the pluralism of a democratic society. If not, then it may before long be seen as a brief interlude of reason and sense in a chaos of media commercialism, bias and opportunism.

The cable revolution, if such it is, is therefore every bit as much about changing attitudes towards broadcasting as about an increase in the number of channels which it is technically possible to provide. Over the past sixty years 'broadcasting' in its public service form has come to mean far more than simply casting a message abroad, so that today we think of it rather in relation to the nature of the service we receive than to the physical activity itself. Consequently it is the changes as much to the character of the television service as to the technology of the transmission system which mean that we are about to go 'beyond broadcasting'.

The White Paper on Cable Systems and Services published in April 1983 (Cmnd 8866), and the cable bill which has been presented to Parliament as a result, have now laid down the ground rules by which cable in Britain will be developed during the next few years. The challenge, as William Whitelaw defined it while still Home Secretary, is 'to catch the tide of technical development while at the same time securing an orderly revolution' (Speech to the Parliamentary Information Technology Committee, 10 June 1982). Yet as we venture towards the cable age it is very obvious that we are not at all sure how long it will take to get there, how many of us will arrive, nor what it will be like when we do. There are enormous areas of uncertainty and disagreement, and many institutions and individuals may well come to regret the changes that cable will bring. As the White Paper admits, 'Today the pace of change has become such that few can with any confidence predict what tomorrow may hold' *(The Development of Cable Systems and Services,* Cmnd 8866, HMSO April 1983, para. 2).

4

This book, therefore, is not an attempt to predict the future. Nor does it particularly endorse one or other of the opposing scenarios described above. The issues raised by cable are so complex, the areas of industry, society and culture touched by it so many and the economics so uncertain that it would be naive to believe wholeheartedly either in the blue sky promises of one camp or the dark cloud forebodings of the other. The intention of this book is rather to describe the debate and place it in the context of actual experience and developments. Part One examines the wider telecommunications background and cable's place within it. It considers the technological, social and commercial pressures mediating cable's growth and the underlying political motivations. In Part Two (Chapters 3-4) the surprisingly long history of cable broadcasting in Britain is chronicled, from the late 19th century up to 1982, taking in the various experiments in cable programming and looking particularly at the debate of the last two years.

North America provides two contrasting examples of cable under a private enterprise system. Part Three (Chapters 5-6) examines the Canadian experience of a private industry which has nevertheless been subjected to considerable government regulation in an effort to control the economic and cultural effects of having the United States as an immediate neighbour. Canada is one of the most extensively cabled countries in the world, and the industry's ability to relay the signals of the American networks has made it a major battleground in Canada's fight for a distinct cultural identity. Meanwhile the United States has led the current cable revolution and is the most frequently cited example of cable at its best and its worst. Developments in the USA have undoubtedly been of major importance in the British debate, so that even if the situations are not wholly comparable this prime instance of privately financed and operated cable at its most advanced and least regulated deserves detailed analysis. Nowhere in the world have conditions for the cable industry been more favourable in recent years than in the United States – although what is good for the industry is far from necessarily good for society. The problems it has faced and the solutions it has found may therefore offer some lessons for the budding industry here. In an extensive Part Four (Chapters 7–15) the many aspects of cable in America are analysed. In the final Part Five the regulatory approach to be taken in Britain will be examined and the prospects and likely next steps considered.

NOTE

Cable is a fast moving subject. The addendum to the Conclusion at the end of this book contains updated information as of 1 March 1984, relevant to Chapters 6, 10 and 18.

PART ONE
The Cable Debate

1 What is Cable?

Electromagnetic communication in the 20th century has taken two largely distinct forms, distinguished by both technique and function. The first – communication between individuals through the transmission of an electrical current along a wire – is the telephone system; the second – communication from one or a few individuals to a mass and undifferentiated audience over the radio airwaves – is broadcasting as we know it. Wire for interpersonal conversation, radio for casting a message abroad, these have been the principal trends, the most economical ways of communicating for such purposes, in terms both of financial resources and of the limited radio spectrum.

Nevertheless, in certain circumstances efficiency and comprehensiveness of service have dictated an alternative approach. For mobile use, interpersonal communication has had to eat into the increasingly overburdened radio waves. The needs of ship to shore, air to land, taxis, emergency services and defence have grown steadily and recently have been added to by car telephones and citizens' band. Indeed, the latest review of how the airwaves are allocated, the Merriman Report in 1982, recommended that space previously dedicated to the broadcasting of 405-line television be given over from 1984 to mobile radio.

Conversely, in areas of poor radio reception, or where the airwaves are already oversubscribed, broadcast communication by wire has been found to be a sensible solution to radio transmission's inadequacies. Cable overcomes the problem of a limited spectrum by physically containing the signals transmitted. However, as a mass distribution method it has generally been thought of as no more than complementary to off-air broadcasting, simply because cable contains the audience as effectively as the signal, limiting it to those who are within its reach and actually connected. In some senses there has been a contradiction inherent in the term 'cable broadcasting'.

We have already seen that the cable revolution entails not only technological change but also changing attitudes towards broadcasting. Equally important is the reassessment of cable's potential which has taken place, the perception of opportunities where once limitations were seen. The cable revolution in large part consists of the recognition that cable's physically restricted reach can be turned to advantage in a number of ways. Firstly, it permits many more channels to be transmitted than is possible over the air. No longer need the capacity of our principal system of mass communication be determined by the radio-transmitting properties of the atmosphere.

Secondly, cable allows a greater degree of control to be exercised over reception than hitherto. Radio transmission is extremely effective at giving the widest possible access to what is transmitted, but its very efficiency renders impracticable the normal laws of sale and supply. Unlike other commodities, programmes cannot be sold – either individually or packaged into channels – to consumers in a straight commercial transaction. Until recently it has been almost impossible to prevent anyone with a radio or television set from receiving whatever programmes have been transmitted, even if they have not contributed towards the cost of providing them. This has restricted television and radio to universal forms of financing, namely advertising and the national licence fee (or in some countries direct government grant from taxation), which have been unable to discriminate between how much different individuals actually watch or listen. At the same time, such methods of raising revenue have mediated a particular form of broad appeal service which may contain something for most tastes but which cannot hope to provide a continuously satisfying diet for any. Nor have they always proved effective in ensuring that consumers of programmes contribute anything to what they watch; in 1983 the BBC lost some £55 million in revenue from licence-fee dodgers.

A further consequence of what is effectively a mandatory levy on every television user is to give broadcasting an enormous economic advantage over other forms of leisure and cultural activity which depend entirely upon market forces for their funding. Britain's four television channels cost the average viewer under four pence an hour in licence fees and advertising expenditure passed on to consumers in the price of goods. As such they represent extremely cheap but good value entertainment which there is an automatic incentive to watch, both because it is inexpensive and because it has nevertheless had to be paid for. There is correspondingly less incentive to pay for or use entertainment services which have to charge their more restricted consumers the full market price. Moreover, as the dominant medium of entertainment and culture in our age, and with the greatest revenue, broadcasting is also the principal patron of entertainers and artists, of actors, musicians, journalists, writers, sportsmen, comedians and other performers. As such it has enormous potential power over the artistic and creative communities and over what forms of culture and entertainment receive its largesse.

10

Broadcasting, simply because it is universally available, has therefore created significant distortions in the cultural market-place. Public service broadcasters argue that it is precisely because they have been divorced from the market that they have been able to cater for minority tastes which the market could not have satisfied. Those who favour a market approach counter with the view that many minorities, both of viewers and within the creative community, remain unserved by a necessarily limited service. The market, they argue, works effectively in other areas of the economy in determining proper levels of supply and demand. Now cable reestablishes the physical link between programme provider and consumer which makes a direct commercial relationship possible even in broadcasting, since programmes can be directed only to those who have paid to receive them. Cable effectively removes the technical and hence economic and moral justifications for differentiating in methods of payment between broadcasting, alternative forms of entertainment and other consumer goods.

The second perceived opportunity which cable offers, therefore, at least where the cable revolution is to be market-financed and led, is that it reintroduces the laws of supply and demand to broadcast communication. This is seen to benefit both providers of programmes and other forms of entertainment, who can now sell them in fair competition at their true market value, and consumers, who can at last demonstrate exactly their preferences in entertainment, information and the entire audio-visual culture of television.

The third and perhaps most important advantage to be seen in cable is that physical interconnection of sender and receiver permits an end to the technical differentiation between person-to-person and mass communication. Cable, if structured correctly, allows every variant of electromagnetic communication – between individuals, from the few to the many and from the many back to the few. It enables the consumer to respond to the services with which he or she is supplied. At a minimal level this may mean simply purchasing access to a particular programme transmitted to whoever wishes to pay for it; at a more complex stage it may involve becoming an active participant in the communication, be it a programme, individual conversation or the transfer of data. Cable, in other words, has the theoretical potential to remove yet another technical determinant of the way we communicate, the artificial alignment of form and function which was described at the beginning of this chapter. The long-term implications of such a development are almost too huge to comprehend. Yet, as we shall see in the next chapter, changes of this kind are already taking place in the broader telecommunications field.

As with all technology, cable's importance lies not in its mechanics but in how it is used. Nevertheless it is useful to understand something of the technology involved as well as of the terminology which has arisen to describe it. Indeed the question of which type of cable technology should be used in Britain has itself been a major area of debate.

Cable systems are divided according to size and nature into two broad categories. *Master Antenna Television* systems (MATV) are those which provide services to the dwellings within an individual building such as a block of flats or, in certain cases, to a housing estate or similar tightly defined group of houses. Recent interest, however, has been centred on the much larger *Community Antenna Television* systems (CATV) in which one cable system serves an entire town or major suburb and where the large number of homes involved suggests the possibility of doing more than just relaying existing off-air signals. The operations centre of such a system is the *headend*. This incorporates (or receives signals from) the broadcast receiving aerials, satellite receiving dishes and studios for local television production. Other signals may come in via trunk landlines or microwave transmission. The signals received by or produced at the headend are processed, amplified and then transmitted to subscribers through the cable system itself.

The concept of *bandwidth* is an important one in attempting to understand the technical arguments behind cable. The greater the bandwidth of a cable the more information it can carry at any moment. The more complex the information which needs to be carried the greater the bandwidth necessary to transmit it. A telex, telephone or audio signal is not particularly complex and so requires a relatively narrow bandwidth (up to 3 kiloherz – that is 3,000 cycles per second). The considerably more complex information contained in a moving television picture signal, however, requires a much wider bandwidth of 8 megaherz (8 million cycles/second) and hence a cable with a greater capacity. Furthermore the current analogue methods of signal transmission may gradually give way to digital forms which, despite their many advantages for ease of switching and reduced error rates, do consume a greater bandwidth for the same amount of information. Transmitted digitally a standard telephone call has a rate of 64 kilobits per second (one kilobit = 1000 'bits' or units of information). Television pictures require a cable capable of carrying a minimum 100 megabits per second.

Most of the existing CATV systems in Britain employ high frequency multi-pair copper cable. The comparatively narrow bandwidth of the high frequency range means that such systems have a limited capacity and are normally designed to carry no more than four to six television channels. As we shall see later we are here paying the penalty for being pioneers in the field. Almost all other systems throughout the world use *copper coaxial cable* which, with *amplifiers* or repeaters at regular intervals to boost the signal, has a much higher bandwidth and thus a larger capacity. In the United States the most recent systems working up to 450 mhz in the UHF band can carry fifty-four video channels on one cable, although the higher the operating frequency the more frequent and complex must be the amplifiers, pushing up the cost. In Britain more stringent technical requirements will limit coaxial capacity to about thirty channels. High-capacity cable systems of this kind are known as *broadband*, as opposed to the narrowband telephone network and multipair cable systems.

Coaxial technology is still developing and in the USA even higher capacities are being talked about. Increasing interest, however, is now being shown in *optic-fibre cable*. This consists of micro-thin glass or even plastic fibres, barely thicker than a human hair and able to transmit light signals with little distortion by using the principle of total internal reflection. The signal to be transmitted is converted at one end of the cable into a series of extremely rapid pulses of light by tiny solid-state lasers or light-emitting diodes, some capable of being switched on and off or of varying their intensity up to 500 million times each second. This extremely complex system of light pulses, allowing a large amount of information to be transmitted, is picked up at the far end by a photodiode and reconverted into an electrical signal for the benefit of a standard receiver. Different types of optic fibre vary in capacity acccording to their purity and core size, with the latest monomode fibres being so pure and narrow as to be able to carry an unamplified signal some 60-100 kilometres without excessive distortion. Indeed, at present capacity is determined more by the equipment at each end than by the fibre itself. Each fibre is so thin that an optic cable with over 100 strands sheathed in a protective casing would be very much smaller than a coaxial cable of a quarter of the capacity. Moreover the technology is still advancing rapidly, so that it will shortly be possible to separate out many more signals from each fibre. The first cable systems to use optic fibres for connecting each home to the trunk line use a relatively large core fibre and analogue rather than digital transmission to carry one to four video channels per fibre. Trunk telecommunications lines will use monomode fibres and digital signals.

Depending on the type and purity of the fibre, optic cable suffers much less from signal loss with distance (attenuation) and distortion than coaxial. Indeed, each amplifier in the latter introduces further distortions, so that in practice there is a limit to the acceptable distance between headend and receiver. The minimal attenuation of optic fibres, by contrast, is of particular value for long-distance trunk cables, though less so in area cable systems. Moreover optical signals, when transmitted digitally, do not suffer from distortion at each amplification; nor unlike coaxial are they susceptible to electrical interference or 'crosstalk' between adjacent cables. Coaxial cable systems have a related disadvantage in that they in their turn can cause interference to services utilising the radio frequency spectrum, particularly if installed above ground. Furthermore, they are relatively easy to tap into, with consequent risk to the security of the information carried, as well as having the standard spark and fire risks of any equipment carrying an electrical current. By contrast, optic fibres are extremely difficult to tap and represent much less of a fire hazard. They are also very light, small and manageable, making them less unsightly if strung on telegraph poles and much easier to thread through already crowded ducts or around an already constructed building.

The future does seem to lie with optic fibres and already a very few cable systems are being built using this new technology. British Telecom has a small 18-home optic fibre experiment in Milton Keynes. However there are disadvantages. The connection of fibres requires extremely precise alignment, which is still difficult in field conditions and costly of time and skilled manpower, particularly on local cable systems with the large number of connections required. Moreover, in such circumstances optic fibre's attenuation advantages are largely wasted. Indeed the process of converting the electrical signal to light and the light back into an electrical signal itself introduces significant distortions, particularly in the case of analogue signals. Above all, whilst such fibres are potentially much cheaper than large copper cables, the associated transmitting and receiving opto-electronic equipment still raises the price in most circumstances above that for a coaxial system, although the overall cost will begin to fall as a result of mass production. For these reasons optic fibres seem certain to be introduced gradually, and then as part of a hybrid optic/coaxial system. Early use could well be for the relatively short local 'drop' cables into each home, using comparatively big diameter, simply aligned fibres, not involving amplification or large numbers of connections and carrying analogue signals. The advantage here is that this part of the system is most likely to be above ground and hence prone to receive and cause interference. In due course the trunk lines will also be made of optic fibres, but of the currently more costly, purer and more difficult to connect monomode variety, carrying digital transmissions.

Even more important than the question of what type of cable to use is that of the best system structure. Although a large number of variations are possible the two which are most debated are *tree and branch* and *switched star*. In the first, which has dominated system architecture until now, signals are transmitted along a trunk cable which at intervals has branches and sub-branches splitting off it, although each has the same capacity as the original trunk. Thus all the services transmitted are available at all points of the cable, with each subscriber using a *converter* placed between the cable and the television set to select the frequency of the service required. Since all signals are available on all parts of the cable, discretionary (pay) channels, central to cable's future development, have to be scrambled. Converters therefore generally also contain a descrambler, or *decoder*, which is activated only in those homes which subscribe to the pay service. In the latest systems each decoder on the system can be individually 'addressed' by a signal transmitted from the headend. In this way the cable operator can add or remove services available to individual subscribers, depending on whether or not they have paid for them. Such systems are *addressable*, with the more complex *two-way addressable* or *interactive* variety allowing each subscriber to send simple individual messages back to the headend – for example expressing the desire to watch and agreement to pay for a particular programme or channel.

The cable network of a tree and branch system is relatively simple, with the complex and costly channel selection and decoding equipment being installed in the subscriber's domestic terminal. This is placed in the home only when he or she decides to subscribe, and there may well be a connection charge plus a deposit which helps to offset the capital cost of the equipment. The initial capital cost to the cable provider is thus limited to the cost of laying the cable itself and building the headend, domestic terminals being installed only as and where they are required with the subscriber helping to defray the expense. Yet, while this is obviously an advantage to the operator when building a system, the presence of expensive converter/decoders in the home makes access for maintenance difficult, and misuse, tampering and theft by the subscriber much more likely.

Tree and branch systems are well established and the technology is readily available. The latter, however, is largely American and there would be few opportunities for British industry to develop an export business. Modern tree and branch systems are capable of providing almost all the two-way services commonly proposed but generally have limited upstream capacity, so that there may be restrictions and delays if too many subscribers wish to use such interactive facilities at the same time. Because the structure differs radically from that of a telephone system it is not suited to interconnecting subscribers or for such advanced uses as a videophone service. Its big advantages therefore are the immediate ones of availability and cost, whilst its disadvantages are those of limited future potential.

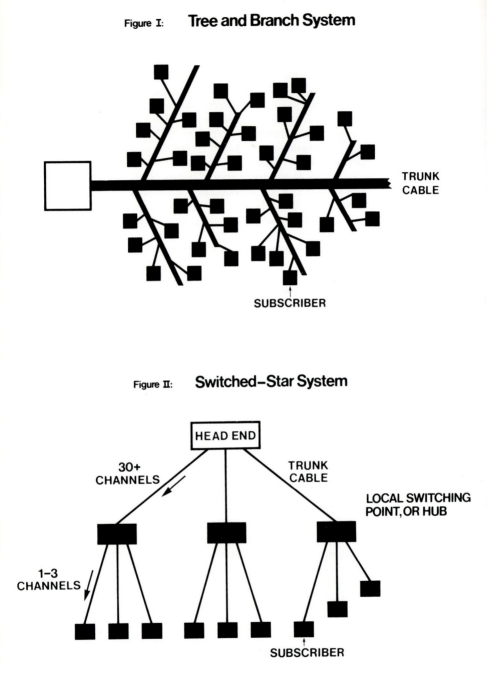

Figure I: **Tree and Branch System**

TRUNK CABLE

SUBSCRIBER

Figure II: **Switched–Star System**

HEAD END

30+ CHANNELS

TRUNK CABLE

LOCAL SWITCHING POINT, OR HUB

1–3 CHANNELS

SUBSCRIBER

Much more flexible and adaptable to future needs is the switched-star system. In this, trunk lines distribute signals from the headend to a number of local *switching points*. From these individual home drops radiate out to subscribers in a star shape, with each switching point, *hub* or node serving anything from twelve to several hundred houses. The home drop cables have a much smaller capacity (three to four video channels) than the trunk, on the principle that at any one time each household will wish to watch or use only a very few of the channels on the system. When the subscriber wishes to see a particular channel he or she uses a relatively simple and cheap channel selector to send a signal to the local switching point, which then switches the requested service along the subscriber's own cable.

Such a system has many advantages. Almost all the complex and expensive converter/switching equipment is placed outside the home and concentrated at the switching point, thereby making access and maintenance much easier and preventing tampering. Moreover, because all signals are not available at all points of the cable, pay services do not need to be scrambled, simplifying the system and improving signal quality. Instead, the switching point refuses to direct particular channels to subscribers who have not paid for them. Clearly this also makes unauthorised theft of signals very much more difficult, as well as increasing the security of return messages from individual subscribers to the headend. For such two-way services as telebanking and shopping this is a major advantage. Unlike tree and branch, switched-star systems include interactivity as an integral feature; upstream capacity can be much greater, while the potential even exists to interconnect subscribers and to develop a videophone service. This, however, is generally regarded as a long term consideration. The structure is better suited than tree and branch to utilising optic fibres, although it can equally readily be constructed of coaxial. Where this is the case, the smaller capacity home drop cables are much less likely to cause interference than the high bandwidth ones of a tree and branch system.

Britain is well placed in the research and development of switched systems, but as yet they are an unknown quantity. Few have so far been built and the technology will not be commercially available before late 1984. Moreover, a much larger proportion of the capital cost is in the system itself rather than the domestic terminals and so must be expended before a single subscriber is taken on to provide some return. Indeed, some of this initial investment will necessarily be wasted, since the operator must have sufficient switching capacity in each hub to cope with all the surrounding houses whether they decide to subscribe immediately, in a few years' time or never. For these various reasons switched systems are currently significantly more expensive than tree and branch, although the higher the proportion of homes that subscribe the more comparable they become. Nor are they yet so readily available.

Tree and branch and switched star are the two principal configurations, but inevitably there are variations. One in particular should be mentioned, since it seems to offer a bridge between the two. This is the hybrid star-structured switchless system. Laid out as a switched-star system, it differs in that the local hub consists simply of ordinary taps rather than switches, with the home drop carrying the full system capacity to each subscriber's terminal. The system operates exactly as a standard tree and branch but has the potential in due course to be upgraded to switched star by the installation of switches at the local distribution point.

THE PHASES AND FUNCTIONS OF CABLE

Cable technology has advanced extremely rapidly in the last ten years and will no doubt continue to do so. This remains, however, just part of a much longer term development. Indeed, cable's growth may be seen in four stages, each characterised not so much by the technology used as by one or a number of the medium's functions. In their *first phase* of development cable systems were evolved to meet three basic needs – to allow the reception of broadcast signals in areas not covered at all by existing transmitters, to improve reception in regions where reception remained poor, and to reduce the number of unsightly roof-top aerials, particularly in new towns and housing estates. Relatively few cable operations around the world are today confined to these three tasks, but Britain's cable industry has been one such.

In North America and certain European countries, however, the way ahead was early on seen to lie in the provision of further services. The *second phase* of cable's growth, therefore, was to allow the reception in areas already served by a television station of signals from other stations too far away to be picked up by ordinary domestic aerials, thereby increasing the channels available to subscribers and extending their choice. With such an added service to offer, cable systems could break out of regions with reception problems and into more heavily populated and hence more lucrative markets. In the United States, for example, this meant predominantly the small to medium-sized towns which might be large enough to support a single television station carrying one of the American networks – say ABC – but not to sustain a second, third or fourth for CBS, NBC and independent programming.

The importation of distant signals was the first of cable's 'value-added' services to make an appearance and was responsible for the second and longest stage of its growth. It was particularly likely to

18

develop where the local economy was unable to afford more than minimum broadcast facilities but where there was an adjacent region with a much richer economy and, in the case of trans-border importation, a common language. The same conditions applied whether signals were being imported from a major American or Canadian city into a small town, or whether they were coming from France and Germany and being imported into Switzerland, Belgium and Luxembourg. Perhaps the best example of this second stage is provided by Canada where, as a consequence, over half of all homes with television now receive their programmes through a cable.

Cable's *third phase* is the result of its ability, given spare channel capacity on the wire, to provide programmes not available at all on broadcast television. They range from local community channels to non-stop film services and can be financed in a number of ways – out of the basic monthly subscription which all cable subscribers pay to receive the service, from advertising on the cable channel, from an additional discretionary subscription (pay-TV), or from a combination of these sources. Services are generally tiered, with broadcast relays, advertiser-supported and community channels being provided as part of the 'basic' service, and additional discretionary tiers carrying the generally more attractive pay channels, particularly films.

Such 'cable origination' services began to play a major role in the growth of cable, particularly in the United States, during the mid-70s, and today some cable systems there offer subscribers a choice of over fifty entertainment channels. More limited programming operations are in progress in Canada, Finland, Switzerland and Britain, whilst a number of countries have small community cable channel trials. However, as we have seen, this third phase is widely regarded as merely the prelude to an altogether larger shift in the very structure of telecommunications. For the *fourth stage* of cable, as yet hardly started, is the point at which the distribution of television signals becomes just one of a wide range of functions which cable systems can undertake, ranging from home security and fire alarms to home banking and shopping, data transfer, electronic mail, energy monitoring and eventually person-to-person voice and videophone facilities.

2 Cable in the Telecommunications Context

Throughout the world today governments, telecommunications organisations, media conglomerates and the cable and electronics industries are preparing for the third and fourth phases of cable. The forces underlying this activity are numerous and complex, encompassing technological, social, commercial and political pressures. Television is being transformed not just because new technologies have become available but also because developments in the structures of industry and commerce, in the nature of work, the mobility of society and the prevailing philosophy of the western world (the philosophy of individualism through personal choice) are combining with and complementing the increased telecommunications capacity of the new systems. As Anthony Smith has commented:

> What happened in the late 1970s was a sudden increase in the potency of telecommunications and in the computing capacity of society that has made it possible for us to reap a whole series of benefits that were impossible when the same technical possibilities existed on a smaller scale. The present 'revolution', if such it is, is one of investment rather than technological innovation, of transformation of scale more than of technological horizon (Anthony Smith, 'Information technology and the myth of abundance', *InterMedia*, January 1983, p.35).

It is important from the outset to recognise that the promised changes to the nature of television as entertainment represent just one phase of cable's growth, and that in its turn cable is just one actor on an altogether larger telecommunications stage. Much of the technology of broadband cable has been available for many years, but it is only under the stimulus of recent developments in satellites, integrated circuitry and computing that it has begun to reveal its full potential. Now it is one of the technologies which seem set to pull down the old divisions between different methods and hence forms of communication.

Increasingly the future is seen in terms of 'information transfer', with an ever more blurred distinction between the various categories of information involved – television and radio programmes, telephone conversations, digitised computer data and videotext information. To take an obvious example, are the BBC and ITV teletext services and British Telecom's Prestel respectively television and telephone services, or should they be regarded as publishing, or something completely new? Where previously the nature of the information transaction also largely determined the transmission system and transmitting agency (wired telephone system and company/PTT for personal point-to-point conversation, broadcasting system and organisation for general programme distribution, etc.), this is less and less the case. Today a television signal may pass through the hands not only of the broadcaster but also of the national PTT or a satellite carrier before being received by a cable system operator for distribution to the home. Two separate wired networks and some form of over-the-air transmission may be involved. Likewise, telephone conversations may make use of microwave and satellite systems. National PTTs are operating cable television systems in France, Germany, Britain and elsewhere, whilst in the United States and now Britain rival companies are able to provide telephone services. Meanwhile, the invention of cellular radio is promising effectively to expand airwave capacity to the point where it may play an integral part in a person-to-person telecommunications network. The technologies and operating organisations of communication are no longer mutually exclusive but can be brought together to meet new requirements.

Just as the technologies and structures of telecommunications are changing, so are the demands upon them. Since the late 1940s telecommunications traffic, both national and international, has seen phenomenal growth. Using trunk landlines and extensive microwave relay networks, the monopoly telecommunications authorities in each country have sought to cope with the communication needs of an ever more scattered and mobile society – the fragmented family, international transactions and increasingly the dispersed business operations of individual companies. Manufacturing industry has steadily moved away from the nineteenth-century centralised factory model, whilst retail chains and banking outlets have spread across each country and across the world. In the United States, while the number of banking organisations remained constant between 1946 and 1978 at some 14,000, the number of their affiliated branches rose tenfold from 4,000 to 38,308. International financiers, insurance companies, computer service industries, electronics manufacturers, hotel chains, airlines and others all have come to depend upon fast and efficient telecommunications operations to maintain routine contact and control over dispersed enterprises. Texas Instruments, the diversified microprocessor and electronics company, has fifty major plants in nineteen countries. The international finance services group, Citicorp, maintains over 2,300 branches in ninety-four countries. Its business depends on its ability to supply thousands of clients with detailed financial information and transactional services at high speed by means of data terminals in each customer's office. Communications within and between organisations and within and between nations has become one of the biggest and fastest growing businesses. Table 1 shows the increasing demands upon the British public telephone system since 1950, although even this excludes the ever larger number of organisations such as ICI and British Steel who have networks permanently leased from British Telecom:

TABLE I

Number of originated effective telephone calls, UK, 1950-82
(Source: British Telecom Statistics, 1982)

Year	Local (millions)	Trunk (millions)	Total (millions)	Continental	Intercontinental
			Voice and Data		
1950	2,940	235	3,175	1	–
1960	3,900	387	4,287	2.8	179,000
1970	8,270	1,352	9,622	14.1	1,600,000
1980	16,000	3,257	19,857	75.2	31,045,000
1982	17,369	3,446	20,806	86.3	45,806,000

Closely connected to these mounting telecommunications requirements has been the tremendous growth of computers and computer services since the mid-50s. As the processing and storage capacity of computers has grown, so has the need for high-capacity transmission systems for the transfer of data. By 1979 there were already 33 million data transactions annually between computer and remote terminals within the UK, and this had more than doubled to 74 million by 1983. The maintenance of complex information networks linking computers, data stores and remote terminals has become a crucial element of modern commerce. The Prudential Life Assurance Company, for example, depends upon a network of 8,500 terminals to provide marketing services, transactional processing and communications to nearly 700 field offices around the United States. In

Britain over 40,000 remote terminals were in operation by 1983. Similarly estimates by the Eurodata Foundation indicate that there were 1.1 million data communication terminals in western Europe by 1981 and that this figure should have nearly quadrupled by 1987. In 1979 data communication between computers was worth some $2 billion to the West European PTTs and should have increased to $8 billion by 1986. Other non-voice traffic – text services, facsimile, teletext, teleconferencing, electronic mail, etc. – should bring the total value for the European market for computing and non-voice communications in the latter year to $20 billion.

The growth of the information industry is reflected in the remarkable expansion of the labour force which is directly involved in handling information or in manufacturing the equipment used in its distribution. In Britain the information sector, which made up barely 10 per cent of the workforce at the beginning of the 20th century, now constitutes some 45 per cent. It includes the obvious categories of journalists, librarians, broadcasters, postal workers, printers and teachers, as well as such less apparent ones as filing clerks, the huge army of secretaries, managers, computer programmers, artists, designers, lawyers, scientists and factory workers involved in making television sets, telephone systems, computers and similar information hardware. What is being created is an information society, where the information-related workforce and the proportion of gross national product that goes to the information and service sectors are greater than in the manufacturing industries which have traditionally been the foundations of the economy. While the latter struggle for survival, it is the computing, telecommunications and information technology industries which have shown the most spectacular growth. Information has become a most valuable commodity and information transfer a major expense for most businesses. Any means of improving transactional efficiency and reducing costs are therefore eagerly sought.

One way to achieve these goals, inevitably, is seen as being to move away from paper-based information systems and into electronic, with consequent savings in time and in the size of the information-handling workforce. Another direction being taken, for example in the United States and Britain, is to introduce a competitive element into the so far monopolistic field of telecommunications carriage. Telecommunications has traditionally been a highly regulated business, monopolised in each country either by a national PTT, such as British Telecom or the West German Bundespost, or by a state-regulated but privately operated organisation, such as the American giant, AT & T. In the last few years, however, a number of deregulatory moves, stimulated by the demands of major telecommunications users and by pressure from electronics industries and others anxious to become involved in such a tremendous growth area, have opened the way for new ventures and new ideas. The increasing traffic in data between computer and computer and between different units of the same company has raised the question of why the means of communication should remain the monopolistic preserve of strictly regulated quasi-public utility organisations, organisations whose services, in any case, are not yet particularly well adapted to data as opposed to voice transmission. Would not competition increase efficiency and reduce costs for these major users?

In the United States AT & T's monopoly was broken in 1969 when the Federal Communications Commission (FCC), which regulates telecommunications, granted MCI Communications permission to provide rival long distance services between St Louis and Chicago. Today, there are some 5-600 similar long distance telecommunications carrier organisations, although AT & T remains predominant. In Britain the process is now just starting, with a Conservative government supporting the view that a single monopoly service cannot and should not supply the full range of services required in an increasingly information-based society. With the British Telecommunications Act of October 1981, British Telecom's monopoly of long-distance business communications carriage has been broken and the independent Mercury consortium, backed by BP, Cable and Wireless and Barclays Merchant Bank, given permission to offer similar services. Now the Government is in the act of privatising BT itself and has already opened up the telephone hardware market to commercial competition.

A further and crucial stimulus to the telecommunications field has been provided by the development of communications satellites, the first of which, Echo I (experimental), was launched by the United States in 1960. In 1963 the first of the truly practicable communications satellites appeared, when Syncom II was successfully placed in 'geostationary orbit' 22,300 miles above the earth, its speed matching the earth's rotation and hence its position relative to the world below remaining constant. Dishes on the ground aimed permanently at one single point in the sky could transmit signals to the satellite, which would amplify and translate them to a different frequency, then retransmit them to other earth stations. Satellites, it appeared, could make terrestrial technologies obsolete, replacing transatlantic cables and substituting domestically for microwave relays and trunk telecommunication landlines. The first satellites were used purely for international communications, however, and it was not until the early 70s that domestic communications satellites were pioneered in Canada and the USA. In the intervening years satellite technology was continually developing, strengthening the power of the retransmission signal, improving the receptiveness of the ground dishes, extending the frequencies which could be utilised and thereby expanding both a satellite's capacity and the geographical coverage of its beams. In particular the 'C' band (4-6 gigaherz) was made available for commercial use, and it is this band which is currently used by all satellite delivered cable channels in the United States, as well as for telecommunications purposes all over the world. More recently the 'Ku' band (11-14 ghz) has been opened up, and the signal strengths required in this instance make possible for the first time reception by small dishes of less than one metre diameter. It is this development which will allow direct broadcasting by satellite (DBS) to individual homes. Already there is talk of exploiting the 'Ka' band (22.5-23 ghz) by the mid 1990s, permitting a further expansion of satellite services.

Yet, far from making landline and microwave relay systems redundant, it was soon realised that satellites needed such terrestrial technologies to carry the signals transmitted and received by the large earth-based dishes to and from their eventual destinations. As satellite capacity has increased, together with the amount of telecommunications traffic, so there has been a concomitant growth in the demand for efficient and high capacity land distribution systems, a demand which traditional telephone technology has been increasingly unable to meet. For the purposes of television transmission current broadcasting techniques are equally quite unable to match each satellite's capacity to receive and transmit up to 24 television signals simultaneously, in addition to further radio signals and other data. By contrast the capacities of satellites and modern cable systems are well matched. As telecommunications demands of all types – voice, video and data – have increased, so has the need for high capacity, 'broadband' networks to handle this greater flow.

In the United States the domestic communications satellite is ideally suited to the new age, and for long-distance communications is economically competitive against microwave and landline. Deregulation of terrestrial common carrier services since 1969 was matched in 1972 when, under Nixon's Republican administration, the FCC instituted an 'open skies' policy permitting commercial companies to own and operate domestic satellites (domsats). Given this opportunity, a number of major interests were quick to enter the field. In 1973 the diversified electronics and broadcasting company RCA began leasing space on a Canadian Anik satellite, and in April 1974 Western Union launched its first domsat, Westar I. This was quickly followed by Westar II and in 1975 and 1976 by RCA's own 'birds', Satcom I and II. Now Comstar, AT & T, Hughes Communications and SBS (a consortium of IBM, Comsat General and Aetna Life and Casualty) are all involved, each one scrambling for a piece of a highly lucrative and very important market. Most recently

Orion and International Satellites have made bids to be allowed to compete with the monopolistic Intelsat in supplying transatlantic satellite services.

Elsewhere, regulation has so far restricted satellite ownership to national and international agencies. In Canada the Anik satellites are now providing a communication and broadcasting link with the northern provinces. In Europe the problems of international agreement, combined with the economics of satellites compared to microwave for the relatively short distances involved, have delayed progress. But even here the European Space Agency, national governments and PTTs are actively considering and developing their response to an environment that appears likely to become ever more competitive. Already there are signs of competition between the ECS satellites of the European Telecommunications Satellite Organisation (Eutelsat) and the Intelsat satellites of the International Satellite Telecommunications Organisation (Intelsat). Significantly, a consortium recently established to provide a film and programme service to European cable systems, and including the British production company Goldcrest, has declared its intention of using an Intelsat satellite in conjunction with British Telecom's new rival, Mercury. Meanwhile, the British Government has approved the UK's first privately financed satellite, Unisat, to be built and operated by British Aerospace, GEC-Marconi and British Telecom and to carry the BBC's two DBS services. Others may follow and the Government has already expressed its desire to encourage greater competition in international circuits. Indeed, in a report to the Government in February 1983 on the future regulation of British Telecom, Professor Stephen Littlechild has even argued the possibilities for a similar private enterprise 'open skies' policy for Europe to that which exists in the United States. The American example and extensive lobbying both by potential service providers and by hardware manufacturers, such as British Aerospace, GEC-Marconi and, in France, Aerospatiale, are clearly forcing the pace.

All over the world governments and major commercial interests are reacting to the new technology and to the ever greater telecommunications demands of both the citizen and business. The tremendous growth of interest in cable is one part of this reaction, a reflection of the need to match terrestrial capacity to that of modern computers, communications satellites and to the requirements of the information society. Recognising the trend, corporate giants who have previously restricted themselves or been restricted to a relatively narrow field of interest, but who have dominated the market within it, are using the new technologies to move into other areas. A new industry, integrated business systems, is being created by the coming together of data processing and transmission. IBM, which has some two-thirds of the world computer market, sees the future in integrated computer processing and data networks. Together with Aetna Life it is investing in satellites and positioning itself to move beyond the computing and office automation fields to which American anti-trust regulation has until recently confined it. Xerox, dominant in copying, is also planning to take the same path into data networks, and AT&T is likewise seeking to develop its traditional telecommunications functions into the area of integrated computer processing and information services. RCA's investment in satellite systems has been mentioned earlier. Already revenues in the USA from local and long-distance data communications exceed $4 billion a year and are growing at an annual rate of 30 per cent.

Although the most apparent and immediate drive to cable television systems has been the perception of a market for new entertainment services, the growing corporate interest in cable is clearly related to the wider telecommunications issues. Coaxial and optic-fibre cable systems have a much greater capacity than the traditional twisted-pair telephone networks and could for some purposes provide a viable alternative to the existing telecommunications monopolies. Indeed the opposition which American cable television operators have encountered from AT&T and the Bell local telephone operating companies, when they have sought to make use of the telephone companies' poles to string their cables, might be regarded by a jaundiced eye as AT&T playing for time, preparing for the conflict between cable systems and the broadband communications network which it recognises it will have to develop.

Meanwhile, media and non-media companies alike have been seeking to enter the cable arena, with America again setting the pace. In the early 70s the mighty American General Electric Corporation attempted unsuccessfully to obtain a broadcast and cable stake by merging with Cox Communications. Cox itself is the tenth largest publishing house in the United States but has taken an even greater interest in broadcasting and cable, so that in 1982 51 per cent of its operating profit of $514 million was from cable system interests. Broadcasters such as Storer, newspaper/broadcasting companies such as Times-Mirror and publishing houses such as Time Inc. have had cable interests for some while, but have greatly stepped up their investment in recent years as when in 1980 the broadcasting and electronics hardware corporation, Westinghouse, bought Teleprompter, then the second largest cable operator in the United States. Time Inc.'s purchase of the major multiple cable system operator (MSO), ATC, in 1978, and its creation of the first pay television network, Home Box Office, have established it in an enviable position in two vital areas of the cable industry. In 1982 47 per cent of its profits came from its cable interest. Since 1980 the largest publishing house in the USA , the Hearst Group, has bought its way into both cable systems and cable channels and is now planning to provide database information services. Likewise, American Express has joined with Warner Communications to create the multiple system operator and programming company Warner Amex Last but not least the ubiquitous Rupert Murdoch, whose News International now also owns Satellite Television (SATU), Europe's first satellite broadcasting service, is developing a number of DBS channels in the States.

The major oil companies, perhaps seeing the future in electronic as much as internal combustion communication, are also preparing to enter the field. Already one American cable channel, the Entertainment and Sports Programming Network (ESPN) is part owned by Getty Oil. Exxon has committed itself to building word processor and mini-computer systems, whilst Mobil has shown clear signs of wishing to move into cable and telecommunications. The trend is repeated in Britain where BP is one of the companies behind the Mercury network. Major interests in the principal British cable companies are already held by large electronics companies such as British Electric Traction, Thorn-EMI and Philips Electronics. These major manufacturers, who have for the most part failed to win any portion of the booming video recorder market, are increasingly concerned by the approaching saturation of the country with colour TV sets and the ending of PAL television system patent protections in 1983, which have until now greatly inhibited Far-Eastern manufacture of sets for the UK. The new technologies, including teletext, direct broadcasting by satellite and cable, are seen as providing new opportunities for the manufacture of appropriate sets and related electronic hardware. Meanwhile Philips, inevitably, is closely involved in cable developments in the Netherlands where, as in Germany, the major publishing houses are also amongst those taking a lead.

Within this broader perspective the prolonged and slowly mounting pressure from cable system operators themselves should not be forgotten. In Britain cable has been an increasingly dead-end business, whilst in Canada cable companies have seen a dual threat to further growth from physical system saturation and from direct home reception of television signals from American satellites. The introduction of DBS in Europe, the United States and Canada between 1984 and 1986 is seen as posing a serious danger to future cable growth, particularly as most domestic consumers are interested primarily in one or two additional pay services only, which DBS can provide quite adequately, and not greatly in the plethora of other options cable has to offer. In the United States other methods of transmitting a large number of channels and of providing pay services are already being introduced, and the National Cable Television Association uses the perceived threat to cable from these as an argument to promote the industry's interests at the Federal Communications Commission.

Everywhere the limitations of the current means of generating revenue from broadcasting services – national licence fees and advertising – are being recognised. To supplement these, entrepreneurs are looking to pay-TV, particularly in America where such services have found a large audience. In Europe also the popularity of video recorders has been taken to indicate a consumer demand for recent and 'adult' films to be made available in the home. Pay-TV offers a new and major revenue source for the cable industry, and it is pay, more than anything else, which has stimulated cable's tremendous growth in the United States during the past seven years.

The technological, social and commercial factors promoting cable are inevitably matched by a number of interconnected political considerations, leading the governments of many developed nations to look favourably upon both cable and pay-TV. Almost more significant than anything else has been other countries' perceptions of cable's phenomenal growth in the United States, together with the visions of a transformed society which arise from it. The prospect of having this pattern repeated elsewhere is alluring, and the fear of being left behind in the race to the new world considerable.

Closely related has been the recognition by all governments that a strong domestic electronics industry is absolutely essential for economic survival and international trading success in the last quarter of the 20th century. Nowhere is this truer than in France, where, even before the its announcement of massive investment in cable systems, the Government was committed to injecting some $20 billion into the electronic sector between 1982 and 1987. Much of this will be via the PTT which is now also to spend some $1.5 billion more on cable systems over the same period. The hope is expressed that cable could create up to 30,000 jobs, although the justification for this claim is not evident. In the Commons debate on the British cable White Paper in June 1983 the Home Secretary, Mr Leon Brittan, expressed a similar belief: 'Cabling Britain will be an investment in tomorrow's growth and jobs and the country's future' (quoted in the *Guardian*, 1 July 1983). Throughout the recession-ridden western world there is a widespread belief that cable and information technology could be important economic rejuvenators. Publicly this is described as a long-term objective; privately it is hoped cable might also act as a short-term stimulant, creating new industries, new jobs and new export opportunities.

Conversely, in a world where economics and information are so closely related, it is not surprising that a common theme is the threat of economic and cultural imperialism if other nations, and particularly the United States, gain too great a lead in either the hardware or the programme production aspects of the information industry. The United States is an intrusive and inescapable neighbour for Canada, an offspring about which Britain has mixed feelings, and a constant and necessary consideration for countries who do not share its language but do make use of its press agencies, its film output and its technology. The publication in November 1982 of the Appelbaum-Hébert Report on Canadian cultural policy implicitly reflects the perennial Canadian concern to retain against enormous odds its own distinct national identity. In the new age information and culture are equated, and a balance of information exchange, indicative of an active culture, is considered as vital as the balance of trade which indicates a healthy economy.

In this respect cable offers a twofold benefit. Clearly it is hoped that cable expansion will boost the domestic electronic and information sectors of industry. But cable also has a characteristic of value in itself, apart from its use as an economic and cultural stimulus. At a time when satellites make possible the almost unlimited crossborder flow of each country's dominant medium, television, cable is a curiously anachronistic, earthbound technology. Countries such as France, Germany and Britain, which until now have kept remarkably tight control of the television signals available to their citizens, will shortly be inundated with those of surrounding countries, beamed down from the latter's powerful DBS satellites. Although the International Telecommunications Union has attempted to protect state sovereignty and preserve the nationalistic character of television in its narrow DBS allocations, it has succeeded only partially. The 'footprint' of a satellite beam aimed at Belgium or Luxembourg, for example, unavoidably overlaps large portions of neighbouring countries, making a mockery of state broadcasting regulations and international copyright agreements. This is a problem which Canada is already facing and which it is seeking to resolve through a policy of regulated cable development; indeed it has long attempted to use cable to control the entry of ordinary broadcast signals from the USA.

Ever since the BBC's earliest days, when its motto was 'Nation shall speak peace unto Nation', broadcasting has been one of the great hopes of the internationalist movement. Equally, cross-border broadcasting has been a concern to governments ever since Hitler ordered that the frequency range and sensitivity of new German wireless sets be restricted so that foreign stations could not be received. Article 19 of the United Nations Universal Declaration of Human Rights expresses the right of anyone to 'seek, receive and impart information and ideas through any media and regardless of frontiers'. Article 59 of the Treaty of Rome is similarly a statement of intention to remove barriers to the provision of services between members of the EEC. Not surprisingly, countries which hope and believe the flow will be more out than in as far as they are concerned, support this concept. Those of the developing nations who see such an internationalist philosophy more in terms of cultural imperialism on the part of the major information-creating states are understandably more hostile. And in practice countries such as France and Germany, while publicly espousing free flow, are seriously alarmed by a trend which threatens radically to change both national viewing habits and sources of information and entertainment.

Yet the forces of technology, commerce and consumer demand seem set to make the trans-border flow of video signals virtually unstoppable. In doing so they will finally remove from national governments the means whereby they can if necessary influence what their citizens watch, namely their ultimate control over all organisations whose television signals are received within a nation's borders. Faced with losing control over the organisations of transmission, some governments are seeking instead, through regulated cable development, to make possible some measure of control over the means of reception, the argument being that viewers connected to cable are less likely to buy their own satellite dish in order to receive unregulated foreign programming. Foreign satellite channels relayed over a cable system can be both restricted in number, if desired, and 'domesticated'. Whether there is necessarily anything invidious about the wish to exercise a degree of regulatory control depends both on the way in which it is implemented and the extent to which traditionally regulated video transmission is or can be equated with unregulated publishing. In any case, each state has its own regulations relating to such issues as the extent and nature of advertising on television, broadcasting standards and obscenity. Given these differences in national morality and law, cable offers one way to maintain a measure of regulatory influence over trends which otherwise challenge the very concepts of the nation state and national identity.

Cable can therefore have a regulatory motive. More prominent in the United States and Britain, however, is the deregulatory trend in broadcasting which, like telecommunications deregulation, reflects the prevailing political philosophy. Maximum individual freedom of choice is seen as being achieved through the workings of the marketplace, a view which in Britain has always been rejected with regard to limited channel broadcasting. Now multi-channel cable appears to offer the potential of greater freedom, of less reliance for information and entertainment upon the programming whims of a limited oligarchy of broadcasters. Together with video recorders, it holds out the prospect of an escape into the market, away from television as a socially homogenising (as opposed to unifying) force. Broadcasting has been about large-scale response to limited options, with inevitable implications for the character of our society. Now cable could allow television to develop into a case of individual, or at least interest-group or socially fragmented response to much greater choice. Like independent television and radio before it, cable in Britain appears to be a move in the direction of a particular philosophy, and that fact has been of crucial importance in the present debate.

Cable has been described as a technology in search of a demand. That the demand exists there can be no doubt, but it is to be found not only in the immediate needs of society but also in the requirements of other technologies, the economic drives of commerce and the political philosophies of governments. Inevitably the relative emphases given to the various factors involved differ widely from country to country and significantly affect both approaches to and experience of cable. In France, West Germany and Japan, for example, with minimal existing cable television systems and effectively no private cable sector, broadband cable development by the national PTTs has a very strong telecommunications emphasis. By contrast, in Canada and the United States privately operated cable systems have already achieved a strong hold as an entertainment medium. Meanwhile, Britain is in the curious position of having little cable yet a powerful cable lobby, including large private companies with considerable vested interests in cable system expansion. It is partly for this reason, but also because the North-American example appears to be making all the running at the moment, that present policy sees cable as essentially an entertainment-led and privately funded phenomenon. As the report of the Government's Information Technology Advisory Panel, which started the current debate in Britain, argued:

> We believe cable to be an essential component of future communications systems, offering great opportunities for new forms of entrepreneurial activity and substantial direct and indirect industrial benefits. However, the initial financing of cable systems will depend upon none of these things, but upon estimates of the revenue from additional popular programming channels. We consider the long-term potential of cable systems for providing new sorts of service to be much more important, but have to accept that cable systems will go through an initial phase when their attraction will be based on 'entertainment' considerations (Information Technology Advisory Panel, 'Cable Systems', February 1982, para. 8.5).

The background to this conclusion and to the British situation will be considered further in the next two chapters.

PART TWO
Cable in Britain: the Historical and Political Background

3 Origins and Development

To most people in Britain cable broadcasting is a new idea, unthought of before 1982 and appearing with satellite broadcasting, teletext and video recorders as just one part of the much broader telecommunications revolution which seems suddenly and almost without warning to be upon us. Yet while the technology of cable television may be advancing rapidly with the development of fibre optics and solid-state lasers, the concept is as old, indeed older than, radio broadcasting itself. Moreover, where today we hear predominantly about the advanced cable systems and services of the United States, cable is very much a world-wide phenomenon, and its origins lie in Europe – in Britain and the Netherlands.

From the earliest days of the telephone, indeed, there was a recognition of its broadcasting potential. In 1894 the Electrophone Company of London was set up to distribute concerts, lectures and church services to homes connected to the telephone. For an annual charge of £10 each subscriber received four pairs of headphones and a microphone through which he could ask to be connected to one of a number of theatres – an early instance, perhaps, of interactive broadcasting. Unfortunately, the technology did not yet match the idea. The service was poor, attracted only 600 subscribers and was abandoned after ten years. Similar systems, however, were established in Paris and Budapest, the first operating until the Second World War, the second offering an all-day news service which ran from the 1890s until the 1920s, thereby predating current American all-news channels by over eighty years.

If these examples of 'pay-radio' were ahead of their time, there was nevertheless good reason for developing wired broadcasting both in Britain and elsewhere. Wireless transmission was, of course, to establish itself in the early 1920s as the dominant form of broadcasting, particularly since for the most part the same organisation both produced the programme and transmitted it. Nevertheless, in many countries where commercial radio stations were prohibited, the national broadcasting organisations were unable for several years to build transmitters for more than the major urban areas. Consequently, wired relay systems were seen as a way in which commercial concerns could legitimately exploit the deficiencies of the broadcasting service. Small operators, often radio-set retailers, could set up a large aerial in smaller towns to receive broadcast signals from more fortunate areas. They could then 'rediffuse' the programmes to subscribers over a wire network. The technical inadequacies and the cost of early radio sets and aerials gave a considerable boost to these 'relay exchanges' as they were known, as did the lack of mains electricity in many of the towns where they were installed. A relay exchange with its own generator could offer a home without electricity good-quality reception of one or two channels – including foreign stations – through a simple and inexpensive loudspeaker unit. Mains electricity and overhead tram wires could also promote the installation of wired relay in modern blocks of flats by creating electrical interference for normal wireless reception. The system certainly had an egalitarian aspect to it, as poor families were more likely to be able to afford a small weekly rental than a lump payment, or even than hire purchase instalments, for an expensive and still temperamental wireless set and aerial. In that respect early developments are reflected in current American experience, for it has been found in many areas that large families with lower incomes are above-average subscribers to cable and pay television. Cable offers a much cheaper way for an entire family to see recent films than would a visit to the cinema.

Relay exchanges first appeared in the Netherlands in the early 1920s. Clear reception of the many foreign stations available was a major incentive and has remained so ever since. In Britain the first exchange was established in January 1925 by Mr A.W. Maton, the owner of an electrical shop in Hythe, near Southampton. For a weekly charge of 1/6d (£65 a year at 1982 prices) he relayed signals from the BBC and foreign stations to about 150 subscribers. Neither he nor fellow system operators showed any interest as yet in producing their own alternative programming, perhaps not surprisingly when even the major radio manufacturers who established the BBC saw little profit to be made in this way. In any case, the Post Office, which then regulated wire and radio broadcasting, was to apply an effective ban on the origination of programming other than by the BBC, a ban which was formalised in 1930.

The relay or 'rediffusion' of existing services was, however, a profitable business by itself. From a total in Britain of 10 exchanges serving 446 subscribers in 1927 the industry grew to 86 exchanges with 21,677 subscribers in 1930 and 343 systems serving 233,554 homes in 1935. This still, however, represented only 3.1 per cent of all radio licence holders. There were particular concentrations of relay exchanges in the northeast, which was poorly covered by broadcast transmitters, and the south coast, which was subject to interference from shipping. In some areas, where relay systems were offered, up to one-third of households subscribed. The exchanges were mostly owned individually by relatively small enterprises, although such names as Rediffusion were already appearing on the scene.

Most early systems in Britain had a limited capacity of only one or two channels, using the audio-frequency technique which required two separate wires to carry one channel. In the Netherlands, however, the profusion of available signals from neighbouring countries led to the building of four-channel relay exchanges. This necessitated eight wires, for the most part strung up on poles along each street. Nevertheless, Dutch local authorities offered few objections, in sharp contrast to the increasing reluctance of borough and town councils in the United Kingdom to accept such eyesores. Whereas in Britain commercially owned relay exchanges were merely tolerated and increasingly regulated, in the Netherlands the municipalities themselves took an early and active interest. By 1939 the Dutch were the most highly wired nation in the world, with some 50 per cent of households being connected. Indeed, in urban areas penetration was as high as 80 per cent.

In Switzerland, by way of comparison, the 38,690 subscribers in 1934 equalled no more than 4 per cent of all households. The story was the same in other European countries which developed an element of wired relay, such as the USSR and Germany, even though in both the latter and Switzerland telephone-based systems were developed which provided up to six channels. This limited European experience was nevertheless greater than the North American, where there appear to have been few if any prewar relay exchanges. Perhaps the American entrepreneurial spirit was satisfied to a much greater extent than in Europe by the commercial broadcasting system which operated there.

The ability of relay exchanges to provide their subscribers with good-quality reception of foreign signals was undoubtedly a major factor in their popularity and hence their commercial viability. However, it was also a source of great concern to the various national broadcasting organisations. In Britain the BBC had been created as a monopoly broadcaster primarily as a solution to the shortage of wavelengths. Nevertheless, once established, it rapidly developed an attitude and an approach to broadcasting in which monopoly was justified as an act of policy. The legal right of relay exchanges not to rediffuse BBC programmes which they considered unattractive to their subscribers, and to put in their place music or variety shows from abroad, threatened both the Corporation's monopoly of 'programming' to the domestic market and the careful balance of education, information and entertainment which it regarded as a primary objective of broadcasting. The BBC could not prohibit ordinary wireless set owners from tuning in to Radios Luxembourg and Normandie, both of which carried music and English-language programmes; but it was most unhappy at the prospect of a relay exchange operator seeking to maximise audiences by deleting all the uplifting fare from the BBC's schedule and replacing it with light entertainment from foreign stations.

From the late 20s onwards domestic relay exchanges were to be a major irritation to the BBC (if hardly a threat), although it actively encouraged their growth in other countries of the Empire and Commonwealth, including the Falkland Islands, as being a good way to extend and improve reception of its Empire service. Today the Corporation is again concerned about the development of cable systems in Britain, but has taken advantage of their growth in the USA to expand sales of its programming there.

Indeed, there are a number of interesting parallels between current arguments over cable and those of the 30s. As now, so then, cable threatened both the existing regulatory structure of broadcasting and the existing balance of programming. Both the BBC and the GPO recognised that the relay exchange had a role in areas of poor reception, but were concerned that it might prove to be a parasite threatening the health of its host. In fact, the Corporation argued strongly that such exchanges as were necessary should be state owned and operated, thereby ensuring control of their output.

On the other side, curiously, one of the most ardent exponents of wired broadcasting from 1930 onwards was a former BBC Chief Engineer, Peter Eckersley. As early as 1925 he had pointed out that wires could be used to overcome the limitation on wavelengths. In 1928 he and his engineering colleagues went further and proposed that the one-channel BBC should itself experiment with relay exchanges in Norwich, Portsmouth and Sunderland. Wired broadcasting, they felt, was potentially 'an undertaking far surpassing the BBC in magnitude' (Quoted by A. Briggs, *History of Broadcasting in the United Kingdom*, Vol. II, 1965, p. 358). As Eckersley told the Corporation's Director General, Sir John Reith, 'It is not impossible to visualise, in, say, twenty years time, complete wire broadcasting, supplemented, it is true, but in minor part, by wireless broadcasting.' Although this visionary proposal came to nothing, it remained with Eckersley, and after his departure from the BBC in 1929 he joined Rediffusion, one of the larger relay companies. One only has to read his book, *The Power Behind the Microphone*, to realise that the vision of cable offered today has a long and distinguished pedigree and that there is little new under the sun.

On both sides the arguments have a familiar ring to them. While the Relay Services Association (the industry's central body in the 1930s) urged that relay exchanges should be deregulated and allowed to originate programmes on local affairs, the BBC expressed grave concern about the possible development of relay conglomerates which produced their own alternative programme schedules. As the *BBC Yearbook* for 1933 warned:

> Each exchange may increase to the stature of a BBC in miniature, and furthermore the possibility must be visualised of several enlarged exchanges being merged under a single financial control. Concerns with sufficient capital would be in a position to buy time on the several continental stations which will sell it, and produce their own programmes abroad on the existing American system (Briggs, op.cit., p.494).

At the root of the debate, however, lay the issue which remains fundamental to British broadcasting and to the future development of cable, namely broadcasting as public service or marketplace. The BBC had been created to make use of a limited resource in a balanced fashion, in a spirit of public interest and for the general public good: 'The BBC has always regarded entertainment as an important part of its work, but it has declined to devote its programmes entirely to amusement. This policy has been upheld by public opinion, and has already resulted in an acknowledged improvement in public taste' (Ibid., p.495). Relay exchanges, by editing BBC output, threatened such a balanced and 'educative' approach.

And why not? Who were the BBC to dictate the nation's listening habits? Should not the marketplace be left to decide public tastes, and could not the commercial relay exchanges do this very effectively? As a former Postmaster General, Lord Selsdon, remarked in 1935,

> The relay companies, if they are to succeed, must give their public what that public wants and, in trying to do so, they have the advantage that, by measuring the relative loads, they can estimate with some approximation to accuracy how many of their subscribers are listening at any given moment to one or other of two alternative programmes (Ibid., p.503).

Yet this was exactly the BBC's point also. It clearly made commercial sense for relay companies always to provide programmes with maximum appeal, and they were able to judge which these were by using power consumption meters attached to their exchanges to assess how many were listening at any one time. In doing so, incidentally, they were anticipating the monitoring capability of interactive cable television by over forty years. But by seeking always to provide programmes with the widest and most general appeal they were also depriving relay listeners of true choice and of minority interest alternatives.

Lord Selsdon's championing of relay exchange interests was also significant. As now, cable was seen as having potential electoral importance. The Post Office and the BBC might be keen to limit the power of relay exchanges, but the Postmaster General himself, as a party politician, was unwilling to be seen to be restricting the individual right of relay subscribers to listen to foreign transmissions. It is interesting to note that the current 'must-carry' rule imposed on cable operators whereby they have to carry *all* BBC and ITV television signals even if this uses their entire system capacity, did not then apply to radio relay. This was despite the fact that many systems still only had a one-channel capacity. The only requirement before 1936 was that all systems wishing to relay foreign programmes had to carry an element of BBC material – but then there were few who would not have done so in any case. Only in that year was it specified that one-channel systems should carry a preponderance of BBC programmes, and that those with two channels should distribute at least one BBC signal (out of a total by then of two) whenever the Corporation was on the air. In the 'golden age of wireless' the BBC's output was not as inviolable as it was later to become.

The debate over wired radio was therefore an interesting precursor of that over cable television. Even the present-day industry's fear of British Telecom's entry into cable TV (and in the USA of telecommunications giant AT & T), is reflected in the Relay Services Association's opposition to the electricity industry using its mains cables for relaying up to six channels, a technique devised by Peter Eckersley in 1931. Indeed, from 1936 onwards the Post Office itself began to experiment with a 'radio-by-phone' system, a move strenuously opposed by the industry.

The parallels go beyond mere argument. The early growth of relay exchanges was not matched in the second half of the 30s, as the industry responded to various broadcasting developments, economic pressures and regulatory constraints. As wireless receiver technology improved, as the cost of sets came down, as the wireless transmitter network was developed and extended, and not least as national and local regulation grew more and more restrictive, so the relay industry saw both its *raison d'être* and its profitability diminish. Between 1935 and 1939 a number of systems were closed down as unprofitable, a trend which was to be mirrored in the 70s when improved television transmitter networks and technology led to a reduction in cable television subscribers. As now, the industry needed a new stimulus if it was to survive. Although that stimulus was eventually to come from television, in the early 40s the industry found an altogether grimmer saviour – the war.

Under war conditions the problems of direct wireless reception in many areas were greatly increased. In order to prevent enemy bombers using domestic radio transmissions as homing signals, transmitter strengths were seriously reduced. In these circumstances the government looked more favourably upon relay interests, and although relay systems suffered severely from bomb damage the industry had, by the war's end, nearly doubled its subscribers to 435,000, mostly in the North and Midlands, South Wales and East Anglia. By 1950 nearly 1 million homes received their radio programmes by wire, representing some 8 per cent of all broadcast licences issued. As the industry grew, so it came increasingly to be dominated by a number of particularly large companies, and this trend was emphasised with the development of cable television, the capital costs of which were inevitably high.

CABLE TELEVISION SYSTEMS

With the introduction of high-resolution television in Britain in 1936 relay operators recognised that sooner or later they would have to start offering this service also. The war halted progress, but by the late 40s several companies were carrying out research into the distribution of television signals by cable, an idea which developed more or less simultaneously but independently on both sides of the Atlantic. On both continents cable television found a market in those towns not yet reached by the national or commercial television transmitter networks, or where reception was still poor. For the first time the electrical manufacturing industry (whose wireless business had been threatened by the relay exchange use of simple loudspeakers) found itself on the same side as relay interests. Cable systems could boost television set sales and consequently a continuing link was forged. Another and even more important connection existed between electrical retailers and cable system operators. Indeed, there quickly developed a two-way integration of interests, as retailers involved themselves in cable and cable operators undertook the sale or, particularly in Britain, rental of television sets.

Cable expansion in Britain, therefore, stimulated by pre-existing relay interests, paralleled the rapid growth of television itself and like television benefited greatly from the increasingly important role of rental in the acquisition of a set. Cable operators saw the opportunity to sell their customers a complete package, renting out not only

41

the connection to the cable but also the television receiver itself. This followed naturally from the normal relay exchange practice of including the cost of the loudspeaker installed in the home in the weekly subscription. In fact, discovering that set rental was a profitable business in itself, cable companies soon expanded it beyond the relatively small cable market and turned it into their major source of revenue. The 50s were to see the rapid growth of such cable and rental companies as Radio Rentals, British Relay (Visionhire), Telefusion and Rediffusion. The last named, already the largest relay operator in Britain, was also to expand overseas during this period, building radio and cable television systems in Canada, Ceylon, Hong Kong, Singapore, Nigeria, Malaya and the West Indies.

The first British cable television system was installed by Link Sound and Vision Ltd in Gloucester in 1951. Before the coming of independent television in 1956 growth was limited, but ITV appears to have given cable a considerable boost. While the number of TV sets in Britain doubled between 1956 and 1961 (largely due to rental amongst the lower income groups) subscription to cable television increased tenfold. By 1966 over 1 million people received their television signals by cable, and by 1972 some 2.3 million. This growth was assisted by the policy of many new town development corporations, such as Milton Keynes, of prohibiting external television aerials.

Yet after the mid-60s the primary reason for cable's existence in Britain began to disappear. Since the 30s, cable had been limited by regulation to the role of signal enhancement. It had been required to relay a certain minimum of BBC (and later ITV) programmes and had been prohibited from originating material of its own or receiving payment for the distribution of any particular programme. Moreover the Copyright Act of 1955 and an agreement forced upon cable operators by the independent television contractors had effectively prohibited the former from making available to subscribers signals not normally available to them over the air. The regional ITV contractors, in particular, feared the notion of 'island hopping', whereby cable operators imported the signal of one ITV contractor into the non-adjacent region of another, thereby destroying the whole concept of regional copyright exclusivity of programming on which British (and American) independent broadcasting is based.

Such constraints upon the cable industry naturally had a severely limiting effect, in that they restricted it to areas of poor reception and relatively high population density. But, so long as signal enhancement remained a necessary and valid function, cable was not actually threatened. However, from 1963 onwards the introduction of UHF-625 line transmissions, of a low-power UHF repeater network in outlying areas and of colour television effectively made a large proportion of the 2,200 cable systems in Britain redundant. At first reception difficulties for UHF colour transmissions actually boosted the industry, but gradually the transmission network improved and by about 1973 the number of cable subscribers had stopped growing. Indeed, after a static period it began to fall and commercial systems lost 140,000 subscribers in five years. The industry was becoming less and less profitable and many companies stayed in it largely for its connection with their rental market and in the hope that cable might soon enter a new phase of development in view of its spare capacity. Heavy capital investment, relatively low returns and low subscriber density made cable at best only marginally profitable. For the year 1971-2 Rediffusion, then one of the world's largest cable operators, made a pre-tax profit of £600,000 on its cable interests, representing only 7 per cent of total profits, by comparison with 54 per cent from its rental and 17 per cent from its broadcasting operations. By 1982 that small cable profit had been turned into an operating loss, and Rediffusion announced that it might have to close down some systems.

Since the early 70s, therefore, the cable industry has made little progress. Currently some 2.6 million households (12.8 per cent of those with TV) receive their television signals by cable. There are 2,300 cable systems licensed by the Home Office, of which 438 are operated by commercial companies or British Telecom, serving 1,484,000 households (7.3 per cent). The remainder are non-commercial systems operated by local authorities, development corporations, housing associations, hospitals and similar bodies. The majority of these are relatively small 'master antenna television' systems. Some 72 per cent of the commercial companies' subscribers are attached to systems which employ 'twisted-pair' wires with only a four or six channel capacity. Almost all of these belong to Rediffusion and Visionhire. The remaining systems employ copper coaxial cable and have a nine to sixteen channel capacity, but with a higher potential. One company, Rediffusion, dominates the cable operating business with between 730,000 and 800,000 subscribers. Together with Visionhire (300-340,000) and Telefusion (158-200,000) it controls over half the present cable market.

Britain is therefore in the strange position of having a low proportion of houses cabled (mostly with outmoded technology) and extremely restrictive regulations, yet a cable industry headed by large and powerful companies, many with diversified interests in electronics, computing, broadcasting and television rental, companies which are well aware of cable's wider potential. Rediffusion, for example, is also a major electronics and television hardware company and has overseas broadcasting interests. A subsidiary, Rediffusion Computers, is the second largest computer manufacturer in

Britain and a leading exponent of viewdata and integrated communications systems. In its turn Rediffusion's parent company, British Electric Traction, has major interests in Thames TV, Capital Radio and the Argus newspaper group. Visionhire is similarly part of the Electronic Rentals Group, whose interests include electronic hardware, television rental and overseas broadcasting. A third of ERG's ordinary shares are owned by Philips Electronics which has its own cable systems in addition to enormous electronics manufacturing interests. A subsidiary, Philips Business Systems, is one of the principal private viewdata suppliers in Britain. Likewise, Radio Rentals, the fourth largest cable operator, with sister companies DER and Multibroadcast, Britain's leading TV and video rental outlet, is owned by Thorn-EMI, whose activities include consumer electronics (TV set and video manufacture), records, films, video software and a half interest in Thames TV. Early in 1982 it strengthened its interest in information technology by buying the Datasolve and Software Sciences companies. Cable was one of the founding interests of many of these groups. Today, despite its past problems, it seems to offer an opportunity to bring together, and integrate, the many and diverse concerns of each.

EXPERIMENTS IN CABLE PROGRAMMING

Not surprisingly, the cable industry has for many years undertaken extensive lobbying of successive governments to allow it to expand beyond the signal enhancement stage. Programme origination, for which extra charges could be made to subscribers or on which advertising could be sold, seemed to be the answer at least for those systems with spare channel capacity. Previous governments, however, have been wary of breaking away from two of the primary tenets of public service broadcasting – that broadcast channels should be equally available to all and that no two television services should compete for the same source of revenue. Consequently, cable companies have been limited to a few brief pay-cable experiments and to community cable channels intended to demonstrate cable's public value and general worthiness.

The first ever cable-originated item was by a radio relay operator who, during the war, was permitted briefly to experiment with special programmes from a war factory. However, this did not lead any further and when the idea was revived in evidence to the Pilkington Committee in 1960 it was firmly rejected. Nevertheless, the Conservative government and its Labour successor did agree to a limited pay-television experiment by Pay Television Limited, a consortium of Associated British Pictures, British Home Entertainment and British Relay, on the latter's systems. This operation, working

44

on the principle of coin-in-the-slot metered television, ran between 1966 and 1968 in the Southwark and Westminster areas of London, where it attracted 9,000 subscribers, and in Sheffield where 2,000 were connected. Income averaged five to six shillings a week per subscriber and the service consisted almost exclusively of feature films, although the original prospectus had talked of sport, 'cultural stimulation and adult education instruction'. In 1968, however, the government rejected a request for the extension or expansion of the service and it closed down with a loss of around £1 million.

The next series of experiments took place in the early 70s and represented an alliance between what one observer called 'the mercenaries and missionaries' (P. M. Lewis, *Community Television and Cable in Britain*, BFI, 1978, p. 16). Calls for community and access television by groups interested in the idea of 'alternative' media matched the strategy of commercial cable operators, who were more than willing to demonstrate the local potential of cable if this would open the door to other more profitable forms of programming such as pay-film channels. A proposal in 1972 by Greenwich Cablevision to provide a community cable service was approved by the Conservative Post and Telecommunications Minister, Christopher Chataway, who also declared his readiness to license a number of other such experiments. Community cable had already been pioneered in Canada during the late 60s (see Chapter 5), and it may have been significant that Greenwich had Canadian backing. Similarly Cablevision (Wellingborough) Ltd, which supplied local programmes to Wellingborough between March 1974 and March 1975, was half owned by the Canadian company Selkirk Communications. Other community channels licensed were operated by Rediffusion in Bristol, British Relay in Sheffield, Radio Rentals-EMI in Swindon and, under a later licence, by CO-AX Cable Communications in Milton Keynes. Greenwich, the first, began in July 1972.

In programming terms these experiments undoubtedly produced some new and valuable ideas and their audiences, while small, were respectable in proportion to the number of cable subscribers. All made extensive use of voluntary personnel and many did what they could to encourage the public access concept (it is interesting to note that BBC2's 'Open Door' programme also started in 1972). Typically between five and ten hours of original material were transmitted each week. Yet, although these experiments offered new types of community programme, no new sources of revenue, neither subscription nor sponsorship or advertising, were permitted. By the time the Government did concede the latter, in 1975, it was too late. Indeed, it had been recognised from the outset that the projects could not pay their way, and this has led to a suggestion that the companies involved had an unwritten understanding from the Conservative government that pay-TV would also get the go-ahead before long. The return to power of Labour in 1974, however, dashed any such hopes and by January 1976 the Bristol, Wellingborough and Sheffield channels had all closed.

Today only Greenwich continues to provide a small but worthwhile community television service of a few hours each week, usually from 6-7 p.m. but with some programmes at breakfast time. The most notable items are a weekly review of local events and entertainment and a regular programme for the Asian community, which comprises 13 per cent of the system's subscribers. The whole operation is run on a shoestring with programmes being entirely produced by volunteers, although the company pays the engineering maintenance costs, other overheads and the annual licence fee of £1,500 which is required from the Home Office in order to operate a community service. The programmes carried advertising for a time, but the audiences proved too low for it to be worthwhile. The decision by Greenwich Cablevision to continue the service must certainly be applauded, but it cannot be taken as an exemplar of the character and possible future development of true community cable.

The community services of the mid-70s did not fail for economic reasons, for they were never designed to pay their way, but their closure was certainly symptomatic of the industry's general malaise. Nor did it seem likely that prospects would improve. Despite strenuous lobbying by the Cable Television Association of Great Britain (CTA), the Annan Committee on Broadcasting Policy concluded in 1977 that cable might be developed gradually as a community service but hardly as a commercial operation. Rather dispiritingly it postulated that a national cable network might develop 'after the turn of the century' (Report of the Committee on the Future of Broadcasting (Annan Report), Cmnd 6753, HMSO, 1977, para. 14.55).

The Labour government of the day, however, was to prove slightly more sympathetic to the immediate needs of the industry. Already in 1975 it had moved to halt the decline, giving cable an added attraction by formally permitting systems with available capacity to carry additional out-of-area ITV signals. It had also made its own contribution to community cable by promoting the local cable experiment in Milton Keynes. Moreover, the CTA was to prove itself a lobbying force which could attract influential support. Speaking in the debate which followed Annan, the shadow Home Secretary, William Whitelaw, argued that the Government should give 'more encouragement in this important and developing area to the Cable Television Association. . . . Surely our purpose here, as in other areas, must be to provide the maximum choice to the viewer' (*Cablevision News*, July 1977, p. 10). Lobbying culminated in a sub-

46

mission to the Labour Home Secretary and his attendance as principal speaker at the CTA's 1977 annual luncheon, an event also attended by spokesmen on broadcasting from both Houses and all parties. By the time the Government gave its own response to Annan in 1978 it was less ready than the latter to believe pay-TV necessarily wrong. Instead it agreed to allow a number of pay-cable experiments, but under 'careful regulation' to ensure that damage did not ensue to the existing broadcasting services ('Broadcasting', Cmnd 7924, HMSO, 1978, para. 175). Pay-television and the less financially viable community channels should, it felt, 'develop side by side'.

This recommendation was subsequently implemented under the new Conservative administration, when the licences for a number of pay-cable schemes were announced by Mr Whitelaw in November 1980. Thirteen were approved, to be run on the existing systems of seven companies (see Table II). Licences were initially for two years and allowed extra charges to be made to those people who wished to receive an additional channel of feature films, entertainment, sport and, it was hoped, an element of local programming. Films, however, had to have a British Board of Film Censors' certificate and could only be shown if they had been registered for public exhibition at least one year previously, the intention being to preserve a theatrical release 'window' for the cinema industry. Channels could not contain 'X'-rated material before 10 p.m. and were also obliged to carry the same proportion of British films as applied to the cinema (then 30 per cent, but now eliminated). Operators could not seek exclusive rights to sporting and entertainment events of national importance, nor was advertising permitted, while the Home Office required that programme schedules be submitted to it in advance for approval. Such restrictions have since been used to question the experimental value of these schemes and their worth as indicators of public interest in cable.

Rediffusion was the first company to offer a pay channel, on five of its systems in September 1981. By the autumn of 1982 all thirteen trials were operational, passing a total of about 343,000 households of which some 102,000 were already subscribing to the basic cable relay service. Some companies have varied the amount charged in order to discover just how price-sensitive such a film channel is. Consequently the subscription for a typical monthly service of two or three films each evening, repeated regularly but with eleven to twelve new titles each month, has ranged from £6.50 to £12. A take-up of 10 per cent of homes passed or 30 per cent of those subscribing to cable was hoped for within the two years of the experiment, but in fact only the five Rediffusion systems taken together have lived up to these projections. Their total of about 8,000 pay subscribers represent some 36 per cent of all subscribers

TABLE II

UK pay-cable TV systems 1981-3

(Sources: Individual Cable operators, July 1983; Post Office Engineering Union Journal, March 1983)

Note: Available figures vary; this table should therefore be taken to indicate general trends only.

Licensed operator	Programme supplier	Location	Number of homes passed	Total sub-scribers Jan. 83	Basic sub-scribers Jan. 83	Pay sub-scribers Jan. 83	% pay to all sub-scribers	% pay homes passed
Rediffusion	Rediffusion (Starview)	Reading	16,380	3,459				
		Pontypridd	6,155	3,375				
		Hull	14,990	5,415	14,090	8,000	36.2	12.5
		Tunbridge Wells	6,726	4,104				
		Burnley	19,600	5,737				
Radio Rentals	Thorn-EMI Video Productions (Cinematel)	Swindon	23,000	10,000	8,500	1,500	15	6.5
		Medway Towns (Chatham, Gillingham and Rochester)	20,000	9,000	8,100	900	10	4.5
			24,000					
British Telecom	Selectv	Milton Keynes	18,000	17,500	15,700	1,800	10.3	10.0
Philips Cablevision	Selectv	Tredegar	6,000	3,500	3,400	100	3	1.6
		Northampton	6,000	6,500	6,100	400	6	6.6
Visionhire Cable	BBC Enterprises (Showcable)	London (various areas)	170,000	23,230	18,230	5,000	22	3.0
Cablevision	Selectv	Wellingborough	8,000	4,500	4,400	100	2	1.3
Greenwich Cablevision	Greenwich Cablevision (Screentown)	Greenwich	26,427	8,177	7,406	770	9.4	2.9

on those systems. About 40 per cent (around 3,200) are people who were not previously connected to the cable system but who have taken it in order to receive the film channel. Taking the thirteen systems as a whole, no more than 17.7 per cent of subscribers have taken the pay service, well below present American experience.

The pay channels for Rediffusion, Radio Rentals and Greenwich Cablevision have been operated by subsidiaries or related companies, and that for British Telecom, Philips and Wellingborough Cablevision by Select TV, a subscription television company set up by Mark Shelmerdine of London Films but now controlled by Robert Maxwell's British Printing and Communications Corporation (BPCC). Although SelecTV did not anticipate profits for three years, the 2,400 total takeup was disappointingly far below the 9,000 considered necessary to break even. Meanwhile, Visionhire's pay channel, Cinematel, has been programmed by BBC Enterprises, which used the experience to promote its successful bid for two DBS channels. Copyright and residual issues, however, prevented any BBC material being used. Indeed, for all the pay experiments a major problem was to find suitable programming at a reasonable price. The terms of the licence prevented films which had been on general release for less than a year from being shown, and there is only a limited stock of items between one and three years old – after which they begin to appear on broadcast television. In 1982, apparently, Central TV on three occasions broadcast a film on the same evening as its transmission by SelecTV. Not surprisingly, therefore, a high proportion of the pay subscribers who asked to be disconnected gave as their reasons high cost and poor service, including too frequent repeats.

A further difficulty was encountered in the cost of material. The major American film distributors proved determined to get a better price for their productions than they have done from pay services in the United States. There they failed to recognise the potential of pay-TV until it was too late. Consequently, in Britain the Motion Picture Exporters Association of America established a minimum licence fee of 43p per subscriber for films under three years old and 21.5p for those over, nearly triple that charged in the US. With monthly programming costs of £5 or more per subscriber, it is hardly surprising that the retail price for an evenings-only service was in some cases almost double the cost of an American twenty-four-hour film channel. Such difficulties only reinforced the view that these trials could give little indication of likely audience interest in a better conceived and fully commercial service.

To the cable industry, watching its subscriber base slowly crumbling, the limited extent and extremely protracted and cautious timetable of the experiments was a case of too little and too late. Welcoming them as it did, it remained concerned about the immediate prospects. Meanwhile, parallel with the pilot projects, a Home Office committee was considering the future development of direct broadcasting by satellite, an issue which closely concerned the industry. Yet its report in May 1981, although moderately sympathetic, nevertheless favoured only a partial role for cable systems and indicated an earliest DBS date of 1986.

The industry's future in Britain appeared even darker by the comparison with events in America, where cable seemed to be enjoying a quite tremendous boom. Reports from the other side of the Atlantic equated that growth with the process of federal deregulation of cable, and this was contrasted with continuing tight controls in Britain. The strength of the industry in North America had another effect: Canadian and American companies began to take an increasing interest in Britain as a potential export and operating market. Within a year of the announcement of the pay-cable projects, representatives of some thirty North-American cable companies had visited the Cable Television Association to learn more about possible openings. Indeed, Rogers Cablesystems and Cablecasting Ltd, the two largest Canadian system operators, established permanent representatives in Britain, a primary objective being 'to raise the level of cable consciousness – particularly among politicians, bureaucrats and journalists' *(Televisual,* December 1982, p.34).

Meanwhile, the Cable Television Association continued its own lobbying efforts and found much support amongst many members of parliament with a broadcasting or technological background. Nevertheless, as late as November 1981, *The Times* could report a statement by Lord Belstead, the Home Office minister responsible for broadcasting, which held out little prospect of immediate progress *(The Times,* 11 November 1981, p.16). Four months later that had all changed; cable became a subject of public debate. Yet the impetus came not from the industry, but from a completely different direction.

4 The Political Debate

Since the early 1970s a small group of MPs of all parties, including Kenneth Baker, Christopher Chataway and the close friend and aide of Mrs Thatcher, Airey Neave, had been pressing government to involve itself more fully in micro-electronics and information technology. For much of the period the Government's primary concern in this field was with the fate of Britain's largest computer manufacturer, ICL. In 1978, however, the then Labour Prime Minister, Mr James Callaghan, was alerted to the much wider implications of information technology (IT), largely as a result of the BBC's *Horizon* programme 'The Chips are Down', which he saw and subsequently arranged for the entire Cabinet to view. As a result the Central Policy Review Staff (CPRS), which had already been urging that greater attention be paid to this question, was set to work on a number of reports, and in particular to attempting to devise some form of central machinery to handle new technology issues, many of which crossed departmental boundaries.

The CPRS continued this work after the Conservative victory in 1979, and Mrs Thatcher's personal attention was secured in particular during a visit to the United States and Canada when she had an opportunity to study a number of new technology developments. The catalyst to this growing Government interest came in September 1980, when the Cabinet Office's Advisory Council for Applied Research and Development (ACARD), established by the Labour government in 1976, presented a report to the Cabinet specifically on information technology. In particular it recommended the creation of a department to co-ordinate policy on computing, telecommunications and information handling and suggested, in view of the IT implications of teletext and mobile radio, that broadcasting should also be brought within this brief. Moreover it expressed its opinion that 'a first class, modern economic communications system is ... essential for effective application of IT' (ACARD, 'Information Technology', HMSO 1980, p.41).

Although it scarcely mentioned cable television, the ACARD Report nevertheless raised speculation that a transfer of broadcasting re-

51

sponsibilities from the Home Office to the Department of Industry (within which any IT department would be placed) would lead to a more rapid and progressive approach. The DOI's function, after all, was to promote industrial initiative, whereas the Home Office saw its role more in terms of protecting society. The report's main impact, however, was to raise government awareness of the industrial and employment potential of IT, the world market for which it valued at some £50 billion a year and growing at 10 per cent annually in real terms. Within weeks a Minister for Information Technology (Mr Adam Butler) was appointed and a special section created within the DOI, although the Home Office retained its broadcasting responsibilities. Consultation between the two departments, however, became increasingly necessary, particularly in relation to decisions on satellite broadcasting. Indeed by the time of the Commons debate on DBS in March 1982, even the Home Secretary was describing the 'opportunities for our industries and jobs' as 'the central factor' in a decision which would radically alter the character of Britain's broadcasting services (Parliamentary Debates (House of Commons), 4 March 1982, col. 418).

In early 1981 Mrs Thatcher promoted Mr Kenneth Baker, long one of the most vigorous exponents of IT in the Commons, to the post of IT minister, and in May gave her personal approval to the designation of 1982 as Information Technology Year. There followed a series of discussions on the best way to pursue the issue, and the PM's close involvement was reflected in the outcome. In July 1981 she announced the formation of an Information Technology Unit in the Cabinet Office itself; it would 'help to promote the use of IT within government and will seek to ensure the overall coherence of Government policies towards IT, particularly in so far as they span the responsibilities of more than one Department' (Written parliamentary answer, 2 July 1981).

In addition, an Information Technology Advisory Panel (ITAP) was established, consisting of leading members of IT industries, particularly computing and electronics. The general train of thought behind these developments was explicitly stated by Mrs Thatcher:

> The Government fully recognise the importance of information technology (IT) for the future industrial and commercial success of the United Kingdom and the central role that government must play in promoting its development and application . . . . In order to ensure that government policies and actions are securely based on a close appreciation of market needs and opportunities, I am appointing a panel of IT advisers who will be available to advise me and my colleagues on all aspects of IT (Ibid).

Perhaps significantly, the Information Technology Unit's secretary, Mr Roger Courtney, was formerly secretary of ACARD, whilst Mr Charles Read, Director of the Inter-Bank Research Organisation, had sat on the working party which produced the ACARD report on IT and was to be chairman of the ITAP working party on cable systems.

The plight of the cable industry and rising government interest in information technology were two converging strands. A third was the growing Conservative determination to encourage private sector involvement in the telecommunications field, as part of its broader commitment to privatisation of suitable public industries. 1981 was notable for the sale of shares in Cable and Wireless and for the British Telecommunications Act. The latter in particular demonstrated the Conservative belief that market forces were better suited to cope with the rapidly changing requirements of the telecommunications field than was a single monopoly network under rigid public control. The decision to allow the Mercury Consortium to provide long-distance telecommunications services in competition with British Telecom was every bit as momentous as a decision to allow cable systems to enter the broadcasting ring. At the same time private companies were given the go-ahead to sell telecommunications machinery – telephones, answering machines, exchanges, etc. – for connection to the telephone network and to provide telecommunications services such as electronic mail and automatic answering agencies. Early in 1982 another significant development was the decision to allow Britain's first privately financed satellite, Unisat, whilst others included a DOI commitment of £25 million over five years to research and development of optic-fibre cable technology. The use of optic fibres was in any case to accelerate in 1981-3, with both British Telecom and Mercury committing themselves to optic trunk telecommunications lines. Indeed, by early 1983 BT was in a position to declare that this was the last year in which it would order coaxial cable for trunk use. The signals from the Government were clear: technology and private enterprise were seen as the foundations of the new information economy.

Converging technologies, converging interests, converging policies; all contrasted sharply with the fact that a multiplicity of government departments still held individual responsibility for increasingly overlapping concerns. The issue of direct broadcasting by satellite was drawing the Home Office into questions of satellite technology which came under the DOI's brief, and the DOI into the Home Office territory of broadcasting. The concept of broadband telecommunications networks which could carry voice, data and video signals as required was presaged by the connection of computers and visual display units/television sets to the telephone network, making ever more artificial the technical and regulatory distinctions between broadcasting, computer services and telecommunications. Some cable televisions systems, betwixt and between, required as many as three separate licences before they could operate – from the Home Office, the DOI and British Telecom – as well as local·authority approval. Meanwhile the advent of Channel Four, pay-TV and cross-media co-financing of films, marked a new and closer relationship between broadcasters and the independent film industry, stimulating further the long-standing debate as to whether the Department of Trade was the most suitable body to watch over the latter.

It was in this 'melting pot' atmosphere of changing roles and responsibilities that the Information Technology Advisory Panel (ITAP) was formed. Its title reflected its IT parentage as did the membership: Mr Michael Aldrich, Managing Director of Rediffusion Computers Ltd, the second largest computer manufacturer in Britain after ICL; Mr I. H. Cohen, Managing Director of Mullard Ltd, a leading electronics supplier; Mr C. A. Davies, Managing Director of Information Technology Ltd; Dr D. F. Hartley, Director of Cambridge University Computing Service; Mr C. N. Read, Director of the Inter-Bank Research Organisation; and Mr C. G. Southgate, the Chief Executive of the Computer Services Division of British Oxygen Co. Ltd.

None of the Panel had broadcast or media experience, and certainly there was no indication that their first task should be to consider cable systems. Nevertheless the decision to do so was born out of needs and circumstances. The ACARD report had described modern telecommunications systems as being 'at the heart' of any large-scale development of information technology and mentioned the French integrated telephone and television experiment in Biarritz, using optic fibres. This view was shared by ITAP's members: the increasing capacity and complexity of computers and computer services made the development of high-capacity transmission systems ever more desirable. Already modern communications within offices required the interconnection of a variety of 'workstations', such as computer terminals, word processors, facsimile machines and advanced telephone systems, on one 'local area network' capable of handling several different forms of communication – voice, data, pictures and text. The obvious requirement was for a system or 'wide area network' of similar capabilities to interconnect separate offices, a function for which the existing telephone system had considerable limitations.

The Panel not surprisingly also shared the Government's views on the liberalisation of telecommunications, which it described as 'a crucial element in the development of IT in this country' (ITAP, *Cable Systems*, HMSO, February 1982, para. 8.9). Moreover it was undoubtedly aware both of cable expansion in the United States and of the British industry's parlous state: as part of Rediffusion Mr Michael Aldrich knew of the problems of its cable arm, as Mr Ivor Cohen did of those of the Visionhire cable subsidiary of Philips, which in its turn owned Mullards. Cable developments abroad, in the USA, Canada, France, Germany and Japan were in any case forcing themselves upon the attention of both the Government and its advisers.

Cable was a logical and necessary subject of study, but the starting point and approach were quite different from traditional enquiries into broadcasting issues. It was significant that those who traditionally provided the bulk of evidence in such enquiries – political parties and pressure groups, trade unions, the film and programme production industry and others who might be termed policy makers and media users – were not solicited for their views, although the BBC and IBA were consulted. Evidence came primarily from commercial interests, including potential investors and operators of cable systems, construction companies, electronic hardware firms and computer software consultants, organisations such as BICC, Greenwich Cablevision, British Telecom, the Cable Television Association, Logica, Plessey and the American Warner Amex Corporation. Whilst the programme production industry was omitted, evidence was sought from companies interested in providing 'enhanced' services such as viewdata and teleshopping – Thomson Data, the Birmingham Post and Mail, Thomas Cook, Debenhams, Great Universal Stores and Tesco. The result was a report which achieved what it set out to do – namely to raise industrial and economic considerations in broadcasting policy to the same level as had traditionally been accorded to social and political issues. The consequence, however, was to arouse the shock and hostility of those, including most of the existing broadcasting interests, to whom social and political considerations (including their own economic future) were paramount.

The ITAP report on 'Cable Systems' was completed and handed to the Government in late 1981 and published in March 1982. Its first paragraph heralded the radically different approach:

Modern cable systems, based on coaxial cables or optical fibres, can provide many new telecommunications-based services to homes and businesses. The initial attraction for home subscribers could be the extra television entertainment channels. However, the main role of cable systems eventually will be the delivery of many information, financial and other services to the home and the joining of business and homes by high-capacity data links (*Cable Systems,* cit., Summary, p.7).

It is this approach and the report's further discussion of the economics of cable, the industrial potential and the broadcast and regulatory implications, which have established the framework of the subsequent debate. In that respect, therefore, and in the alacrity with which the Government took its analysis to its own heart, the ITAP report has been brilliantly successful.

High-capacity cable systems, ITAP argued, could provide a wider selection of services more efficiently than traditional broadcast and telephone networks. New types of television programme could be produced for specialist and minority audiences – for ethnic, religious, educational and cultural subgroups as well as for truly local community interests. A wider choice of conventional television programmes could also be provided as well as very recent films to those who wished to pay extra for them. Advertising could benefit as producers of specialist products found it easier to target their particular specialist audience than the undifferentiated mass which commercial broadcasting currently supplied. New information services on the videotext principle would also become available, as would new ways of buying and selling through electronic viewing and ordering of goods – everything from groceries to houses. This would save both time and precious natural resources, as it would reduce people's need to travel. In a similar fashion, 'in serving homes and businesses alike, a cable system makes possible new work relationships' (Ibid., para. 2.10). Cable could offer everything from the transfer of digitised business data to the continuous monitoring of a home security alarm system, and all much more efficiently than existing 'narrowband' telephone lines.

Other countries, ITAP pointed out, were already very actively involved. Both France and West Germany were undertaking large scale optic-fibre systems trials, while in Japan an experimental optic-fibre interactive system was already in operation. In all countries the growth of satellite broadcasting would promote cable growth as people sought to receive these additional services without the bother of a multiplicity of individual household antennae. Above all, the United States was showing the way ahead:

> Until 1975 the FCC closely regulated the programmes that cable systems could show, for example limiting their showings of films to those more than three years old. However, most of the regulations were withdrawn in 1975 .... Cable subscribers have grown from 9 million or so in 1975 to the present 18 million, and there is no sign of this ceasing. (Ibid., para. 3.2. The first sentence, it should be noted, is factually incorrect – see Chapter 7.)

Meanwhile, the UK cable industry was in a state of decline and over 5,000 jobs could be lost shortly if that decline was not halted. To ignore cable would be to condemn an industry; to embrace it would be to open the way for industrial and economic regeneration on a huge scale. To cable half the country would necessitate capital investment of at least £2,500 million and additional expenditure of £1,000 million would go into information, security and other cable-related services. A large domestic market would be provided for cable equipment manufacturers, computer hardware and software companies, programme and enhanced service providers and producers of office equipment and other information technology systems. Cable, the ITAP members believed, was as inevitable as information technology itself, and both needed to be promoted. To do so would be to minimise imports and open international markets. While conceding that some countries would protect their indigenous cable and IT industries, the report concluded that there would be 'sizeable export opportunities' (Ibid., para. 5.10).

The message that cable could have major industrial benefits and a 'substantial' effect on employment was certainly very welcome to a government facing over 2.5 million unemployed and a slump which seemed to be getting progressively worse. But how could the money be found and who would want these new services? 'We have no doubt,' ITAP reported, 'that funds would be available from commercial sources to finance the installation of cable systems . . . . Cable systems offer large business opportunities with good chances of profit. We can see no need for public funds to be used to establish them' (Ibid., paras. 5.15, 5.16). Moreover, video recorder sales in Britain indicated consumer interest in additional programming.

> If experience in the USA is any guide, households will pay upwards of £10 monthly for additional [basic and pay] TV services . . . . Additional income could come from advertising and perhaps sponsorship. Even with less than 100 per cent pick up of the system, there would appear to be sufficient income from subscribers to give a reasonable return on capital (Ibid., para. 5.16).

Additional income would come from the other services cable could offer, such as information, security and shopping. Cable could be profitable, but only in certain circumstances. The lesson to be learnt from the American experience was repeated in the British context: 'Private sector funding will only be available if the range of programmes and services permitted on cable systems offer sufficient revenue-earning potential. There is a direct connection between the degree of broadcasting "liberalisation" established for cable systems and the possibility of private sector investment in them' (Ibid., para. 5.18).

Investment and profitability would also depend on the types of cable system constructed. It would be cheapest to use copper coaxial cable laid out in a 'tree and branch' configuration. To do so, however, would be to encourage use of American equipment, already tried and trusted. By contrast, optic fibres were likely to be too expensive and uncertain initially, although their cost and reliability would both improve rapidly. It was pointed out, however, that Britain was currently in a leading position with regard to technology of the 'switched-star' type, which also had a number of technical advantages over the traditional tree and branch pattern. Switched-star systems using copper coaxial cable, it was argued, became economically comparable to tree and branch when over thirty-five channels were involved. ITAP therefore expressed the view that certain technical standards might be established, preferably to allow subsequent connection between individual cable systems. In its desire to get systems built, however, the Panel proved itself ready to compromise:

> We would not want possible long-term considerations to delay the investment required now if United Kingdom industry is to benefit from cable systems. The technical standard developed for cable systems should ensure the interconnection of local networks and should not pay undue regard to any eventual integration into the national telecommunications network (Ibid., para. 5.19).

The Information Technology Advisory Panel could not ignore the fact that the expansion and 'deregulation' of cable services had enormous implications for current broadcast and telecommunications services, as well as for other media. The tenor of its argument, however, was that, while effecting a social and economic revolution, cable could well leave existing services largely intact. It pointed to previous occasions when fears had been expressed that new services would endanger and lower the quality of old – as when commercial television started in competition with the BBC. Yet such fears had proved groundless; quality had been not just preserved but actually improved. Careful thought now could ensure that the effect of cable was the same. In any case, the Panel believed that the BBC would always retain a dominant position in broadcasting, partly because of its historical status and partly because, as the report conceded, cable was unlikely for many years to reach more than half the population. Not only would the national licence fee continue, therefore, but in addition the BBC could supplement its income considerably by selling programmes to cable companies for repeat showings.

Nor would cable competition for audience and advertising revenue necessarily harm commercial television revenue. It was admitted that cable would mean the end of the long-established broadcast

58

dictum that there should not be competition between channels for the same source of finance. The new channels would, however, enable many more companies to advertise on television: 'These might either be firms with a local customer base, for whom national or regional advertising is irrelevant, or with a specialised market, who would wish to advertise on channels directed to that market' (Ibid., para. 6.9). In the United States, indeed, cable system growth had actually been 'accompanied' by an increase in advertising income for the national off-air commercial networks. (The fact that at that time cable channels had attracted minimal advertising revenue and so had not yet begun truly to compete with national off-air networks was not mentioned.) The very positive conclusion was that 'commercially, cable systems are an opportunity, not a threat; they would provide new sources of income for broadcasting, they could enable programme producers to make better use of their accumulated material, and they offer the possibility, with their interactive facilities, of wholly new types of programmes' (Ibid., para. 6.15).

A further objection which ITAP anticipated was the view that all channels needed to reach the maximum audience for greatest profitability and that this would lead to the 'lowest common denominator' effect, with each one showing only programmes with mass appeal. The Panel's look at American experience produced the conclusion that in fact the new cable channels were the ones which contained the most specialised and least 'homogenised' fare. Narrowcasting to specific interest groups could therefore work: 'We envisage that most of the other channels [besides existing services] to be provided on cable systems would provide for more specialised or local needs, or would be devoted to information and data transfer services' (Ibid., para. 6.17).

The final issues which ITAP addressed with regard to cable's impact on broadcast services were the questions of 'siphoning' and 'disadvantaging'. The Annan report had expressed concern that many people would not benefit from cable and pay-TV, either because they could not afford the extra cost or because they lived in areas it was uneconomic to cable. Such people might well suffer if existing services were adversely affected by cable, particularly if programmes were 'siphoned off' to the new channels. The loss of major national sporting events to cable was the principal concern, as cable companies might be able to outbid existing broadcast services for the rights to these. ITAP agreed that measures would have to be taken to prevent this happening, but its ready recognition that a large proportion of the population might never be able to receive cable services demonstrated the implicit view that cable was very much a luxury item and not a public service which should be available to all.

As for the other media and telecommunications interests, ITAP recognised that cable's local character held potential dangers for the local press and radio, although once again it argued that these were in a good position to benefit by involving themselves in the new medium. For the film industry, cable equally held both great potential for new material and possible threats from a large influx of programming from the USA. Finally it was admitted that British Telecom had considerable experience and resources as well as access to underground ducts for cable laying. The obvious conclusion, however, that BT should be encouraged to build a national cable network, did not suit the commercial and political approach so far taken. The report argued, therefore, that whilst BT should contribute it should not dominate cable development.

In view of subsequent criticism of ITAP as a commercially inspired, wholly deregulatory report it should be noted that it specifically recommended the further consideration of a number of regulatory issues – questions of ownership, monopoly, licensing of systems and penalties for non-compliance. Moreover, it took up and rejected the view that the multiplicity of channels a cable company offered gave it the same status as a book publisher, needing only to be subject to the laws of the land on obscenity and libel, and not to the specific regulations of traditional broadcasting: 'Cable systems are local monopolies, and therefore the operator would potentially have considerable control over the information and programme services reaching the community. Therefore, some form of regulatory structure will be required' (Ibid., para. 6.21). What regulation there was, however, should recognise the needs of investors and be liberal in intent: 'The aims must be to remove the barriers to private investment in cable systems that at present exist, to allow reasonable (although not absolute) freedom for entrepreneurial flair and in so doing to give a great stimulus to large parts of the IT industry' (Ibid., para. 8.9).

The nub of the Panel's argument was that speed was essential in determining cable policy lest the existing industry disappear and Britain be subsequently forced to depend on foreign hardware. Rapid cabling would be more probable using private investment than public money; this did, however, depend on the service provided being made sufficiently attractive to draw in cable subscribers. For although the long term interactive and information technology potential of cable systems was the principal objective, it was their character as an entertainment service which would be the initial chief attraction. The Panel therefore recommended that urgent studies be undertaken into the regulatory, financial and technical issues, so that policy could be formulated within the tight timetable which it proposed.

The ITAP report had put the principal points for the pro-cable lobby. A number of others could also be made. In particular, the potential benefits of increased channel availability could be reinforced. More channels held the potential not only for increased programming *to* specialised audiences but also *by* new and different sources – by independent producers, educational bodies, public institutions, local community groups, welfare bodies, particular interest groups and even ordinary individuals. More space should make access to television easier, resulting in a more 'democratic' use of the medium. Moreover, the new channels ought to react more accurately than existing services to the viewing preferences of their audiences, as a direct result of the activities of the market. With pay-television, in particular, people would demonstrate their preferences by paying or not paying for particular channels or even for individual items. The operation of market forces would thus lead to programme policy being determined by audience interests, rather than by broadcasting organisations' crude perceptions of mass mores and tastes, by the needs of advertisers to reach large audiences and by the cultural and social aspirations of those who manage the broadcasting duopoly.

Some proponents of cable take their argument further and do indeed press the publishing analogy. According to this view a cable operator is in the same position as a book publisher, for the most part simply putting out the productions of others. Like a publisher he has to make a profit. His decisions on what to 'publish' are therefore determined by his assessment of the audience's desires and his understanding of what the market will support. He is in the position of any other retailer of goods. Regulation of programming is surely redundant where the market supplies its place. Nor is strict balance and impartiality necessary, as the public will be able to choose as it pleases from the wide variety of opinion available on cable, as it currently does from the diverse national press.

Other deregulatory arguments challenge a different regulatory assumption. Most of those interested in the debate, including the ITAP Committee, have accepted automatically that, in line with all experience, franchises would be awarded to specific cable operators to provide services to specific areas. The capital-intensive economics of cable, it is conceded, make it a natural monopoly business in any particular locality; some form of regulation is therefore required to ensure the best possible service and to prevent this monopoly being abused. By contrast, a number of economists have argued that cable is very much a non-essential luxury good and that therefore it enjoys no local monopoly. On the contrary, it is in direct competition with other luxury goods, entertainment services and information sources –

newspapers, the cinema, the pub – for the consumer's disposable income. Consequently, neither regulation nor local area franchising is necessary. Cable will have to prove itself in direct competition and the market will ensure the proper level of penetration and service which it reaches, proper in relation to the consumer's degree of interest in it.

The channel choice argument can also be expanded. If cable operators are no longer bound by the need to programme channels to suit general tastes, and if consumers can make a choice to receive only what they pay for, then, it is argued, it becomes possible to extend the range of moral and political standards conveyed beyond that which is currently considered acceptable on broadcast television. Cable could more truly meet the evident national demand for more 'adult' programmes and films, as well as enabling extreme social and political viewpoints to be aired. At long last individual tastes and predilections would not be limited by society's concepts of what is or is not morally acceptable. Television, the great homogeniser, would at last be able to contribute to the search for individual freedom and self-realisation which has been such a feature of western culture in the last twenty years. This trend would be enhanced by the increasing incidence of homes with several television sets, thereby releasing the family from the confines of a communal 'fireside' and giving each member freedom to pursue their own programming interests. One of the most telling American examples used by cable exponents has been a comparison of what is available at any one moment on cable television in Manhattan with the choice at the same time in Britain. The example is also used to demonstrate that cable does not lead to a reduction in quality programming. (See Tabel III opposite.)

Two important qualifications need to be made to this comparison. What is not pointed out is that thirteen of the twenty-five Manhattan channels cited are simply relays of existing broadcast stations and therefore not a product of cable. Moreover, of the remaining cable channels, all but two pay-TV and one advertiser-supported channel are running at a very considerable loss. Current variety in the United States is not so much the result of cable profitability as of the continuing fight between service-providing companies to get and hold on to a piece of the market. How many and which will survive is still unclear.

Despite this caveat, the vision which a deregulated cable network offers remains extremely attractive, and so it needs to be if it is to supplant the widely held view of Britain's regulated broadcasting services as already the best in the world. When a nation has something which is good there is an inevitable and understandable resistance to change, lest in trying to make what is good better it destroys

62

TABLE III

TV viewer's choice in New York and London
at 9.00p.m. on 7 June 1982

Source: A. Neill (ed.) The Cable Revolution — Britain on the Brink of the
Information Society, London 1982.

Manhattan Cable	*BBC/ITV*
1. *M*A*S*H*	1. News
2. *Black Ghetto Life* (documentary)	2. *The Hitch-hiker's Guide to the Galaxy*
3. *Sister, Sister* (film)	3. *Minder*
4. Merv Griffin (talk show)	
5. *The Kennedy Years* (documentary)	
6. Baseball	
7. Spanish Play	
8. Variety Show	
9. *Adam and Eve*, with Nureyev (dance)	
10. *Attack* (film)	
11. Spanish Drama	
12. *Orpheus* (opera)	
13. International Education (public access discussion)	
14. Seminar on Nuclear Arms	
15. Baseball	
16. *Bye, Bye Birdie* (film)	
17. *Danger UXB* (drama)	
18. *Dog Day Afternoon* (film)	
19. Gymnastics	
20. Classified Advertisements	
21. Royal Ballet	
22. Folk Art (discussion)	
23. Chinese Cooking	
24. News	
25. *The High Country* (film)	

the equilibrium of the whole and brings everything tumbling down. Cable clearly has to justify itself. But at the same time one can legitimately ask whether everything is as it should be in the existing broadcasting system. The answer, inescapably, is that it is not. Although Channel Four has to some extent reduced the problem, independent producers have traditionally had difficulty in gaining access to the medium, whilst the duopoly has effectively limited the amount that independents and sports promoters can get for their product. Similarly, public access is very limited, truly local television nonexistent and minorities only poorly served, often only at the unsociable margins of each broadcast day.

Since the existing organisations have to take account of social rather than individual tastes and values, there is much that television could show but which is considered unacceptable. Equally, because of the need to maintain the cost of television at a socially acceptable price, there is much material – current feature films or programmes with only a very limited appeal – which it simply cannot afford to show. Perhaps the largest category of excluded material, because taken to the extreme it comprehends all experience, is that which off-air broadcast television does not have the *space* to show. At present television lacks freedom, money and space. Consequently it serves most of the people some of the time, but it certainly does not satisfy all requirements at all moments. The debate in Britain over the last two years has been about whether in practice, given the economics of broadcasting, cable do any better.

THE REACTION TO ITAP

The ITAP report set the character of the subsequent debate and drew attention to the principal industrial, economic, social, broadcasting and regulatory issues. In fifty-four pages, however, it could not hope to resolve them. While much of the press took ITAP's conclusions at face value and eagerly sought to confirm them by looking to America, others, including political interests, unions and broadcasting organisations, took a more sceptical view. To both the latter and the cable industry, the principal ITAP message had been 'deregulate', although their reaction to this message was very different. For its part, the government embraced ITAP's philosophy. As William Whitelaw declared in the subsequent Commons debate, 'The Prime Minister has made clear the government's determination to secure the advantages that cable technology can bring to this country' (Parliamentary Debates (House of Commons), 22 March 1982).

In line with ITAP's recommendations, a number of interdepartmental committees were immediately established to consider in more detail the technological, commercial, economic, broadcast and telecommunications aspects, involving the Home and Cabinet Offices, the Treasury and the Industry, Environment, Employment and Trade Departments. Moreoever, in a move which was widely seen as a mark of traditional Home Office caution, but which actually did no more than follow ITAP's agenda, the Home Secretary appointed an independent committee to investigate the broadcasting implica-

64

tions. Headed by former Cabinet Secretary Lord Hunt of Tanworth, the three-man committee also included Sir Maurice Hodgson, retired chairman of ICI, and Professor James Ring of the Imperial College of Science and Technology and a former member of the IBA. The Government's approach was made quite clear by the inquiry's brief:

> To take as its frame of reference the Government's wish to secure the benefits for the United Kingdom which cable technology can offer and its willingness to consider an expansion of cable systems which would permit cable to carry a wider range of entertainment and other services (including when available services of direct broadcasting by satellite), but in a way consistent with the wider public interest, in particular the safeguarding of public service broadcasting; to consider the questions affecting broadcasting policy which would arise from such an expansion, including in particular the supervisory framework; and to make recommendations by 30 September 1982 (*Report of the Inquiry into Cable Expansion and Broadcasting Policy,* Cmnd 8679, HMSO October 1982, p.1).

Thus in the space of a few days the debate had moved beyond the question of whether or not cable should be permitted and encouraged to expand. Although there was still little if any evidence of consumer demand for new channels and services, the IT lobby, looking to overseas developments and to perceived opportunities in Britain, had forced the pace. The issue was no longer 'whether' but 'how', 'how much' and 'how quickly'. As Roy Hattersley subsequently commented, 'We delude ourselves if we think there's a possibility of preventing or frustrating' the coming of cable (quoted in the *Sunday Times,* 5 September 1982).

So forceful had been the alliance between the IT lobby and the Government that traditional broadcasting interests had had little opportunity to consider or reassess their own viewpoint. To many groups on the margins, indeed, it was almost the first time they had heard of cable. In his request for submissions to the inquiry, Lord Hunt himself laid down the basic regulatory arguments. Previously regulation had been justified because broadcasting used a limited resource – transmitting frequencies – and involved bringing into the home a powerful medium with great potential to influence or offend people. Cable removed the limited resources argument and so brought television closer to the situation of the press. Nevertheless arguments for a degree of regulation remained:

> a) cable is different from the written press, not only because there is almost bound to be an effective monopoly in any given local area, but also because a large part of the country will continue to depend on off-air services for the foreseeable future;

b) an expansion of broadcast services by cable could damage the quality and range of public service broadcasting, on which viewers who cannot receive or do not wish to pay for cable services would continue to depend, by obtaining exclusive rights to national and sporting events etc., or by attracting audiences (and in the case of ITV advertising revenue) away from broadcast services and leaving them less able to provide the range of programmes now offered;

c) regardless of the medium of transmission, television programmes brought direct into the home have a power, an intimacy and an influence which justifies supervision (Reprinted as Appendix A of the Hunt Report, pp.40-44).

In view of these concerns, the Inquiry invited comments on a number of specific issues, including the ownership, operation and financing of cable, the protection of existing broadcast services, the cinema and domestic production industries, the maintenance of programme and advertising standards and the degree and character of regulation necessary. The result of this request was 189 submissions from all manner of bodies, including broadcasting organisations, unions, cable operators, potential investors, advertising interests, newspapers, publishing houses, American and Canadian companies, the churches, government departments, economists, producers, film organisations, the cinema industry, computing and telecommunications interests and political organisations. For many it was their first real opportunity to comment on ITAP and consequently some of the most valuable evidence came in the form of challenges to or defences of the Cable Systems report. While questions of principle remained important, it had become equally vital to determine the likely realities of ITAP's vision.

Not surprisingly, neither British Telecom nor the telecommunications unions were ready to concede cable to private enterprise without a fight. While BT described itself as 'uniquely placed' to play a major role, the Post Office Engineering Union (POEU) pointed to BT's television transmission, telecommunications and cable experience, to the economies of scale and standardisation which a national network would allow, to BT's existing infrastructure of ducts, poles and switching points and, most tellingly, to its ability to cross-subsidise the construction of less economic rural cable systems from the profits of urban ones, thereby ensuring the more rapid creation of a truly national network. ITAP's suggestion that coaxial cable be used initially was also condemned as short-sighted when the extensive commercial application of optic fibres would quickly bring their cost down to realistic levels.

Such differences of opinion about public or private investment reflected more than personal interest or differences in political philosophy. They also indicated scepticism about one of ITAP's fundamental assumptions – that the information revolution could and would be entertainment-led. Information and other services surely had to sink or swim on their own merits, not on the back of entertainment. Of the information being created by the information sector barely 6 per cent is actually for domestic consumption (newspapers, printing, broadcasting, etc.); the remainder is entirely contained within business and industry. Investment in more efficient information working practices and in IT technology is consequently of primary interest to business, not to the domestic consumer. Indeed, the enormous size of the information-handling workforce is now one of the major obstacles to increased productivity and to more efficient use of capital; consequently it is in such areas that investment in information technology must and presumably will be greatest. Where then is the logic in arguing that the information revolution will arrive by attracting domestic consumers to buy additional entertainment services? Entertainment services on cable are hardly the crucial IT fuse which the ITAP report suggests, although without them there would certainly be little incentive for private investors to build cable systems in residential areas. As many critics pointed out, a publicly funded network could more readily be placed in the broader IT perspective, as part of a national telecommunications resource designed for all the information needs of society.

Not only was the concept of an entertainment-led revolution questionable, but so was its economic viability. As one submission to Hunt declared, 'Just because a service is technically feasible, it does not mean that large numbers of people will buy it' (Evidence of A. Ehrenberg and T. Barwise, p.7). The lack of success of BT's Prestel service was referred to as evidence of the average domestic consumer's minimal requirements for data, whilst the high take-up of video recorders cited by ITAP was taken to indicate more the desire of viewers to watch broadcast programmes at times other than when they were transmitted than a widespread demand for new types of programme. The growth of cable in the United States was explained by poor reception, the low quality of programmes and excessive and intrusive advertising, factors which did not apply in Britain. In a period of deep recession and high unemployment, therefore, just how willing would the City be to invest the sums necessary for extensive cabling, particularly given the long-term return which the industry seemed to entail? With 51 per cent of BT itself coming on the market, if the Conservatives remained in power, would not this be a far more attractive investment? The POEU quoted *Financial Weekly*: 'The Government . . . is living in cloud-cuckoo-land if it believes the private sector will generate the £2.5 billion which the Information Technology Advisory Panel estimates will be needed' (*Financial Week-*

ly, 26 March 1982, quoted in POEU, *The Cabling of Britain*, p.28). Moreover, if people were interested in new entertainment channels but not in videotex and the similar enhanced services cable could offer, then other technologies – direct broadcasting by satellite, low-power television or terrestrial microwave systems – could do this much more cheaply.

The belief that the economy, employment and exports could be significantly stimulated by such means was similarly queried. The major developed countries would encourage their own cable and electronics industries in the same way that Britain was preparing to encourage hers. If an overseas sales market did develop, it would inevitably be dominated by Japanese, American and Canadian technology and companies. At the same time, the overwhelming domination of film and TV production by the USA, and the relative cheapness of this product, implied a likely trade deficit on the programming for cable, at least initially. The National Electronics Council Working Party on Technological Opportunities in Broadcasting pointed out another problem: 'Technology is advancing rapidly and many relevant standards have yet to be agreed internationally . . . There is thus a danger that by moving too fast the UK could go it alone and lose out on export markets' (Report of the National Electronics Council Working Party, May 1982, p.18). European attempts to market the video recorder too early in its development – by Philips, Telefunken and the ICI, Ilford and Rank consortium – had had just this effect, leaving the way wide open for the Japanese influx, using Japanese tape formats which now effectively excluded almost everything else. As for the argument that cable might create up to 20,000 jobs, Professors Ehrenberg and Barwise of the London Business School argued that if this could only be achieved at the expense of lowered broadcasting standards then it was not worth the price. What 50 million people did for an average of twenty-five hours each week – watch television – was more important than what 20,000 did for thirty-five hours a week, namely work: 'The basic consideration has to be that television is of far greater social than economic importance' (Evidence of A. Ehrenberg and T. Barwise to Hunt Inquiry, p.8).

Ehrenberg and Barwise also addressed the question of how much money might be available for programming. Precious little, they felt, would come from advertising. Evidence from the United States suggested that advertising revenue would not grow in proportion to increased advertising capacity. American television has four or five times as much advertising as British, yet, relative to the USA's size and wealth, advertising revenue is only about one and a half times as high as here. The cable channels which might be profitable are the mass appeal, predominantly pay-TV, film and sports ones.

Ehrenberg and Barwise's conclusions for 'narrowcast' and community channels were therefore dire:

> The revenue potential of narrowcasting to specific minority groups is small: such groups mostly watch general television (like everybody else). The scope for minority *interest* programmes will also remain small: television, whether cabled or off-air, is a slow and inflexible information medium. Achieving the production standards that we all now expect is also very costly . . . for similar reasons there is virtually no scope for producing local access and community programmes which people will actually watch (Ibid.).

Much of the evidence of Lord Hunt's committee was concerned with the potential effect of cable on the existing broadcasting services. The IBA in particular pointed out how invidious and difficult it would be to have unregulated cable channels operating side by side and competing for audiences and advertising with regulated off-air services. It reminded the Committee that less than two years earlier, in 1980, Parliament had imposed the most detailed regulations ever, regarding franchise awards and programming, upon the independent television companies and particularly upon Channel Four. The IBA's codes on the portrayal of violence and on family viewing policy were cited as examples of where regulation was clearly necessary to protect the interests of child viewers. While identical codes could not be placed on cable there should not be wide discrepancies in standards: 'If cable services went ahead on a totally different basis, there could all too easily be a gradual erosion of requirements on existing services, without Parliament having taken a deliberate decision that this was acceptable' (IBA initial evidence to Hunt Inquiry).

A related cause of changes in programming was described by Ehrenberg and Barwise in a paper prepared for the IBA and BBC. The more programmes there are to choose from at a given point in time, the more viewers tend to select one of the easier and more relaxing entertainment programmes, rather than an intellectually or emotionally demanding one. The audience for the latter then inevitably drops, and without reasonable audiences the justification for showing such material declines, most of all on ITV where advertising revenue from small audiences would be minimal. Without regulation of content the range of programmes available to everyone is therefore diminished by the very act of increasing channels.

With the BBC's evidence, questions as to the practical consequences became mingled with questions of principle. Public broadcasting, it argued, enshrines three concepts – commitment to excellence, enrichment of choice and widespread access. Traditionally regulation has shielded public service broadcasting from the forces of the marketplace; consequently it has been possible to fund the whole range of programmes and services on their merits and not exclusively in terms of their popular appeal. The result is a national asset which would nevertheless be rapidly eroded if unregulated cable services were permitted an operating philosophy of 'quick-kill methods of financial control, a cynical view of public taste and no concern for social side-effects' (BBC evidence to Hunt Inquiry). Excellence would deteriorate if cable operators were allowed to seek a quick return through cheap programming, particularly imported from the USA. Choice would also be reduced if operators could compete with the networks for major sporting events and popular programmes:

> If, unlike the networks, these operators have no commitment to a wide range of programmes, they will be able to concentrate their resources on blockbuster attractions .... The resulting auction faces public service broadcasters with a cruel dilemma. They must either commit a disproportionate amount of their resources to matching the bids of the cable operators – thus impoverishing other areas of programming – or see the majority deprived of such star attractions in favour of a paying minority (Ibid.).

That minority would also be a geographically restricted one. Only prosperous and heavily populated areas would be cabled for a long time to come. People in poorer and less dense regions would have no access to cable services. Cable would become a socially divisive force: 'If cable becomes symbolic of what Mayfair can have but Brixton cannot, what Metropolitan Man may enjoy but Rural Man is denied, then one more social tension will be generated in an uneasy age' (Ibid.). The edge of this argument was somewhat blunted when it was discovered that in fact Brixton was one of the few areas already cabled and part of a pay-cable experiment. Nevertheless, the same argument was used in many other submissions.

One issue upon which Lord Hunt specifically invited comments was the ownership and operation of cable systems. The ITAP report had argued that investors would only be interested if the owner of a cable system could also take responsibility for operating it, thereby protecting his investment and obtaining the benefits of potentially higher and quicker returns from actual operation. Few would be interested in merely owning the system and leasing its use to others as though a common carrier. By contrast, the regulatory lobby almost without exception proposed a separation of system owner and operator, just as in commercial broadcasting the IBA owns and maintains the transmission system but the independent contractors actually operate the programme services. In this way, it was argued, the problems of system owners enjoying an effective local monopoly and control over the material transmitted could be reduced and cable *operators* brought more easily to account. Regulation was required to prevent the abuse of monopoly power. While admitting that operators would actually produce very little of what they transmitted, the IBA, BBC and others argued that they would control all the available channels in any area. And the IBA made a further salient point in response to the argument that a multiplicity of channels rendered unnecessary the traditional broadcast requirements of impartiality and balance in programming: 'The number of services that can be provided as a result of cable will be greatly increased; but the number will in theory as well as in fact be finite. Considerations of limited access will still be relevant' (IBA initial evidence).

A final potential monopoly problem was identified by a number of observers. ITAP's arguments for a more market-based approach to cable assumed the existence of a free market, something which in the context of the capital-intensive cable system and electronics industries could not be said to exist. It was pointed out that the financial and organisational resources required would lead to domination by a few companies, as indeed was already the case both in Britain and the United States. Moreover, those companies involved, such as British Electric Traction (Rediffusion), the Electronic Rentals Group (Visionhire) and Thorn-EMI (Radio Rentals), all had a vertical integration of interests which would inevitably influence supposedly market-based decisions. As one commentator put it, 'a market economy for cable will in all probability be no more than the public articulation of the private needs of commercial giants. The call for deregulation of cable by the cable industry is in reality a call for boards' (M. Tracey, 'Wrapping up Cable', *Stills*, Vol. 1, No.5, 1983, p.15). This train of thought raises the issue of the objectives and motive forces underlying our broadcasting system. For sixty years broadcasting has been organised around the central principle of 'public service'. Is that central principle now to be changed to one of 'market force'? The Broadcasting Research Unit's Working Party on the New Technologies pointed out to Lord Hunt: 'You can only ultimately choose between a system that is regulated in the broad social interest and has as its core a notion of "public good", and a system that is regulated on the basis of commercial criteria and has as its core a notion of "private good" ' (Evidence of BRU Working Party on the New Technologies to Hunt Inquiry).

The issues raised in this debate were therefore of four kinds: questions of principle, of likely impact, of practicability and of the best approach to cable. While many submissions were expressing their concern at the idea of rapid and unfettered cable growth, an equal number sought to add weight to ITAP's conclusions. Where the

BBC argued as a question of principle the need to preserve national events for 'free' off-air television, Charterhouse Japhet, the merchant bankers, argued the equally strong principle that it was the promoters of such events and not the general public who owned the television rights and should be able to sell them to the highest bidder. In response to the view that the power and influence of television in the home justified regulation, Charterhouse pointed to the distinction between 'free' and 'pay' television where the viewer makes a conscious decision to buy a particular service. There is no difference between the latter situation and the purchase of pre-recorded video tapes or books and magazines, none of which are regulated beyond the normal confines of the law. Charterhouse also had something to say about fears for the future of existing services. It pointed to the position, strength and wealth of the latter and suggested that, with only limited penetration, cable could remain a 'permanent poor relation' (Evidence of Charterhouse Japhet to Hunt Inquiry). In a similar fashion, the British production industry could hold its own against imported material without the need for import restrictions; experience had shown that British viewers preferred British-made programmes, despite the popularity of certain American productions.

One of the most influential pieces of evidence on the likely impact and practicability of cable came from the Institute of Practitioners in Advertising. In a passage cited in the Hunt Report, the IPA estimated that advertising revenue on cable services could reach £120 million (at 1980 prices) by 1995 and that previous experience had shown that advertising expanded whenever new media were introduced to accommodate it, as with independent radio and free newspapers. In any case there was scope for an increase in the ratio of UK advertising volume to GNP (1.34 per cent in 1980), which if raised to American levels (1.6 per cent) could generate a further £500 million in advertising revenue. The IPA argued that previous fears as to the effect of new media on the advertising revenue of existing services had always proved unfounded, and American evidence indicated that this would also be so for cable.

Pearson Longman, the diversified publishing and communications company, was equally bullish on cable but not quite so sanguine. Cable could take advertising away from the local press (in which it has extensive interests), a possibility which led it to argue that such newspapers should be allowed to take a financial interest in cable systems. This pragmatic approach was reflected in its response to fears of monopoly control of cable systems and channels of communication. Ownership and operation of systems should, it felt, not be compulsorily separated, nor should there be limits on how many systems a company could control. The extremely high costs of construction made any serious concentration of power most unlikely. If it did eventually transpire that a few major corporations held an excessive share of the market, then legislation might be introduced to separate the provision of programmes from the operation of systems. This had been done in the United States film industry in the 50s, when the major film studios/distributors had been required to sell off their enormous cinema chains for the same reasons.

The heat generated by the arguments on both sides was exacerbated by the ambiguity of the central term being used – 'deregulation'. From the comments of some 'deregulators' and from misleading reports of American deregulation many took it to mean no regulation at all. To others, including some of the most ardent exponents of cable, it was apparent that a total lack of regulation was neither possible nor entirely desirable. At the very least, most potential system operators favoured the awarding of franchises for specific areas so that two companies could not attempt to 'overbuild' each other – that is, to lay two cable systems in one place. Consequently, few took the term to mean anything other than 'less regulation' and this was equally the Government's view. Following an ardently pro-cable speech at the 1982 Edinburgh Television Festival, Kenneth Baker himself indicated a number of areas where regulation would be necessary:

> Of course we must have some sort of regulation. However, to hold back the cable process because it might not reach everyone in the country right away is really holding back progress . . . . And, at any rate, I am an optimist. I believe that we will have the whole nation cabled from Land's End to John O'Groats within ten years. Regulations can see to that without reducing the investment potential of the private sector (Quoted in B. Murphy, *The World Wired Up*, 1982, p. 129).

The questions at issue, therefore, were how much regulation and of what kind? Everyone awaited the Hunt Report.

LORD HUNT REPORTS

The Inquiry into Cable Expansion and Broadcasting Policy presented its report to the Home Secretary on 28 September 1982. In it three questions were addressed: should cable be subject to regulation, if so of what kind and how could public service broadcasting best be preserved? The answers were a cause of immediate jubilation in the cable camp, confirming that few if any had expected total deregulation or even felt it to be necessary. For although it suggested that a number of initial ground rules and a degree of continuing 'oversight' were necessary, Lord Hunt's Committee also made it clear that the latter should be neither too detailed nor too inflexible. It further stated that a formal franchising procedure would be desirable and that a national cable authority (not the IBA) should be established, but that once franchises had been awarded oversight should be reactive rather than constant.

In particular four functions to cable provision were identified:

a) The cable provider – the owner and installer of the physical cable system;

b) The cable operator – the manager of a cable system who puts together a package of cable services to sell to subscribers in that area;

c) The programme or service provider – the person who assembles a block of programmes into a channel or provides a particular service (e.g. security) for sale to or through the cable operator;

d) The programme maker – who produces individual programmes.

In some evidence the case for licensing the cable system owner and the programme provider had been put; but the report argued that the key figure would be the cable operator who, through his packaging and marketing skills, would ultimately be responsible for the success or failure of the whole system. There should therefore be no need to license or restrict ownership of the other functions. The operator, however, should be licensed for ten years initially and eight thereafter.

To avoid political or ideological bias it was argued that central and local government bodies, political parties and religious groups should be excluded from cable operation. To prevent excessive concentration of media power, press, radio and television companies should be allowed only a minority interest, as should foreign companies. The Committee felt, however, that fears of excessive power being wielded by a company which both owned and operated a system were overstated. The only limitation necessary was to mandate that an owner/operator would have to sell or lease his plant to another operator if he was ever deprived of his operating licence, thereby ensuring continuity of service to the consumer. Unhelpfully, but perhaps sensibly, Lord Hunt considered the question of whether Britain should be cabled by British Telecom or by private money to be outside his brief.

The fears of the BBC and IBA were not rated very highly. Although the Committee admitted that forecasts of how much advertising revenue cable might attract were 'hedged around with uncertainties', it did not feel that independent broadcasting revenue would be seriously affected. Nor did it believe that BBC and ITV would lose any significant proportion of their audiences to cable channels, even to the film services. In any case, if cable was going to succeed it would need both to be popular and to attract advertising revenue. The only significant protective measures the Inquiry proposed, therefore, were to prohibit cable from obtaining exclusive rights to a limited number of national events, and to ban the form of revenue known as pay-per-view, which the BBC had argued would allow cable to outbid the existing services for particularly appealing films and sporting events. On the whole the Hunt Committee preferred to be optimistic about cable's impact.

No limit was proposed for the number of channels an operator might offer. The argument that BBC and ITV would be forced to compete with cable on a more popular level to the detriment of serious programming was also not considered significant. Consequently, the Committee did not feel that the traditional broadcasting requirements of range and balance in programming were necessary for cable, although it did suggest that the franchising process should take account of the need for programme diversity. Similarly, impartiality on individual channels was not essential (other than in news), although there should be no bias over a system as a whole. If a pay channel could be electronically locked it should be allowed to show films with a British Board of Film Censors '18' (X) rating at any time of the day. The Committee did, however, accept the view that 'the place of television in the average family home is such that restraints on pornography and violence are required additional to those imposed by the law of the land' (Hunt Report, para. 72). Channels which could not be locked, therefore, were to be subject to current broadcasting standards of taste and decency, and advertising was to conform to the existing IBA code, although not pre-vetted as at present.

In its desire not to stifle cable at birth the Committee had proposed minimal protective measures for broadcasting services. The same attitude marked its recommendations on production. It recognised that cable would need to buy in programmes from abroad, particularly the United States, to fill the available channels. It therefore recommended that no maximum quota of foreign material be imposed, as was presently the case for off-air television. Again the tone was optimistic: the Committee had 'faith' that the British film and television industry would expand to satisfy the market.

The Hunt Report's recommendations on operating requirements were, therefore, a radical departure from previous practice. But, in its various references to the franchising process, the Committee made it clear that operators should take account of the public interest. A number of 'hopes' and 'expectations' were expressed, although it was admitted that how much was possible would depend on particular circumstances. It anticipated that certain technical standards would be imposed, including interactivity and a minimum system capacity.

To avoid excessive monopoly power there should be a diversity not only of programming but also of programme sources. Some channels should be available for lease by companies not associated with the system operator. There was a 'presumption' that all systems would offer children's programmes, education and a community service and even that cable operators should 'accept responsibility for ensuring and financially assisting some community participation in cable programmes' (Ibid., para. 71). The franchise-awarding body should also have certain expectations regarding the speed, order and, most ominously for potential cable providers, the geography and comprehensiveness with which an area was cabled:

> The franchising body will need to take into account the comprehensiveness of the cabling within the area concerned, so that it is not restricted to streets where a majority of occupiers are likely to pay for cable. It could also speed up the widespread development of cable and avoid what is known as 'cherry-picking' by seeking in some cases to combine less attractive localities with those carrying the best commercial prospects or even by asking large consortia which bid for a prosperous area to provide a separate cable system in a less promising area elsewhere (Ibid., para. 86(a)).

The Committee therefore expected much from the franchising process, which it expected would be competitive. Thereafter the cable authority would have oversight only from a distance, but with the power to impose additional regulations or even remove an operator's licence if, in extreme cases, he abused his position or failed to live up to his promises. Given these potential sanctions and the relatively short franchise terms proposed, detailed regulation, including the regulation of charges to customers, seemed unnecessary.

As a former Cabinet Secretary, Lord Hunt's speciality was in finding a path between apparently irreconcilable viewpoints and in guiding the way towards consensus. In the days following the publication of his report the question most frequently posed was whether in fact he had succeeded, in his own phrase, in 'squaring the circle'. The inevitable conclusion was that, clever as the report was, he had not. As one commentator put it, 'Lord Hunt has driven a huge hole in the UK's traditional concepts of broadcasting .... Lord Reith must be turning in his grave' (Arthur Sandles in the *Financial Times*, 13 October 1982). The cable lobby's satisfaction was only lessened by the ban on pay-per-view and the short licence period recommended, and it set out immediately and successfully to persuade the government that on these issues Hunt had got it wrong. To the IBA, by contrast, the regulatory authority proposed was 'a toothless watchdog' (Lord Thomson, Chairman of the IBA, *Sunday Times*, 17

October 1982), while to Alan Sapper of the ACTT the report was a 'predictably abject and grovelling document, ridden with spurious compromises' (*Film and Television Technician*, 1 November 1982). Perhaps most pertinently *The Scotsman* described Hunt's rather vague 'hopes', 'expectations' and 'presumptions' as 'too pious by half; more than wishful thinking will be required if the worst excesses are to be avoided' (*Scotsman*, 13 October 1982).

For the problem was that Hunt had brought no certainty into the debate, provided no answers. All remained speculation. As he admitted himself, cable was 'a leap into the dark' (Hunt Report, para. 13). To the Committee this had been a justification for flexibility of approach; to others it was confirmation of the need for caution. Hunt has left uncertain the likely impact of cable on audience sizes or on advertising revenue for ITV, Independent Local Radio, the cinema or the local press. He had admitted that some programmes and sports events would be siphoned off to pay-TV from broadcast, despite the ban on pay-per-view. He perhaps assumed too much in believing that BBC and ITV would be able to maintain programme quality and hence audiences in the face of competition. Writing in the *Observer*, John Birt, Director of Programmes at London Weekend Television, argued that if ITV lost audiences it would have 'no choice' but to shift away from peak viewing time programmes which added variety to the schedule but erned low ratings. Moreover, resources would be transferred to peak-time programmes at the expense of off-peak minority items – which currently consumed over half of ITV's production budget (*Observer*, 5 December 1982). Even more vehemently, R.W. Wordley, Managing Director of HTV, queried why, in a competitive environment, the ITV companies should contribute either to the Exchequer levy or to the various worthy but unprofitable causes they presently did, including Channel 4 (*The Times*, 15 October 1982).

In his turn, Alasdair Milne, the BBC's Director General, doubted whether the list of 'protected' national events proposed could be made to work, whilst Lord Hunt's belief that an 'X'-rated, electronically locked channel could really be childproof was widely treated with scepticism. Perhaps above all the view that an unprotected British production industry could compete against cheaply 'dumped' American products was rejected as quite unrealistic. When cable operators could buy off-the-shelf American drama for anywhere between £500 and £15,000 an hour, where would be the incentive to commission or produce British material at upwards of £100,000 an hour? Equally dubious was the idea that franchisees would be prepared to take on less attractive franchises in return for being given profitable ones. Cable was already a high-risk, long-term return venture; could the cable authority actually require a company to lose money on a project?

Ultimately a person's reaction to Hunt had to depend on his state of mind. A pessimist would see little chance of all Lord Hunt's assumptions being realised; an optimist could share in Hunt's confidence in the flexible approach. For it was an almost inevitable characteristic of the subject that all should remain uncertain. The Hunt Committee could not hope actually to resolve the issues it addressed, and this problem was exacerbated by the approach it took. By interpreting its brief very narrowly and not even attempting to consider the technological, interactive, economic, industrial or wider social implications which ITAP had raised, it left issues crucial to the whole debate completely unconsidered. Nor did it consider BT's role in cable, a subject of central political and economic importance. Although the various interdepartmental committees were sitting in private to consider some of these questions, there remained no authoritative public statement, no considered investigation of ITAP's various assertions. All remained speculation.

LOOKING TO NORTH AMERICA

The cable debate in Britain has therefore been characterised by vehement assertions on all sides, assertions as to the technology's economic, entertainment, community, telecommunications and democratic potential, and of its likely fatal consequences for existing broadcasting institutions, other media, the British production industry and even for national cultural identity and social unity. In the heat of the argument there has been overemphasis, overconfidence and overreaction as each lobby has fought to influence major political decisions. Glib phrases have been coined and new terminology invented to describe complex issues, while in one beautiful, telling, but essentially emotionally based image the opponents of rapid cable development have been likened to medieval monks and barons – the vested interests of the age – debating whether or not to permit the Renaissance (Peter Jay, 1982 Edinburgh Television Festival).

That the public debate has so far remained at this essentially emotional level is perhaps inevitable, given the underlying differences in social and political philosophy. In any case, prophecy is an uncertain business at the best of times and there has been all to little concrete experience on which to base opinions or decisions. As yet it has proved difficult to supply real answers to the many practical issues raised: issues as to cable's economic viability, the prospects for the concept of narrowcasting and community channels, the consumer demand for cable services – both entertainment and enhanced – and the implications for the national economy. Naturally, in the months since cable became a live issue and a likely prospect much detailed research has been carried out on all sides as to the particular situation in Britain, with the major players – the prospective investors, cable operators and service providers – taking a hard look at where the opportunities lie and making their plans accordingly. What those opportunities, plans and perceptions might be, and how cable seems likely to develop in the light both of them and of the regulatory structure now being established in the cable bill, will be considered in Part v of this book.

Nevertheless, throughout the debate of the last two years and even during the early 1970s, one of the most common references on both sides has been to the North American experience, as providing the only significant examples of market-led cable in its third and fourth stages of development. There has been a constant flow of reports from the United States first of the tremendous choice which cable provides, of the crucial importance of deregulation, the reality of narrowcasting, the demand for pay-film channels and the highly advanced interactive cable systems now being built, only to be followed by tales of the industry's severe economic difficulties, the failure of two cultural channels, the poor quality of cable programming, the unwatchable character of access and community services, but the nonetheless serious impact which cable is having on the fortunes of the broadcast networks. Meanwhile, from Canada there has been evidence of a different and more regulated approach to cable and pay-TV, and of the experience of a relatively small country (in terms of population) sitting in the cultural and economic shadow of a mighty and common-language neighbour, with a traditionally weak production sector but a large and increasingly powerful cable lobby.

Inevitably there are dangers in trying to make direct comparisons between different societies and circumstances. Cable television in the United States, as in Canada but unlike Britain, enjoys the solid foundation of widespread poor broadcast reception, an unequal distribution of broadcasting stations across the country and a consequent demand for the importation of distant signals. It is fortunate in that respect in having a large number of distant signals readily available and in a common language, thanks to the structure of American broadcasting which results in each town or city of any consequence having its own network-affiliated and wholly independent stations. Moreover, one reason for the success of pay cable is seen as being a consumer reaction against excessive advertising on television (in some cases up to sixteen minutes in seven breaks each hour) and of a demand for higher-quality programmes. This contrasts with less intrusive advertising in Britain (seven minutes each hour in fewer blocks), two advertising-free channels and a relative, though far from complete, satisfaction with the programmes available.

The high take-up of pay-film channels in the USA may also be related to their cost which, thanks to advantageous agreements with the major film distributors, are significantly lower than in Canada or Britain. At the same time, the average consumer's disposable income is higher in the United States and the amount already spent on receiving television (without cable) much lower, there being no national licence fee and a relatively small incidence of television set rental. Meanwhile, where cable in the United States has grown without significant competition, in Britain video recorders are already seeking to satisfy the demand for the latest (and raciest) films in the home, and the BBC and ITV DBS services should provide the full convenience of a film channel.

The strength of demand for cable in Britain may therefore be somewhat less than in North America and, because of different technical standards, the capital cost rather more. But it is nevertheless interesting and worthwhile to study the experience of cable elsewhere and at some length. Canada and the United States, after all, offer the two principal examples of cable in its next stages of development and provide the only real practical experience on which to draw. That experience covers the whole gamut of issues currently being debated – the system economics, the character of cable services, 'narrowcasting', the importance of cable advertising revenue and of pay-per-view, the nature of community and access channels, the significance of the various enhanced services and the effect of cable's growth on the broadcasting, cinema and production industries. In particular, they provide evidence of system and service priorities in a market-based industry of the likely character and relative potential of the various new services and of the character and viewing habits of a cabled audience.

The widely differing perceptions of events across the Atlantic have been central to – even major motive forces within – the British debate, and are worth studying for that reason alone. But, despite the differences, there will undoubtedly be points of similarity, lessons to be learned from similar or different approaches and points on which one may use the comparison to analyse the impact of cable per se, irrespective of its cultural environment. Together, Canada and the United States offer valuable insights into the character of cable development and of countries undergoing major changes in their media and telecommunications systems.

PART THREE
The Canadian Experience

5 Canada's Cultural Dilemma

However cable develops in Britain, it seems certain that we will have to face the same problems of audience fragmentation and of an influx of foreign and particularly American programming which Canada has had to contend with for over thirty years. Canada is the second most highly cabled nation in the world after Belgium although, like Belgium, there has until recently been little cable origination of programmes. Canadian cable's roots are partly in improved reception, as in Britain, but also largely in importing common-language distant signals (the second phase of cable's growth), predominantly from the United States. Indeed, Canadian broadcasting policy is conditioned – even formed – by the overwhelming presence of its neighbour, so that a natural consequence has been a deep concern, reflected in its regulatory approach, to retain and promote some form of national identity in the face of such a presence. Over 80 per cent of the Canadian population live within 100 miles of the American border, however, and the realities of this situation have had a greater impact than somewhat abstract cultural aspirations. Although regulation has been imposed to promote both Canadian broadcasting and production, the Canadians themselves have consistently demonstrated a strong interest, even a preference, for material from the United States. Consequently, the Government has had to find a path between accepting the reality of US cultural imperialism and forcing a Canadian cultural chauvinism which appears antithetical to the rights and wishes of its own citizens. This is the background to the statement by Francis Fox, the Communications Minister, in early 1983 that 'within a healthy and viable Canadian broadcasting system Canadians are entitled to as much choice in programming as possible.' But, he added, 'I also firmly believe that "choice" for Canadians is meaningless unless it also includes programming which reinforces the cultural heritage of all Canadians' (Department of Communications, 'Towards a New

National Broadcasting Policy'. February 1983). Inevitably cable's role as an importer of foreign signals has made it one of the major battlegrounds.

Cable first appeared in Canada in 1949 when Rediffusion of Britain brought its wireless relay service to Montreal, recognising, perhaps, that here was the future. When Canadian television began in 1952, Rediffusion started a television relay service. Only one broadcast signal (CBFT) was available initially, however, and between 1952 and 1954 the company supplemented this with a channel programmed by itself and offering films and locally produced entertainment and news. When Montreal's second television station, CBMT, started up in 1954, this first-ever cable channel was closed down as being commercially unprofitable. Broadcast signal relay was easier and cheaper, and by 1955 the system, serving the remarkably high number of 58,000 subscribers, was importing American TV channels as well. Already in 1952 another pioneer system in London, Ontario, had been set up to bring in the only available television signal, from Cleveland, Ohio.

Clearly American television was a potent attraction, particularly since few Canadian cities yet had more than one or two local signals available to them. Some cities particularly close to the US border could already receive American stations off-air, and this proved only to be an incentive to those with poor reception or too far away. Not surprisingly the Canadian cable industry had the full backing of American broadcasters. American stations close to the border supported anything which extended their reach; advertisers on these stations were favourably disposed for the same reason, as were the US networks. A number of American broadcasters, including CBS, even entered the Canadian cable business and injected much-needed capital. Because early systems were built largely to relay American signals, their growth was as much in the major Canadian cities as in rural areas and small towns without their own television station. Penetration of television homes was therefore proportionately high, and by 1968 some 13 per cent (710,000) were served by nearly 300 systems, an indication incidentally of the significantly larger average size of systems than in Britain (and the USA).

This easy cross-border flow of American signals naturally had considerable implications for domestic broadcasting policy. The Canadian broadcasting system laid down in the 50s had been built on the assumption that each market could only sustain a certain number of commercially financed television stations. But now this influx threatened to upset the equation by fragmenting the audience. Indeed, it was significant that the profits from French-speaking TV stations in 1963 exceeded those from English, despite the fact that the French-Canadian population made up only one-third of the total.

Not surprisingly, it was the English-language stations which were hardest hit by signals from across the border.

The Board of Broadcast Governors (BBG), responsible for regulating the Canadian broadcasting system, had beeen directed to provide 'a varied and comprehensive broadcasting service of high standard that is basically Canadian in content and character' (1958 Broadcasting Act). Regulation of the minimum amount of Canadian-produced programming which Canadian stations had to carry could not, however, limit the amount of American material Canadians watched. Cable circumvented such cultural objectives; and yet, faced with this threat, the BBG was able to do little, as cable had not been regarded as broadcasting at the time of the 1958 Broadcasting Act, remaining curiously the responsibility of the Department of Transport. Moreover, when it seemed likely in the early 1960s that the Government might move to bring cable within the BBG's jurisdiction, there was considerable political protest. Cable was giving a large number of people a service they wanted, it was argued, and should not be restrained. All the Department of Transport was able to do, in an effort to preserve the concept of broadcasting as a local service, was to insist that all local stations be carried and to restrict cable systems to relaying only the signals which could be picked up off-air by their large headend antennae, prohibiting the importation of really distant signals by microwave. The intention was to set a new limit to the total number of signals available in a market, but the effect was merely to slow development in the more northern provinces where large towns, and hence broadcasting stations which could be relayed, were less frequent. In major cities such as Montreal, Toronto and Vancouver, where a large antenna could already pick up several American stations, it was in fact only after this rule came into force that subscriber levels began to grow by leaps and bounds. Between 1965 and 1968 the number of subscribers in Vancouver grew from 29,933 to 114,095, giving a cable penetration of TV homes in that city of almost 40 per cent.

REGULATION IS IMPOSED

By 1968 it was clear that a new approach to broadcast regulation was required, as the policies enunciated in the 1958 Broadcasting Act were simply not being achieved. Consequently, in that year an entirely new body, the Canadian Radio-Television Commission (CRTC), was set up, replacing the BBG and taking this opportunity to absorb cable regulation into its brief, namely to create an integrated Canadian broadcasting policy. The new commission became responsible for awarding the franchises for new cable systems, for determining the conditions upon which existing licences would be renewed and for regulating the rates operators might charge. To keep cable operators on their toes, the CRTC followed the same licensing practice as for broadcast stations, by granting franchises for only five years at a time, with renewal being made dependent on performance. Community programming was permitted, but not pay-TV or advertiser-supported cable channels. Additional steps were designed to ensure that cable systems gave priority carriage to Canadian stations, particularly local ones, and in 1970 the CRTC announced that it would not license cable systems where this might 'seriously inhibit local programming, cause the financial failure of a local station, or prevent the extension of Canadian service' (Quoted by D.R. Le Duc, 'Cable TV control in Canada', *Journal of Broadcasting*, Autumn 1976, p.439).

Regulation, however, could not readily counter consumer demand. While attempting to protect Canadian broadcasters by cable regulation, the CRTC had to accept that it could do little directly to limit how much American television Canadians watched. Indeed, in 1973 it admitted a 24 per cent overall increase in the amount of viewing of American stations during the previous four years. In the early 1970s cable and newly licensed independent stations continued to fragment the audience. In Calgary, for example, the national public network, CBC, and the independent network CTV were the sole stations available in November 1970, with 42.7 per cent and 57.3 per cent of viewers respectively. By November 1977, with 77.1 per cent of all homes connected to cable, ten stations shared the audience, six of them American and taking over 29 per cent of viewers. CBC's share had dropped to 15.5 per cent, although the CTV audience remained the largest at 37.1 per cent. The greater number of Canadian independents, unfortunately, actually reduced the average viewing of Canadian programmes, since they also carried a high proportion of American material. A new station in Edmonton in 1974, for example, caused a reduction of the audience for Canadian programmes there from an already low 37 per cent to an even worse 29 per cent.

Caught at an early stage of development, as in Britain, cable's growth might have been severely restricted. By now, however, it was too late and the industry was providing a popular service which no amount of concern for cultural integrity could contain. The decade after the CRTC's creation saw cable's greatest growth, at an average annual rate of 13 per cent. Indeed by 1976, systems provided television to 3.1 million cable subscribers, some 47 per cent of television households. In large part this represented the expansion of existing systems and their increasing penetration in already cabled areas; whereas in 1968 44 per cent of homes passed by cable were connected, by 1976 this had grown to 67 per cent. The expansion of existing systems also reflected the nature of the industry in Canada – a relatively limited number of cable operators developing increasingly large systems, with a very few controlling an ever bigger sector of the market. Thus by 1980 Rogers Cablesystems had amalgamated with or absorbed two other major operators, the Premier Company and Canadian Cablesystems, and provided service to 1.3 million subscribers – well over a quarter of the entire Canadian market. Cable had become, in the space of a few years, the fastest growing and most profitable sector of Canadian communications. Rates of return could be as high as 40 per cent, whilst the average was about 24 per cent, nearly double that enjoyed by Canadian television broadcasting stations.

A NEW APPROACH

Cable was the horse which had bolted, and it was the Canadian public itself which had opened the stable door. Not even such regulatory constraints as a prohibition on pay-TV and on selling advertising, a very short five-year franchise and the regulation of the rates operators might charge had held it back. Recognising the inevitable, the CRTC now took the decision actively to use cable to promote as many of the objectives of Canadian broadcasting policy as were still workable. In a statement of February 1971, the Commission declared itself to favour a policy which would 'integrate cable television into the Canadian Broadcasting System, avoid disrupting the system, enhance the capacity of the system to produce programs, and finally permit a rigorous development of cable television and of the whole Canadian Broadcasting System' (CRTC, 'The Integration of Cable TV in the Canadian Broadcasting System', 26 February 1971, p. 7). To this end, it gave tacit approval to cable's further growth, while at the same time making certain 'suggestions' which would protect existing broadcasters. This attempt to find a satisfactory compromise position, it must be said, has had mixed success.

To minimise the effect of audience fragmentation, for example, the CRTC boldly attempted a piece of legalised piracy. In its programme-substitution ruling it allows a local broadcaster who is showing a particular programme at the same time as it is being shown on an American or distant Canadian station, to require any cable system relaying both signals to substitute his own broadcast for the other. This ensures that the audience for each transmission sees his advertising rather than that sold by his American or distant Canadian rival. The intention is to protect the broadcasting industry, but a side effect has been to damage the interests of Canadian producers, since it encourages the purchase of American shows and their transmission in peak viewing hours at the same time as they are being broadcast on American stations. The result is a reduction in the amount of Canadian programming in prime time. Relegated to the margins, Canadian productions attract lower audiences and less advertising revenue.

From the broadcasters' point of view this particular ruling has proved reasonably effective and, for the cable operators, relatively simple to implement. Considerably less successful has been the even more piratical 'commercial deletion' proposal and ruling. In a policy statement of July 1971 the CRTC suggested that cable systems might actually delete commercials from American stations and replace them with advertisements sold by the Canadian television stations in their area. This was effectively an invitation to Canadian stations to steal American signals and to obtain advertising revenue from programmes for which they had not paid. The audience might be lost, but not the profits.

It was a clever idea with more than an element of tit for tat in it, paying the American stations back for having placed themselves quite deliberately on the US/Canadian border. Unfortunately, the complexities of commercial deletion were enormous, as systems had no forewarning of where commercials might appear in a programme and no knowledge of how long they might last. Objections came not only from the American networks and border stations but also from the Canadian cable operators themselves, who made it abundantly clear that the idea was unworkable. Despite a 1973 ruling that all systems should be capable of deleting foreign television commercials, resistance has been very considerable, and only Rogers Cablesystems in Toronto carried the idea through with any success. In 1976 the Canadian parliament attempted to reinforce CRTC policy by denying business expense tax deductions on advertising which Canadian firms bought on US stations for transmitting into Canada. Nevertheless, commercial deletion has found little favour, and today is effectively in abeyance.

The CRTC has similarly had little success with its 1971 proposal that cable systems which enjoyed a certain level of revenue per mile of cable should pay for the programmes they relayed from Canadian stations. The purpose of this proposal was to ensure that a proportion of the considerable relay revenues were pumped back into Canadian production – the promotion of the Canadian production industry and a high level of Canadian content on Canadian stations being two of the Commission's primary objectives. Inevitably, however, the question of cable payment for programmes has become inextricably bound up with broader copyright issues and with the proposed copyright bill which, ten years later, is still under discussion. Unlike American cable systems, Canadian operators are still in the enviable position of paying nothing for any of the broadcast programmes they relay.

Cable regulation must be seen as part of a wider broadcasting policy. The promotion of Canadian production has always been a major concern of the BBG and CRTC and this has led them to impose a number of content requirements on broadcasters. Their problems with cable, however, have been matched by the difficulty of enforcing these regulations, which are seen by television stations as reducing both audiences and profits. The first attempt to mandate a statutory minimum of programming which was defined as Canadian was made by the BBG in 1960, but was toned down almost to the point of worthlessness following strong protests by private broadcasters. The same pattern was repeated in 1971 when the CRTC required that Canadian programmes fill 60 per cent of the broadcasting day, including the prime-time evening hours, with a further limitation that only 30 per cent of material could come from any other single country. A series of relaxations followed and by 1972 the Canadian quota had been reduced to 50 per cent (60 per cent for CBC) in primetime, which had also been generously redefined to run from 6 p.m. to midnight. The limit on programming from any one country was abolished and the period of measurement increased from three months to a year.

The result has been the relegation of Canadian material, largely news, current affairs, sport and cheap quiz and chat shows, to the daytime, the margins of primetime and the summer months when viewing is traditionally low. Peak viewing hours are filled with American shows, a tendency which is exacerbated by the programme substitution ruling applied to cable. Even with these watered-down requirements there have been suggestions that the independent broadcasting stations and the commercial network, CTV, do not fulfil their quotas, nor promote any significant amount of indigenous drama. The stark fact is that in 1982 nearly three-quarters of all English-language viewing time by Canadians was spent watching American programmes (largely entertainment shows and drama) on Canadian and American stations. 96 per cent of the drama – films, soap operas, detective series and serious plays – shown on Canadian television was foreign (American and British predominating). The CRTC's view is that the situation would have been even worse but for content requirements, and it is certainly the case that domestic news programmes, sport, current affairs and documentaries are well represented in the Canadian quota. It is equally evident, however, that there is a natural demand for home-grown news and sport, which there is not for Canadian drama and entertainment; or, to put it another way, Canadian culture is competitive and appealing in the political and sports arenas, but not so much in drama, comedy, entertainment, etc. High production costs and expensively produced American drama cheaply available leaves Canadian broadcasters no incentive to produce their own.

It is evident therefore that the CRTC's power over broadcasters and cable operators is restricted, despite the five-year licence and rate of return regulation. In fact, even these apparently powerful instruments of regulatory control have their weaknesses. The five-year licence, for example, is certainly valuable in providing the opportunity for a regular review of performance; and the CRTC undoubtedly has a wealth of experience and knowledge, together with an established set of regulatory criteria, by which it can determine what may be expected of a particular cable operator in the circumstances of a particular system. It is upon these criteria that it awards franchises in a competitive process. However, in order to give investors sufficient security to commit the substantial sums involved, the renewal procedure has not been made competitive, thereby placing the licensee *in situ* in a very strong position. Clearly there is a major disincentive for the CRTC to remove a miscreant operator's licence if there is no-one immediately available to replace him and to maintain the service to consumers. Nor has the solution of separating system ownership and operation, as mentioned by Lord Hunt in Britain, been seriously considered in view of the relatively low programming/operating requirements upon systems. Short-term licence renewals have been known, but beyond a certain point the CRTC is constrained by the need to consider consumers' immediate needs. In practice, no broadcasting station or network has ever lost its licence. Equally, only one cable system has done so, in Glovertown, Newfoundland in 1981, where the CRTC determined to make an example of an operator who had installed a satellite dish illegally to supply American pay-TV channels to subscribers. The CRTC not infrequently attaches requirements for better performance to licence renewals, as a quid pro quo for higher profits. But in general these requirements have not been rigorously enforced.

In like fashion the CRTC does not regard the primary objective of rate regulation as being to keep rates low and to prevent monopoly abuses, but rather to help in evaluating how systems are contributing to Canadian broadcasting objectives. Because the CRTC does hope that the private cable industry will promote certain cultural aims, it has to take into account that industry's expectations of a worthwhile profit. Indeed, without constant vigilance the CRTC is in some danger of being 'captured' by and becoming too sympathetic towards the industries it regulates, as the BBG before it was accused of becoming.

A good example of the CRTC's rate regulation dilemma is provided by its experience of community programming on cable. As with many other of its cable policies, this may be described as a partial success in those areas where cultural objectives happen to complement commercial incentives. Canada is very much the birthplace of the community and access channel, with the first occasional programmes on local affairs appearing on cable systems in the mid 60s. These early efforts were done very much on an amateur and shoestring basis, a simple studio being equipped for $10,000 and programmes produced for under $100 an hour. Production quality was poor, although probably little worse than some of the efforts of the local television stations.

Parallel with these developments were the activities of the National Film Board of Canada and the 'Challenge for Change' project. This was an attempt during the 60s and early 70s to involve problem communities in the making of films about themselves, and thereby to use film as a mirror and an instrument in the process of social change. These films were commonly shown in local halls rather than on cable systems, but it soon became evident that involvement in such projects could significantly affect the way a community viewed itself. One consequence was the appearance, all over the country, of voluntary community communications associations, themselves part of the international movement during the 60s towards grass-roots politics and citizen action.

The evidence gathered from the 'Challenge for Change' project, particularly in the case of the inhabitants of Fogo Island, off Newfoundland, was to have a major influence upon the newly created CRTC. In its first major policy statement, in May 1969, and increasingly thereafter, it encouraged cable systems to undertake local community programming, thereby pursuing the long-stated objective of localism in broadcasting. If the importation of distant signals was inevitable, then the cable system which made it possible should also be used to promote the use of television as a community tool, thereby encouraging the identification between community and broadcaster which had been originally envisaged. No new sources of revenue were allowed to finance such channels, although the provision of community services was undoubtedly taken into account when system operators requested increases in their basic rates.

For their part, cable operators greeted the CRTC's suggestion with considerable sympathy. By March 1972 a survey of eighty-five systems revealed over 1,500 hours total of local programming being transmitted each week. Items included local sports, civic meetings, news, amateur dramatics and discussions of local events, whilst

91

evidence from one system suggested that 24 per cent of cable subscribers did watch the community channel occasionally. By 1979 some 380 systems transmitted over 1,000 hours each day, and in 1982 community programming consumed 7.9 per cent of the industry's gross annual revenue.

Cable operators must certainly be given credit for sincerely believing in cable's community role. At the same time they are well aware of the public relations value of involving themselves in the lives of their community and of appearing to add something material to Canadian programming, rather than simply helping to swamp Canadian culture with American imports. The likely supplement to the basic amount they can charge consumers is also an incentive. Perhaps most significant is the fact that such programme origination enables operators to justify the distinction between themselves and common carriers of signals, such as the telephone companies. As programmers they cannot be subjected to the set rate of return regulation by which common carriers in a monopoly environment are tied. The CRTC can and does set limits to the amount operators may charge for their service, since in practice they do enjoy a monopoly in the area in which they operate. But that regulation is relatively lenient, allowing considerable freedom as to the methods and levels of profit achieved. Local origination is therefore regarded as something of a safeguard against common carriage restrictions. It is also a constant advertisement of cable's additional potential.

Community programming reflected a growing concern on all sides, if for different reasons, that cable should be more than just 'a technically sophisticated distribution system for imported programmes' (CRTC Annual Report 1971/2, p.22). It did not, however, represent a complete success for CRTC policy. While the industry commits 7.9 per cent of its gross annual revenue to community channels, it has always resisted the CRTC's view that this should be a full 10 per cent. Nor has it been enthusiastic about the idea of providing yet more services free to subscribers. In 1975 the CRTC suggested that operators provide special programming channels to carry government and other non-commercial information films, sponsored material of a limited nature, foreign films in their original language, amateur films and re-runs of Canadian-produced off-air broadcast programmes. At this the industry balked. Forbidden as it was from selling advertising or charging extra for discretionary channels, any additional programming would merely eat into revenues while providing little return from increased subscribers. Although a number of special programming channels have appeared in the last three years, these are either supported by federal or provincial grants or are set up as loss-leaders to promote the commercial case. For the most part operators have resisted adding new services for no new return.

Canadian experience up to the early 1980s provides a good example of the second stage of cable's growth. Despite apparently formidable regulation, the industry enjoyed a great measure of success, founded almost entirely on the importation of American programming. Indeed, by 1977 fully 62 per cent of English-speaking Canada had access to four American channels, whereas only 45 per cent had four Canadian. Content quotas could not apply when channels were merely being relayed from across the border, and the fact that many Canadians could pick these signals up off-air effectively prevented the CRTC from taking measures to prohibit their reception and relay to others. In the absence of new types of programming – as in pay-TV film channels – Canadians demonstrated a strong demand for greater choice at any one moment from amongst the existing programme range. People do not like to be tied to the scheduling of a very limited number of broadcasters.

Recognising an almost unstoppable force, the CRTC in the 70s permitted basic cable growth while attempting by specific regulation to use it for the broader aims of Canadian broadcasting policy. To an extent it sought to use it (without much success) as a means of extending some measure of political control beyond broadcast transmission to reception. In all such objectives the results have been mixed. Nevertheless, it would be wrong to suggest that Canada demonstrates the ineffectiveness of regulation. Certainly, complex rules are not always successful and can have undesirable side effects, as in the programme substitution ruling. Nor can they counter strong consumer demand or powerful, consumer-supported commercial pressure. At the same time, regulation can do something to channel those consumer demands and commercial pressures in the cause of wider cultural objectives. The problem comes in attempting to promote cultural aims which have little immediate commercial or consumer appeal – a lesson, perhaps, for those who believe that community, access and educational channels and information services will happen without either strong commercial incentives (in the shape of consumer demand) or substantial support from public money.

Above all, therefore, Canada illustrates the problems inherent in attempting to reconcile conflicts between consumer demand, commercial incentives and cultural objectives. As the Federal Cultural Policy Review Committee commented in 1982:

> The inherent conflict here, as in many other areas of cultural policy, is between an industrial and a cultural strategy. If the airwaves, cable systems and other common carriers are to be

exploited to achieve the largest possible addition to gross national product (GNP), then cultural and artistic objectives are impediments to those who benefit from a larger GNP and who will then seek to have the impediments reduced . . . The tendency of federal cultural policies, so apparent in the licensing practices of the CRTC, to stress the complementary nature of these [industrial and cultural] goals instead of their competitiveness is generally counter-productive *from the point of view of culture.* (Report of the Federal Cultural Policy Review Committee, Canada, November 1982, p. 286. My emphasis.)

Certainly the Canadian broadcasting and cable industries have had to accept certain responsibilities where cultural concerns are involved. But equally those seeking to promote such concerns are having to come to terms with what is possible in a commercial environment, an environment in which the pace is now being forced yet again.

6 Into the Third Phase

By January 1983, 505 cable systems served 4.6 million Canadian subscribers, representing almost 60 per cent of television households. Cable penetration of homes passed was a remarkable 75 per cent. About 80 per cent of homes are passed by cable and many of the rest are too remote and scattered to be economically reached. System revenues exceeded $350 million (Canadian) in 1980, with fixed assets of some $390 million; the industry has long been highly profitable. Yet, despite this, cable operators have for many years been concerned at the industry's long-term prospects. With the country steadily approaching effective cable saturation, the future growth of cable purely as a signal enhancement, relay and community service is limited. Recently a new threat has appeared in the shape of direct home reception of television signals from American satellites. Although receiving dishes several feet in diameter are currently necessary, these can be bought for as little as $3-5000. There are estimated to be well over 10,000 already operating, until recently illegally. The consumer demand for yet further programming does seem to exist.

Since the late 60s some systems have provided additional attractions (and tried thereby to increase penetration and revenue), firstly with community channels, and secondly with what are known as 'converter services'. Most Canadian cable systems' twelve-channel capacity is limited not by the coaxial cable itself, but by the capacity of the domestic television receiver. By providing an additional electronic box, or converter, systems can offer between ten and twenty-three further channels. Many of these are used to provide simple information services – a clock, an alphanumeric news and weather service and a stock market ticker. The cable operator can gain revenue from converter rental and possibly attract additional subscribers. By 1981 some 47 per cent of cabled homes which had a converter service available took it, but this still represented only 19 per cent of all Canadian homes.

Converter services did not greatly increase the industry's revenues, while community channels for which the subscriber paid nothing extra could only be a drain on them. Nevertheless, these services did show the way ahead. If the cable industry was to continue to grow, it would have to provide additional services from which it did receive substantial revenues. Since the early 70s, therefore, the Canadian Cable Television Association has pressed to be allowed to provide additional discretionary pay channels and advertiser-supported services. At first the CRTC resisted this move, which it again regarded as a threat to the structure of Canadian broadcasting. As with cable itself, however, the Commission has come gradually to appreciate that regulation cannot stop a combination of technological advance, social demand, commercial pressure and external circumstance. Wider telecommunications policy, in any case, is forcing the pace. Canada's progressive approach to telecommunications technology – the pioneering of geostationary domestic communications (4/6 ghz) and direct broadcast (12/14 ghz) satellites, the development of the Telidon second generation viewdata system, work on digital PABX exchanges and on optic-fibre technology – all signal the inevitability of change, as do the problems experienced in guiding and exploiting this telecommunications lead to best advantage.

Cable is clearly part of the changing environment, and both individual companies and federal departments have sponsored research programmes and experimental projects. In September 1979, Canadian Cablesystems (part of Rogers) began an experimental 300-home interactive cable system in London, Ontario, to test equipment and determine demand for two-way television, polling and security services. From the results obtained, Rogers' engineering division and its computing arm, Cableshare, have designed a commercial security service which is now being offered on its Syracuse system in New York State. Meanwhile, an optic-fibre experiment has been under way since September 1981 in Elie and St. Eustache in rural Manitoba, financed by the federal Department of Communications and the Canadian Telecommunications Carriers Association and operated by the Manitoba Telephone System. Using switched technology, the 150-house project carries television signals, telephone calls, teleshopping facilities and the Telidon service through the same fibre. The notion of carrying all services in one cable appeals where the scattered nature of the housing makes installation of several wires prohibitively expensive. In such low-density areas, the normal ban on telephone companies also providing cable television in the regions they serve is waived and the consequence seems certain to be a lowering of the housing density figure at which it is considered economic to provide cable services. Another utility service which can be provided in this way is electricity. This experiment is also designed to test how well optic fibres can stand Manitoba's climatic extremes, between $+35°$ and $-40°C$. On an altogether larger scale is the fully commercial optic-fibre trunk network being laid down by the Saskatchewan Telecommunications Co. Costing $56 million, it will stretch 3,200 kilometres and connect the fifty major cities and towns of the prairie provinces. Separate cables will carry television and telephone signals. The final local links to the home, however, will be by coaxial cable in view of its tried and trusted and still cheaper technology.

In the last few years, therefore, the CRTC has had gradually to modify its approach to additional cable services, in response to the changing environment. As an extension of its special programming channel policy, it began by licensing a number of specialist channels largely on an experimental basis, although once again it prohibited advertising or additional subscriber charges. Most significant has been the national relay of the proceedings of the Canadian House of Commons, a service produced and financed by the CBC. Other projects have also had external support. Galaxie, an experimental children's channel provided by Rogers to a number of systems in Ontario, is part financed by the Ontario Department of Education. Equally, both Ontario and other provincial governments support local educational channels of a limited character. Meanwhile Rogers, which is very much in the forefront of the lobby for additional services, has offered a service of French programming called 'French for Canadians'. A larger venture by a consortium of cable operators in Quebec is known as 'La Sette'. This receives TDF programming by satellite from France and transmits it nightly. In Montreal Télécable Videotron has also been allowed to experiment with a number of special interest channels, including arts, entertainment, educational, sports, children's and hobbies. None of these experiments is a commercially viable operation. Yet in permitting them the CRTC has shown its increasing flexibility, as it did also in December 1981 when it approved a number of applications for the cable distribution of non-programming services such as security, energy meter reading, videogames, videotex and teleshopping, all on an experimental basis. An application to provide a classified real estate advertising channel was, however, denied.

PAY-TV COMES TO CANADA

Such 'experiments' represented a testing of the water. With pay-TV, however, the CRTC finally took the plunge. In 1980, after much hesitation and delay, it accepted the need for Canadian pay services to counter the threat from American satellite-delivered channels. A number were licensed in 1982 and began operations in early 1983, while also in March 1983 the Communications Minister announced his intention to approve advertiser-supported cable services.

In finally deciding to permit Canadian pay services, the CRTC was mirroring its previous landmark decision of the early 70s. For just as then it had learnt that cultural objectives could not benefit from an unrealistic attempt to stifle cable itself, so now it recognised that only by embracing pay-TV and the expansion of cable services could it continue to promote those objectives. American 4/6 ghz services were already available in Canada and DBS channels would soon reach 90 per cent of the Canadian population. As the Federal Cultural Policy Review Committee concluded:

> Restrictions are not the solution. In the long term no government or regulatory agency can, or should, prevent the public from obtaining access to the foreign programmes and services it wants. *But if Canada is to retain a programming presence in its own broadcasting and telecommunications system, it must use all its technological and creative resources to provide Canadian programs and services that Canadians want to see and hear, programs that are competitive in quality with those from other countries* (FCPRC Report, cit. p. 285, committee's emphasis).

The decision to license Canadian pay-TV services was therefore taken with long-standing cultural objectives very much in mind. By licensing a number of pay services to be delivered predominantly by cable, the CRTC is able to maintain regulatory control over their character. Yet at the same time it can strengthen their marketability against American pay channels by stipulating that the latter be prohibited from cable relay. The incentive for the average citizen with Canadian services available on cable to opt instead for direct delivery from American satellites is thereby greatly reduced. Recognising the near impossibility (and political invidiousness) of attempting to restrict or prohibit direct American signal reception, the CRTC and the government are seeking to minimise its attractions. As before, so now the strategy is to use cable's appeal to the consumer as a tool in the pursuit of wider regulatory objectives.

This fact is made even clearer by the CRTC's decision to restrict the number of pay services in any one region to four. More than this, it feels, would fragment the market and revenue too far, and so prevent any from investing in new production. As it declared in its Pay-TV Decision of March 1982:

> Through its capacity to generate revenue, pay-television should contribute significantly to the broadcasting system by increasing the diversity of programming ... and by enhancing the quality and distinctiveness of Canadian programs. Pay-television should provide new opportunities and revenue sources for the program production industry in Canada, particularly for producers currently unable to gain access to the broadcasting system (CRTC Decision 82-240, p. 9).

Licences were therefore awarded to First Choice Canadian Communications to provide two national twenty-four-hour film and general entertainment services in English and French; Lively Arts Market

Builders (C-Channel) for a national cultural service (performing arts, arts films, children's programmes); five regional film and entertainment channels and to one regional multilingual service.

In making these awards the Commission has attempted to learn from previous experience. Perhaps most importantly it has expressed its determination in future not to renew licences if services fail to meet their promises. The future of pay-TV in Canada may largely depend on the CRTC's strength of will in this respect. The conditions it has imposed as regards Canadian content also represent a new approach. The national and regional entertainment channels are required to devote 30 per cent of their programming hours to Canadian material initially, rising to 50 per cent by the fifth year. In addition the CRTC has specified that a set proportion of gross revenues and of total programming budgets must be spent on acquiring Canadian items, the exact proportions varying according to the licensee. Furthermore the general entertainment pay services have been required to spend a certain percentage of their budget on Canadian drama, in an effort to stimulate a category of production which is currently badly under-provided for by broadcast channels. First Choice, for example, must devote 75 per cent of its gross revenue to programming, while 45 per cent (60 per cent of its programming budget) must go to Canadian material. Moreover, 50 per cent of all money spent on Canadian programmes must be on drama. It is notable, incidentally, that the CRTC has now also told the CTV commercial broadcasting network, as a condition of licence renewal, to transmit a specified number of hours of 'original new Canadian drama' each year, whilst the CBC has declared its intention of increasing its Canadian content to 80 per cent.

A natural concern of the CRTC is the likely impact of pay on existing broadcast services. Although it has not imposed any formal anti-siphoning measures, it did make it clear that a major influence in its choice of licensees was the type of programming they proposed and their assurance that they would not seek material of a traditional broadcast character. C-Channel, for example, which commenced operations on 1 February 1983 and collapsed five months later in June, offered a unique package of theatre, opera, dance, serious music, some superior children's programming, foreign films and critically acclaimed popular films such as *Chariots of Fire*. The Commission stipulated, however, that feature films should occupy not more than 40 per cent of its schedule and that not more than 5 per cent should be given over to those which were amongst the top thirty grossing films in the Canadian market during the previous three years. The Commission was similarly impressed by First Choice's promise to place a 'substantial emphasis' on the development and exhibition of Canadian drama and live theatrical events but not to show (or pirate from broadcasting) any significant amount of sport (Application of First Choice Canadian Communications to the CRTC,

20 July 1981, pp. 1-7). First Choice also argued persuasively that it would not draw significant audiences away from broadcasting:

> We will concentrate our efforts on a relatively limited number of original hours, with maximum production values, and repeat them very frequently. The result will be a service in which our audience may watch us only a few hours per week, *but these hours will be special events of extraordinary value, and can be watched entirely at the convenience of the viewer's schedule* (Ibid., pp. 1-5).

In its evolving broadcast and cable policy the CRTC has also shown a desire to prevent the formation of groups with multiple interests in production, distribution and exhibition. For this reason, it rejected applications for national pay licences from companies with major broadcasting, cable and production concerns; equally those regional licensees with production interests have had to agree not to make use of them. Consequently, the pay-TV services are not undertaking any in-house production, but are relying upon buying in, commissioning and co-financing projects. All services have made a commitment to commissioning a large proportion of their Canadian material from regional production companies outside the major production centres of Toronto and Montreal. In this again the CRTC is seeking to stimulate a regional industry and programming which is distinctively provincial. The policy of separating production from distribution has been most recently reflected in the Federal Cultural Policy Review Committee's radical recommendation that the CBC itself should cease to produce its own material, with the exception of news. Likewise, the desire to prevent the development of significant cross-media conglomerates is further reinforced by a government decision to deny daily newspaper owners any interest in broadcasting stations within the same sphere of operation, something which until autumn 1982 was permitted.

ECONOMICS AND PRODUCTION POTENTIAL OF CANADIAN PAY-TV

Pay-television has therefore come to Canada in a highly regulated form and ostensibly with high cultural and political objectives. In contrast to Lord Hunt's conclusions in Britain, the CRTC has decided to license the service providers on the principle that if pay-TV is to further such objectives the Canadian market can sustain only a limited number of channels. Indeed, many in the industry feel that even so it has licensed too many, and the fate of C-Channel seems to confirm that view. Initial projections for the latter did appear bright. Capitalised at $14 million and at a wholesale price to cable operators of $8 a month, it needed only about 250,000 subscribers, some 5-6 per cent of all cabled homes, to generate a break-even revenue of

$19.2 million a year. According to its president, Edgar Cowan, each percentage point of penetration above 7 per cent would have returned about 50 per cent on invested capital. Programme costs were expected to be about $66 million over five years so that the channel would have contributed a small but very useful $35 million to original Canadian cultural production. Yet it rapidly proved to be seriously undercapitalised, while its evening schedule of 40 per cent performing arts, 40 per cent films (largely foreign) and 20 per cent children's programmes managed to attract only 27,000 subscribers by June, well short of the 60-70,000 projected for them. Few question that, like the American cable culture channels, CBS Cable and the Entertainment Channel, which failed in 1982 and 1983 respectively, the quality of the service and of the programmes on offer was high and played little part in its demise. More probable is the simple if unhappy conclusion that the audience for this type of service simply did not exist in sufficient numbers, or at least not among cable subscribers. At the very least, it is clear that it required more time and resources than were available to find and attract an audience.

C-Channel's failure should not, of course, be taken to spell doom for the other more general film and entertainment channels. Nevertheless, their success is also by no means assured. Indeed, many critics have questioned whether in imposing content and other requirements the CRTC has not placed too heavy an imposition on all the licensees from the start. Their collapse, one by one, could result in yet another ignominious failure to achieve the desired cultural ends and open the way for full-blooded American pay services. At a typical retail price of $15-16 they are considerably more expensive than their American equivalents and there can be no doubt that this is partly a result of the content requirements imposed on them. How far this will deter subscribers is still uncertain, although it is likely that few will take more than one of the channels available. Since the major appeal of such services is, inevitably, American films, Canadian content may at the same time make them less attractive. Another factor in the high retail price has been the major Hollywood film studios' determination to obtain more profitable deals with Canadian pay-TV companies than they managed with their American counterparts. This has forced First Choice and others to accept higher rates than they would like for the American films which are their primary attraction.

Adding these considerations to the current very poor state of the Canadian economy and to the weak condition of the production industry, many observers wonder at the viability even of two general entertainment pay channels competing in each province. Initially it was thought that the CRTC would license only one national film channel, and no regional; indeed the disadvantage of competing services was convincingly demonstrated by First Choice, who showed that it would both force up the price of programmes and reduce the overall amount available for them. Distribution and marketing costs would more than double, but total revenue would be reduced by at least $90 million over four years. The logic is that in a limited market the number of directly competing outlets should be restricted in order to maximise production spending. However, in this case the CRTC's concern to prevent any one company from holding excessive market power overrode its desire to give the largest possible boost to the production industry.

If the surviving companies were to meet their initial projections, then the pay-TV business would look attractive both for themselves and for the Canadian production industry. Based on American experience in areas where pay-TV was introduced to an already cabled market, general estimates are for a take-up by over 40 per cent of cable subscribers, with 2-3 per cent of previous non-subscribers also being drawn to the new services. Independent surveys in Canada also indicate a likely 40 per cent take-up, an estimate supported by the fact that the country is per capita one of the largest film markets in the world. Although the various pay-TV services are currently distributed to cable systems only via low-power satellite, it is anticipated that a further 1-2 per cent of homes not passed by cable may take a service direct by satellite dish. At a wholesale price to cable operators of $9.25 and a retail price to subscribers of $15.95 per month, First Choice calculate that it requires only 500,000 subscribers (11 per cent of cabled homes) to be profitable.

Equally, the capital costs of providing a pay-TV channel consisting primarily of theatrical films should be comparatively modest. In its application for a licence, for example, First Choice estimated an initial hardware expenditure of under $4 million, with annual costs thereafter of $100,000. Although the marketing start-up costs have been considerable, the business was expected to have a positive cash flow in the first year of full operation. Consequently, the initial capitalisation considered necessary was relatively low, at $18 million. Programming, of course, has required considerable early investment in Canadian production; but equally programming costs are related to the number of subscribers at any moment, so that once the fixed costs of delivery, marketing and overheads have been covered, the fees from additional subscribers (less programming costs per subscriber) represent profit.

If the various services do achieve the hoped-for penetration, then the amount spent on programming should be significant. In its licence application First Choice estimated that even with 24.5 per cent penetration it would be spending over $65 million per annum

102

on programming, of which $40.4 million would go to Canadian material. The regional services between them would be spending slightly less. Although total programming budgets will therefore be rather smaller than that of the CBC, the repeats policy of all services should permit them to pay more per programme. Indeed, First Choice has already been spending up to $400,000 an hour for the Canadian pay-TV rights to made-for-pay movies.

A major problem with Canadian productions in the past has been their lack of international, predominantly American, appeal. This has been largely a function of their production values, and is thus something of a vicious circle. Canadian producers and broadcasters, forced to recoup most of their costs from the domestic market, cannot afford to produce high-quality product capable of being sold abroad. This is the corollary of the argument that Canadian viewers prefer American drama because of its superior production values, whilst broadcasters prefer it because of its cheapness in relation to its actual production costs. In order to get round this problem, which has seriously inhibited the Canadian production industry, the Government in 1974 introduced the Capital Cost Allowance Program whereby investors in Canadian production could write off their entire investment against other income. The result was a false boom in which the inadequate Canadian content definitions were wilfully abused in order to provide tax shelters in programming made to look as American as possible. The market became over-supplied with films and as a result many were never even released theatrically. Since then the independent production industry has enjoyed a roller-coaster existence, with a feature film surge in the late 70s, followed by a slump in 1981. Less than half of the independent production industry's revenue has come from domestic television, thereby leaving it decidedly unstable and dependent on the vagaries of theatrical film release and overseas sales.

Pay-TV again could make a major difference to this situation. International co-production and concentration of revenue into a more limited number of programmes than has traditionally been the case in broadcasting should permit higher production costs and hence more appealing presentations, to both the domestic and international markets. The character of the programming required – feature films, made-for-pay films and specials – should itself mean a break from broadcast production values. Moreover, the CRTC identified the area of script and concept development as one which urgently required greater funding. Consequently, First Choice are putting 5 per cent of total revenues into a Canadian Creative Development Board set up to provide financing in the early stages of programme projects. Although the competitive environment will mean that the $13 million per annum originally envisaged will not be reached, the sum involved could still be substantial. Pre-production licence payment and co-financing deals will undoubtedly make it easier for producers to obtain the 'upfront' money necessary actually to make a film or programme. The inevitably close relationship between Canadian and American pay-TV distributors will also assist the introduction of Canadian product into the US market, as lack of distribution contacts and expertise has long been a major problem for Canadian producers.

The expanded American market is, in any case, looking for new programmes and has already recognised the real advantage of Canadian material. With both American and Canadian operators looking for domestic pay-TV rights to new productions, an obvious trend has been to pool resources and to co-finance, and this has largely meant Canadian product in view of the Canadian content requirements. In any case, the exchange rate in 1982 and 1983 meant that an American company making programmes in Canada enjoyed a 15-20 per cent discount on its money. By using a Canadian crew, director, location, a proportion of Canadian money and other qualifications, a largely American-financed production can be counted as Canadian under the Canadian content rules and so be made at lower cost. At the same time, a Canadian content label enhances its value to Canadian pay and broadcast TV companies, in view of their content requirements. For a typical drama series, for example, the latter might pay $15,000 per episode without that label, but up to $70,000 with it. In co-production deals the Canadian pay-TV companies are showing themselves willing to put up between a quarter and half as much as the American, as in the 1982 special concerts by country and western singers Crystal Gayle and Dolly Parton, financed by First Choice and the American Home Box Office. In this way HBO may get a programme costing $1 million for $750,000 while First Choice gets it for $250,000. The American rival to HBO, Showtime, has undertaken a particularly large number of productions in Canada, including the 'adult' entertainment shows *Bizarre, Romance,* and *30 Brompton Place.* HBO's first ever made-for-pay film, *The Terry Fox Story,* was also made in Canada and co-financed by the regional pay service Superchannel and the commercial broadcasting network, CTV. Unusually for such co-productions it was also on a Canadian subject.

The penalty paid for attracting American sales could be the loss of exactly that distinctive Canadian quality which the CRTC is seeking. In these early deals Canadian crews and bit-actors have been used, but the stars have largely been American. Vancouver has masqueraded as Seattle, and the Canadian producer of the Showtime/First Choice co-financed adult drama series *Romance* has admitted that he had no artistic say in what was essentially an American-controlled Canadian production. In a highly controversial deal First Choice has also made an agreement with the American Playboy Channel to co-finance $30 million worth of Playboy material to be made in Canada and count as Canadian content. With such projects as *New Orleans Stripper* planned, only the presence of the 'playmate' of 1982, who happens to be Canadian, gives them an indigenous element. Moreover, while First Choice is putting up only about a quarter of the budget, the content rules are said to have enabled it to claim the entire $30 million as expenditure on Canadian content. Superchannel, its main regional rival, appears to have kept slightly closer to the spirit of the content requirements, but even so its principal investments in Canadian production include *Louisiana*, a five-hour mini-series shot on location in the USA and set during the American civil war, and *Blood of Others*, shot on location in France and starring Jodie Foster. Not surprisingly, additional funding for these projects is coming from Home Box Office and Antenne 2, the second French television network. In the case of *Louisiana*, qualification as Canadian content is assisted by the fact that its star, Margot Kidder of *Superman* fame, is Canadian-born. However, as Superchannel's chairman, Jon Slan, has stated, 'Our Canadian programming must be programming the world will pay to see' (Quoted in *Variety*, 23 March 1983).

The reality of the Canadian situation, whatever the CRTC might wish, is of a relatively small and weak independent production and film industry, heavily reliant on American money and with a serious lack of internationally known talent (stars, directors, etc.). Indeed, the CRTC's belief that there is sufficient talent to support regional production centres was dismissed by two of its own commissioners, who dissented from this part of its pay-TV licence decision. Given the problems of significantly expanding the Canadian production industry, a likely development, already evident, is the growth of a relatively limited number of core companies who will provide a large proportion of the pay-TV companies' original programming. Companies who have produced good material for pay-TV will be favoured with future projects. Broadcasting companies with under-utilised production facilities are already involving themselves in productions for pay, often on the understanding that they receive the subsequent broadcasting rights. CBC has also now expressed its readiness to become involved in pay-TV deals.

The attempt to impose certain minimum regulatory requirements is therefore fraught with difficulties. Inevitably there is a danger that content definitions based on a points system, assessing such factors as financial backing, stars, other actors, director, producer, writer, lighting, camera crew, music director and location will not determine actual content. Consideration of the need to attract foreign money and foreign sales will predominate. Given that a long-term objective of such content rules must be not only to employ a country's actors and production talent but also to establish and build an identifiable, strong, yet attractive national screen identity, Canadian efforts are still far from satisfactory.

THE PROBLEMS AND PROSPECTS FOR PAY AND CABLE

From the evidence of their first few months, it is clear that the Canadian pay services have placed the CRTC is a considerable dilemma. By June 1983 the first rush of subscribers had ended and growth had become more gradual. Indeed, there was a higher than expected number of disconnections during the summer. As of September 1983, First Choice had about 220,000 subscribers to its English-language service and 40,000 for the French; Superchannel, its main rival in the heavily populated provinces of Ontario and Alberta, had 142,000; TVEC, its French regional competitor in Quebec, 22,000; and the services in the more sparsely populated and remoter provinces an estimated 10-20,000 each. Numbers are still growing, but slowly, and none of the services is yet close to its break-even point.

Total pay subscribers, therefore, probably number no more than 12 per cent of all cable subscribers, perhaps enough for one service, but certainly not sufficient to provide the major financial commitment to Canadian production which First Choice by itself had been predicting. Again, of course, it must be emphasised that these are still early days. Nevertheless, time is not limitless for the pay services; the two principals, First Choice and Superchannel, have both admitted that they are already seriously overextended and, in an ominous development in June 1983, both froze their current Canadian production projects in an effort to retrench. Several companies, including First Choice, have sought additional funds to compensate for heavy losses. Meanwhile, the regional companies are simply too small as yet to put significant amounts into production. Not surprisingly, all the services have been putting pressure on the CRTC to reduce its content requirements in the early years.

The future character of pay-TV in Canada will therefore depend on the continuing will of the Government and the CRTC to pursue certain cultural objectives, and on the strength of the domestic market. If that market proves weak, then the financial pressure upon pay-TV operators to reduce their commitment to Canadian production and to share production costs with American services will intensify, as will the incentive to emphasise tried-and-trusted American, or American-style product. The CRTC may deem jobs for Canadian actors and production crews to be more important than a

Canadian screen identity, and Canada may remain 'Hollywood in the North'.

The situation is still constantly evolving. At the time of writing, however, there were signs of a continued tough stance by the regulators. Indeed, the CRTC has moved to tighten its definitions of Canadian content for both feature films and other programming, declaring that 'productions in which non-Canadians are the only principal performers will not be accepted as Canadian and the addition of Canadians in minor roles will not be sufficient'. Canadians must also have a 'significant involvement' in artistic and financial control. Meanwhile, the furore over Playboy programming has stimulated a move towards an ethics code, although it has always been accepted that pay channels would show restricted films. The dilemma in such regulations, the conflict between industrial and cultural objectives, is only too obvious. As one independent Canadian producer has commented, 'Canadian content was an industrial policy, but now it's thought of as cultural policy and it's having a negative effect. TV is very much a two-way street and this new strategy could result in shows seen only in Canada' (Michael Hirsch of Nelvana Productions, quoted in *Variety*, 6 April 1983).

Meanwhile, other aspects of broadcasting and cable policy are also in a state of constant adaptation to changing circumstances. After hearings on broadcast Canadian content during 1982, the CRTC has announced changes to Canadian broadcasters' responsibilities, toughening up the requirements for Canadian drama during the true primetime hours of 7.30 to 10.30 p.m. The Commission is also considering introducing the same revenue-related quota to broadcast companies as the pay services currently have to meet, the exact proportion being tailored to the ability of each licensee to pay. In order to stimulate the production industry further, the 1983 Canadian budget introduced for the first time a tax on cable and pay-TV subscriptions, the money raised being put into a new programme development fund. This tax of 6 per cent of subscriptions, which will be passed straight on to the subscriber by the cable operators, will cost the former an extra 50 cents a month, or $1 if they take a pay service. In all it should raise $35 million in the first year to support production, rising to $60 million by the fifth. Moreover, for every dollar paid from this fund a producer will have to find two from private sources, so that the total amount brought into production by this means could be $100 million each year. To complete its regulatory requirements and ensure that broadcast television as well as pay will benefit from this new production initiative, the Government has stipulated that features and other programmes produced in this way must be shown on broadcast television within two years of production. By such means the Government is attempting to recycle some of the money put into the distribution technology of cable to boost the production industry and to bring it and the new pay channels closer to the broadcast services.

Having taken the decision to permit pay-TV services in order to forestall widespread and direct reception of American pay channels such as HBO, it could only be a matter of time before the Government and CRTC decided also to approve Canadian advertiser-supported cable channels. This they did in February 1983 and it is expected that the first will appear by 1985-6. As with the pay services, it will be for the CRTC to license applicants wishing to supply such channels, and it has already made it clear that it will only approve special-interest services. General channels which seek to emulate ordinary broadcast stations, provide little new and succeed only in grabbing some of the latter's audience will not be permitted. Services must add to the variety of programming on television. Again the hope is that they will provide a Canadian substitute for the various American advertiser-supported services now available on satellite, particularly the news, sports and children's channels. The authorities have evidently realised that unless they do give the go-ahead for this development, many people may well consider it worth their while to bypass the cable and go for direct satellite reception. Indeed, in an effort to ensure that cable remains the preferred method of receiving services, the Communications Minister has even decided to approve the cable-carriage of up to five American advertiser-supported channels, but only where Canadian equivalents prove not to be feasible. If this seems rather like inviting unwanted guests in to prevent them gate-crashing, it is interesting to note that the move is actually approved by the CBC and independent broadcasters. They accept that their future now depends on viewers' continued subscription to cable, on which the broadcast services receive priority carriage. Unless cable provides as much variety as direct-satellite reception, therefore, they could lose access to a considerable proportion of the audience. The Minister has emphasised that the new services must be Canadian if at all possible, and several are being planned. But it is still very far from certain that there is sufficient advertising revenue in Canada alone to support them. The outlook in this respect is less than propitious, and most people accept that they will probably turn out to be little more than slightly 'Canadianised' adaptations of existing US offerings, consisting predominantly of an American feed with occasional Canadian inserts.

Yet even if this does happen, the argument goes, it is still preferable that Canadians should see Canadianised channels with some Canadian programmes – appropriately regulated by the CRTC – than that they should turn directly to unregulated, fully American services from DBS and domestic satellites. Faced with external pressures and consumer demand, the Government and CRTC are being forced into steps it is unlikely they would otherwise have taken. Central to their strategy is continued control of the principal means of distribution/ reception – cable – in an effort to pursue the regulatory objectives of a distinct Canadian broadcasting and production industry, whilst also satisfying demand for more choice. The hope is that, given stimulation from the new pay channels, broadcast programme development fund, revenue quota requirements and capital allowance incentives, Canadian programmes may find and sustain an identity and a quality which makes them popular and profitable in their own right. In the meantime, content quota rules and the requirement upon all cable systems to give priority carriage to Canadian services over their American equivalents is as much as the CRTC can do, short of telling Canadians what they may or may not watch. Indeed, the Federal Cultural Policy Review Committee came close to favouring mandatory cable when it suggested that all houses passed might be automatically connected 'to give encouragement to Canadian creativity by providing our creators with enlarged audiences. Recommending a favoured position for Canadian-based channels within the cable television system is a major step in this direction' (Op. cit., p.32).

The Canadian broadcasting scene has been and is being changed out of all recognition by the development of cable. While the objectives of the 1978 Broadcasting Act remain the same as before – 'to safeguard, enrich and strengthen the cultural, political, social and economic fabric of Canada' – the strategy which is seen as most likely to bring them about has radically altered (Section 36, Broadcasting Act, 1978). The Act is no longer even appropriately named; off-air Canadian broadcasting is becoming just part of a much broader visual media environment. Canada is an international broadcasting and multi-channel television country where none of the existing broadcast institutions, not even the CBC, has achieved an established position in the hearts or viewing habits of the community. With many channels offering much the same types of programming and without any particular production strengths, it is not surprising that there has been considerable audience fragmentation. In 1980, CBC's English-language service received only 18 per cent of the audience, CTV 30 per cent and the American networks 32 per cent between them. With some 40 per cent of programmes on Canadian stations being American also, and dominating primetime, the average viewer sees far more US than Canadian material. Without content quotas and other incentives there is little doubt that the Canadian production industry would have suffered still further. Even with quotas it is noticeable that although domestically produced news and current affairs have retained their appeal, Canadian 'drama' occupies only 2 per cent of the peak hours between 7.30 and 10.30 p.m. The Canadian experience demonstrates the care with which content quotas need to be defined if they are not to be abused or evaded. Nor do they do more than provide the maximum opportunity for domestically produced programmes to be seen. In a multichannel society there will always be plenty of alternatives, including foreign DBS, if quota programming shows itself to be worthy but dull.

Canadian policy is designed to minimise the attractions of the latter option, to impose adequate controls without destroying audience appeal. In a constantly evolving environment it is hardly surprising that results have so far been mixed, leading to frequent suggestions of regulatory weakness. Yet the CRTC is contending against considerable problems – a powerful, intrusive neighbour, strong consumer demand for greater choice, a traditionally weak and unstable production industry and broadcasting institutions which have largely failed to establish a particular regard amongst Canadian viewers. It is for these reasons that cable has itself become a major weapon in the regulators' armoury. Today the CRTC's broadcast and cultural objectives positively require it to expand and use cable in its own cause. Canada's paradox is that the solution to its problems is seen to lie in the very technology which first aggravated them.

PART FOUR
The United States

7 The Coming of Cable

To write about cable in the United States today one needs both a good stock of superlatives and a sense of proportion. It has more cable systems than any other nation and the largest multiple-system operators. Among its recent urban franchises are the first commercial interactive system and the one with the greatest channel capacity. The USA enjoys the greatest number of cable entertainment channels. Generic television is being developed there in its most extreme form, with nationally distributed non-stop news channels, sports channels, channels for women, youth, blacks, Hispanics, the religious, the health conscious, the film fan, the soft- and hard-core porn patron, the video game addict, the politico, the lover of culture, the deaf, the businessman, the country and western music enthusiast, children and the family which wants good, wholesome American entertainment. At the local level, community, ethnic community (Chinese, Italian, Greek, etc.), local government, educational, public access and leased access channels are available in many systems, as are regional sports channels. Cable is very big business; indeed with over 33 million subscribers by the end of 1983 there are more homes connected to cable systems (excluding communal aerials on blocks of flats) than in the whole of Europe, Canada, Japan and Australia combined. It is not surprising therefore that both the exponents and opponents of cable development in Britain look to the USA for their evidence. Equally, it is not surprising that in such a large and varied industry it is possible to find examples to suit every case. Cable, we are told, is viable and highly lucrative – or it is not lucrative at all, and almost all the companies involved are losing enormous sums. It is run by opportunists out for a quick buck, or by people with a public-spirited desire to further the aims of localism and community access in broadcasting. It provides specialist audiences with specialised programming and special product advertisers with exactly their target audiences. Yet most people continue to spend most of their viewing time watching ordinary network television, while advertisers prove reluctant to believe the promises made for the concept of 'narrowcasting'. Cable provides new material of great variety, or it is a parasite, providing repeats, films and thirty times the usual rubbish. It successfully meets individual tastes, or cynically exploits and panders to all manner of sexual appetite.

Generalisations of this kind are both inaccurate and unhelpful, and it is therefore necessary to approach the American experience with caution. This is not because nothing can be gained from looking at specific issues, but precisely because that experience has been so widely used to prove and disprove the various arguments within the British cable debate. Nowhere is this truer than in the discussion of cable deregulation in the United States, which has been frequently seen as a cornerstone of the industry's growth and an exemplar for other countries.

The commercial locomotive of television's development in the United States during the 40s left many less heavily populated areas without any television service at all, or with only the poorest reception. The American NTSC transmission system was in any case particularly susceptible to interference, a shortcoming of which cable entrepreneurs could take advantage. Indeed, the deficiencies of the broadcasting system and structure were so evident that a number of individuals conceived of cable television more or less simultaneously and independently. Consequently, rival claims to be the father of cable abound. In Lansford, Pennsylvania, a local radio and television set retailer, R.J. Tarlton, found it difficult to sell his stock when the nearest television transmitter was sixty-five miles away in Philadelphia, with the Allegheny mountains in between. In 1949 he experimented with installing individual antennae on the mountain top for each set owner, and in 1950 built what was probably the first full master antenna system in the United States, with a master antenna capable of receiving good-quality pictures from three television stations and a coaxial cable linking it to each subscriber. By using a cable rather than any form of (at that time illegal) relay transmitter, he avoided complications with the Federal Communications Commission which regulated broadcasting, avoided interference problems with other stations, made possible the reception of more signals, provided himself with a new, assured and regular source of revenue and ensured his own virtual monopoly of the television market in Lansford.

Not surprisingly other entrepreneurs in hilly or similar regions of poor reception followed suit, and twelve years later there were 800 systems providing service to some 850,000 subscribers. As in Canada, signal importation was soon added to signal enhancement as a staple function of the cable system, and from the mid-50s onwards towns which could support one or two stations of their own, but no more, became prime targets for operators offering to double or treble the customary choice. Indeed, as late as 1971 some 20 per cent of the American population could receive no more than two off-air television signals, a consequence partly of geographical position and partly of the strategy of the national regulatory body, the FCC.

For the first decade of cable's growth the FCC regarded it simply as a signal enhancement service and so a useful complement rather than a threat to broadcasting. Consequently it remained unregulated. Indeed, many of the worst examples of profiteering took place during this period, when unsupervised operators charged consumers in poor reception areas, who had no other way of obtaining the ever more socially prestigious and desirable television service, exorbitant rates to be connected to the cable system. Revenues from connection charges alone could be triple the total capital cost of the entire system, before monthly subscription fees were considered.

The significance of these early unregulated years, as in Canada, was considerable. They gave the industry time to develop its signal importation role to an extent which prevented the FCC and CRTC from subsequently cracking down on systems and depriving subscribers of these imported channels. By contrast, the early experience in Britain with relay exchanges led to an immediate prohibition on signal importation before cable television had even got under way. Subscribers lost nothing they had had before and cable operators were deprived of a most valuable weapon, consumer support. It is an ironic reflection that the British cable industry lost out in part because of its pioneering initiative.

REGULATION AND 'DEREGULATION'

As with the governments in Britain and Canada, however, the FCC's primary objective when it did first become concerned at cable's growth was to protect and promote already formulated broadcasting policy, if necessary by restricting possible developments in alternative directions. Since 1952 federal policy had been to encourage local station growth through the granting of new UHF station licences, in addition to the already existing VHF system. The objective was to reduce the effective broadcasting oligopoly enjoyed by the three national networks – CBS, NBC and ABC – and to introduce a greater element of localism into television. This strategy, however, was never to work satisfactorily as for many years thereafter most domestic television sets were not equipped to receive UHF, while even for those which were reception remained difficult.

Although cable helped to improve reception, its increasing use for distant signal importation into relatively small markets threatened to fragment the audience of the financially highly insecure UHF stations already in situ and to render unviable further UHF expansion. At first the FCC believed itself unempowered to take cable into its control. By 1962, however, the situation was becoming too serious to ignore and the Commission took the first tentative steps. Emboldened by court decisions in its favour, in 1965 it brought cable systems which received distant signals by microwave link within its regulatory purview. In 1966 it went further and, in a forlorn attempt to buttress its crumbling broadcasting policy, brought all cable systems under its authority.

Already, however, it was becoming clear that the Commission's aim of extending local station choice by encouraging UHF growth was commercially unrealistic, even without the threat of cable. The majority of UHF stations had in any case been established not in the smaller towns but in the major markets where there was most likelihood of commercial success. In 1968, therefore, the FCC recognised that cable might actually have a useful role to play in extending choice where UHF stations had not been established and, like the CRTC in Canada, determined to use it for its own ends. Effectively abandoning its UHF policy in the smaller markets, it decided to allow cable expansion in these, with safeguards for existing local stations. Its objectives of diversity and localism were transferred to cable systems, whose right to originate material themselves was accepted. At the same time, however, the Commission imposed a de facto ban on further cable growth in the top 100 urban markets, where it considered that diversity could still be achieved through existing UHF policy.

This ban has frequently been represented as a freeze upon further cable growth, resulting in a period of stagnation until its removal in 1972. That it significantly delayed cable's entry into the most lucrative markets there can be no doubt. The top 100 contained 87 per cent of all TV viewers in the United States, only a small proportion of whom had been cabled beforehand. Already it was clear that cable operators were being attracted to the major cities where there was potentially most money to be made, and in fact San Diego and Manhattan in New York were both cabled at this time, having received waivers to the ban in view of the major off-air interference problems which they suffered. Without this FCC restriction, cable would have reached the major cities much earlier.

These four years were nevertheless a valuable period for the cable industry, during which it consolidated its base and gained strength. Since the mid-50s a number of individual operators had begun to expand their operations by building new systems in other towns, a trend which was to lead to the rise (as in Canada) of the Multiple System Operator (MSO). Increasingly cable's apparent profitability attracted major investors, including some of the largest broadcasting companies – Cox, Storer and CBS itself. Already broadcasters were hedging their bets and, with other MSOs, looking to the day when cable would be allowed into the major cities and be able to provide additional non-broadcast services.

The late 60s were consequently years of consolidation and growth in the small and medium-sized markets. In 1965 there were 1,570 cable systems serving 1,575,000 subscribers, or 3 per cent of US television households. By the end of 1972, 7,300,000 subscribers (11 per cent of homes) received their service from 2,991 systems. By 1971 cable was growing at the rate of some 20 per cent per annum, faster even than in Canada. Additional automated services which may have attracted some subscribers – stockmarket tickers, clocks and rolling weather reports – also began to appear, as did community and access services. The first public access channel was operated between 1968 and 1970 in Dale City, Virginia, being financed and run by the Junior Chamber of Commerce. Access and community requirements were similarly included in the 1970 Manhattan cable franchises and a large number of systems began to provide channel time for educational and local government items. Community programmes for children, pensioners and others were produced and the National Cable Television Association began to make annual awards for 'cablecasting', as it was coming to be known. When in October 1969 the FCC proposed that larger systems be positively required to provide local programming and access facilities, the industry successfully opposed the idea because of the element of compulsion involved, even though the pill was sugared by the Commission's decision to allow advertising on such channels. Yet by 1973 fully 20 per cent of systems were originating local programmes, although only 17 per cent would have been affected by the FCC's proposed ruling.

The FCC spent the years between 1968 and 1972 in an attempt to reassess its existing broadcasting policy and to formulate a coherent approach to cable regulation through a series of rule-making proceedings. In 1970, for example, it judged that the involvement of the three major broadcasting networks in cable system ownership was against the public interest, and so ordered CBS, the only one so far to have bought systems, to divest itself of its cable subsidiary, Viacom. In general, however, its attitudes towards cable were changing and for much the same reasons as those of the CRTC in Canada. Consequently the FCC's 1972 Cable Television Report and Order, setting out a comprehensive approach to cable regulation, recognised cable's inevitability and, as in Canada, reflected a growing determination to use it as an opportunity rather than to oppose it as a threat.

It recognised, firstly, that by extending and improving the reception of UHF signals cable could actually promote the viability of such stations. The ban on cable's entry into the major markets was therefore lifted, this being the single most important deregulatory move in cable's history. At the same time, the belief was maintained that each market could only sustain a limited number of stations, and that these would be threatened by excessive signal importation. Accordingly, limits were set on the number of distant signals that might be brought in, the maximum figure being set in direct proportion to the size of the market. These distant-signal carriage limitations remained in force until 1980 and were widely claimed by the industry to have further hindered its growth. In fact, it is evident that they never proved to be a significant restriction and may even have promoted the development of other non-broadcast cable services by ensuring that many systems retained unused capacity. Their removal did not lead to a sudden increase in the number of such distant signals carried, even though these and pay-TV were proving to be the cable services most attractive to subscribers.

Although the 1972 rules removed the effective freeze on CATV growth in the major markets, it did impose other major regulatory requirements. In particular, it set down a range of standards with which cable operators had to comply in building systems. Complex rules were also imposed regarding signal carriage and the relay of programmes into the market area of a broadcast station which already had exclusive local rights to that material (properly known as the network programme non-duplication and syndicated exclusivity rules). Restrictions on the ownership of cable systems by local telephone companies, the broadcasting networks and broadcasting stations in the immediate vicinity of a system were set out. Moreover, in order to further the FCC's wider vision for cable, all new systems with more than 3,500 subscribers were required to have at least a twenty-channel capacity and interactive potential. These same systems were also obliged to provide up to three channels free for public access, educational and local government use, as well as undertaking an element of cable-originated programming themselves. With regard to pay-cable channels, which were just beginning to be considered, systems were to be prohibited from showing films which had not been on general release within the last two years, as such older material was a staple diet of independent broadcast stations. Sports events which had traditionally been shown on broadcast television were also to be excluded from pay-cable.

It is this comprehensive set of rules for cable which has over the past ten years been the subject of the process known as 'deregulation'. Cable deregulation in the United States has in fact been just part of the broader deregulation of telecommunications by the federal government, a trend which started under Nixon's Republican administration and continued during the Democratic interregnum of

118

President Carter. In Britain the proponents of cable have emphasised the apparent correlation between cable's rapid growth in recent years and the almost wholesale federal deregulation of the industry. Yet, although it is evident that many of the restrictions in Britain will need to be lifted if cable is to progress further, it must be said that the American experience appears on closer examination to be something of a red herring. Some of what has been 'deregulated' was not in practice regulated initially. Equally, a number of deregulatory moves do not deserve the description, being merely a transfer of power from federal to local authority.

The programme origination requirement, for example, succumbed to industry pressure before being implemented. In any case, programme origination continued to grow apace without compulsion and the FCC's ruling, having been suspended, was deleted entirely in 1974 as unnecessary. In a similar fashion the federal court victory by pay-cable service Home Box Office (HBO) over the FCC, resulting in the deletion of the latter's pay-cable content restrictions in 1977, was not as crucial as has been claimed. It rapidly became apparent that the principal attraction of pay services was not the older films the FCC had sought to protect for independent broadcasting stations, but precisely those more recent films to which the content rules had attempted to confine them. Some sporting events, notably boxing contests, have been siphoned off to pay-cable from the networks, but it was only in 1982 that the pay channels also began to take an interest in previously networked television series. The removal of the content rules did give them some greater programming flexibility, but in no way was it crucial to their growth nor influential in their programming character. As for the regulation of pay-channel fees, which has always been within the FCC's preserve, it has never considered it necessary or desirable to do so. Clearly deregulation in all these areas was not what it seemed to be.

By contrast, many of the regulations remained in force throughout the 70s, including the period of cable's accelerating growth. The FCC's technical requirements and its access rules (modified in 1976) were deemed unconstitutional by the Supreme Court only in 1979. The complex rules regarding distant-signal carriage restrictions and programme exclusivity similarly survived until 1980, while only in 1983 did the FCC begin to consider the necessity of its cross-ownership rules. Throughout the 70s cable systems were being built in a still heavily regulated environment which the subsequent period of rapid deregulation has done much to obscure. Until 1983, moreover, 'deregulation' related only to federal control, while the powers of local authorities during the franchising process and in regulating basic cable rates remained very considerable. Local authorities have always been responsible for awarding the cable franchises within their own jurisdictions, doing so, however, in accordance with a federally established set of technical performance standards. Yet when in 1977 the FCC deleted all but one of its franchising standards, as part of its deregulatory process, local authorities showed themselves very ready to adopt equally or more rigorous requirements, which the increasing competition between cable companies for those franchises only exacerbated. Today the FCC's sole franchise regulation is actually designed to protect cable system operators, being a limitation of the annual franchise fee a city can charge an operator, that limit being 3-5 per cent of the latter's gross revenue. In the period of cable's fastest growth, between 1977 and 1983, the franchising environment has been even more exacting than that which existed before. (The Cable Bill of 1983, which is before the House of Representatives at the time of writing, will reduce the local authorities' power somewhat, particularly in basic rate regulation and franchise renewal, but still leaves them in control of the initial franchising process.)

It is therefore simply not appropriate to discuss the expansion of the cable industry in relation to the full process of the deregulatory movement. Nor, in view of their wholly dissimilar regulatory starting points, is it possible to use America as an exemplar for deregulation in Britain. All one can conclude is that in both Canada and the United States, given the incentives of imported distant signals and (as we shall see below) pay-TV, the cable industry grew rapidly in spite of extensive regulatory constraint. At the same time, it is evident that without the acceptance of programme origination in 1968 and the lifting of the major market ban in 1972 the American industry would not have achieved its phenomenal growth of the last few years.

For phenomenal that growth has been. In its third decade cable entered its third phase. While the improvement of signal reception and the importation of distant signals remained significant factors, the driving force of that growth was increasingly cable's ability to provide special services which offered the viewer significantly different programming to that on off-air television.

THE COMING OF PAY AND SATELLITE SERVICES

The relaxing of the ban on cable's further entry into the top 100 American markets led to a sudden surge of franchising activity as cable companies perceived the tremendous prizes to be gained. Inevitably this scramble was accompanied by a degree of bribery and corruption, a development which opponents of the industry have used to disparage it as an unscrupulous and mercenary business, but which in truth merely demonstrates the dangers in any highly com-

120

petitive franchising process of this kind, particularly at the local level. In a bid to gain the best franchises, potential system operators fought to gain the favours of the local city officials who awarded them, and this unhappy trend reached its nadir when the chief executive of the largest MSO, Teleprompter, was gaoled for bribing officials in Johnstown, Pennsylvania.

Yet the early 70s proved to be a false dawn. Cable companies over-reached themselves in the worsening economic conditions and attempted to build systems in markets where basic penetration did not produce enough cash flow even to service debt. Teleprompter almost went bankrupt and so did many others. Some systems for which the franchise had been awarded were never built, as in Southgate, California, and others proved much more costly than anticipated. By 1974 the industry as a whole was only marginally profitable and in 1975 depreciation and interest charges consumed 90 per cent of its cash flow.

A number of factors turned cable's fortunes around. Not least was the increasing public, political and commercial knowledge and expectations of the 'new' technology, fired in part by the publication in 1971 of the Sloan Commission report, 'On the Cable: the Television of Abundance', and by books such as Ralph Lee Smith's visionary and influential *The Wired Society*, which appeared in 1972. Even more important was the improving economic climate. Because the industry is highly capital-intensive, any reduction in interest rates can have major benefits. This is exactly what happened between 1976 and 1979, combining with the slowdown in system building (as a result of companies' financial problems) to steady the industry's debt. The financial market's growing enthusiasm for cable, moreover, allowed an increase in equity rather than debt financing. Most crucial, however, was a significant increase in revenue growth. In the short term this resulted from a concerted industry effort to persuade local regulatory authorities across the country to permit basic subscriber rate increases. In the long term, however, it was a result of the discovery at last of a successful formula for the packaging and distribution of pay-television and other additional services.

The idea of pay-television using scrambled broadcast transmissions had been around in the USA since the 30s, although prohibited in practice by the FCC. In the early 50s an experimental pay-cable service in Bartleville, Oklahoma, proved a financial failure as did many others attempted by Zenith, Avco, CBS, RKO and Paramount. The first experimental broadcast subscription channel, operated by Zenith and RKO in Hartford, Connecticut, between 1962 and 1969, equally failed to attract sufficient revenue. It did, however, lead to the FCC's decision in 1968 to permit broadcast pay-TV on a commercial basis.

121

Although subscription television had been seen predominantly as an adaptation of broadcast services – as a means to promote UHF station profitability – the emphasis began to switch to cable in the early 70s. Cable subscribers were already used to paying monthly charges and in some systems to receiving non-broadcast channels, although without making extra payments. Moreover, cable operators who were not on a sound financial basis were keen to generate additional revenues. A number of new marketing ploys also proved important. Earlier schemes had been founded on the belief that subscribers would prefer paying on a per-programme basis rather than with a monthly fee for an entire channel. The technology, however, had proved complex, while the method of billing had brought home to the consumer how much he was spending each time the pay service was turned on. The first successful pay channels were based on the recognition that a package of premium films, sold together more cheaply than if they were sold individually, and billed on a monthly basis, was seen as a far more attractive deal by the purchaser. Like a biscuit assortment, there might be a number of offerings which were not particularly wanted, but it was the variety at the price which appealed. Pay-channel operators also soon realised that in this way they could sell less popular films or programmes on the backs of other more attractive ones.

The second major discovery was that on pay cable, unlike broadcast television, it was possible to repeat material several times a month and yet sell this cost-cutting exercise and simple solution to shortage of programming as a positive consumer convenience. Finally, it was recognised that the operation of a pay service was a business distinct from running a cable system and should be organised separately. Having made this distinction the conclusion was obvious: the economics of a pay-cable network, supplying the same programmes to several cable systems, were much more attractive that serving one only. The economies of scale could be considerable.

Home Box Office, owned by Time Inc., began a pay-cable service on 8 November 1972, when it relayed a live hockey match and a film from its New York centre to the 385 pay-cable subscribers of Wilkes Barre in Pennsylvania, using microwave relays and trunk telephone lines in the same way that broadcast stations are interconnected. By 1974 it had become the first true pay-cable network or distributor, providing a service to thirty systems. The channel was sold to any system that wanted it, irrespective of whether it was owned by Time. Typically it showed two films each evening, or a film and a sporting event, often live from Madison Square Garden. A similar service was begun by Warner Cable in 1973, and by 1974 was serving ten of its own systems. Later this became The Movie Channel and was the first to be offered twenty-four hours a day. Other early pay services were provided by TheatreVision, Optical Systems Corp. and Viacom.

Home Box Office was hardly an instant success. After two years it had about 57,000 subscribers and was still losing money. The microwave and line distribution (and in some cases physical transportation of tapes) was complicated and geographically limiting, whilst the major film studios were cautious and unwilling to let HBO show their more recent films, in case it reduced their box-office appeal. The enormous resources of Time supported it, however, and in 1975 the radical decision was taken to distribute programmes by satellite, making HBO available across the continent to all systems. This was a brave and unprecedented step, following on the launch of the first private domestic communications satellite, RCA's Satcom I, earlier in 1975, itself a consequence of the FCC's 1972 decision to permit commercial satellite operations. For the lease of the satellite transponder alone Time committed itself to spending $7.5 million over five years.

The decision was all the braver because few if any cable systems yet had their own satellite-receiving dishes. Indeed, until then it had been normal practice for a satellite operator also to own central transmit-and-receive dishes and to distribute signals to individual users by microwave and landline. HBO created a demand for continuous satellite reception (and reception only) using dishes owned and operated by cable systems. Yet the cost of the 9-metre dishes approved in FCC guidelines was still over $80,000 in 1975, far more than most systems could afford. Fortunately in December 1976 the FCC responded to appeals to approve 4.5 metre receive-only dishes (TVROS). With the growing cable interest in HBO the cost of these smaller TVROS began to drop dramatically, to as little as $25,000 in 1977 and $10-15,000 in 1979. In 1983 mass production economies allowed prices of $3,500-5,000. The resultant growth was remarkable, from about 500 cable system dishes in 1977 to 1,300 in 1978, 2,500 in 1979 and 4,800 by early 1982. Today over 90 per cent of all cable subscribers have access to satellite-distributed services.

Two further elements helped to turn HBO into the extremely profitable operation it has become. As the studios recognised the money to be made from pay, they began to supply films more attractive to subscribers. Previously HBO had been pinched between studio caution about releasing recent films and FCC regulations regarding older ones. In fact, by the time the FCC's rules were overturned in 1977, HBO already had a positive cash flow and was looking to satisfy audience demand for premium films. The second major factor was the joining of HBO on Satcom I by the first superstation, WTBS Atlanta, in December 1976. The owner of this ordinary independent television station, Ted Turner, recognised the appeal of distant-signal stations to basic cable subscribers and saw how easy system operators would find it to take his signal together with HBO. He also created the 'per-subscriber' form of payment, whereby system operators paid him a few cents a month for each subscriber on their system, in return for his signal. The extra channel could be added to the basic package at no extra cost to subscribers and at minimum cost to the operator. Meanwhile Turner was able to charge advertisers national rates while continuing to put out a cheap diet of old films, syndicated series and Atlanta sport. With two services available on one satellite, the economics of buying a dish became much more attractive to system operators. A TVRO for one service might cost $25,000, but the extra equipment to pick up a second service added only another $3,000. Each channel therefore cost $14,000 in capital outlay, and as others became available on the same satellite and as TVRO costs fell, the outlay per channel was reduced to a few hundred dollars.

Thus by 1977 prospects were set fair for a new and more sustained cable boom. Interest rates were declining, enthusiasm on all sides was high, new cable programme services and sources of revenue were becoming available across the nation and at ever lower cost to cable operators. In 1977 barely 17 per cent of television homes were connected to cable systems and only two satellite-delivered cable services were available. Yet in the years since then American cable systems and services have grown at such a rate and in an atmosphere of such optimism that the impact has been felt around the world.

8 Cable Systems: Boom or Bust

The improving economic climate, the prospect of new revenues for cable from pay services and even from advertising sold on the other new channels, revived all the earlier 'blue-sky' visions and stimulated a further and sustained period of system building. Between 1975 and 1980 cable stocks rose a remarkable fortyfold on average, and revenue growth exceeded 20 per cent per annum. Before building picked up again pretax income gains of 50 per cent or more were achieved. In 1978 a new and startling discovery was made in Thibodaux, Louisiana, when many cable subscribers, offered the choice of HBO and a new rival pay service, elected to take both. The revelation that subscribers would take two or more pay channels increased operators' optimism still further, and the economics of prospective systems were increasingly calculated on the expectation that well over 50 per cent of an operator's return would come not from basic fees but from his slice of the multi-pay cake. Today some 40 per cent of systems offer between two and ten pay services.

Pay channels were also seen as the key to selling cable in the major urban areas already well served by off-air broadcasting stations. Everything seemed to be fitting into place as major companies began again to fight for the right to cable the remaining major markets. The competitive scramble, the optimistic gold-rush atmosphere which characterised the late 70s, resulted in a sellers' market for the city authorities which awarded franchises and induced a remarkable improvement in the general specification of new systems. Authorities came to expect, almost as a minimum requirement, fifty-four-channel interactive systems with extensive access, community and educational facilities. In major cities 'institutional loops' for business and public institutional data traffic have become common features of franchise bids, and these have led to the stories cited in Britain of 214 channel systems, as in Boston. So keen were companies to obtain franchises that bidding standards became somewhat loose, relying increasingly on unproven sources of revenue – particu-

125

larly extreme levels of multi-pay, but also pay-per-view, advertising, interactive banking, teleshopping, security services and business traffic. All manner of ploys have become common to gain franchises. In Sacramento this included lobbying on behalf of the losing contender, Warner Amex, by the former US President, Gerald Ford, now on the board of parent company American Express. Elsewhere, losing applicants have been known to sue the city authorities on anti-trust grounds, as in Houston and Dallas.

System growth in the last few years has reflected the mood of optimism. Between 1975 and 1983 the number of activated systems increased from 3,506 to around 6,200. More significantly the average size and capacity of systems has risen also. In 1978 only 100 systems had over 20,000 subscribers and only one over 100,000 (San Diego, with 153,000). Three years later the figures had more than doubled. Whereas in 1978, before most new systems had come on-line, only 556 had more than a twenty-channel capacity, five years later this had grown to 1,896. Then the large number of old and small systems meant that at least two-thirds of subscribers had access to twelve or fewer channels. By 1983 well over two-thirds were on systems with more than twelve.

Optimism was also reflected in the complexity of the new technology. In particular, Warner Amex's Qube system, first installed in Columbus, Ohio, in 1977, provides a two-way interactive service which allows home security services, six channels devoted entirely to pay-per-view programming, programmes in which the viewer can participate and even voting from home on local issues. The capital cost of such a system is considerable and Warner Amex have yet to break even on the venture. Nevertheless, they have subsequently bid successfully for and are building a further seven major urban franchises, including Cincinnati (sixty channels), Dallas, Houston, Pittsburgh (eighty channels), parts of St Louis and Chicago and one of the New York franchises. All offer the Qube interactive service. Other system operators are just beginning to make use of optic fibres (as in Denver) and AML multi-channel microwave (e.g. Houston) for relaying signals from the central headend to local hubs, while in Alameda, California, Times-Fiber have been awarded the franchise to build the first fully optic-fibre switched system in the USA. Equally interesting from a British point of view is the hybrid optic/coaxial switched system to be built by Storer in Miami, since this is a technology which is also to be marketed here and which is claimed to be economically comparable to entirely coaxial systems. The majority of systems now being built are at least one-way addressable, meaning that the operator can provide or block particular services to individual households from the headend, without having to send an engineer to the home. Not surprisingly, construction costs have soared and have frequently exceeded budgets. Four years ago a typical system might be a one-way thirty-five-channel aerial plant, costing $8,000 a mile. By 1982 dual-cable plant costing $18-20,000 a mile had become more common.

The competitiveness of the franchising process and the consequent power of local authorities has undoubtedly been responsible for this rise in standards and hence in costs. The city of Detroit's minimum expectations when inviting bids in August 1982 are representative of many. Offering the operator a large market of 471,000 homes, it asked for a two-way residential cable system of at least seventy-two channels and an additional institutional cable to interconnect businesses and municipal, educational and medical buildings with at least twenty 'upstream' and twenty 'downstream' channels. It also required a minimum of ten access channels (two public, four governmental and four educational) and six production studios, with an obligation to increase both as usage increases. A franchise fee of 5 per cent of the operator's total revenues is to be levied and a further 3 per cent devoted to supporting public access programmes. The operator is to have five years to build the entire system and must wire a certain number of low-income communities each year to ensure that he does not just skim the profitable cream. A few systems are even being asked to provide a free 'universal' service to all homes passed. In Chicago, thirty-six channels, including off-air relay and access channels, are to be provided in this way, whilst 20 per cent of total channel capacity is to be set aside for access.

Even so, completion has frequently raised bids well above the stipulated minimum. One of the applicants for Detroit is offering 126 channels and an additional sixty-one channel institutional loop. In Boston the winning applicant, Cablevision, offered double the institutional network capacity required and proposed a remarkable fifty-two-channel basic tier for only $2 a month. This will include not only relays and access channels but also some of the satellite-delivered cable services. Frequently these cheap or free basic tiers contain little that anyone really wants to watch and are offset by high installation costs ($40 in Chicago). The Boston basic tier is notable in that it does offer worthwhile programming at low cost, whilst an additional twenty satellite-delivered channels (excluding any pay services) will be available for just $5.95.

Another feature of the industry is extensive cross-media ownership. Just as in the 30s to 50s publishing interests moved into broadcasting, so more recently both they and others have moved into cable. Consequently, the principal MSOs are for the most part simply branches of larger media enterprises. ATC, the second largest MSO, is owned by Time Inc., with interests in magazine and book publishing, forest products and, of course Home Box Office, HBO's sister-channel Cinemax and the advertiser-supported USA Network. Group W Cable is part of Westinghouse, the major broadcasting station owner, fifth largest electronics manufacturer in the USA and parent of the cable services Home Theater Network (movies) and The Nashville Network (country and western music). Other MSOs in the top ten include Cox, another major broadcasting and publishing company, Storer (broadcasting and Delta Airlines), Times-Mirror (major publisher and broadcast station owner), Viacom and Warner Amex. Warner Communications, which owns Warner Amex with American Express, has enormous publishing, film production, record and leisure interests and owns Atari, the largest video games company. Other major publishers with cable interests include Newhouse, Knight-Ridder, Dow Jones, the Tribune Corporation and the New York Times Company. In fact, by 1982 some 30 per cent of all subscribers were on publisher-owned cable systems.

The full extent of cross-ownership in cable systems is revealed by Table IV:

TABLE IV

Percentage of cable systems with cross-ownership interests, June 1981. (Multiple-interest ownerships are counted in each relevant category.)
(Source: TV Factbook, No. 50, 1981-2, p. 84a)

Broadcasting	38.3
Newspapers	15.7
Book or magazine publishing	11.8
Programme production or distribution	20.9
Cinema	3.1
Telephone companies	3.2
Municipal	0.5

Such a situation naturally leads to fears that one company could completely dominate the media within a particular area. Consequently the FCC has so far maintained a number of regulations to prevent this. Several states specifically forbid newspaper ownership of cable systems within the same market, whilst the FCC has similarly restricted telephone companies in order to prevent them taking unfair advantage of their control of ducts and utility poles and of their cross-subsidisation opportunities. Only in 1981 was this last rule relaxed so that telephone companies could offer cable services in uncabled rural areas – areas which ordinary cable companies would regard as too sparsely populated to be economic. Interestingly, as a result eighty-six co-located operations were approved in 1982, each serving communities of no more than 2,500 homes and with fewer than thirty houses per cable mile. Indeed, where most cable com-

128

panies regard thirty to forty homes per mile as the minimum density they could cable, and then only if the overall franchise averages at least 100 a mile, one telephone company in West Virginia has considered it economically viable to cable an area with an average density of just nine houses per mile. Whilst this demonstrates the potential economic advantages of telephone companies in any direct confrontation with cable, it also suggests that by such means the fear of cable as an essentially urban phenomenon and therefore geographically divisive could be resolved.

The investment necessary for these large and complex systems is enormous. The 220,000-home Denver franchise will cost the partnership of ATC, Daniels & Co. and local investors $80-100 million to provide a 220-channel-capacity, interactive service with a fifty-channel $3.75 basic tier. Additional tiers will provide further advertiser-supported and pay channels. Each Chicago franchise (there are five of between 188,000 and 271,000 homes) will take up to $175 million to build. Warner Amex is spending some $100 million to wire Dallas (400,000 homes) and a similar amount for Cincinnati. When costs per mile can rise to $100,000 for underground urban systems, it is not surprising that the average cost per subscriber (at an assumed 50 per cent penetration) has risen from $4-500 in 1980 to $7-800 in 1983. The cost of a relatively simple fifty-four-channel headend can be upwards of $750,000, and even the expense of applying and lobbying for a franchise commonly exceeds $1 million.

What are the most significant factors in determining a system's capital costs and operating expenses? Analysis of the economics of recent franchise awards by National Economic Research Associates (NERA) has revealed that in an average tree and branch system the distribution network itself (excluding subscriber feed lines) and headend equipment account for 55 per cent of all capital costs, the converter/decoder equipment in the home takes some 37 per cent, with 8 per cent for subscriber feeds. The most significant factors determining the capital costs of the headend and distribution system are its channel capacity, the overall size of the franchise and local wage rates for construction. Interestingly, the proportion of the system which is laid underground has only a moderate effect on its cost, since it is frequently possible to use existing ducts, while the right to use telephone poles can be expensive. The view that in Britain systems will be more costly because a higher proportion of each will be underground may therefore be mistaken, while lower average wage rates than in the USA will also be significant. Similarly, the idea that housing density is a major factor in system costs appears to be doubtful, at least down to suburban levels. The cost of digging trenches where necessary and of installing ducts is highest in built-up city areas and much lower in suburban, with the difference apparently compensating for the lower housing densities (and therefore fewer potential subscribers per mile) in the latter.

Turning to the 45 per cent of capital costs which are essentially subscriber-related – the converters and lines into each home – the most important influences, predictably, are the number of households which subscribe and the capacity of the system (the larger the capacity the more complex and expensive the converter/decoders). Finally, on average some 36 per cent of operating expenses are taken up with the system operator's payments for pay services. The most important influence on these is the retail price to subscribers, since the pay-service providers generally charge operators a percentage of the retail rate. Other operating expenses (installation, maintenance, administration, etc.) are primarily determined by the number of subscribers on the system.

The competitive and local character of the American franchising process is frequently criticised for leading to impractical bids. Operators claim that local authority power forces them to promise more than they know for certain they can provide, and there is certainly some truth in this, given the enormous complexity of estimating a franchise's viability, its capital costs over a five-year build period, the rate of penetration and the take-up of pay services. To attempt to forecast profitability over the typical fifteen-year franchise is an almost impossible task. Consequently, efforts are already being made by many operators to renege on franchise terms, while in several cases the rate of construction has not matched the timetable specified in the franchise. Usually franchise agreements contain penalty clauses for delayed completion, and these can prove extemely costly to a dilatory operator. Yet if the operator has promised a system technology which subsequently proves to be beyond the state of the art, or services which are simply not cost-feasible, there is little the city authority can do. It does not pay to penalise the operator too much. The New Orleans franchise agreement contains all the necessary penalty clauses, yet this has not induced the franchisee, Cox Cable, to meet its obligations.

Similarly, there are arguments against the authority levying large franchise fees. In some cases fees have exceeded the amount it costs a city to regulate the cable operation – the ostensible reason for such a fee – and have been put into its general fund. Since the operator merely passes these costs on to the subscriber, this becomes little more than an indirect tax. In many instances the franchise fee or an additional 'royalty' (as in Boston and Chicago) is used to defray the costs of the various public and local government access channels. Although this is generally considered a more acceptable use of such funds, it does mean that cable subscribers are financing a number of channels in which most viewers seem to take little or no interest.

130

A further area for criticism in the initial franchising and subsequent local authority supervision of systems is in the regulation of rates. In order to prevent system operators taking advantage of their local monopoly position to make excessive profits, authorities have until now controlled the charges made for basic services, although the FCC effectively prevents any regulation of rates for pay channels and the more recent enhanced and business services (burglar alarms, etc.). Yet experience in other monopolies in the United States – energy, transport, telecommunications – has demonstrated just how limited is the success of rate regulation in terms of price and performance efficiency, whilst inflation means constant appeals for rate revision. In practice, cable rate regulation has become a political weapon and a cause of much tension between operators and city officials. The former argue that, as a luxury good, cable does not need rate regulation, since market forces will operate effectively, and this argument seems to have been accepted in the 1983 Federal Cable Bill. Indeed, since 1979 the State of California has allowed cable systems to operate without rate regulation if they meet certain requirements, most notably a minimum twenty-channel capacity, community programming, fifty cents per subscriber per year to be devoted to community channels, and up to three of the latter to be provided, with provision for more if usage warrants it.

Franchising and subsequent regulation is clearly of the greatest possible complexity. Commonly over two years may pass from the moment a franchising authority draws up its initial ordinance (specifying minimum expectations and laying the ground rules of regulation), through to the request for proposals, the evaluation of bids, shortlisting, public hearings, final selection, negotiation of the provisional licence and then of the final licence, until the time when the first foot of cable is laid. Some idea of just how many issues have to be taken into account can be gained by looking at the contents pages of a franchise agreement. Appendix I describes the background to the Boston franchise and lists the contents of the provisional licence. Large as the system is, the issues raised and points specified are not untypical of a modern franchise. What is noticeable is that where a city devotes significant resources and energy and establishes a full-time team to the business of franchising and subsequent supervision, it tends to reap commensurate rewards. Compare Boston, where there is a permanent forty-strong cable office, with Houston, where cable is regulated by the public utilities department which is also responsible for transport and refuse. Houston, with only two access and community channels, is now trying to win back some of the ground it lost in a very unhappy and somewhat doubtful franchising 'carve-up' in 1979.

Inevitably the tremendously competitive franchising process of the last few years has tended to favour the larger and more financially secure companies. As a result the industry appears to be increasingly dominated by a limited number of powerful multiple-interest conglomerates. Given the varying size of systems there would not be much point in the FCC's limiting the number a single company can own, as it has done with broadcasting stations. But nor has it put any upper limit on the size of a company's subscriber base. Consequently, although there are nearly 5,000 cable systems in operation, the top fifty MSOs alone account for 65 per cent of all subscribers, and the top ten for a remarkable 40 per cent.

Such concentrations within the industry have naturally been criticised as leading to excessive monopoly power, but in general the attitude being taken is not to legislate or act against something until it manifests itself in practice. In any case, there are already a number of checks and balances against extreme horizontal integration, both natural and imposed. The Justice Department can, for instance, prohibit mergers on anti-trust grounds if they are likely to lead to excessive concentrations of power, while the FCC can effectively do the same by refusing such a company a cable relay licence (normally granted automatically). But, in any case, not even the largest MSO, currently TCI, yet serves more than 7 per cent of cable subscribers — a total of 2.2 million homes, or barely 2.6 per cent of television households. Moreover, in the most recent franchise contests it has been local consortia rather than the major MSOs which have made the running, as the latter's already heavy capital commitments prevent them expanding still further.

A more serious problem is that of vertical integration, in which a large MSO also has programme service interests – as several do. Where this is the case it is certainly possible, as we shall see in the next chapter, for one MSO to carry his own programming but exclude that of a rival service provider. Indeed, in such circumstances there is a risk that the success or failure of a programme service may depend not on subscriber interest but on the readiness of a few MSOs to give it access to the large blocks of subscribers whch they control. In this way a system operator's local monopoly effectively gives him the ability to determine what cable services will or will not be made available to subscribers, a position of potentially enormous economic and intellectual power.

According to a recent estimate only about 10 per cent of all US television households (which comprise 98 per cent of all households) are still in areas where a cable franchise has not been awarded, and since these are predominantly in such major markets as Chicago, Washington, Philadelphia and Detroit, even they are currently under negotiation. A large number of franchises awarded in the last two years are in the construction phase and growth should remain rapid for some time as they come on line. In 1982 some 8 million addition-al homes were passed, equivalent to 10 per cent of all US house-holds. Subscriber growth has been equally remarkable. In the early 70s numbers were increasing by about 70,000 each month. By 1976 this had grown to 140,000 and by 1980 to 180,000. In the next year new systems and rising penetration in old led to 430,000 additional subscribers being connected each month. In 1975 under 30 per cent of households were passed by cable, but by 1983 this figure had grown to 65 per cent. More importantly, whereas in 1975 some 43 per cent of homes passed actually subscribed, by 1983 this had grown to 56 per cent. In many systems penetration is even higher, and in a few exceeds 70 per cent. Most spectacular was the overall rise from 46 to 52 per cent between 1980 and 1981, as a large number of new cable channels became available. As cable's attrac-tions grew, so did interest in it; the economics of cable began to look even better.

The pay-film channels have been a major reason for subscriber growth. In many new systems over 90 per cent of subscribers take at least one pay service in addition to basic. In 1975 barely 3 per cent of cable subscribers received a pay channel, but by 1980 this had grown to 42 per cent and by 1983 to 59 per cent. Pay services are still not available on some of the older systems; discounting these, therefore, over 65 per cent of basic subscribers who have a pay service available take it. The number of pay subscriptions rose at 143 per cent the rate of basic in 1981, and the average pay subscri-ber took 1.3 pay channels. In many new systems, such as Storer Cable's in Houston, the ratio of pay units to basic is over 200 per cent.

In absolute terms, therefore, by the end of 1983 there were 83.7 million television households in the United States and over 34 mil-lion cable subscribers. This represented a 40 per cent cable penetra-tion of TV homes. Some 23 million pay units were sold, representing over 17 million individuals. Estimates for continued growth vary, but it is widely expected that TV homes passed will exceed 80 per cent by 1985 and those taking cable television total about 50 per cent. In 1982 the average monthly basic subscription was $8.46 and the average pay fee per channel $9.56. Industry revenues were climbing at an average of nearly 30 per cent per annum and totalled $4.5 billion, of which $1.9 billion came from pay services, some 43 per cent of the total. Within three years 50 per cent of revenue is likely to come from pay.

DOUBTS AND PROBLEMS

Although recent growth has been phenomenal, it has not been

unalloyed. Basic penetration has generally met expectations but in many urban systems lags at under 30-40 per cent or less. Equally, new subscribers may begin by taking several pay channels but tend then to cut back to one or two only. Most importantly, the industry's ever-mounting debt, reaching $5 billion in 1982, has become increasingly costly to service as interest rates have soared. In 1981, the most recent year for which full figures are available, industry revenues totalled $3.6 billion, with operating expenses of $2.4 billion, leaving an operating income of $1.2 billion or a 33.4 per cent margin before depreciation, amortisation, interest and taxes. Yet, after depreciation and interest, net income came to only $40 million before tax.

The nature of the industry means that long-term fixed-rate financing is not available, while the 1980-81 equity boom in cable stock did not raise sufficient money to finance the major franchises which are now being built. The cost of construction is rising and in some cases has reached $1,000 per subscriber (plus depreciation and interest). At 40-50 per cent basic penetration, this means a necessary monthly income per subscriber of $40-50, most of which will have to come from pay services and other new sources of revenue. Boston's franchise, in which the basic and first tier of advertiser-supported channels costs $8, is calculated on the basis of an average $35 per subscriber per month at 40 per cent penetration. Yet the industry average is only $18-19, with Cablevision on another of its systems having the highest income per subscriber, but still at under $30. Inevitably, basic and pay subscriptions are regarded as the major sources of revenue, but poor results for advertiser-based channels have led to scepticism as to whether advertising will prove a significant revenue earner for system operators. Meanwhile, delays and complications in producing addressable converters, the hardware that makes pay-per-view possible, are seen as delaying yet another source of income.

1982 also saw the recognition of 'churn' and signal theft as major problems. 'Churn' − the percentage of subscribers who decide to disconnect from the cable service − is currently running at about 3 per cent of basic customers every month (over 30 per cent per annum), and 4-5 per cent of pay subscribers (50-60 per cent per annum). New subscribers are more than balancing this loss to the industry, but in many franchises churn is seriously hindering growth. In Syracuse, for example, a system activated in March 1978, basic connections grew rapidly to 50 per cent (32,000) in 1981, but since then have risen barely 1 per cent. In the 1981-2 period 9,000 new subscribers took the HBO pay service, but even more disconnected, giving a net loss and a churn of 41 per cent of the 22,330 total. Nationally some 840,000 basic and 850,000 pay subscribers are disconnecting each month, a loss to the industry of about $174 million.

A major cause of 'churn' is social mobility. People move house, disconnect and reconnect – not a permanent loss to the system but an expensive one, since most operators subsidise the cost of connection. In Syracuse 22 per cent of disconnects represent people moving out of the area, 23 per cent moving within. Thirty per cent simply do not pay their bill. Operators are unwilling immediately to disconnect someone who may only be in temporary financial difficulty and generally give up to ninety days grace. During this time they nevertheless have to continue paying channel providers for their services to recalcitrant subscribers and this represents additional expense. The net effect of churn, particularly in non-addressable systems where engineers have to be sent out to disconnect a house, is a considerable loss to the operator.

Almost as serious is signal theft. Although pay-TV signals are generally scrambled it would appear that many subscribers have managed to tap the signal of simpler systems without payment. At Cox Cable in San Diego, the nation's largest system, basic signal theft is estimated at 15 per cent and pay at 13 per cent, an annual revenue loss of some $8-12 million. In Storer's Houston franchise theft is as high as 20 per cent in some areas, and 10 per cent is a figure quoted by many other operators. This is a particular problem in apartment block complexes where access to the cable makes tampering relatively easy. Nationally signal theft has been quoted at five to six per cent both of basic and of pay, equivalent to lost revenue for system operation of $392 million and for service providers of some $96 million.

The unhappy economic state of the industry has given it an opportunity to complain about a number of thorns in its flesh, particularly the cost of regulation, the power of the cities and the threat from alternative distribution technologies, including DBS and over-the-air subscription television (STV). All, it suggests, could endanger cable's viability. A much-cited survey for the National Cable Television Association concludes that over 20 per cent of a new cable system's expenditure, and hence subscriber revenues, can be attributed to regulatory and franchise requirements – to access channel provision, licence fees, additional engineers' expenses, staff costs and the various 'must carry', 'network duplication' and 'sports blackout' rules. Armed with this analysis, the industry has strongly backed the cable bill presented to Congress by Senator Barry Goldwater which, despite certain compromises forced upon it by the National League of Cities, will limit the power of city authorities over cable operators in future. Its effect could be greatly to reduce operators' obligations and expenses.

The issue of alternative methods of distributing television signals is one which deserves particular attention, since it opens up the possibility of supplying additional services without the necessity of cabling at all. Off-air subscription television (STV), using available UHF frequencies, can supply one or two pay channels to relatively large markets. The signal is scrambled at the transmitter to allow only subscribers with decoders to receive it. By 1982 there were over twenty such STV stations serving at least 1.5 million subscribers. Multi-point distribution services (MDS), which transmit at micro-wave frequencies, have also been allowed to supply a single channel of pay-TV and serve about 500,000 subscribers. Like single-channel STV, MDS has until now been relatively limited in what it could offer. But as from May 1983 the FCC has reallocated frequencies to allow two MDS operators in any market to provide up to four channels each, making this service more competitive against multi-channel cable and DBS. Moreover, by comparison with either of these, the capital costs are minimal — perhaps $1-2 million for the transmitter and $150 per home for the receiving antenna and decoder. As a result of this policy change the FCC has been inundated with over 20,000 applications to provide multi-channel MDS.

It has also accepted a number of applications by prospective DBS operators, who between them could provide thirty to forty additional channels right across the nation. The first three, United Satellite Communications Inc. (owned by Prudential Insurance and General Instrument Corporation), Satellite Television Corp. (Comsat) and Inter-American Satellite Television (backed by Rupert Murdoch), will use medium-powered satellites (11.7-12.2 ghz) which can be received by 1.2 metre dishes, and should be providing five channels each by 1984. In any case, apartment block owners are already putting larger three-metre TVROs on their buildings to provide tenants with existing satellite services (Satellite Master Antenna TV, or SMATV systems), thereby circumventing the local cable system. In the still uncabled Bronx area of New York, for example, one large apartment complex is having its own 120-channel SMATV system installed which will by itself serve 15,000 homes, thereby depriving Cablevision, the newly franchised cable operator, of valuable poten-tial subscribers. Even individual home-owners are installing these larger TVROs. According to the industry, at least 30,000 homes were equipped in this way by 1981 and annual sales are running at between ten and 20,000 dishes. A private TVRO has become some-thing of a status symbol. Meanwhile the FCC's decision to permit low-power television stations within the contours of existing broad-cast station signals has led to a deluge of over 12,000 licence applica-tions, many for low-power subscription TV services. Finally, after a slow start, video recorders are proving increasingly popular.

136

Not surprisingly the cable industry is making much ·of the threat which these new distribution technologies pose. Of course existing single-channel MDS and STV cannot hope to compete with multi-channel cable where the latter enters a market first and at a comparable price. But where the more easily installed over-the-air services arrive first, as in Los Angeles, they have managed to capture a reasonable proportion of potential subscribers and even to retain 5-15 per cent of the market once a competing cable system is available. According to a survey for the NCTA, by Browne, Bortz and Coddington, most viewers' needs are satisfied by five channels in addition to broadcast network services, while interest in further channels drops sharply even with only marginal increases in the consumer price. The industry's conclusion is that, when available, five-channel DBS, MDS or STV, offered at a lower rate than fifty-channel cable, could attract a significant share of the market. Given the tight financial situation of many new cable systems, even a 5 per cent drop in the ratio of subscribers to homes passed could affect profitability, as it would involve a loss in net income of rather more than 5 per cent due to cable's high fixed costs.

A particularly sore point for the cable industry is that while it is bound by municipal regulation, franchise fees, access requirements and similar restrictions, these other services can compete freely once a federal licence has been granted. SMATV operators in particular, not even needing a federal licence, can enter an urban market and skim off a large proportion of the lucrative apartment block sector, while a cable operator is still negotiating his franchise. Moreover, the normal franchise requirement that a standard cable subscription rate be applied throughout a system means that some subscribers pay more than it costs to supply them, while others pay less. This creates a price inefficiency in high-density areas and so makes STV, MDS and other such services more attractive there than is economically justifiable. From this the industry argues that cable is unfairly hindered in a competitive environment and so should be no more regulated than the alternative distribution systems. In 1977, it is pointed out, cable had 95 per cent of all pay-TV subscribers, but by 1982 STV had taken 12 and MDS 3 per cent.

The financial difficulties of many of the satellite-delivered cable services, although unrelated to system profitability, conspired in 1982 with growing awareness of churn, signal theft, regulatory costs, high construction expenses, excessive franchise promises and competing technologies to create an air of despondency amongst both cable operators and investors, a mood which spread across the Atlantic as quickly as the earlier optimism. News of the slowdown in franchising bids by major companies has led to doubts about urban system profitability, although it actually reflects more the excessive demands

of city authorities, as well as the franchise successes of MSOs elsewhere and their inability to raise yet further capital. The necessarily
very high construction and franchise start-up costs have completely
absorbed internally generated cash flow. While the industry's
revenue has soared, heavy capital costs mean delayed profits.

REASONS FOR OPTIMISM

Given these mounting and cumulative problems, the inevitable question now being asked is whether, even in the United States, cable
can be a profitable business. Certainly, for many of the newest
systems the return will be very slow and uncertain. A number of
particularly competitive franchises may well have been seriously
overbid and will prove a problem if calculated on the assumption of
a higher than 200 per cent pay to basic ratio. Some, as a result, may
end up with rather fewer services or a less ambitious technical
structure than originally promised. Recently, for example, Times-
Mirror declared that it could not build the Brookline, Massachusetts, system as bid and sought to sell its franchise rights. The
chief executive officer of Warner Amex has similarly admitted that
the company made a loss of $46 million in 1982 and will lose at least
$25 million each year in 1983 and 1984. It is said to be trying to
renegotiate its Qube franchises in order to escape some of the more
optimistic and futuristic promises made in the heat of the contest.
According to Pittsburgh's Bureau of Cable Communications, Warner
was 'totally unrealistic in its original projections. . . . In many cases
the expenses [in building the Pittsburgh system] were underesti-
mated by several hundred per cent' (reported in *Broadcasting*, 11 July
1983, p.8). As a result the city has had to allow an increase in
subscription rates to help Warner reduce losses to acceptable levels.
Storer Communications may even have to sell some of its television
stations to meet its cable commitments. Indeed, many companies are
already swapping cable systems with each other in order to concentrate their interests geographically, thereby allowing economies in
centralised billing, maintenance services and even microwave interconnection between systems for regional area advertising or combined headend facilities.

   The present mood, in other words, could best be described as
'realistic', a recognition after the heady rush to win franchises at any
cost that costs are in fact going to be very tight indeed. The wired
society will come, but rather more gradually, hesitantly and with
many more pitfalls along the way than the public relations 'hype' of
the last few years would have us believe. This is not, however, to say
that the many problems now being encountered are insuperable.
Even where a high pay ratio is crucial, evidence suggests that

take-up can be boosted by sophisticated marketing techniques, the tiering and packaging together of pay channels and by improved after-sales service. The art of a good operator is undoubtedly in putting together the most attractive *package* of services, and in this respect he may well be helped by the current trends towards prog-ramme exclusivity and increased differentiation between the various pay services (see Chapter 10). In any case, systems which rely on multi-pay remain the exception. Most franchises awarded before 1980 were still bid on the assumption that basic subscriptions would continue to be the foundation of profitability, and, where this is the case, financial difficulties should be only temporary. Improved in-terest rates are helping and most MSOs also have a base of highly profitable older systems, as well as other non-cable interests, which can be used to offset early losses in new franchises. Cablevision's systems are financed through limited partnerships in which losses may actually be welcomed in order to offset tax on other more profitable businesses.

Nor are problems such as signal theft and churn quite what they seem. In the newer addressable systems (almost certain to be the standard in Britain) signal theft is considerably more difficult than in those which employ the older and simpler 'trapping' devices for their pay services. Moreover, the financial consequences of churn, particularly of geographical mobility, are greatly reduced when a subscriber can be disconnected at the headend by a simple computer instruction. Addressability is becoming the norm in new systems not just because it allows greater flexibility of programming and pay-per-view, but also for hard economic reasons of improved operating efficiency.

The crucial importance of packaging services and of marketing in order to improve subscriber satisfaction and reduce churn is now being recognised by an industry which in the past has tended to let such matters take care of themselves. The unscrupulous selling methods of cable salesmen paid on a commission basis, for example, has been identified as a major reason why subscribers become dis-illusioned within a short time of first taking cable. They are simply promised more, for example in the differentiation between the films on separate pay services, than they receive. A number of operators now recover the commissions they pay their salesmen if new subscri-bers disconnect within six months. Others revisit subscribers a month or two after connection to discuss any problems or sources of dissatisfaction and to attempt to resolve them. Apparently minor factors, such as the difficulty of reaching the cable operator by telephone when a fault develops, can be a major cause of churn. The presentation of the monthly bill and the problem of discovering what is on each of fifty channels, are also important. By paying greater attention to such issues, basic churn can be reduced noticeably, although high geographical mobility remains an inevitable problem.

Nor is the estimated cost of regulation as cited by the industry a particularly useful figure. The clear implication of such a calculation is that without regulation operators would not provide such access and community channels, nor carry certain local broadcast signals. Yet few would deny that as a local monopoly they do have responsibilities both to the community and to the broadcasting service. Subscribers may be subsidising community and access channels they rarely watch, but it is equally true that they rarely watch the majority of channels (and programmes) which they pay to receive as part of the overall cable package. If operators wish to package services together to sell more of them, then they can hardly complain about the inclusion of community and access channels. As one defender of regulation puts it, operators should regard this expense not as the cost of regulation but as the cost of responsibility (Frank Greif, Chairman of the National Association of Telecommunications Offices and Advisors, quoted in *Cable Age*, 26 July 1982, p.18).

The issue of alternative distribution technologies is more problematic. If any, particularly the multi-channel ones, prove to be significantly cheaper than cable, then they could certainly draw away a proportion of those for whom such a consideration is important. But their main impact will be in areas still not cabled, or just possibly where cable systems are old and of very limited capacity. In general, cable has a considerable historical and economic headstart over all other distribution systems, bar free off-air broadcasting itself. Moreover, in sheer cost per channel, and so far often even in absolute terms, cable undoubtedly offers a cheaper deal. Indeed, research by the ELRA Group contradicts that carried out for the NCTA by demonstrating that although few people watch more than five channels on a regular basis, the fact that additional services are available is valued highly. Cable's extra capacity gives it a considerable status advantage, and its ability to perform a variety of functions is also appreciated. As ELRA concludes, 'there is more consumer demand for multi-channel services than cable's competitors can meet either singly or collectively. Each new variety of service adds to the perceived value of cable . . . the perceived benefits of state-of-the-art interactive cable systems with a hundred or more channels far outweigh their costs in the eyes of potential new cable consumers' (ELRA, 'Consumer interest in interactive and pay-cable services', press release, June 1982).

The evidence is therefore contradictory, and the prospects for each alternative will in any case vary. SMATV systems are certainly posing an early problem, but cable operators such as Warner Amex in Dallas are now themselves learning to supply apartment blocks with

SMATV systems until they can be cabled properly. Multi-channel MDS, if it is able to provide service very much more cheaply than cable, could prove an irritation; but it is handicapped by reception problems and by the need for any receiving aerial actually to be in line of sight of the transmitter and not obscured by obstructions such as trees or buildings. In both high-rise urban and wooded or hilly rural areas MDS is at a major disadvantage. Meanwhile, DBS should certainly appeal where cable is unlikely ever to be available, but it cannot hope to compete seriously with the package of services offered by a modern cable system. Many people, as in Britain, see it becoming a supplier of additional channels for cable distribution in cabled areas. As for STV, few observers, including STV operators themselves, now believe that its share of the pay-TV market can be sustained. The figures quoted earlier merely reflect the fact that since 1977 STV has taken advantage of the growing interest in pay-film sevices to enter non-cable markets, markets into which cable is now steadily encroaching. Indeed, during 1983 several STV stations closed down in the face of cable competition and its subscriber base fell by a third, so that its future generally seems doubtful.

Finally, owners or renters of video recorders (VCRs) are also proving to be those most interested in cable, suggesting that the two are not necessarily competitive. Of interest to the British situation is the potentially disturbing discovery that video-recorder homes which regularly rent videotapes (mostly films) are only half as likely as other video-recorder households to subscribe to cable. Tape rental, in other words, could prove a major alternative, particularly given the greater range of films available in this way. As ever, however, it is necessary to assess such findings carefully. Homes with videos are still heavily concentrated in the major urban areas, many of which are as yet uncabled. This will undoubtedly have affected the relationship of tape-renting to cable-subscribing video-recorder users adversely. In general, the signs are that for the 75 per cent of video homes which rarely rent films cable and video recorders will be seen as complementary.

High capital costs and interest rates, occasionally slow take-up, excessive churn, signal theft and alternative distribution systems which cream the market have all contributed to cable's recent problems and will take time to be surmounted. None the less, it would be unduly pessimistic to suggest that such difficulties are fundamental or that they cannot be resolved. Indeed, the situation varies widely from franchise to franchise, a function as much of the reasonableness of the original agreement and the skill of the operator as of the economic climate. Certainly, cable system operation involves extremely high early risks and capital costs which, if not estimated accurately in advance (perhaps more a case of inspiration than

141

calculation), can lead to a much slower turn-around than expected and even to an inability to meet commitments. Time Inc's Manhattan Cable, for example, licensed thirteen years ago, only achieved annual profitability in 1979-80. Group W's system in North Manhattan, licensed at the same time, is still losing money. Yet overall the outlook for the cable system industry would seem to be one of 'cloudy at first but bright later on'. Already falling interest rates and the fact that system construction has passed its peak of capital expenditure have begun to ease the situation. As leading analysts Donaldson, Lufkin and Jenrette conclude, 'there is no serious threat to the health of the cable industry as a whole, although individual systems or companies may indeed run into problems. Most of the industry's other difficulties are ones of timing that will eventually be corrected' (Donaldson, Lufkin and Jenrette, *Industry Viewpoint*, October 1982, p.4).

What this means, however, is that for the time being at least, the industry will primarily concern itself with resolving the problems in its principal revenue-earning areas – basic subscriptions, pay and multi-pay. As we shall see later, many companies are keen to involve themselves in almost any and every potentially profitable business which can be carried on through a cable. But at present, faced with the sober realities of enormous early capital expenditure, the industry as a whole will continue to place greatest emphasis on the business which is known and trusted as the basis of profitability, namely entertainment.

For Britain the American cable systems industry offers many lessons – that cable is neither an easy way to make money nor an electronic panacea, that deregulation is almost inevitably a relative term (but the rate regulation is not necessarily beneficial) and that local franchising can lead to unsatisfactory and unrealistic awards. It demonstrates the heavy capital costs involved, the innumerable early problems and the need for construction timetables to be included in the franchise agreement. It suggests that, contrary to belief, there is probably little danger of excessive horizontal integration across the industry but that vertical integration of interests may be more of a problem. Pay services are likely to be a major revenue earner, but multi-pay is less certain and will depend largely on the variety of what is on offer. Churn is certain to be an important consideration and a significant factor in deciding whether or not to install an addressable system. While American experience cannot give any direct indication of cable's economic prospects in Britain, it may provide clues as to the factors which are most important in determining its capital costs, operating expenses and revenues. Above all, it shows that skill in packaging and marketing cable are crucial to its success; overselling is almost worse than underselling, since it leads to unrealised expectations and a reaction and positive antipathy on the part of consumers which is subsequently very difficult to overcome.

For the American industry the immediate questions are specific ones: will Cablevision be able to persuade 40 per cent of Bostonians to pay an average $35 a month? How quickly will Storer and Warner Amex in Houston resolve their signal theft and SMATV competition? What new marketing methods will prove most effective in reducing churn? Will Group W be able to lift its Manhattan system above the currently unprofitable subscriber base of 38 per cent? How quickly will additional sources of revenue become available and how important will they be? Last but not least, which services will prove most attractive and profitable? The highways are being built; what traffic will use them?

9 National Basic Services

UNLIMITED ENTERTAINMENT?

It is an obvious but none the less important truism that the average cable user is interested not in the politics, mechanics or economics of the system but in what it delivers. The subscriber's concern is with what new services are available, which of these in particular satisfy his requirements and how much they will cost him. Although we shall consider these services in their totality, therefore, it should be borne in mind that for many the full potential of the cable cornucopia remains a distant prospect. Barely three per cent of American cable subscribers yet have any form of addressable or interactive service available. Some 40 per cent will have access to twenty or fewer channels and 20 per cent to twelve or less.

For those fortunate enough to be on advanced, large-capacity, interactive cable systems the variety is indeed impressive. Since HBO showed the way, a plethora of satellite-distributed cable networks have appeared. Some of these continue to provide general entertainment programming of a broadcast character, particularly the superstations like WTBS. At another level are the general entertainment channels of particular value, in other words the mainstream pay services which carry a wide variety of premium feature films and entertainment specials to appeal to a broad range of tastes. More specialised, but equally anxious to gain a catholic viewership, are two channels which offer a mixed bag of special-interest segments, an approach known as 'piggy-backed' or 'consolidated' narrowcasting. But by far the largest category of nationally distributed cable networks consists of those aimed at particular audiences of interest or concentrating on a particular theme. They range from news to adult film channels.

To complete the list of what is on offer there are the locally originated services. Most prominent, of course, are the relayed networks, public broadcasting service and independent stations. The majority of systems also offer local community and public access channels, some with additional educational, local government and leased access channels. A few operators do still programme some entertainment channels themselves, usually unique to their own sys-

144

tems and knows as 'standalones'. In addition, there are an increasing number of channels of regional interest, particularly sports. Finally, the majority of enhanced and business services, where available, are locally run, although they may be organised by or tap into a national operation.

These enhanced and locally originated services will be considered in Chapters 11 and 12. The most popular cable services, however, are undoubtedly those which are distributed nationally. The switch to satellite distribution had confirmed HBO's success and it reached 1 million subscribers and profitability by the autumn of 1977. By the end of 1983 over 12 million took it. Ted Turner's WTBS also showed itself to be highly lucrative, reaching 26 million cabled homes in August 1983 and making over $18 million profit the previous year. Two further services followed HBO and WTBS on to the satellite in 1977, nine in 1978 and ten more in 1979, filling Satcom I to capacity. As of January 1984 four satellites carry some forty television, nine radio and seven text services, with another fourteen being planned.

This apparent abundance needs to be qualified, however. Firstly, few of these services are profitable and it is widely expected that several will fall by the wayside. Already one superstation, KTVU Oakland, has returned to normal broadcast status, whilst two cable-only services, CBS Cable and RCA's The Entertainment Channel, have closed down. Two others, Daytime and Cable Health Network, have merged, as have two of the news channels. As has already been pointed out, abundance is to some extent a result of the competition between rival services to capture a piece of the market while matters are still in a state of flux.

Secondly, it is important to distinguish between services and channels. Twenty-one of the television services are full twenty-four-hour channels, and another five or six operate for most of the prime-time evening period. The remainder are only available at certain times of the day, or even once a week. Cable operators frequently run two or three of these services, or even segments from them, on one channel, the effective result being a single continuous service. Manhattan Cable, for example, 'piggy-backs' segments of Nickelodeon (children's programmes), Modern Satellite Network (consumer information) and ARTS (culture). Likewise, five of the nationally distributed text services are carried on the vertical blanking interval of WTBS, the total capacity being no more than that available on one channel of the BBC's Ceefax teletext service.

Thirdly, repeats and duplication of programmes account for much of the material shown. Almost all services rely heavily on multiple showings of items in order to fill their space. Even CNN2, one of the non-stop news channels, transmits live for two hours and then repeats the entire block. Other services may reschedule programmes but repeat them frequently, in some cases up to ten or twenty times in one month. Moreover, five of the major channels are premium film services which currently duplicate much of the material they show. Although one or two are able to show some films and other programmes on an exclusive basis, the majority of items are still duplicated, occasionally even appearing at the same time on the same night on separate channels. It is hardly abundance when some channels show the same programmes.

The final proviso is that, despite 'piggy-backing', the large majority of cable systems are quite unable to receive or carry every available service. Barely a quarter of systems yet have two or more TVROs. Those with only one can receive signals from one satellite alone – a maximum of twenty-four video channels. Almost invariably operators with a single dish point it at Satcom IIIR, which now carries Home Box Office and WTBS, thereby giving other services on the same satellite a considerable advantage over less fortunate rivals. In large systems with plenty of available channel space it is normally in the system operator's interests to take as many of the free and advertiser-supported services as possible, since the cost per subscriber for the additional receiving and processing equipment is marginal by comparison with their potential value in attracting or holding on to even a few subscribers. On the other hand, decreasing marginal benefits may make it less financially sensible to carry every available pay service, as we shall see later.

But, for many of the existing systems, such cost-benefit considerations are academic, since they have limited channel capacity and the most basic equipment for delivering pay services. Moreover, broadcast relay, community and access channel obligations take much of what capacity there is; even Manhattan Cable's thirty-five possible channels are not sufficient, since fully seventeen are used in this way. Consequently, the system operator is placed in the position of electronic gatekeeper, deciding which services it is in his interests to take. This is particularly significant where a company owns both systems and services, giving it the opportunity to exclude rivals. When Times-Mirror, TCI, Cox and Storer introduced their Spotlight pay channel into their own cable systems in 1981-2, for example, they did so by compulsorily switching subscribers from rival film services HBO, Showtime and The Movie Channel, these being removed for a time from the services on offer. Clearly subscribers do not always have free choice, although system profitability will ultimately depend on consumer satisfaction with what is available. But then subscribers lacking a competitive alternative are unlikely to disconnect their entire cable package because they are not offered one or two particular services.

146

Despite these qualifications, the number and variety of networked video services remain impressive. Table v is a complete list as of December 1983. The numbers of households reached and pay subscribers are as of July and are of course constantly rising. The figures shown give an indication of the networks' relative sizes.

Broadly speaking, therefore, there are seven religious, five premium film/entertainment and five news/information services. Three are ethnic channels and another three broadcast superstations. Two each supply adult, music, cultural, family and mixed special-interest programmes, with individual services for children's programmes, women's health, sports and educational material. Nationally distributed pay-per-view events are offered on an occasional basis. Although not carried nationally, the regional sports networks should also be included; at least eight are operating or planned, often owned by consortia of sports teams, in areas such as Chicago, New England and Houston.

Although it is useful to categorise cable services by their character in this way, in practice the issue of finance tends to dominate. After all, cable has the potential to offer so much that between system operator and subscriber there may be several different contractual arrangements, ranging from basic services on various tiers, through pay and pay-per-view, to leasing of line capacity for business use. To the system operator the financial situation is even more complex. Amongst the services he may offer are relayed distant broadcast stations for which a copyright fee is paid; community and access channels supported partly from subscribers' fees and partly from the general community purse – from a local authority's educational budget, for example; 'free' channels financed by voluntary contributions from viewers; 'per-subscriber' supported services where the system operator pays the service provider a few cents per month for every subscriber on his system; combined per-subscriber/advertiser-financed channels; ones relying entirely upon advertising for their income; discretionary pay services; occasional pay-per-view events or, on a few systems, permanent pay-per-view channels; and business services financed in a number of ways. Some of these services the system operator is offered free by a national distributor, but without any opportunity of himself earning revenue from them. Others he has to pay for, merely passing on that cost to the subscriber. Still others he may be paid by the provider to carry, or given advertising space on them to sell. Finally, with pay and pay-per-view he can add a retail price element on to the wholesale charge and so earn considerable revenue in that way.

Character and finance are therefore the two central strands in any consideration of American cable services, and the remainder of this chapter will consider those which are generally offered as part of the

TABLE V

Satellite-distributed video services, December 1983

Method of finance	Name	Nature of Service	Households reached, July 1983 (in millions)	Operating hours	Satellite
Free/voluntary contributions	Alternative View Network	Religious programming, including talk, shows and drama	0.13	Sun. 8 a.m.–1 p.m.	Satcom IIIR
	Eternal Word Network	Catholic religious and entertainment programming	1.1	7–11 p.m.	Satcom IIIR
	National Christian Network	Multi-denominational religious programming	1.4	6 a.m.–8 p.m.	Satcom IV
	National Jewish Television	Programming for the Jewish community	2.5	Sun. 1–4 p.m.	Satcom IIIR
	PTL – The Inspirational Network	Christian entertainment, news and specials	7.5	24 hrs	Satcom IIIR
	Trinity Broadcasting Network	Christian programming	2.9	24 hrs	Satcom IV
Per-subscriber	ACSN – The Learning Chapel	Educational and community service	3.2	6 a.m.–4 p.m.	Satcom IIIR
	C-Span	Live coverage of US House of Representatives, and current affairs	13.5	24 hrs	Satcom IIIR
	Nickelodeon[1]	Programmes for children and teenagers	11.4	8 a.m.–9 p.m.	Satcom IIIR
Per-subscriber/ advertising	Black Entertainment Television	General entertainment programmes for the black audience	3.8	8 p.m.–2 a.m.	Westar V
	Cable News Network	Continuous news and features service	19.2	24 hrs	Satcom IIIR
	CNN2 – Headline News	Continuous news bulletin service in half-hour bulletins, available also to broadcast television and radio stations	3.8[2]	24 hrs	Satcom IIIR

ESPN – Entertainment and Sports Programming Network	Continuous sports coverage and sports-related programmes, with morning business news section	26.0	24 hrs	Satcom IIIR
Nashville Network	Country music entertainment	7.4	18 hrs	Westar V
USA Cable Network	Broad-based programming for special-interest groups – children, women, sports	17.5	24 hrs	Satcom IIIR
WGN Chicago	Chicago independent broadcasting station	10.1	24 hrs	Satcom IIIR
WOR New York	New York independent broadcasting station	4.7	24 hrs	Westar V
WTBS Atlanta	Atlanta independent broadcasting station	26.0	24 hrs	Satcom IIIR
Advertising — Arts	Cultural programming – music, drama, dance, etc.	9.5	9 p.m.–3 a.m.	Satcom IIIR
Christian Broadcast Network (CBS)	Entertainment and family programmes, and a daily Christian segment, the latter financed by viewers' contributions	20.3	24 hrs	Satcom IIIR
CHN – Cable Health Network[3]	Continuous health and fitness programming	10.7	24 hrs	Satcom IIIR
Daytime[3]	Magazine-type programmes for women	9.5	1–9 p.m.	Satcom IIIR / Westar V
Financial News Network	News service primarily for broadcast television featuring stocks and financial news. The 'household-reached' figure indicates those systems required to relay FNN as a broadcast signal	6.5	10 a.m.–5 p.m. Mon.–Fri.	Westar IV

[1] Has now decided to accept advertising.
[2] Takeover of SSC in November 1983 will probably have added some 6 million households.
[3] Now merged into The Leisure Channel.

continued overleaf

TABLE V – *continued*

Method of finance	Name	Nature of service	Households reached, July 1983 (in millions)	Operating hours	Satellite
Advertising cont.	Modern Satellite Network	Consumer information programming aimed at women	7.1	10 a.m.–1 p.m.	Satcom IIR
	MTV — Music Television*	Non-stop rock music, using promotional videos	8.6	24 hrs	Satcom IIIR
	SNC — Satellite News Channel	Continuous news service in eighteen-minute bulletins. A joint ABC/Westinghouse venture in response to CNN	5.0	24 hrs	Westar V
	SPN — Satellite Program Network	Varied special-interest programming, including women, health, business and nightly 3½ hours of subtitled French material	5.3	24 hrs	Westar IV
	SIN — Spanish International Network	Spanish-language entertainment programmes	3.8	24 hrs	Satcom IV
	The Weather Channel	Continuous coverage of national, regional and local weather	7.1	14 hrs	Satcom IIIR
			Subscribers		
Pay	Bravo	Cultural programming — music, dance, international films	0.08	8 p.m.–6 a.m.	Satcom IV
	Cinemax	Film and entertainment programming, owned by Time Inc., as complementary service to HBO	2.0	24 hrs	Satcom IIIR

Channel	Description		Hours	Satellite
The Disney Channel	Family programming from the Disney studio, started April 1983	n/a	16 hrs	Westar IV
Eros	Adult film channel (R-rated films)	0.2	12 p.m.–5 a.m. Thurs., Fri., Sat.	Satcom IV
Galavision	Spanish-language films, variety and sport	0.12	4 p.m.–3 a.m. 24-hr, Sat., Sun.	Satcom IIIR
Home Box Office	Premium film and variety service owned by Time Inc.	11.0	24 hrs	Satcom IIIR
HTN Plus (Home Theatre Network)	Family films and travel programmes	0.18	4 p.m.–4 a.m.	Satcom IIIR
The Movie Channel	Premium film service, owned by Warner-Amex.	2.3	24 hrs	Satcom IIIR
The Playboy Channel	Adult films and specials (R-rated)	0.4	8 p.m.–6 a.m.	Satcom IV
SelecTV	Premium film and entertainment service, directed largely to broadcast TV market	n/a	24 hrs	Satcom IV
Showtime	Premium film and entertainment service owned by Viacom	3.9	24 hrs	Satcom IIIR
Spotlight	Premium film service owned by Times-Mirror, Storer, Cox & TCI	0.75	24 hrs	Satcom IIIR
Pay-per-view				
Don King Sports and Entertainment Network	Occasional sports, concerts, film events	n/a	occasional	Satcom IIIR

* As of July 1983 ATV also charges a per-subscriber fee.

basic cable package, being financed either by voluntary contributions, per-subscriber payments or advertising. In the next we will
consider pay services and pay-per-view.

'FREE' SERVICES

Without exception the services provided free and without carrying
advertising are all religious, ranging from the Catholic Eternal Word
Network to National Jewish Television. This apparently wide spectrum of beliefs obscures the fact, however, that it is the evangelical
fundamentalist sects which predominate through the Inspirational
Network, Trinity and the very much larger free/advertiser-supported
Christian Broadcast Network. Since, in any case, relatively few
systems carry every religious network, the overall effect is hardly
balanced, and the essentially right-wing tendency of evangelical
fundamentalism adds to the problem. Using chat shows, variety and
other wholesome programming, evangelists such as Rex Humbard
(the World Outreach Ministry) and Moral Majority leader Jerry
Falwell seek both spiritual and financial support, a source of much
concern to local churches who argue that the networks are taking
contributions away from them.

PER-SUBSCRIBER SERVICES

Per-subscriber-financed services can only be a drain on the resources
of the system operator, so that there has to be good reason for his
taking them. In the case of The Learning Channel and C-Span this
can hardly be because of their popularity. The former is worthy but,
given its low reach after four years, has to rely on cheap programming. It can, however, be combined with local items to create an
educational and community channel which fulfils system operators'
franchise obligations or imparts a sense of social responsibility. This
is also very much the reason for the wide take-up of the Cable
Satellite Public Affairs Network (C-Span), which gives full coverage
of the debates in the House of Representatives, committee sessions,
party conventions and similar events. Some might think that its
uninterrupted coverage of the National Conference of Catholic
Bishops takes a too optimistic view of public interest, but there can
be no doubt C-Span provides a valuable democratic service. It is
valued both by audiences interested in particular issues and by
competing cable system applicants, who offer it in order to demonstrate cable's value to the local politicians who award franchises. In
1983 its total budget for a twenty-four-hour service was only $4
million and although it is still making a loss, it seems only a matter
of time before it reaches the critical number of subscribers necessary

to support what is, after all, exceedingly cheap programming. A second channel is intended eventually to televise the proceedings of the US Senate.

System operators' motives in offering Nickelodeon (the children's service) can similarly be somewhat devious. Not least it is recognised that it appeals to and satisfies adult consumer guilt at buying cable for its other programming. Parents wishing to subscribe for the sports, daytime or film channels are able to justify the purchase as being for the children. Given an absolute dearth of quality children's programmes on the three broadcast networks, Nickelodeon does fulfil a basic need and is an example of cable programming at its best. Entertaining and educational, but not at all didactic, this Warner Amex service produces or commissions about 60 per cent of its material, such as 'Pinwheel', and buys other programmes from Britain, Canada and elsewhere. Almost all of Nickelodeon's output is receiving its first American airing, although puppet work such as 'Pinwheel', and costume drama like *The Adventures of Black Beauty* from ITV, will have a continuing and repeatable appeal to successive generations. Cartoons, long condemned by the children's television lobby, are used only when they are of particular quality and informative; they are in any case mostly too expensive for Nickelodeon's present limited programme budget.

In 1982, after three years in operation, Nickelodeon was earning about $10 million a year. But with programme costs of some $10 million also, plus staff, distribution and marketing expenses, it is still heavily in debt. It is also facing a challenge from The Disney Channel, which shows typical Disney fare, the USA network (which is far less particular in the type and worth of children's programmes it shows), and even from Home Box Office which is developing children's material. One of Nickelodeon's principal selling points in the past has been its total lack of advertising. Faced with continuing debts, however, it decided to accept advertisements as of October 1983, although only between programmes rather than during them. This is also something for which system operators have been pushing so that they could sell local advertising in order to recoup the per-subscriber fee they currently pay for the service. Some critics are already suggesting that it is the beginning of the long slide into commercialism, with an inevitable lowering of programming standards.

Yet, although this decision is a sign of continuing problems, prospects do look bright. As one of the services most commonly offered on a new system and as part of the basic package, Nickelodeon's universe is expanding by some 3-400,000 a month. With a monthly per-subscriber charge of fifteen cents it should become profitable within the year, with a 14 million universe and revenues of

$25 million. It has the added advantage of sharing certain distribution, marketing and administration costs with Warner Amex's other programme operations, Music Television and The Movie Channel. As ever in cable, the economies of scale can be considerable, particularly for a high fixed but low incremental cost business such as this. The important question for Nickelodeon, therefore, is not whether it will survive, but whether in a competitive and commercial environment it will win through with its early high quality and original praiseworthy objectives intact.

PER-SUBSCRIBER/ADVERTISER-SUPPORTED SERVICES

While there was still a shortage of satellite services their providers could afford to charge system operators a per-subscriber fee as well as selling advertising. Consequently most of the early basic services used this dual form of finance, including WTBS, the USA Network, the Entertainment and Sports Programming Network (ESPN) and Cable News Network (CNN). Subsequently the enormous increase in the number of services available and the competition between them to get on to cable systems of limited capacity induced many of the newer ones to offer themselves to system operators without a per-subscriber charge or even to pay operators to carry them. As financial losses have mounted, however, there has been something of a move back to a combination of advertising and per-subscriber revenue.

The three 24-hour superstations – WTBS Atlanta, WOR New York and WGN Chicago – all charge the systems which carry them a per-subscriber fee, in addition to selling advertising space as ordinary broadcasting stations. Indeed WOR and WGN are technically 'passive superstations' in that there is no connection between the broadcast stations themselves (which earn revenue from advertising) and the companies which retransmit their signals nationally via satellite and charge cable operators a per-subscriber fee. All three stations offer typical broadcast fare – numerous repeats of network series and up to forty old films of indifferent quality each week. In addition all carry extensive local sports coverage so that each has an element of regional appeal. WTBS, for example, covers live games of the Atlanta Braves (baseball) and Atlanta Hawks (basketball), both teams owned by Ted Turner himself. It also has an exclusive agreement for live coverage of National Collegiate Athletics Association football games.

By buying programmes at local or relatively cheap rates and selling advertising at a charge in proportion to its total reach, WTBS took some $90 million in advertising in 1982. This was in addition to the $30 million per annum obtained from a ten cents monthly fee for

154

its 25 million homes reached. However the 1983 rise in copyright fees which systems pay to carry distant broadcasting stations, including superstations, has induced many system operators to drop the latter in favour of other, cheaper satellite-delivered non-broadcast services. Both WOR New York and WGN Chicago have suffered from this. In any case neither is in the same league as WTBS. By contrast WTBS's success has allowed Turner to expand in other directions, acquiring a film production company and creating the first twenty-four-hour news channel, CNN, in 1980, and its sister service, CNN Headline News, in 1982.

Combining news bulletins, sport, weather and informational features, CNN provides an enjoyable mix of the serious and entertaining. Features range from 'Moneyline' to gardening and car maintenance. CNN2, by contrast, is a rapid all-news service with a half-hour schedule and is offered not only to cable operators but also to broadcast television and radio stations. As a result it is available continuously to some four million cable subscribers and as a half-hour news bulletin to over 60 million viewers of 110 broadcast television stations. Indeed, Turner now describes himself as a programmer rather than specifically as a cable network provider. CNN and CNN2 use the same news resources and employ entirely non-union labour at below standard rates. Staff turnover is consequently high; yet the services provide valuable training for students out of college and command considerable respect. Certainly CNN's operations have worried the three broadcast networks into providing overnight news programming, whilst ABC and Westinghouse joined forces in 1982 to produce Satellite News Channel (SNC), which was conceived very much as an ABC response to Turner.

In order to attract operators away from the earlier established CNN, which charges a per-subscriber fee, SNC was offered free and even paid operators to carry it. Yet despite this CNN continued to dominate and SNC quickly found itself in financial difficulties, lacking both viewers and advertising revenue. In eighteen months it lost $30 million and in October 1983 was taken over by CNN and closed down. The only two American cable news services now operating, therefore, are both owned by Ted Turner and are run from the same news centre in Atlanta, Georgia. CNN attracts a large proportion of the advertising money presently coming into cable (perhaps because it is said to reach a better educated and more affluent audience) but it is still not profitable. In 1983 it probably lost about $6 million, and before that had accumulated losses of $43 million, while CNN2 continues to lose heavily. WTBS's profitability kept Turner's overall losses down to $3.4 million in 1982 and profit in 1983 should reach about $12 million, but outstanding debt is higher and it is clear that the company has only just survived by dint of being first in the field and by relying on a combination of advertising revenue and per-subscriber charges. Indeed, given the relatively small effect that SNC had on CNN's subscriber numbers, it would appear that the per-subscriber fee charged earns Turner more revenue than it loses him system operators.

The whole question of dual forms of payment is a highly contentious one. A number of executives argue that, as with newspapers and journals, both advertising and some form of direct payment are essential ingredients of overall income. As the President of Warner Amex Satellite Entertainment has stated: 'It has become increasingly apparent that in today's marketplace both operator fees and advertising revenues are necessary income sources for basic cable services to thrive and prosper.' (Quoted in *Cable Age*, 6 June 1983, p. 126). Others feel that, CNN notwithstanding, per-subscriber charges dissuade more system operators from taking services than they earn. The USA Channel, already one of the largest, intends to drop its per-subscriber element in 1984 and rely on advertising. ESPN, by contrast, dabbled with payments to systems but has now reverted to and increased its per-subscriber element in order to reduce massive losses, confident that its popularity with cable subscribers will prevent this policy damaging its attractiveness to system operators.

These two channels have amongst the largest audience reaches of the cable services. USA is one of two which provide a number of varied segments of special-interest programming. Started in 1977 primarily as a carrier for Madison Square Garden Sports, it expanded to offer at other times Black Entertainment Television (now separate), Calliope children's programming and the 'English Channel' showing material bought from ITV companies. Currently it features broad-based 'magazine' programmes for women during the day, Calliope in the early evening and sport in primetime. The 'English Channel' segment appears several times a week and *Coronation Street* daily – there is, after all, twenty-one years of life on 'the Street' to catch up on! Now a twenty-four-hour service, USA has doubled its advertising revenue annually since 1981 and seems likely to approach $30 million in 1983. In 1982 it was the fourth most successful cable network in attracting advertising revenue and seems to have found a sound if unadventurous formula in providing large blocks of mainstream programmes to potentially very large audience segments, namely men, women and children. Although it is growing steadily, losses are still heavy and it is said to need a 25-30 million reach in order to succeed. Perhaps the strongest evidence that it is likely to survive, however, is the fact that Time Inc., quite the most astute company in cable at present, bought one-third of the network in 1981, Paramount and MCA being the other two partners. USA's philosophy is summed up by its president, Kay Koplovitz, who has

156

said that its programmes aim to be 'the most desirable and not the least objectionable' (Quoted in *Broadcasting*, 13 September 1982, p.8). Indeed, it seems consciously to be emulating broadcast network programming, describing itself as 'the fourth network' and buying up old network series.

ESPN is now the largest cable network, with a 26 million reach (87 per cent of cabled homes). It offers a wide variety of sports coverage from football, baseball and ice hockey to athletics, golf, boxing and motor racing. Events can be shown in their entirety rather than through edited highlights, but until recently the items covered have been essentially in the second rank of interest for most Americans – minor league games, the earlier stages of tournaments, obscure sports and foreign events. The three broadcast networks have so far retained the rights to major occasions and tournaments, although a new joint-venture agreement with ABC, which owns 15 per cent of ESPN, may allow the latter to offer items to which ABC has the rights, on a pay-per-view basis. The broadcast audience may gradually lose access to live sports coverage as much through such agreements as through competitive siphoning by cable. In any case, many teams are forming regional consortia to take their games off the local independent stations which have run them in the past and to sell them on pay-TV. Supporters without pay-TV will have to attend the games themselves. In every sense, therefore, cable has the power to bring the gate back into American sport, and the sports industry is already feeling the financial benefit.

Despite ESPN's size, it remains in financial difficulties, with a $20 million loss in 1982 and an anticipated $10 million loss in 1983. Without a per-subscriber income of more than $32 million, its debt would be higher still. The increasing cost of sports rights is one factor, but of particular importance is the lack of audience and advertiser interest outside primetime. A twenty-four-hour service seems a good idea, but sport is not durable programming and so does not allow multiple repeats. Nor has it proved particularly attractive to the predominantly female afternoon audience. Consequently, daytime advertising interest has been low. Faced with only a 30-40 per cent take-up of advertising space outside primetime (and 60-70 per cent in), ESPN has been forced to change tactics, emphasising health and fitness programmes and women's events more in the afternoon (skiing, skating, gymnastics, etc.), and, most significantly, leasing a two-hour morning segment to another cable service called Business Times, an early morning business news and information service for executives. This lease brings ESPN significantly more income than it could get from selling advertising at that time, yet provides Business Times with a large universe very cheaply. Already the latter has found a small but very important and adequate audience, as well as financial and business-service advertisers who are only too keen to reach such people before work each morning.

The specialised character of the audience for each special interest service is something which all the service providers emphasise. ESPN, in its sales talk to advertisers, emphasises that its audience contains a higher percentage of males aged between eighteen and forty-nine than the broadcast networks, and that they tend to be better educated and to have a higher income than normal. Like CNN it implies that it reaches an audience of particular value to the advertiser, and not surprisingly one of its main users is the beer manufacturer Budweiser. ESPN is undoubtedly one of the most popular of basic cable services, but whether this is saying much is doubtful. It now claims an average primetime audience rating of two within the homes it reaches, yet this still means only just over half a million households viewing at any one time, with considerably fewer for most of the day.

ADVERTISING ON CABLE

Although systems operators value CNN and ESPN sufficiently to pay a per-subscriber fee, most of the more recently established basic satellite services such as Daytime and the Weather Channel are more specialised and so less individually important. For this reason, as mentioned above, many have offered themselves free to operators, as well as giving the latter an opportunity to sell local advertising space. At the same time, these newer networks have had to compete for the advertising dollar against the longer established and for the most part much larger per-subscriber/advertising hybrids. In 1982, including the three superstations, there were nineteen cable services seeking advertising revenue. Between them they earned about $242 million in advertising revenue, of which some $32 million was spent at a local level and so went to system operators rather than the service-providing companies. It is worth comparing this with the $6 billion that the three broadcast networks took and the $12-13 billion which broadcast television earns overall from advertising. Cable advertising is as yet a drop in the advertising ocean, and one which has to be shared amongst all too many services. Yet of these the three superstations took some $107 million in 1982 while just three of the cable-only services – CNN, ESPN and USA – probably took about $73 million, leaving barely $30 million for the thirteen remaining. It is unlikely that any earned more than $5 million.

These figures are naturally extremely disappointing and worrying for the industry, whose initial projections for advertising growth were much higher. ARTS, the Hearst/ABC cultural service, for example, took just one-seventh of the revenue anticipated in its first year. Yet the budgets of such services are considerable; at the top end CNN and ESPN's annual expenditures are certainly over $50 million, while other twenty-four-hour services probably cost some $20-30 million each. Those with fewer hours, such as ARTS and Daytime, or similar and cheaper programming – the Weather Channel and Music Television (MTV) for example – are proportionately less expensive. All are cheap by comparison with traditional broadcasting, yet few are close to profitability. Competition is extreme and costs higher than expected.

Moreover, advertisers have exhibited their traditional caution towards a new medium, not knowing quite what to do with it. Certain advertising agencies have advised television advertisers to put 5 per cent of advertising budgets into cable, to compensate for the audience being lost from the broadcast networks, but only 10 per cent of their clients have spent anything on it at all. Indeed, the whole television environment for advertising is changing and many advertisers are unwilling to commit themselves until they see the trends. The increasing number of channels makes it more difficult to reach a mass audience, while pay and per-subscriber TV effectively remove a proportion of viewers from the advertisers' reach. Video recorders, as they grow in popularity, allow people to time-shift programmes and fast-wind through the advertisements, while the proliferation of remote-controlled TV sets encourages channel-switching during advertisements. Videogames and home computers also occupy television time. There is a fear that for a variety of reasons the audience is escaping from the advertiser. Nor is the situation helped by the admitted inadequacies of existing audience research methods in tracking viewing habits in a multi-channel environment.

The arguments used to attract advertisers to cable emphasise its particular values in such a changing world. Homes with pay cable, it is pointed out, will also have basic services and are likely to spend some time watching them. Advertising on cable should therefore regain some of the lost access to pay-cable viewers. Cabled families are in any case better off than non-cabled and so more attractive to advertisers. The incomes of Warner Amex subscribers are on average 39 per cent higher than the median national income. More particularly, special-interest channels are seen to reach particularly valuable demographic groupings. Almost every cable service from ARTS to ESPN argues that its audience is 'upscale', i.e. better educated, more affluent and with a greater disposable income than average. This is the type of person who is normally considered a light television watcher and is therefore difficult for the advertiser to reach. ARTS, for example, points out that 27 per cent of its employed male viewers earn over $35,000 a year (compared to the national average of 11 per cent), 65 per cent are college graduates (national average 18 per cent) and 75 per cent hold professional or managerial jobs (32 per cent). Similarly Daytime, the afternoon service for women also owned by Hearst/ABC and now amalgamated with the Cable Health Network, tells potential advertisers that 'The Daytime woman is a family woman in the active buying years .... She spends 31 per cent more on grocery/household items than the national average' (Daytme promotional literature, 1982).

A corollary to this argument is the one that audiences motivated to seek programmes of special interest to them on cable have a higher than average interest in their content and therefore a greater interest in related advertisements. Advertisements are even seen as a consumer service rather than an irritation, just as in specialist magazines. Cable Health Network research demonstrates that pharmaceutical advertisements are better remembered by its viewers than by normal television audiences. The argument is also supported by cable's higher than normal success in direct-response advertising. Indeed, some services argue that because their audiences are of greater value to advertisers than large undifferentiated masses, so the cost of advertising on them should be higher than normal, comparing more with the high advertising charges of specialist magazines than with ordinary television. Consequently, ARTS costs-per-thousand-reached are three times those of broadcast television or even of the less specialised ESPN. The ill-fated CBS Cable cultural channel is said to have charged up to seven times as much per-thousand for some programmes as the broadcast networks. CNN, however, adopts a different stratgey and offers cheaper advertising rates than broadcast television. In effect it is subsidising advertisers from its per-subscriber revenue.

Meanwhle, because cable still has relatively low penetration and reach, absolute costs of advertising are lower than on broadcast television, opening the way both for new advertisers and for more frequent advertising by others. Given their extremely low audience ratings, advertiser-supported services are trying to wean advertisers away from their reliance upon cost-per-thousand efficiencies and absolute numbers, and to emphasise that cable reaches large audiences over a period of time. CNN is watched by 39 per cent of those to whom it is available at least once in any week (its cumulative rating) although its average primetime rating is only 1.5 per cent. As a percentage of TV households in the United States, its rating (in June 1982) was even worse, at 0.3 per cent. Nor surprisingly, therefore, services such as CNN argue that weekly cumulative ratings are as valuable as average audience levels.

The low cost of advertising and programme production on cable also opens the way for advertisers to sponsor or even produce programmes themselves. As one advertising agency states, 'Advertisers who are seeking a tailor-made programme environment for their commercials can now custom-create it for themselves on cable' (*Television in Transition*, Doyle Dane Bernbach, 1982, p.Y-3). Bristol Myers, for example, produce a two-hour daily health and fitness programme on the USA Network, called 'Alive and Well', in which it places advertisments and information about its health and beauty products. In this way, cable blurs even more the division between programme and advertisement. On the Modern Satellite Network, a morning consumer information service aimed at women, an advertiser can pay to be the guest on a half-hour chat show. Cable also allows longer length overt commercials, or 'infomercials', in which a product's features can be explained in more detail. One agency, J. Walter Thompson, is even experimenting with four continuous 'infomerical channels' on a system in Peabody, Massachusetts. The remarkable finding has been that viewers actually browse through these channels, often watching three or four seven-minute infomercials at a time. Perhaps this is a commentary on the quality of the other thirty to forty available channels, but the experiment's success has led to its expansion into other systems on a national basis.

Cable apparently has the potential to provide new and more efficient ways for advertisers to reach new and more specific audiences with more effectively packaged messages. For those who believe this to be the case, it is only a matter of time before advertisers overcome their initial reluctance and begin putting even larger sums into cable. Others are more doubtful about cable's promise. Alternative analyses of the cable audience call into question its demographically fragmented character. According to the audience research company A.C. Nielsen, the average primetime rating of all basic cable-only services combined in 1982 was just 4.3 per cent in homes which also took a pay channel, and 2.9 per cent in basic cable homes. Ratings during the day were even lower. The 'mainstream' cable channels, such as USA, ESPN and CNN, naturally attracted the largest viewership, with little left for the others.* Even on a weekly cumulative basis, while ESPN and USA are watched at least once by half those who can receive them, most of the more specialised services, such as SIN, the Spanish channel, or even the Satellite Program Network which presents a wide variety of special interest program-

---

*This average combined figure can, however, be somewhat misleading, since it assumes that each basic network reaches 100 per cent of cabled homes, although none does so and few cover even 30 per cent. Thus twenty services, including per-subscriber and free, averaging 25 per cent cable-area coverage, could each have a coverage-area rating of 0.8 in pay homes and 0.6 in basic – still low but individually better than the combined average ratings figures suggest.

mes, are seen by no more than 20 per cent. On an absolute basis, in May 1982, CNN, one of the largest and most frequently used services, had an average audience at any moment of only 152,000 homes and a cumulative weekly audience of 5.3 million out of the 13.5 million homes then in its universe.

The narrowcast argument justifies such small audiences (in broadcasting terms) by emphasising their specialist character and high appeal to advertisers. Of crucial importance, therefore, is the advertising rate that can be charged, which in turn depends on the audience's demographic character. Evidence seems to suggest, however, that the larger part of the specialist service audience is not the normally light viewer who has been consciously attracted to programmes of particular interest, as these services like to suggest. Rather it is those people who watch most television anyway. This mirrors earlier findings that the audience for the educationally and culturally orientated public broadcasting service is composed largely of heavy television users rather than those who otherwise watch little. Narrowcast cable channels, in other words, are not really attracting the new and hard-to-reach audience promised, but the same audience as before, spreading their viewing over more services. Cable television subscribers are known in any case to be heavier users of television than non-subscribers, suggesting that the desired light TV audience is still eluding cable entirely. Nor do people appear to be more selective in their viewing habits than hitherto. A number of studies suggest people are as likely to watch a programme at random, because it is on at the time, as they are consciously to select one in advance. As one cable consultant has concluded, 'people tend to watch "television" rather than "television programmes" or "television services"' (P.H. Lemieux, *The Multichannel Media Environment*, private study, 1983, p.6).

Service providers are correct in arguing that cable subscribers tend to be more affluent and are more likely to have children (therefore spending more) than non-subscribers. In that respect the cable audience is more attractive to advertisers. But whether it is significantly more attractive is more doubtful. Studies of specialist magazines, relating various costs-per-thousand to demographic groups reached and to actual purchasing responses, suggest that non-specialist journals are as efficient an advertising medium as specialist ones which charge higher advertising rates. Similarly, if a special-interest cable service charges double the cost-per-thousand of a broadcast service because it claims to attract double the proportion of a certain demographic group, then by the same argument the broadcast service can argue that it is not only as *efficient* and economical a buy for the advertiser but also a better one, since its reach is much greater than cable – which in any case currently penetrates

162

less then two-thirds of homes passed. Indeed, by this argument broadcast television has another advantage over cable since it not only reaches the immediately desired audience as efficiently as cable services, but also is seen by additional demographic groups – normally considered the wasted audiences for the advertiser – who may nonetheless contain people ready to respond to an advertisement not directed specifically to them.

Special-interest service providers can of course argue, as do specialist magazine publishers, that the particular character and content of their programmes give added potency to the advertisements within them. People appreciate advertisements more when they are placed in a related rather than a random context, as the Cable Health Network research mentioned above indicates. That this is true is common experience. Yet it must be remembered that the viewers of special-interest services are equally amongst the heaviest television users overall. Consequently, they are also the most exposed to television advertisements. The competition for their attention is therefore considerable and their exposure to unrelated random advertising high. Perhaps this may turn out to be one of the narrowcast services' best selling points for advertisers – that they are actually better at making an impression upon the heavy viewer. But in the American environment, where programme sponsorship and the practice of relating the product advertised to the programme content are already normal features of broadcast television, this is hardly a strong argument or one unique to cable. Conversely in Britain, where such practices are not common, it may prove a strong incentive to advertisers.

The truth is that in terms of advertising efficiency, which is what advertiser-supported narrowcast services are all about, cable may bring fewer advantages to the national advertiser than is often claimed. Such services may come to rely upon the continuing subjective judgements and inefficiences inevitable in trying to measure advertising's effectiveness. Yet even here two-way cable, with its opportunities for instant response purchase, promises to make it easier to assess an advertisement's power actually to make people buy a product. Ironically, cable's potential to take the intuition out of advertising decisions may also reveal the advertising inefficiencies of its own narrowcast services.

A number of qualifications need to be made to this otherwise rather gloomy picture. Extrapolating from existing data, it is possible to calculate the potential revenue for services once cable has reached a more mature penetration of television households than at present. By 1986 at least 50 per cent of homes should be cabled and by 1990 60 per cent, although subsequent growth will probably be more gradual. In March 1983 ESPN's charge to advertisers averaged about

$6 per thousand viewers (the same as the broadcast networks) for a thirty-second spot, of which there were up to fourteen each hour. ESPN reached 87 per cent of cable homes and had an average 2.0 rating in primetime, whilst the much smaller ARTS reached 27 per cent only (8.3 million out of 31 million) and appears optimistically to have claimed a 1.0 rating. Both are likely to increase their penetration of cabled homes, however, as the average channel capacity of cable systems is increased, so that figures of 90 per cent and 45 per cent respectively may be assumed by 1986, and 95 per cent and 60 per cent by 1990. Their ratings are unlikely to change dramatically, given the amount of competition. Assuming ratings of 2.0 or 3.0 for ESPN and 1.0 or a more realistic 0.8 for ARTS, we can calculate their potential average revenue per hour in primetime at 1983 prices and this is shown in Table VI.

These figures represent average *potential* revenue in the *peak* period only. Average revenue throughout the television day will be very much lower, with reduced audience ratings and fewer advertising spots sold. Moreover, as their reach increases so there will be pressure to offer discounts and lower costs-per-thousand, in line with traditional broadcasting practice. Taking the most favourable case, however, ARTS could take $18,000 in revenue per peak hour in 1983, $42,800 in 1986 and $73,900 in 1990 (all at 1983 prices). ESPN could receive $45,000 per-peak-hour from advertising in 1983, $99,800 in 1986 and $136,400 in 1990.

These figures clearly bear no comparison with the costs of broadcast network programming. In primetime the networks spend some $6-800,000 an hour, and, even spread across the entire day, their programming and distribution costs average $125,000 an hour. But equally there is no real value in making such a comparison. ARTS in particular depends heavily on multiple showings of items and on a great proportion of bought material (some 75 per cent in 1982). It goes out only during the late primetime hours, with a repeat of its three-hour block after midnight. On present figures it is clearly still making a loss; but if it maintains its present policy of short service cheaply programmed, continues successfully to persuade advertisers that it is worth three times as much per thousand as the ordinary broadcasting services and manages to sustain losses for a few more years, then it should eventually see revenues which compare favourably with the amount Channel 4 in Britain, for example, has to spend each hour (about £25,000 on average). This conclusion matches the assertions of ARTS executives that the service should be profitable by 1986-7, five years after it started.

ARTS, is fortunate, of course, in having plenty of cultural programming available off the shelf from Europe and little competition for it (keeping the purchase price down). The failure of the rival cultural service CBS Cable was due in no small part to its extraordinarily high

TABLE VI

Potential average advertising revenue per hour in primetime for ARTS and ESPN, 1983-90 (all at 1983 prices)

Service	Date	Cable penetration of TV households[1]	Service penetration of cabled homes	Average primetime audience rating	Average primetime audience	Estimated cost-per-thousand for thirty seconds	Potential primetime advertising revenue per hour[3]
ARTS	March 1983	37.2%	26.8%	0.83[2]	68,900	$18.00[2]	$14,900
				1.0	83,000	18.00	18,000[2]
	1986	50	45	0.8	158,000	18.00	34,100
				1.0	198,000	18.00	42,800
	1990	60	60	0.8	273,000	18.00	59,000
				1.0	342,000	18.00	73,900
ESPN	March 1983	37.2%	87%	2.0	540,000	6.00	45,000
	1986	50	90	2.0	792,000	6.00	66,500
				3.0	1,188,000	6.00	99,800
	1990	60	95	2.0	1,083,000	6.00	91,000
				3.0	1,624,000	6.00	136,400

NOTES

1 It is assumed that there were 83.3 million TV households in March 1983, rising to 88 million in 1986 and 95 million in 1990.

2 In March 1983 ARTS was charging up to $1,500 for a thirty-second commercial, giving a possible revenue per hour (with twelve spots) of $18,000. At an assumed cost-per-thousand of $18 (triple the broadcast rate) this indicates a claimed rating of 1.0. ARTS charges start at $1,250 for thirty seconds, indicating an assumed rating (at $18 per thousand) of 0.83, and giving a potential revenue per hour of $15,000.

3 This is an average potential, since certain programmes may receive higher ratings and others lower. Some ESPN football games have received a five rating, for example.

programming costs, the result of its high proportion of original rather than bought-in material and its more ambitious twelve-hour schedule. A major cause of its downfall was also its placing on the wrong satellite and therefore its unattractiveness to system operators. Cultural cable seems likely to be a good example of the cautious tortoise beating the extravagant hare. As one executive of Hearst Cable Communications has stated, as far as cable programming is concerned, 'One of the arts of winning is durability, spreading out your resources for a long stretch rather than pouring it all out at once' (Raymond Joslin, President of Hearst Cable Communications Inc., personal interview, 30 November 1982).

ESPN, of course, is a twenty-four-hour service and able to repeat material less frequently than ARTS because of sports programming's relatively short life. With much of its night and daytime advertising space unsold and minimal ratings outside primetime, its average revenue per hour across the day must be low indeed. It does, however, have important additional sources of revenue in its per-subscriber fee and lease payments from Business Times, while the extremely low-grade nature of much of its material (such as full coverage of a 500-mile endurance motor race) also means that programme costs outside primetime are kept down.

Given the right mix of advertising and a per-subscriber fee which both brings in revenue and can be used to keep its advertising rate at a competitive level, ESPN should eventually turn around, although neither it nor ARTS seem likely to become major revenue earners. Figures which initially might appear rather depressing therefore actually demonstrate why Hearst/ABC and Getty/ABC consider both ARTS and ESPN to be long-term viable concerns, ARTS because of its relatively unambitious character and ESPN largely because of its dual form of financing. For both, everything now depends on their staying power, a steadily expanding reach, at least a minimum level of audience interest and increased advertiser response.

On current evidence, audience interest in such basic services does indeed look small, rising to a maximum of a combined average 4.3 per cent rating in pay-cable homes during primetime. The current problems in measuring audience shares in a multi-channel market, however, are widely acknowledged, and one or two indications place previous assumptions in doublt. It is evident, for example, that ratings figures, while low, are increasing, as is shown by Table VII opposite.

As people become used to these new services, therefore, so ratings seem likely to rise. Moreover, this trend should be further stimulated as average system capacity grows, leading to basic cable-only services making up an even greater proportion of the total number of channels on offer. Indeed, the current channel limitations of many systems are a serious hindrance, not least because of the industry's traditional function

166

TABLE VII

Primetime (8-11 p.m.) audience ratings for non-pay, cable-only services combined,
1980-82
(Source A.C. Nielsen, Nielsen Television Index 1982)

	1980	1981	1982
In all households	0·5	0·9	1·4
In basic-cable households	1·7	2·2	2·9
In pay-cable households	1·9	2·8	4·3

of importing distant broadcast signals. Satellite service growth has undoubtedly been hindered by the ready availability – and considerable popularity to cable subscribers – of ordinary independent broadcast stations, a factor which will not apply in Britain. The 1983 rise in copyright fees payable by systems for importing broadcast signals has induced many operators to reduce the number of stations they carry, opening up space for more basic satellite services. Nevertheless, the majority of systems continue to have insufficient channel capacity.

Other evidence already presents basic cable audience figures for all services combined more favourably than hitherto. A survey by A.C. Nielsen of audience shares (the proportion of the actual television audience at any moment watching a particular service) in Columbus, Ohio, and San José, California, discovered that in cabled homes basic services averaged a 16.4 per cent share between 9 a.m. and 11 p.m. during the week and a 24 per cent share between 9 a.m. and 4 p.m. at weekends. Relating this to known overall weekday viewing levels still gives a total-day rating of only between 4.4 per cent and 5.7 per cent in cabled homes, although this is some three times the figure of 1.3-1.9 per cent which an earlier Nielsen survey had discovered in 1981. That the figures released were given in the form of *total day shares* also suggests that the *primetime ratings* were less favourable. Yet the same survey also showed that, at 16.4 per cent, basic services combined had a higher audience share than did pay services or independent broadcast stations (10.3 per cent and 15.8 per cent respectively), in direct contradiction of earlier studies. If this is so, it does indicate a greater popularity for basic cable services than previously thought, a fact which may encourage more advertisers to put money into cable.

Estimates for the growth in total advertising revenue for cable vary and certainly expectations have not yet been met. By 1990, however, it is widely agreed that revenues should be up to $1.8 billion, with some optimists even predicting $3 billion, assuming that basic services together attract about 10 per cent of the evening audience. RCA study predicts a 43 per cent annual growth rate in cable advertising revenue, with a $3.5 billion total in 1990. Some 40 per cent of this revenue should be from local advertising and go to the system operator – in line with present proportions of advertising between broadcast networks and local stations – leaving $1-1.8 billion revenue for the services themselves. On these figures, and taking into account the per-subscriber income of several, it seems reasonable to assume that at least the twenty-four-hour services should be profitable by 1990 and probably more, with a number of limited-hours operations also viable. Exponents of cable advertising point to the eight years of losses which even the ABC broadcast network had to endure before achieving profitibility,and to the fact that most cable networks have been established only since 1980. What is certain is that like the cable system industry the present rush into basic services provision has little to do with making a quick profit and everything to do with staking a claim.

Already a few services are close to breaking even. Almost without exception they are ones with additional sources of revenue. As mentioned earlier, CNN is approaching the break-even point. The Christian Broadcasting Network is also reported to be just profitable, although a proportion of its programming it supported by voluntary contributions. Perhaps most interesting is the Satellite Program Network (SPN) which attempts, like the USA Network to provide a variety of special-interest segments but in a rather more adventurous manner. Indeed, SPN has two interrelated objectives, firstly, to provide this 'consolidated narrow-casting' service, and secondly, to sell its airtime to programme producers and distributors who otherwise have no access to a national cable audience. This latter approach reflects the business of its parent company, Southern Satellite Systems, a telecommunications carrier. As with USA, much of its daytime programming is aimed at women, including large blocks on health and hobbies; but it also carries financial and business material, while until the autumn of 1983 each evening was dominated by TeleFrance USA, a three-and-a-half-hour block of subti-tled French material packaged separately by Gaumont Films, Radio Monte Carlo and Sofirad. This, however, failed to attract sufficient advertising revenue and has now ceased operations. Programmes from other Mediterranean countries (extremely cheap to buy, of course) adds to SPN's culturally orientated and 'upscale' reputation. The recent introduction of a seven-hour daily pop video block, however, combined with TeleFrance's collapse, may be evidence of a move into the mainstream. SPN's universe remains small after four years in operation. Yet, despite advertising revenues of only $2-3 million in 1982, SPN is thought to have made a profit in 1983, due almost entirely to its sale of airspace. SPN, in other words, doesn't just get its programmes free; it actually gets paid to show them. Meanwhile SIN, the Spanish network, is profitable only because it is also transmitted by 217 Spanish-language broadcasting stations (five of which is partly owns), whereby it reaches 90 per cent of its 25 million universe.

What conclusions can be drawn, therefore, from the experience so far of advertising on cable? It is obvious firstly, following on from the last point, that the earliest services to become profitable have additional sources of revenue. In the early stages, when there are as yet few services available, systems are willing to pay a per-subscriber fee, and this can be particularly valuable in boosting revenue, holding advertising rates down and cushioning the service provider against insupportable losses until advertisers begin to take a serious interest. Indeed, mainstream services which system operators consider particularly desirable can maintain a per-subscriber charge even when a multiplicity of services are available, as ESPN and CNN realised.

Additional sources of revenue generated by the service itself are of course essential if the operating company is relatively small in media terms. This is the case, for example, with SIN, SPN, and even TBS (CNN and WTBS). Otherwise it is undoubtedly the case that basic services need to be backed by large capital resources if they are to sustain the early losses. In practice, the majority of new services are owned by large corporations, as shown in Table VIII overleaf.

Large corporations are more likely than smaller independents to be able to support continued losses. Nevertheless, not even they can afford to throw money away. Bad planning, extravagant expenditure, unrealistic forecasts of consumer and advertiser interest, use of the wrong satellite and, not least, lack of long-term commitment, were all factors in CBS Cable's rapid downfall, less than a year after start-up and with losses already exceeding $40 million. That CBS could sustain such losses was undoubted; less certain for it was any significant improvement in the situation within the foreseeable future. More likely to stay the course are the more modest efforts such as ARTS, which in any case piggy-backs with other services and so does not consume an entire and extremely valuable system channel, and even the Weather Channel, which does seem to have found a need. Some 40 per cent of homes reached by it tune in at least once a day and, remarkably, for an average of fifteen minutes.

The Weather Channel is a fourteen-hour service, yet although its losses are high its outlay remains modest because of extremely low programming costs. The same is true of ARTS and even more so of Music Television (MTV). This twenty-four-hour rock music channel gets high-quality material free of charge by using video promotional tapes supplied by the record companies. It is the ultimate in continuous advertising, selling advertisements between the video promotions. This is not to say that it does not provide a worthwhile and popular entertainment service, but merely that its widely anticipated early turn-around will owe much to the special circumstances of its

TABLE VIII

Ownership of advertiser-supported services

Service	Parent company
ARTS	Hearst/ABC
BET	Independent
CBN	Independent
CHN/Daytime	Viacom/Hearst/ABC
CNN	Turner Broadcasting System
ESPN	Getty Oil/ABC
FNN	Independent
MSN	Independent
MTV	Warner-Amex
Nashville	Westinghouse/WSM Inc.
SPN	Southern Satellite Systems
SIN	Televisa SA (Mexico, 75 per cent)
USA	Time Inc./Paramount/MCA
Weather	Landmark Communications Inc. (publishing, broadcasting, cable)

low operating costs. Even so its parent company, Warner Amex, decided in June 1983 that they would start charging a per-subscriber fee in order to boost its advertising revenue, which had not met expectations. However the increasing popularity of MTV among the 12-25 age group has not been lost on other services, and, in addition to SPN, WTBS and BET have both introduced large blocks of pop-video programming into their schedules, while the pay services are increasing the number of concerts they show. MTV originated the idea, but now everyone is jumping on the bandwagon.

If MTV, which gets much of its programming free, has found the going rough, other services such as the recently amalgamated Daytime and the Cable Health Network, which of necessity produce a large proportion of their own material, have had even more difficulty. Daytime's aim has been to provide a complete afternoon service for women and as a result has repeated material infrequently (for cable), perhaps up to four times a year. Inevitably, it has had to keep costs down as far as possible and so to rely very largely on magazine-format studio chat shows. Despite its claim to offer a different audience to the advertiser, in practice there has been very considerable competition for the 'upscale' woman's attention, including USA, SPN, CHN, and even ESPN and CNN, which both direct their afternoon programming in that direction. CHN has been placed in a similar position, committed to producing more original hours of programming than any other network and so forced to rely largely on low-budget talking heads. This in its turn seems certain to have reduced audience interest even though for its small viewership CHN has proved to be one of the most satisfying services. Like Daytime it has had rivals to its women-oriented morning and afternoon programming and other rivals (of a different nature) to its late-night health items for single and married adults. CHN seems to have been born as much because of confidence in the enormous advertising budgets of pharmaceutical companies as because it filled a programming gap. But advertisers, however rich, still want audiences, and consequently there was not much surprise when, firstly, CHN declared that it would broaden its appeal by introducing health-related situation comedies into its schedule, and, secondly, when in June 1983 Daytime and CHN announced their decision to merge into one twenty-four-hour 'lifestyle' service. This will provide programmes ranging from fashion and cookery to health and family counselling.

It is clear that the majority of narrowcast channels are being driven back to the traditional broadcast network practice of addressing the majority audience at particular times – women during the day (with some morning business information), families and men in the early evening and 'adults' later on. Twenty-four-hour services use their off-peak hours to repeat material, or even, as in ESPN's case, lease it out to another service. Indeed, either through the activities of individual cable system operators of within certain services (e.g. USA, SPN), the idea of 'piggy-backing' blocks of programmes of interest to different audience segments on one channel seems to have found a place. Yet if this becomes standard practice, then the convenience argument for continuous and separate narrowcast services will be greatly diminished.

Perhaps the most notable feature of American narrowcasting is just how broad the supposedly narrowcast segments are. Narrowcasting is not about particular interests, about gardening or golf or cooking. Rather it is about demographic groupings, about women (particularly), men, children, teenagers, certain large ethnic divisions and upper socio-economic markets. One J. Walter Thompson advertising executive describes it not as narrowcasting but 'target-casting'. For, above all, basic cable narrowcasting is about marketing. Markets of particular attraction to advertisers receive particular attention. Interest groups within these broad categories have to continue to search for programmes which satisfy their interests amongst the mass of material which does not, and often continue to find them only in the non-primetime hours. On the sports channels, for example, primetime continues to be dominated by the major sports. A twenty-four-hour service generally means that primetime material is repeated during the day and overnight, rather than that minority interest material, traditionally relegated to the daytime, receives a primetime slot. Primetime remains a service's best opportunity to win the largest possible audience.

In practice, narrowcasting can never be directed to the narrowest of interests, to a solitary subject or to one individual. Of necessity an audience is composed of a multiplicity of different personalities, each with a variety of requirements which change constantly with changing moods. No narrowcasting service therefore can either afford to dedicate itself to a single subject area or by itself hope to satisfy even one individual's tastes. On the contrary, each service must seek logically to maximise the number of individuals or special interests to which it appeals, whilst alienating as few as possible within its chosen target group as a result of the broadness of its approach. In any case, the truth is that even members of minority interest groups spend most of their time as parts of majorities watching majority interest programmes. If a service is to reach any significant audience at all, therefore, its output as a whole must of necessity have a relatively broad appeal. This is why a host of special interests are still served together under such general headings as 'women' and 'sport', and also why so many services are seeking the largest potential audience grouping at any particular time of day. It is an irony of narrowcast services that they have discovered the logic of audience maximisation within their overall services and even within different parts of the day as surely as the broadcast networks found it for individual programmes. Indeed, it is significant that the few basic services which do concentrate on just one subject area, day and night, deal with the two or three subjects which have an almost universal and not at all narrow interest, namely news, weather and music.

This is not to say that many services do not include programmes of considerable interest and quality. ARTS buys and presents expensively produced cultural programming, while MTV shows complete rock concerts and BET provides news and current affairs of particular interest to a black audience. Daytime's most famous programme included a bare-breasted woman explaining how to look for breast cancer, certainly a first for afternoon television in the USA. These basic services can provide more programmes going further and into greater detail than traditionally, as well as much more of just the same as ever. But despite some widening of the boundaries of what is possible, limits do remain, defined not so much by social mores (although these are important also) as by the requirements of audience maximisation within a broad demographic group. The inevitable result is compromise – not so much 'narrow' as 'less-broad' cast.

The economics of narrowcasting are equally uncertain. It would seem that services supported entirely by a per-subscriber fee are as much a consequence of the politics of franchising (e.g. C-span) and marketing psychology (Nickelodeon) as of economic logic and consumer demand. Similarly, at best a question mark hangs over the logic of narrowcast services financed entirely by advertising, since few appear to reach either a significantly new audience or the desired one more efficiently. If advertisers reject the arguments behind paying premium rates or accept only a relatively low premium for narrowcast audiences, then services such as ARTS and CHN/Daytime will find it very much more difficult to survive. In particular, they will be in competition with hybrid per-subscriber advertising-supported services offering lower advertising rates, in some cases for a not dissimilar audience. These hybrids will, however, have to prove their value to the system operator if they are to be retained despite free alternatives, and this again necessitates a relatively broad appeal. Generally speaking, it would appear that the prospects of significant advertising revenue for cable services by 1990 are fair, largely because of the need to offset the audience losses certain to be experienced by broadcast television. But what is rather more doubtful is whether this increased revenue will validate the concept or confirm the practice of advertiser-supported narrowcasting.

LOCAL ADVERTISING

An important question for system operators is just how lucrative advertising on cable services can be for them. Can it in fact contribute significantly to system revenue or is this an illusory dream? In 1981 barely $21 million was taken in local cable advertising, just 23 per cent of the total advertising revenue from cable. Such low sums by comparison with basic and pay contributions have led some observers to suggest that cable advertising will only ever be of marginal importance to system operators. Nevertheless, this still represented a 53 per cent growth in revenue over 1980, a very positive trend which was continued in 1982, with revenues of about $32 million. More importantly, a major reason for this low total revenue was that only 436 cable systems actually tried to sell local advertising, either on the national cable networks which offered space or on their own local origination channels. Given their lack of experience in this field, many consider that it would not be worthwhile to employ the necessary sales staff. Those which are doing so tend to be amongst the larger systems, including Manhattan Cable, and many have already found it a moderately profitable and worthwhile business.

Local advertising on cable as opposed to broadcast networks has both advantages and disadvantages. For the truly local advertiser, such as local retailers and garages, cable's community-sized reach is ideal, far more appropriate than even the regional reach of independent television stations. Even for the national advertiser, advertising on local spots can have major benefits since specific geographic areas can be targeted, areas which often have a uniform demographic character (such as a particular area within a town or city). Test marketing is also greatly aided by cable's ability to provide the advertiser with small test-bed audiences, allowing experimentation not only with new products but also with different advertisements, testing the effectiveness of various formats and messages.

On the other hand, many cable systems are simply too small to reach a viable advertising audience, particularly for advertisers who are actually seeking a regional scope. For these an important development is the regional 'interconnect', where a company is formed to insert and transmit advertisements within the networked services but at a regional level and serving a large number of local cable systems. In this way small systems can avoid the costs of their own sales staff, production facilities and automatic ad-insertion machines, but reap the benefits of local advertising while joining together to serve a larger area than they could independently. The scope and flexibility within such an arrangement is tremendous and made more so by the ability of such interconnect companies, such as the Bay Area Cable Interconnect in San Francisco with twenty-eight systems, to bring together advertising not only on several systems but also on several different networked cable services. By treating several systems as one, and several cable services also effectively as a single service, an interconnect of this kind can build up a sizeable audience for the advertiser.

Such interconnects depend on microwave distribution or in a few cases on the physical transportation of tapes. Not suprisingly, many are now taking advantage of the regional network they have developed to distribute not just advertisements but regional programming as well. The Bay Area Interconnect, for example, was started by Gill Cable of San José as a natural complement to its regional sports channel. Community programming of a regional character or interest can also be distributed in this way. Clearly there is a danger that in the drive for such economies of scale the local character of cable may be lost, but there can be no doubt of cable's ability to create and define particular audiences to a much greater degree than ever broadcast television could, with consequent attractions to the advertiser. The costs of advertising to such geographically and demographically defined audiences is remarkably competitive, matching in some cases the advertising costs of local radio rather than broadcast television.

Interconnects, of which there are now some thirty to forty, are one obvious development. Another is agreement between cable systems and local newspapers or radio stations to sell advertising space jointly. Both newspapers and local radio have a wealth of experience

174

and contacts in local advertising, as well as a full-size advertising sales force. Such a connection is in the interests of both cable operator and newspaper or radio owner, since the latter is generally keen to become involved in the new medium. This is particularly the case where the system operator has introduced cable classified advertising, although this is still very limited and only really viable where there is plenty of available channel capacity. Anyone who believes that cable is a good medium for classified advertising, however, has clearly not sat in front of a television set watching an endless rolling caption. Where there is space to allocate specific channels or times to certain types of advertisement (cars for sale, houses, help wanted, etc.) then there may be some value, as there could be in interactive advertising where a viewer is able to request only specific types of information on the viewdata principle (houses in a particular area and of certain size, for example). Otherwise, cable's only advantage over the press is its ability to update information more rapidly, deleting items already sold. Manhattan Cable offers a classified service and claims a positive sales response. What is does not do is earn significant revenue from the service.

Manhattan Cable is, however, the first individual system to earn over $1 million in local advertising revenue during 1982, although Bay Area Interconnect took over $2 million. Manhattan's revenue represented only a fractional sale of the 55,000 local spots that it had available on its various channels during the year, indicating not only the potential which exists but also continuing advertiser caution. The local advertising lobby point to previous examples to justify their optimism: local television and radio stations both started slowly as advertising mediums, with the former rising from only $280 million in 1960 to $3 billion in 1980 and a probable $6 billion by 1985. If this is the time scale involved, however, local advertising will remain a peripheral business to the average system operator for some time to come.

In their estimates of turnover, few cable operators are yet looking to advertising for a significant contribution. At Syracuse Cablesystems it formed less than 0.8 per cent of income in 1982, the first year in which it had been attempted. Yet, despite better than expected response, the operator's estimates for 1985 still anticipate that it will provide under 1.5 per cent. The mso Daniel and Associates estimate that local advertising could at present bring in about $6.50 per subscriber each year, that is barely fifty cents a month. This compares with average monthly basic subscriptions of $8 and pay charges of $9. One of the most optimistic projections is made by Cablevision in Boston, which estimates that it could derive 5.5 per cent of revenue from local advertising in 1984 ($1.50 per subscriber per month), rising to 9.6 per cent in 1986 ($4 a month) but drop-

175

ping back and stabilising at about 7 per cent in the early 1990s. Thus it would certainly be a useful component in overall revenue, but in no way compare with basic and pay subscriptions. A number of operators, interestingly but unexpectedly, have found that the sale of advertising in their printed programme guide can actually be as useful a revenue source as trying to sell space on their channels.

As ever, estimates of local cable advertising revenue and its rate of growth have greatly exceeded the reality. At present it seems unlikely that it will ever provide more than a relatively small proportion of a system operator's income, perhaps between 5 per cent and 10 per cent at most. Nevertheless there are signs that more and more systems are beginning to recognise it as a profitable and worthwhile operation, if hardly a major revenue source. As penetration of homes increases, as more cable interconnects are developed and as interactive cable opens new opportunities for advertising, so cable's value as a local advertising medium will become more evident. What seems certain, though, is that however quickly it does grow it will lead to a new level of complexity and subtlety in the continuing struggle of advertisers to reach their prey.

10   Pay and Pay-per-view

To most new cable subscribers the principal reason for subscribing is
in order to receive the pay channels available, primarily those showing relatively recent, uninterrupted and uncut films. Indeed, without
pay, the cable industry would not be enjoying its present enormous
expansion nor entering the cities as rapidly as it is. If cable before
HBO was all about broadcast relay, today it is first and foremost
about pay and multi-pay (the selling of several services to a single
subscriber), with pay-per-view seen as yet another potential gold-
mine for the industry in the not too distant future.

At present some 59 per cent of basic subscribers take one or more
pay services, but the proportion is very much higher in new systems
where consumers have been introduced to cable itself and to pay at
the same time. Attempting to market the latter in older systems
where people are used to cable as a broadcast relay service has
proved more difficult. Nevertheless, over the industry as a whole,
cable growth has more than been matched by pay. In 1981 the
number of pay subscriptions increased by 69 per cent and in 1982 by
43 per cent, rising at 143 per cent the rate of basic. New cable
subscribers, in other words, were taking an average of 1.4 pay
services. At least one pay channel is now available to all but 500,000
(1.6 per cent) cable subscribers on older and smaller systems, and
well over half have access to two or more. We have already seen that
in some of the newest systems the rate of pay to basic can exceed
200 per cent, with over 90 per cent of cable subscribers taking pay.
Whether these levels can be sustained, however, or reached in older
systems now introducing multi-pay, is more questionable. The disconnection of pay services is presently increasing, particularly in
multi-pay markets, as subscribers come to appreciate the similarity
of many of the services and the limited extent to which they can
actually use them.

The response of the pay services themselves to this problem will
be considered later, but within the cable system industry the whole
concept of multi-pay is under serious discussion. No one doubts that
pay is likely to be the most lucrative individual source of revenue to

system operators after basic charges for the foreseeable future. But whether it is in their interests to offer as many pay services as they can to subscribers is more doubtful. Maximising subscriber choice is not necessarily the best way of maximising system revenue, and it is naturally the latter which remains their first concern. Most multi-pay systems offer substantial discounts to subscribers as an incentive to take more pay channels. Beyond the level of three or four services, however, it is being discovered that that discount has to be so high to persuade people to buy as to almost wholly eliminate the system operator's percentage of the proceeds. In 1981, in systems where only one pay service was offered, take-up averaged 41 per cent of basic subscribers, and when two were available this pay/basic ratio rose significantly to 70 per cent. Where three were offered the ratio again rose sizeably to 104 per cent. But thereafter increased take-up was small. Where five pay services were available the ratio of pay to basic reached only 115 per cent. The costs and complexities of administration of multiple pay services and the high churn rate at these levels makes the value of offering more than three services very marginal indeed, even in the newer addressable systems.

The implications of this finding are naturally considerable. It may well be in the system operator's interests actually to restrict the number of pay services he offers, effectively cutting out those channels of more marginal interest – predominantly the more specialised services – from access to their market. While it is still early days in the experience of multi-pay, there can be little doubt that this 'gatekeeper' function of cable systems and the continuing problems of 'churn' will be major factors in determining the character and success of the various networked pay services.

Turning to those services, of which there are currently twelve offered nationally, one can see the same division between general entertainment and specialised services as in the basic services, and the same proportionate consumer interest. Besides Home Box Office, there are four mainstream services which carry a wide variety of premium feature films and in some cases sports and entertainment specials, to appeal to a broad range of tastes. The two owned by Time Inc. – HBO and Cinemax – alone account for 66 per cent of all pay subscriptions (other than regional and local pay services), with HBO having a massive 55 per cent all by itself. Cinemax, now the third largest service, has been designed by Time as a sister service to HBO in multi-pay markets, offering complementary programming. Showtime, the second largest with just over 4 million subscribers, was put on the satellite by its parent company Viacom in 1978, and Warner Amex's The Movie Channel (2.4 million) followed in 1979. In 1983 it was agreed to form a joint venture to manage both Showtime and The Movie Channel although the Justice Department prohibited two of the major film studios – MCA and Paramount – from buying their way into Showtime on anti-trust grounds. Meanwhile, in 1981-2 the major multiple system operators, Times-Mirror, Storer, Cox, TCI and Cablevision, started Spotlight, an all-film channel which, with 750,000 subscribers, is currently not offered to systems other than their own.

A number of trends are already becoming apparent. The first is that all these services are owned by major multiple system operators. Given that each MSO will offer his service as the first pay choice, or market it in some preferential way, each mainstream channel has a sizeable assured potential subscriber base. Warner Amex may offer HBO in its systems, but it gives prime place to The Movie Channel, just as ATC (Time) does to HBO and Cinemax.

Given the system operators' gatekeeper powers, there is a considerable advantage for a service which has a large number of them already on its side. Even so this may not be enough. HBO, very lucrative, is estimated now to have profit margins of 20-25 per cent. Other than HBO, however, only Showtime and Cinemax are making a profit. Showtime broke even in 1982 when subscribers topped 3 million, and is thought to have made between $30 and $40 million in 1983, beginning to recover some of the earlier losses. Cinemax, with 2 million subscribers, went into profit after only 1 million had been reached, but only because it is put together by HBO personnel and marketed jointly. Marketing costs are inevitably high; HBO spent some $20 million on this in 1982. Moreover, as a complementary service to HBO, Cinemax shows older films or big films later on, so that programming costs are much lower. The same joint operation advantages should become available to the currently unprofitable Movie Channel when its operation is combined with Showtime. There seems little doubt that the two will become complementary services like HBO and Cinemax, showing different films from one another each month.

Another obvious feature is that with their combined audience of over 14 million HBO and Cinemax have much greater power and financial leverage when negotiating for pay-TV rights to feature films than their competitors. A long-standing complaint both of HBO's rivals and of the film studios has been its excessive power and position, allowing it to gain pay-TV rights to films at advantageous rates. Again economies of scale are important. While The Movie Channel pays an average twenty-five cents per subscriber to film distributors for a typical feature, Showtime, with nearly double the number of subscribers, pays twenty-two cents, and HBO, with double the two combined, is said to pay only seventeen cents. Often it can even force film distributors to accept a flat licence fee, since in absolute terms this will still exceed anything the other film operators can pay. The real blockbuster films, however, can in each case command significantly higher rates.

All these mainstream services are twenty-four-hour and all rely upon theatrically released feature films as the basis of their programming. Each shows some 300 films every year. The film industry, however, is simply not geared to satisfying such a demand and a major problem is the lack of adequate material. The major studios turn out only some 120-140 films a year of which perhaps fifty receive a good national theatrical distribution. Even fewer are the number of really attractive box-office successes produced annually, films which are crucial to the pay services if they are to persuade subscribers that their entire package is worth buying. Perhaps fifteen to twenty of these appear in a good year, giving all the pay services together an average of no more than two each month. These are the films which grossed over $20 million at the box office and whose reputation is sufficient attraction in itself.

Consequently, there has had to be considerable duplication of films between services, such that HBO, Cinemax, Showtime and TMC showed the same five films a total of fifty-seven times during the evening hours of September 1983. All the services use consumer convenience as an excuse for repeating items up to fifteen times each month. This last strategy, however, has proved double-edged. Certainly subscribers do regard six or seven evening repeats of a film within one month as a positive feature. But beyond that point the 'convenience' rapidly becomes a severe irritation, and excessive repeats is cited as a major reason for disconnecting. Another way to make up the programming complement is to put out older and second-grade films described on the advertising brochures as 'classics' and 'golden oldies'. Some may be; others differ little from material equally available on the broadcast networks and independent stations. One possible development is the attempt by some pay services to buy exclusive rights to entire film libraries and the truly classic films such as *Casablanca* and *Stagecoach*, thereby removing them permanently from broadcast television. Already HBO has considered buying Warner Bros' pre-1950 feature film library (including *Casablanca* and *The Maltese Falcon*), even though the amount of pre-1970 material it shows has so far been small. The Disney Channel, a more specialised service, has now bought exclusive rights to several classic Chaplin features, preventing their being shown on free television.

HBO has avoided where possible the showing of films which have already been over-exposed on broadcast television. The result however is that many of the films it does show are ones which were not originally well received and have long been forgotten. Indeed, a number were never even released theatrically because they were

180

considered certain failures or received only a very short run. A similar ploy used by the now defunct Entertainment Channel was to show the pilots of television series which were never made because of poor audience response but which, according to the pay service, did receive critical acclaim. By such devices is old material reworked.

More significantly, in an effort to pad out their programmes and also to differentiate themselves from their rivals, the major pay services have been moving towards the policies of 'exclusivity' and 'made-for-pay'. Showtime, often marketed as a second service to HBO in multi-pay systems, now emphasises that each month only 6 per cent of its material duplicates that on HBO. Cinemax naturally makes similar claims. Like much advertising hype, such statements reflect a distorted truth. A film unique to one service one month may well have been on two others the previous and on all of them the next. According to industry observer Paul Kagan, fewer than half the films which HBO, TMC and Showtime showed between July and September 1982 were unduplicated by each other during that three-month period. Exclusivity of this kind has relatively little meaning, since only a few blockbuster films have sufficient subscriber attractiveness to make their exclusivity to one service a matter of concern to the others.

HBO, however, has now become sufficiently powerful to buy the exclusive pay rights to certain feature films for up to a year after they are first released to pay. Taking the theatrical exhibition period into account, this means that subscribers to other services may not see a film until two years after its first release. This is a serious problem when pay's major selling point is that it shows premium films while public interest in them is still strong. HBO has already shown *On Golden Pond*, *Annie* and several other box-office successes on an exclusive basis. Indeed, it is now heavily committed to the policy of pre-buying pay rights, before even a film has been made. In 1982 it gained exclusive rights to four Columbia Pictures films a year for four years. By January 1983 it had bought exclusive pay rights to no fewer than thirty-seven (40 per cent) of the 106 films due to be released by major studios MCA, Paramount, Columbia, 20th Century Fox, Warner Bros, MGM/UA and Orion Pictures. Among the top-grossing films to which it has exclusivity are *Tootsie*, *The Dark Crystal*, *Sophie's Choice*, *Six Weeks* and *Frances*. This ability to give its subscribers first the films they really want to see is one reason why HBO is now taken by about 75 per cent of homes which receive pay, even if this has to be as second service where Showtime or TMC receive preferential marketing by Viacom and Warner Amex.

The major film studios have become ever more disturbed by HBO's power. Increasingly it is in a position to preempt them or force their hand on the question of pay rights, so that they actually receive less for such exclusivity than if a film was sold to all the pay-services on a non-exclusive basis. Yet where they refuse to sell to HBO at the price it is offering they lose even more. Much more importantly, the rise of the pay-television programming company between the studios and the exhibitors (cable systems) has effectively deprived the former of the opportunity to extend their own distribution role into this new business. Traditionally the film studio/distributor has taken about 60 per cent of the cinema box office revenue, leaving the exhibitor 40 per cent only, plus ancillary sales (popcorn, screen advertising, etc.). The pay-TV proportions, however, are rather different. Although exact percentages vary according to the number of subscribers delivered by a system and the value of the film, on average the system operator (exhibitor) will retain 45–50 per cent of the monthly subscription of, say, $10. With 40–60 per cent of the remainder being retained by the service provider as distributor, this means that studios may receive no more than 20–25 per cent of the subscriber's fee, very different from the 60 per cent they received from theatrical release as producer and distributor.

Slow off the mark to take advantage of the rise of television in the 50s, the studios were equally reluctant to become involved in or encourage the pay-TV industry when it appeared in the 70s, believing that it would seriously reduce box-office takings. Such uncooperativeness backfired and today they are desperately trying to get into a business which before long should indeed overtake the theatrical box office as a film's principal source of revenue. In 1979–80 MCA, Paramount, Columbia and 20th Century Fox attempted to create their own pay service, called Premiere, on which they could give their own films a nine-month exclusive showing, thereby depriving HBO of its advantages and of much of its material. However, the plan was judged by the Justice Department to be anti-competitive and illegal, and it fell through. The same happened in 1983 with MCA, Paramount and Warner Bros seeking to buy their way into the Showtime/TMC venture and emphasising that on this occasion their products would be offered to all the pay services on an equal basis. This would certainly have made it more difficult for HBO to insist upon low and exclusive pay rights, since studios would have had an alternative outlet in which they themselves had an interest. Yet although the Justice Department has so far blocked major entry by the film studios into pay-TV distribution, the relationship between producer and distributor does seem to be reestablishing itself. Already Columbia has formed a close partnership with HBO, which has also bought Orion Pictures and announced the creation of a new studio with partners Columbia and CBS. If ever the major studios were able to buy their way into pay-TV distribution a likely consequence would be increased competition for exclusive pay rights and a general rise in the price of film licence payments. In other words, the pay subscriber might well find himself paying more for fewer premium films on each service. Almost certainly, pay services unaffiliated to major studios, such as Spotlight, would find themselves in a more difficult position. It is worth noting, therefore, that the two principal British pay film channels currently being developed both include major Hollywood studios as significant shareholders.

While the relationship between the pay services and major film studios/distributors is still in a state of flux, both HBO and Showtime have increased the amount of non-theatrical feature film material in their schedule. HBO claims that almost half its output consists of sports events, made-for-pay films and entertainment specials, including concerts ('Elton John Plays Central Park'), Broadway shows (largely comedies and musicals) and occasional documentaries. During 1983 and the first half of 1984 it will have a hand in twenty-four made-for-pay films and by 1985 aims to show some eighty pre-bought and made-for-pay films exclusively a year. In particular, it has been successful in picking up the rights to special sports events, notably boxing contests. Showtime's schedule is similarly up to 40 per cent non-theatrical film, and it has already aired its first made-for-pay movie, *Falcon's Gold*.

Until recently both services' non-theatrical material was primarily one-off. The problems of churn, however, are now persuading both to move into what one executive describes as 'addictive programming', namely series. The relatively low production costs of these are also an incentive in this direction. HBO sees comedy as a potential draw as well as strengthening its 'brand image'; it had five series scheduled in 1983, including the American-licensed version of *Not the Nine O'Clock News*, and *Fraggle Rock* by Muppet-creator Jim, Henson.

Showtime is moving even further in this direction with at least eight series during 1983, including comedy, soaps and drama. Such items tend to be franker and more risqué than would be possible on broadcast television, and Showtime in particular has capitalised on this with its adult comedy *Bizarre* and its adult soaps *Romance* and *33 Brompton Place*, all made in Canada. Even its flagship 'made-for-pay' series, *The Paper Chase*, bought after the Public Broadcasting Service had dropped the broadcast version, contains 'adult situations'. Its film policy, in any case, is to show more 'R'-rated (18) films than HBO. Showtime and HBO executives make play of the greater artistic freedom which pay allows, being discretionary services, and Showtime certainly has tried to put out a number of 'difficult' stage plays. But for the most part artistic freedom is a euphemism for characters swearing more openly and taking more of their clothes off more frequently.

An important question concerns the real quality of the programming on these pay services. Despite growing subscriber numbers, their annual revenues remain small by comparison with those of the broadcast networks, which now take some $2 billion each. How then can their output possibly match the quality of traditional television? As far as the films they show are concerned, of course, the production budgets involved reflect the numerous outlets and stages of their release, from cinema to broadcast television, so that the pay-TV licence sum paid is only one element in the overall equation and still far from the most important. With HBO's and Showtime's ventures into original programming, however, the onus is far more on them to ensure its quality. In almost all cases such programmes remain the result of co-financing – for example, with the Canadian pay services, the major studios and even the Public Broadcasting Service. Nevertheless, as the principal and initial outlet, the pay services are responsible for a large proportion of the production costs. Even HBO's total programme budget in 1983 was only a little over $300 million, whilst Showtime's was only about $100 million. From this, each had to pay both film licence fees and whatever was necessary for original programming.

Yet because of their repeats policies the pay services actually require considerably less programming than a broadcast network, with the result that the price they can pay for particular items frequently equals and even occasionally exceeds what the broadcast networks could afford. HBO can now certainly outbid the latter for individual sports events, and it finds special occasions particularly attractive to viewers and so good at increasing subscribers. This is one reason for its emphasis on boxing contests, some of which have been watched by up to half of all homes taking HBO and particularly by men, who tend still to be the members of the household who decide whether or not to subscribe and who pay the bills. Both HBO and Showtime are also now in a position to buy up or create drama series at prices almost equal to those the broadcast networks pay. In 1982 HBO bid for the comedy series *Taxi*, previously aired on ABC. Although it lost it to NBC, it is said to have offered $460,000 for each half-hour episode, a price comparable to what it pays (multiplied up for increased length) for a successful feature film. *Fraggle Rock* is similarly said to have cost $300,000 an episode. Showtime probably paid an average $500,000 for each of seven episodes of *The Paper Chase*, although the price of its adult soaps may have been as low as $30-60,000. As for the made-for-pay films in which both are investing, the budgets vary between $2 million and $5 million, cheap by theatrical film standards but more than most made-for-TV films. All of these are expected to have subsequent sales to broadcast television and overseas. In general, it would seem that both HBO and Show-

184

time are increasingly in a position to pay for quality programming, particularly through co-financing. Both, however, are seeking to escape from the traditional production inefficiences of the major studios by looking elsewhere, including Canada and Britain.

The impact of cable on the production industry will be considered further in Chapter 14. Assuming, however, that exclusivity and made-for-pay programmes do become an ever more prominent feature of these services, their character will obviously change. In any case, as video recorders grow in popularity the convenience of repeats will be reduced still further and the need for additional material become stronger. While premium feature films and more adult content will continue to differentiate pay-TV from the broadcast networks, therefore, there may well be an increasing emphasis on a network type of schedule, lacking only the advertising and clean wholesomeness which are the prevalent features of broadcast television. Not that frankness and explicitness will go too far; HBO and Showtime are every bit as keen to appeal to conservative middle America as they are to the more 'sophisticated' audience. In their desire to seek the largest possible subscriber base they differ not at all from the broadcast networks' search for the largest audience, a desire and search with profound consequences for the overall character and moral values they each present.

Each mainstream pay service will therefore seek to differentiate itself from the others by exclusives, 'made-fors' and its own series, creating its own identity in the manner of the broadcast networks while also retaining broad appeal. In any one market, moreover, it seems likely that there will be a tendency towards complementarity of service, as with HBO and Cinemax or Showtime and the Movie Channel, rather than direct competition between the mainstream offerings. The latter leads to disgruntled subscribers who only take one service, whereas the former opens the way for the maximum degree of multi-pay, with each service being taken for its particular, but widely appealing programming, both films and 'made-fors'. Differentiation helps to maximise multi-pay, and multi-pay benefits both service providers and system operators.

Differentiation, however, is not the same as specialisation or narrowcasting. Six of the satellite-distributed pay services may loosely – very loosely in some cases – be termed specialised in that they have a less than broad appeal. In the case of four of them, they are specialised only in that they represent the two side of the media morality compromise, serving those who want to go further than the mainstream services or those who feel that even these have gone far beyond the bounds of acceptability. Westinghouse's Home Theatre Network Plus provides twelve hours of wholesome family programming, primarily feature films (suitably cut if necessary to eliminate any offensive language) and thoroughly innocuous travelogues. This clean approach reflects Westinghouse's corporate image – it sold its half interst in Showtime when the latter started to include 'adult' content. The Disney Channel, started in April 1983 and with over 300,000 subscribers by the end of the year, is a sixteen-hour service programmed largely from the enormous Disney library and partly with other material, all of it in keeping with the Disney image. Another example of a major studio entering the pay-TV field, this venture represents a $70 million investment by Disney. The company has been steadily withdrawing its product from broadcast television in order to reserve it exclusively for its own service. Although its personal library is large – 160 feature films, 450 cartoon shorts, 561 episodes of Mickey Mouse and over 200 hours of television programming – this will hardly be sufficient to fill a complete channel. 60 per cent of programming is films, although the classic feature cartoons such as *Snow White* are not being used lest they be videotaped and so lose their continuing theatrical re-release value. Another feature is the daily 'Epcot Magazine' which gives wide publicity to Disney's latest and most expensive leisure complex.

Disney is a family rather than a children's channel and has certainly been conceived on an ambitious scale. System operators may be tempted to offer it both for itself and as a franchising sop for a pay channel at the other end of the spectrum. Quite apart from the two networked porn channels – Eros and the Playboy Channel – a large number of system operators do still programme their own service of this kind or use one of a number of regional services. A few even go beyond the R-rated line and show films which in Britain do not receive a licence. Some operators claim that over half of their cable subscribers take such a channel, but on average no more than 10-20 per cent of subscribers take them on systems where they are offered. Certainly both Eros and Playboy have found the going tough, with the latter in 1982 suffering a very high disconnection rate of up to 7 per cent a month. It is not surprising, in these circumstances, that the rival Penthouse organisation has decided not to go ahead with the pay service which it was planning. The implication is that a general channel such as HBO or Showtime, which includes semi-pornographic material in the late evening as part of a wide variety of programming, is more popular than one which offers an unrelieved diet of sex. Playboy, owned by the Playboy organisation and a number of MSOs, had about 560,000 subscribers by December 1983 or 10 per cent of cabled homes on systems served. It is said to require 750,000 to make a profit, but has already covered costs by ancillary sales to Canadian First Choice and through video cassettes. Such other outlets are expected to account eventually for over half the operation's revenue. Since Playboy provides only a five-hour block day, which is repeated overnight, its operating costs are in any case low by comparison with HBO or Showtime. It shows both R-rated films and a video version of the magazine, and, under its former name, Escapade, was put out jointly with Bravo, a culture pay channel, in order to make it more respectable. Opposition to such channels has, not surprisingly, been considerable and some system operators have been reluctant to carry one lest it endanger their licence renewal.

Bravo is now sold separately and the relative lack of interest in it is unfortunately all too evident. Its ten-hour overnight service is taken by only 140,000 subscribers in 100 systems and its principal appeal appears to be the large number of international and classic films it shows. Its relatively unambitious efforts have allowed it for the time being to survive its separation from Escapade (where previously it ran only three evenings a week), but its future must depend on an increase in the number of systems which offer it. Like the ill-fated Entertainment Channel it is relayed on a less popular satellite, Satcom IV. The Entertainment Channel, owned by RCA and the Rockefeller Center Inc., closed down after only ten months in operation and with losses estimated at over $35 million. More than any other it demonstrated the problem of trying to sell a non-film service. Offering a totally exclusive programme of BBC material (40 per cent of its schedule), original American series, 'classic' domestic and foreign films and adaptations of Broadway stage plays, it found it almost impossible to create a clear identity to sell to cable subscribers. The result was a take-up of under 50,000 for a service whose break-even point was at least 1.5 million. In systems where one or two pay services were offered, they were the mainstream ones; where several were available, it was still the mainstream film services which were taken by subscribers. Where it was bought as a third or fourth service, churn was quite unacceptably high. As the Entertainment Channel's chairman, Arthur Taylor, admitted, the service 'encountered a multi-pay marketplace that was developing much more slowly than anyone had anticipated' (Quoted by the *New York Times*, 6 March 1983).

Unlike the Entertainment Channel, Galavision, the last of the nationally distributed pay services, does have a well-defined market, being the Spanish-language equivalent of the premium film channels. Owned by SIN, Galavision's eleven-hour service is just breaking even with 120,000 subscribers, although it is having problems all of its own. Disconnections are now matching new subscribers, so that the service is not expanding at all. One reason is the poor economic circumstances of many Spanish-Americans, but most important is straightforward disenchantment with the high number of repeats. It would seem that with the few Spanish channels available to them,

Hispanics use Galavision on a far more regular basis than subscribers to the other pay services use those. Foreign-language minorities, in other words, look to the new cable channels to provide a complete service and not to complement other channels, with the result that multiple repeats simply are not tolerated. Consequently, Galavision is having to become a more continuous service, presumably with increased programming costs but also, it is hoped, with more subscribers.

So far the number of specialist pay channels is strictly limited, although one might also include the regional sports pay services. Westinghouse plans to connect the latter into a national pay-sports network, starting in April 1984. Once again, as with advertiser-supported channels, the lesson seems to be that the slow, steady and modest effort, attempting only a few hours a day and offering relatively little original programming, is most likely to stay the course until system capacity and cable penetration is sufficient to create large enough minority audiences. So far specialisation appears to have been not so much in terms of subject interest as of moral standpoint, with Disney and Playboy representing the opposing camps. What does seem likely, as with basic cable, is the growing importance of ancillary sources of revenue. Not surprisingly, the mainstream film services, such as HBO and Showtime, are already under pressure from advertisers to accept advertising, particularly since the former is now regularly attracting a 12 per cent rating or 18-20 per cent share of the primetime audience in homes which take it, figures comparable to the average broadcast network. All have so far refused these suggestions, making the absence of commercials a poisitive selling point. For the smaller services, however, any additional source of revenue will be welcome. Playboy in particular earns money from video cassettes and has declared its intention of accepting programme sponsorship. The regional sports pay services equally all sell advertising space, thereby helping to keep subscriber charges down to $2-5 a month only. Disney in its turn is one vast marketing operation continually selling itself in all its multifarious guises. The lesson for specialist services seems to be that, since they will only ever be of marginal value to most subscribers, so they must only be of marginal cost by comparison with the mainstream channels. This in its turn means a relatively modest operation. Conversely, all must offer essentially unique programming and in some cases a low proportion of repeats, both circumstances which raise their costs. Disney's ambitious service, with almost entirely exclusive programming and high subscriber fees matching those of HBO and Showtime, certainly demonstrates its aspirations but has also led many observers to doubt its prospects. It also suffers from being unconnected to any MSO, none of which therefore has any special incentive to promote it.

However pay-TV develops, it seems unlikely that there will be any significant number of specialised services for many years to come. Most probably pairs of complementary general entertainment services will establish themselves as the two-pay tiers which most subscribers take first, with the regional/national sports channel becoming the third most popular. At present only some 10 per cent have three pay-services, while those which are commonly taken as the second and third choice, notably Cinemax and Playboy, have very high churn rates. That there will be cable subscribers with alternative preferences or prepared to take four or more pay channels is not in doubt, but whether it will be worth a system operator's while to offer many additional minority services seems unlikely. Small markets do seem to exist for soft-porn and family channels and possibly, on systems with a heavy Hispanic subscribership, for a Spanish-language service. What we are talking about here, though, even in the moral aspects, is a demographic division. Systems in traditional middle-American towns will find it neither economically viable nor politically sensible to offer Playboy, while Home Theatre Network Plus or even Disney may find it difficult to gain access to low-capacity systems in more sophisticated urban areas. Where pay cable is concerned, community mores may well prove of greater significance than individual wishes. Equally, the interests of the mainstream service providers and system operators will be best served by an increasing degree of differentiation and exclusivity, so that subscribers will have either to pay for ever more mainstream services or lose many of the films and programmes they presently enjoy, at least until the exclusive licence for a film expires.

Pay-TV can and does provide new and different programming to the majority and even to some large minorities. But it is not yet about narrowcasting or the satisfying of minority tastes. Pay-TV is about maximising profits for service providers and system operators. A major argument for pay is that market forces will determine the value of special-interest programming to minorities who, by paying the requisite sum, will be able to receive programmes to suit their tastes. Yet in practice other factors intervene to prevent pay channels fulfilling the logic of this argument. Clearly, up to a certain point, it is to a system operator's advantage to try to satisfy the minority interests of individuals who might not otherwise have taken cable or a pay service at all. But in most cases members of minorities also exhibit majority tastes, and it is economically more sensible for the operator to attract them by satisfying these. Only when a section of the community served by a system is truly distinct, of a certain critical size and attracted in no other way is it necessary for the operator to offer a new carrot. And in practice such sections or minorities tend to be demographic ones – people separated by a foreign language, for example, or people normally hostile to cable and even to television on moral grounds. The latter is a group which operators are naturally keen to catch; if they can do so by offering Disney or Home Theatre Network then it may be worthwhile to do so. It is of course right that such groups should have channels tailored to their entertainment needs. But present pay services are hardly specialised. The pay channel is simply not a sufficiently subtle or sophisticated device to serve more than broad interests. For the possibility of anything more we must look to the concept of pay-per-view.

PAY-PER-VIEW

Pay-per-view, which allows subscribers to pay for individual programmes only, is one of the big unknown factors in cable. Estimates as to its likely growth and the degree of interest in it vary wildly. While Warner Amex sees it as a normal part of their service, offered on a daily basis, others believe that consumer willingness to pay the sizeable sums involved may restrict its use to six to twelve times a year. Where industry analysts Donaldson, Lufkin & Jenrette estimated that two-thirds of cable subscribers would be on addressable systems by 1990, making pay-per-view relatively easy, another leading consultant believes 15 per cent only to be more likely. Hard evidence gives no clearer a picture, for the various experiences of pay-per-view events have received very mixed responses.

Pay-per-view is also the centre of more rarified economic argument. To some economists, 'over-the-air "free" and per-channel pay methods of delivering programmes fail the test of economic efficiency. The inefficiency occurs because neither system can reflect the intensity of demand consumers hold for individual programs. Utilisation of a per-program pay-cable delivery system solves this problem' (T.F. Baldwin, M.O. Wirth and J.W. Zenaty, 'The economics of per-program pay cable television', *Journal of Broadcasting*, Spring 1978, p.146). By this argument, pay-per-view means that diversity and choice in programmes will match exactly the degree of interest in them. Others, however, point out that the extra cost of providing such programmes to all rather than to the few who pay for them is nil, yet to make them freely available deprives the latter not at all. As public goods which all consumers could enjoy equally, therefore, pay-per-view programmes (and pay-per-channel) suffer from a 'zero price inefficiency' (Ibid., p.148). In strict economic terms it would seem that per-channel pay-TV is the least efficient method of providing the programmes viewers actually want, while a mixture of commercial and per-programme television is the least inefficient. Once again, however, the system operator's interests have intervened. After the early experiments with pay-TV on a per programme basis had

190

proved disappointing in the early 70s, system operators rapidly moved to per-channel (such as HBO) when it was discovered that considerably more revenue could be gained in this way, which in any case required a far less complex and expensive technology.

Today, with pay-per-channel established as the principal pay-TV mechanism, system operators, service providers and programme producers are all beginning to look again to pay-per-view to see if this can be an additional (rather than an alternative) revenue source. To the film studios and to concert and sports promoters, in particular, pay-per-view is welcome because it puts pay-TV back on a true box-office basis. Consequently, the producer's share of the proceeds can be calculated exactly as a proportion of what was grossed. Under the pay-channel system it has been necessary to assess the licence fee of each film on the basis of its earlier theatrical success and the relationship of this to its likely cable popularity – hardly an accurate method. The major studios are also well aware that only 20 per cent of the population buy 80 per cent of the cinema tickets sold each year in the USA, and that these are overwhelmingly in the fourteen to thirty-four age group. Even more than the pay-channel services, pay-per-view should be able to draw back the older audience to the true box office, without their having to leave home.

The studios are equally determined not to be preempted a second time by the establishment of independent pay-per-view event distributors, cutting into their share of the pay-TV 'box-office' take, as they were in the case of Home Box Office. If pay-per-view is to depend largely on their product (feature films), then they want a hand in its distribution. Exactly the same attitude is being taken by professional sports promoters such as Don King, who are also now referring to their players and events as 'product'. Indeed, in the few pay-per-view events organised so far, the promoter/producers have been demanding anything from a 50 per cent to an 85 per cent share of the total take, in line with traditional box-office proportions. In some cases, it may be that they will deal direct with system operators, cutting out the middleman. More likely, however, are the developments of a number of pay-per-view distributors with individual studios, promoters and others involved in each, and each distributing their own product exclusively. Once again, such exclusivity will probably mean less access or higher cost for the subscriber. Don King has already formed such a company for sports events as has ABC in conjunction with ESPN. ABC is also looking to partnerships with MSOs such as Cox in order to distribute other pay-per-view items on their systems. The USA network is planning to offer occasional pay-per-view films for its owners Time, MCA and Paramount, as are Viacom and Showtime, while HBO is actively considering the possibility.

The main problem so far has undoubtedly been the very few systems which are really equipped to offer pay-per-view events in which individual houses can select to receive one particular programme. There are three methods of delivering pay-per-view, using two-way addressable systems such as Qube and Cox's Index, one-way addressable, or, on older systems without any addressability, 'disposable traps'. The latter are devices which viewers purchase from the cable operator, plug into the back of the television to unscramble the pay-per-view event signal, but which 'self-destruct' after two days. They are an expensive and unsatisfactory method of delivery and require a premeditated decision on the subscriber's part to watch an event. One-way addressability similarly requires a telephone call from the subscriber to the system operator asking to have the signal unscrambled. Both methods therefore lose a considerable proportion of the 'unpremeditated' or impulse audience which is widely believed to make up some 60 per cent of those watching any programme. The cost of the disposable trap has in any case made it so far unprofitable for most non-addressable systems to offer pay-per-view events, although several have done so on a very occasional basis.

Estimates vary as to the number of homes now capable of having individual programmes addressed to them. According to the Paul Kagan *Pay-TV Newsletter*, there were only some 500,000 on cable systems by July 1982. Other estimates suggest that by March 1983 there were some 2.3 million addressable homes, although at least 1 million of these were on broadcast subscription television systems. The largest STV operator, Oak Industries, also produces addressable converters and has some 35 per cent of the pay-per-view audience itself. Severe problems in developing reliable addressable equipment, however, have seriously delayed further expansion, while system operators who are still amortising their non-addressable converters are naturally reluctant to take on further expense for a technology whose revenue potential remains unproved. By March 1983 there had been ten pay-per-view events nationally distributed, including the heavyweight boxing championship fight between Larry Holmes and Jerry Cooney in June 1982, live rock concerts by the Rolling Stones and The Who, and the films *Star Wars* and *The Pirates of Penzance*. Prices to the subscriber ranged from $10 up to $30. Early evidence seemed to augur well; the Holmes/Cooney fight attracted almost half the potential subscribers and earned some $9 million. Several systems discovered that subscribers made such occasions into television parties, with Warner Amex estimating an average nine people per television set for the Leonard/Hearns title fight in September 1981. Also in 1981 the Rolling Stones concert attracted 25 per cent of the potential, while *Star Wars*, despite its long theatrical release and extensive video piracy, still drew a remarkable 30 per cent in September 1982. 324,000 homes paid an average $7.50 to watch it earning $2.43 million for 20th Century-Fox and the system operators together.

Subsequent events, however, have not been so favourable, and subscriber levels have dropped down to and even below the economic minimum for system operators, whose marketing expenses on such occasions are very considerable. The concert by The Who distributed by 20th Century-Fox attracted only 14 per cent of the 2 million to whom it was offered, whilst the Broadway musical, *Sophisticated Ladies*, did even worse with only 11 per cent being prepared to pay an average $15. In February 1983 a $10 pay-per-view showing of *The Pirates of Penzance*, on the opening night of its cinema release, attracted about 125,000 subscribers, only 10 per cent of those to whom it was offered. Universal made about $600,000 from the event, compared with about $225,000 from the cinema box office on the same night. For system operators, however, profits were small if any. The result has been some cooling of interest amongst the latter and an insistence on at least 50 per cent of the gross revenue. Indeed, ATC have suggested that an addressable system with 40-50,000 subscribers and with a pay-per-view take-up of 15 per cent will only barely break even if it receives 40 per cent of a retail price of $15. At any lower price it is not worth its while.

Such results, if they continue, may well delay the upgrading of older systems to addressability. The majority of the urban systems now being built, however, have one- or even two-way addressability as a franchise requirement. In any case, it is being recognised that the high cost of installing addressable equipment is justifiable in terms of its greater operational and administrative efficiency, irrespective of its pay-per-view potential. Addressability has great advantages to operators offering several levels of multi-pay because it makes it easier to cope with the high levels of churn they experience. To the pay-per-view distributor, therefore, this likely growth in the market holds out great prospects. If estimates of 30 million subscribers on addressable systems are realised by 1990, then even a 10 per cent take-up at $10 would reap $30 million, half of which would go to the distributor. Even if a more likely 20 million are addressable by 1990 then a 30 per cent take-up of a major film or sports event at $15 (as with *Star Wars* and the Holmes/Cooney fight) would gross $100 million.

For the system operators the lessons at present seem to be that special pay-per-view events need to be chosen carefully and marketed intensively. As one-off events each needs considerable promotion, which in the case of addressable systems must be continued right up to the moment they are shown in order to catch the impulse viewer. Such events also need the broadest appeal and cannot be put too close together. Low take-up of events of truly minority interest may prove profitable on a national scale to the promoter/distributor, but much less so to the individual operator. Events which lend themselves to communal viewing by groups of friends sharing the cost can attract much interest, but there is a danger that this will reduce the number of individual households paying. Perhaps what most needs to be investigated is what price subscribers will be prepared to pay on a regular basis. A number of individual systems are offering pay-per-view programming, largely films, more frequently than the national efforts. Cablesystem's system in Portland, Oregon, is showing up to six films each month at prices between $4 and $8, whilst the Bay Area Interconnect is regularly achieving a 15-20 per cent response for films costing $3-4.

Most interesting, however, are Warner Amex's Qube systems, which have taken an altogether different route. All these two-way addressable systems include a number of channels wholly dedicated to continuous transmission of films and other programmes on a pay-per-view basis. In its most mature Qube system in Columbus, Ohio, it had just over 60,000 subscribers by the end of 1982, of which 44,000 took the Qube interactive tier, giving them access amongst other services to six pay-per-view channels. When it was activated in 1977 it had ten, but four have been replaced since then by advertiser-supported services and the undoubtedly more profitable pay channels, including HBO, Showtime and Warner Amex's own Movie Channel. Viewers can watch any of the pay-per-view channels as and when they want and are automatically billed for a programme after they have been watching it for two minutes (calculated cumulatively, to prevent their avoiding payment by switching channels and back again every minute). All the channels are lockable to prevent unauthorised use by children, although neither the system nor parental watchfulness has proved infallible.

Three of the pay-per-view channels are programmed twenty-four-hours a day with recent feature films, generally several months ahead of their appearance on the pay networks. The cost of watching a film on these channels is a very tempting $2.50 to $4.00, although the special events described above, which are also shown whenever available, cost considerably more. Warner Amex also programmes local special events, such as Ohio State football games. A fourth channel, which rather remarkably has proved quite popular, is described as 'Drive-in Movies' and offers non-stop 'B' pictures at $0.50-3.00 each. The fifth, and undoubtedly the most popular, is a continuous adult film service. Lastly and most interesting is the Live and Learn channel which contains informational and educational programming. Amongst the items on offer are series on cooking, learning golf and playing the guitar, and viewers can watch either individual programmes for $1 or pay a discount price of up to $10 for a complete series. This channel currently relies on very cheaply bought or produced material, and certainly the subscriber base is not yet large enough to finance more. As new Qube systems are built, however, and as Warner Amex's total Qube subscribership increases, so the size of minority groups within the whole may make better programming practicable. With 500,000 Qube subscribers in Warner Amex's various systems a not too distant objective, even a 1 per cent minority interest could raise $100,000 for a programme by paying just $2 each. For a relatively small ethnic minority, such as the Italian or Chinese communities, the prospects seem fair for at least some programming directed to their needs in this way.

Warner Amex's newer Qube systems in Pittsburgh, Cincinnati and Houston also carry four to six pay-per-view channels, suggesting that at this number there is sufficient interest for them to make money. Indeed, according to one senior Warner Amex executive, the film channels were all profitable in 1982, with even Live and Learn probably breaking even. The latter is worth offering in any case as a franchising ploy and to counter the inevitable criticism arising from the more lucrative 'adult' film channel. Exact figures as to the operation's viability are naturally not released. One important factor, however, is Warner Amex's overall and wholehearted commitment to Qube itself and to exploiting all its interactive opportunities. Another is its built-in ability to promote and market the pay-per-view services on a continuous basis, thereby heightening subscriber awareness of what is on and available. This heightened awareness and daily experience of pay-per-view by subscribers makes it much easier and cheaper to promote special events. On the other hand it may also reduce the excitement and incentive actually to watch them; only 18 per cent of Columbus's Qube subscribers watched the Holmes/Cooney fight, less than half the average elsewhere.

Having been operating full pay-per-view channels for six years, Warner Amex seem to be finding the right mixture of broad appeal and 'adult' films at a reasonable price, a varied, barely viable but extremely cheap-to-programme educational channel and occasional special events. A survey in February 1982 indicated that 60 per cent of Qube subscribers had used the pay-per-view channels and that those who did so had a higher satisfaction rating with the programming they received than normal. Although churn levels are much higher than Warner Amex would like, take-up of the Qube interactive tier in its new systems is said to be reaching 85-90 per cent. Perhaps most encouraging and interesting is the fact that Columbus's pay-per-view channels are estimated to be generating an average $8-10 a month per Qube subscriber, equal to the fee from another pay channel.

The situation in the newer Qube systems, where subscription to pay channels is over 200 per cent of basic subscribers, is still very fluid, with high churn levels. Early indications, however, seem to suggest that subscribers welcome a combination of pay and pay-per-view channels and that use of the latter does not significantly reduce subscription to the former. Pay-per-view, in other words, is indeed an additional source of revenue rather than an alternative to pay-per-channel. That other MSOs also believe this to be so is evident from the intended introduction of a regular pay-per-view facility into certain of their systems by Cox, Cablesystems (Rogers), Cablevision and others.

Warner Amex's experience of pay-per-view is of course far from typical. In any case, the operational expenses of such pay-per-view services will be higher than for a normal pay channel, although the cost of providing interactivity itself is covered by the monthly $5.50 charge for the Qube tier. Nevertheless, if Warner Amex really is deriving $8-10 per month per Qube subscriber from these channels, then this could amount to a worthwhile proportion of its revenue. Given the huge levels of investment necessary to build these inter-active systems, even an additional 5-10 per cent to its revenue could be significant. Optimism should not, however, be taken too far; it is surely worth noting that Cablevision, whose Boston system will also be fully interactive, making possible regular or continuous pay-per-view, does not anticipate deriving more than 2.3 per cent of its revenue from pay-per-view over the next ten years. Indeed, as the system develops it sees under 2 per cent as an average figure.

The greatest growth in the next few years is in any case certain to be in one-way addressable systems, able to offer occasional pay-per-view events but not suited to the Qube approach. With several national distributors for pay-per-view items now being established, it seems certain that the number of such special events will rise until several are available each month, ranging from new films to major sports events. ABC's successful bid for exclusive broadcast coverage of the 1984 Los Angeles Olympics has not entirely precluded the possibility that some heats might be sold first through its pay-per-view distribution system, while the growth of the pay-per-view mar-ket by 1988 makes this almost a certainty for the Summer and Winter Olympics that year. If the most optimistic estimates are realised, then by 1990 some two-thirds of cable subscribers could be on addressable systems, each paying $9 a month for pay-per-view events. Such a situation would bring in some $37 billion annually, with pay-per-view becoming cable's most important source of re-venue after basic subscriptions and pay channel fees. Once again, however, Cablevision, not normally noted for a pessimistic outlook, is less confident. Its figures suggest an income per subscriber of barely $12 in an entire year by 1990. If this is a more accurate reflection of demand, annual pay-per-view revenue nationally would be only some $420 million, even with two-thirds of cabled homes addressable. In any case, no one currently believes that it would be worthwhile for an operator with a one-way addressable system to offer individual pay-per-view programmes at a price acceptable to the subscriber if take-up falls below or even averages 10 per cent. The implication is that for most subscribers pay-per-view will remain a means of satisfying majority tastes, often with programmes previously delivered free on broadcast television, as with boxing championships or the Olympics. Only on dedicated pay-per-view channels, and then only to a very limited extent, does there seem any likelihood that minority interests will begin to be considered.

11   The Local Element

Because cable subscribers spend most of their viewing time watching either the broadcast stations or the newer cable networks, there has been a natural tendency to play down the local services which many systems now provide. About 80 per cent of systems originate their own programmes or provide access facilities of various kinds, although they are no longer legally required to do so. Some still find it worthwhile to put together their own pay or advertiser-supported channels, or 'standalones', while most claim to do at least some community programming. In the larger capacity systems 'leased access' is becoming a not uncommon feature, whereby anyone can buy airtime for a relatively limited sum, put out a programme and, if they wish, attempt to sell advertising space to recoup their costs. Finally worth at least a mention are the automated text services – programme guides, local news and information, weather reports and other items.

The tremendous competition for urban franchises in the last few years has resulted in a remarkable improvement in the community and local services which are offered. Not untypical are those being promised by Cablesystems Pacific (50 per cent owned by Rogers) in Portland, Oregon. Now being completed, its sixty-nine programmed channels (others are available when there is programming for them) are to include not only almost every satellite network but also community, educational and local government services and a number of 'theme channels' incorporating national and locally originated material. In addition, five public access channels will be programmed from four studios or live from any of thirty location points. Each can be directed to any of three separate community areas within the franchise, giving the potential for up to fifteen separate programmes at any moment. Most of the 'theme' and community channels should be interactive and are to include children's, senior citizens', local cultural, local sports, multicultural, local 'humanities', environmental, black and deaf services. Alphanumeric television guides, weather, community bulletin boards and shopping information are to be supplemented by access (for those who pay extra) to the Canadian Telidon videotext data bank, with appropriate local pages added. This latter service, however, is so far offered only experimentally to a few subscribers and utilises the telephone line because of delays in obtaining interactive converters.

This, of course, is one of the most recent systems with a high channel capacity, but supporters of community programming argue that even one local or access channel opens up new opportunities for community involvement. Yet, given the increasing importance of nationally distributed cable services, just how realistic are such beliefs, just how valuable such channels? Cable appears to be following the same path as broadcasting, that is away from localism. With such a variety of national services (including the broadcast networks) proving so popular, can locally originated services really serve a useful purpose?

STANDALONE CHANNELS

Technically, standalone channels include all local-origination programming put out by an individual system operator, but in practice a distinction is made between services about local community issues or with community involvement (local-origination or community channels), and those consisting of films and similar commercially produced material packaged together by the system operator as a significant revenue-earning operation. Columbus's pay-per-view channels, for example, could be regarded as standalones, while its other locally produced community channels are considered to be local origination.

Most standalones are hold-overs from the period before systems bought TVROs to receive networked services. To most system operators the bother and cost of assembling a package of programmes, negotiating film rights, receiving and despatching tapes on time and inserting reasonable-quality continuity and promotional announcements between programmes is not worth the return, requiring as it does extra staff, equipment and administrative effort. A number, however, have become used to putting together their own channels and find it a financially profitable and personally rewarding exercise. Again the opportunity exists – this time for the system operator – to cut out the middleman distributor and thereby reduce operating costs. Certain systems, moreover, recognise a potential market within their particular area which no networked service satisfies. Colony Communications in Rhode Island, for example, have found a particular interest in a 'classics' (i.e. old) film channel amongst local college students and are able to sell sufficient advertising to support such a service. Group W's 'Uptown' in Manhattan similarly offers a cheap pay service with a strong special-interest and foreign-language film element to appeal to a number of low-income ethnic communities. Meanwhile, Gill Cable in San Francisco finds it considerably more profitable to programme two pay channels – one family, one R-rated – itself than to take HTN Plus and Eros or Playboy. Such locally packaged services are potentially more responsive to consumer demands and tastes and, it is hoped, can therefore promote higher than normal satisfaction and lower churn rates.

Such tailoring of a service to a particular market certainly seems to have been responsible for the considerable success of Group W's Z Channel, which it offers on a pay basis in its Los Angeles and other Southern Californian systems. Begun in 1976, it provides a mixture of current, classic and 'serious' films to a Californian audience with a particularly high interest and involvement in the film industry. Since February 1982 Group W has also sold HBO, Showtime and The Movie Channel on its systems; yet Z has held its audience of about 86,000 and continues to outsell any of the others. While its programming costs are higher per subscriber than average, reflecting its small size and particular mix of programming, Group W has managed to keep other operating expenses to a minimum. No effort is made to sell the service to other system operators, nor to attempt any major marketing within the systems which offer it, while the whole channel is put together and operated by a team of only five. Its success in California has tempted Group W to offer it nationally, but they have so far accepted that the local conditions responsible for that success are unlikely to be repeated elsewhere, particularly since it would be entering markets already dominated by HBO and others.

Given a sufficient market and an unsatisfied demand, it can clearly pay to offer tailor-made standalones. Consequently, many of the franchisees in the new and larger urban areas are now proposing to programme their own pay, pay-per-view and advertiser-supported services, believing that there is money to be made if such channels remain under their control. A possible development is the channel assembled in blocks from a variety of sources including the national cable networks, bought-in and locally produced programmes. In Portland, for example, the children's channel contains segments from Nickelodeon, Calliope (USA), the Canadian Galaxie service and local programmes. In this way the operator retains greater control over his output, reduces his per-subscriber payment for Nickelodeon and gains the opportunity to sell his own advertising in whatever quantity he is able. Those who believe that the economics of cable programming necessarily lead to entirely nationally networked services should consider the ability of the cable operator to pick and choose his programme sources and the advantages it gives him, not least in his power over the competing service providers.

200

Local origination (LO) or community channels are those containing programmes actually produced by the system operator or generally under his direction. Although they may rely extensively on the voluntary efforts of members of groups within the community, they differ from access channels in that both channel and programme policy remain under the editorial control of the system operator or a nominee (such as a community channel foundation). The operator is usually also responsible for financing the channel, and consequently many services of this kind contain advertising. In recent franchise contests LO and access channels have been areas where competing companies have sought to outbid each other in an effort to impress the city authorities with the many community benefits they would provide. While the average television viewer may be more interested in receiving HBO and CNN, there is no doubt that for the local officials who award franchises the words 'local', 'community' and 'access' have been powerful attractions. Consequently, it would not be overly cynical to suggest that, despite Rogers' consistent commitment to community programming, Portland's large number of local-origination services owe as much to an anxiety to win the franchise as to a belief that LO can be financially profitable. In fact, the approach taken in this instance is an extremely clever, sensible and interesting one, since only one channel relies entirely on locally originated community programmes. Other LO material, produced almost entirely by community bodies, such as sports associations, film societies and ethnic groups under the operator's guidance, are to be inserted into the appropriate 'theme' channels, which will be programmed mainly from national services. The result is a large number of channels with a cheaply produced local element, but not relying on the attractiveness of such local programming to draw either viewers or advertisers.

Elsewhere, dedicated community channels are more common, but evidence as to their popularity is mixed. Systems seeking extra channel space to add a new satellite-delivered network have un-doubtedly been tempted to 'piggy-back' it on to a relatively little used or watched local-origination service. In Audubon, New Jersey, New York Times Cable has introduced Daytime into its LO channel. Manhattan Cable similarly placed Nickelodeon, Daytime and ARTS on its LO service and now produces at most only a few hours of local programming each month. Even Rogers' Syracuse system carries MSN and Daytime on its LO channel during the day, although from 5 p.m. onwards each evening it is cleared for community program-mes. Once again the distinction between a channel and a service needs to be made; it is simply unrealistic to expect most cost-

201

conscious cable operators to create non-revenue-earning programmes unless either there is a minimum requirement imposed by the franchise or there are alternative benefits to be gained from doing so.

Having said that, such benefits may be more powerful than they might appear, while many operators are even beginning successfully to sell advertising on certain types of programme. It is easy to dismiss philanthropy as a motivation for commercially minded operators; yet in their effort to expand beyond signal relay they have been arguing cable's community potential for so long that there is a strong conviction and incentive to prove the validity of the case. Few, anyway, would dispute that, if community television does have a value, either cable or low-power TV are the means by which it will be realised. The recognition that community TV has a useful public relations value is also of vital importance. The community members most likely to appear on or come into contact with the LO service are also most likely to be its dignitaries, opinion leaders, organisers and others whose support is essential to the cable operator at refranchising time. As for the general public, just to see a television camera on the street or even to be interviewed for a vox pop item is to feel more involved in the dominant medium. LO is as important to the operator for the community peers who appear on it as for those who watch.

The ability of LO to attract new subscribers is also appreciated. People are drawn by the opportunity to watch family or friends on television or to see the local high street through a TV screen. The interest which the elderly have in the local community, for example, is a strong incentive to provide an LO service, whilst those from upper socio-economic groups who otherwise disdain cable and television also demonstrate a higher than normal taste for local news. The implications are clear for an operator seeking the marketing strategy most likely to increase penetration. A local origination channel containing regular local bulletins, or even CNN or SNC with a local news insert, could attract normally light viewers and senior citizens at least on to the basic tier, even though there has so far been a lower than average take-up of cable amongst the over-65s.

Cable is in any case better suited to truly local news than either existing television stations or local radio. A survey in 1976 showed that satellite towns and suburbs around American cities, relying on their broadcast stations for their own television, received a disproportionately small amount of news and information about themselves (W. C. Adams, 'Local Television News Coverage', *Journal of Broadcasting*, Spring 1980, pp. 253-65). The city of Pittsburgh contains less than one fifth of the total population included within its television market, which in all comprehends 698 distinct local government units (towns, suburbs etc.). Yet it received 40 per cent of all broadcast local news coverage. McKeesport, the largest nearby city with over 40,000 inhabitants, received only five minutes of news attention in five hours of local bulletins during one week. Bethel Park, the next largest suburb, was not even mentioned on two of the three stations studied and received an eighteen-second mention on the third. By contrast the majority of cable systems cover much smaller areas and usually a limited number of distinct communities. Even where several communities are served, newer systems are capable of selectively directing specific programmes to its individual subsections. In any case a local-origination channel gives time for separate bulletins to be transmitted to different communities and even in different languages if desired. Whether such community news bulletins, broadcast monthly, weekly or even daily, can really help to create a sense of community identity, as some believe, seems doubtful. But they may at least help to prevent local communities from being subsumed entirely within the all-enveloping metropolitan sprawl.

Early efforts at local news programming seem to have had encouraging results. Palmer Cablevision in Naples, Florida, has produced a nightly half-hour bulletin each weekday since 1970. Remarkably, a survey by Nielsen in 1980 revealed that it received a 23 per cent share of the audience amongst the system's subscribers at its 6 p.m. showing, an audience share exceeded only by the local NBC affiliate station. With four repeats of the same bulletin each evening, its total audience is likely to have been even larger. In this case, however, costs are shared with two local AM and FM radio stations owned by the same company. In Wichita and Kansas City the cable operator produces a similar but independent half-hour nightly bulletin which receives a 34 per cent share (25 per cent rating) of the system's 13,500 subscribers. The programme has also attracted advertisers and sells twelve thirty-second spots per half hour at $15-20 each. With a potential weekly income of $1,200 the operation still makes a loss, but in a larger system with more subscribers and therefore a higher spot charge such a bulletin could pay for itself. This stage has almost been reached in the Massachusetts town of New Bedford and Falls River, where Colony Communications has some 37,000 subscribers (53 per cent penetration). Its news team of six produces a daily bulletin for $1,800 (1980 figure) per week. Perhaps most interestingly it is transmitted both in English and in Portuguese, as the area has a high proportion of recent immigrants. Co-operation comes from the local Portuguese newspaper, with other news items being sent from Portugal by a government agency. Such a co-operative effort and an audience with such a particular and hitherto unserved need gives the cable operator a tremendous opportunity. Advertising space is fully booked and sales do cover the immediate weekly expenses, although hidden costs (studio overheads, etc.) mean that the profit only appears on the balance sheet and not in the bank. Nevertheless, if a local news service can break even or nearly do so, then its unseen revenue potential – the additional subscribers and goodwill it generates – undoubtedly makes it well worth the effort. That effort and expense can in any case be greatly reduced by a co-operative agreement between the system operator and the local newspaper or radio station, which will already have both news-gathering and advertising-sales resources. Indeed, many systems which do not yet have a televised news bulletin do provide or lease an automated channel to the local newspaper or papers to provide a local news text service. Moreover, where a news bulletin does not completely pay for itself some local authorities have agreed to a suitable adjustment to subscriber fees to make up the difference, thereby giving the operator an incentive to provide the community with its own television news. The only questionable point in the whole issue of local cable bulletins is the extent to which a system operator could abuse his local monopoly position.

The category of LO programming which is produced most widely and which receives the greatest interest is coverage of local sports. High-school football games, inter-school tournaments and college sports, for example, all have a guaranteed audience and appeal, as well as lending themselves to sponsorship by local businesses. Inevitably any parent whose child's school has a game televised has a strong incentive and is strongly pressed to take cable. Moreover, the audience for such televised school games is an attractive one to the advertiser. One system in Florida, for example, covering high-school football games on two channels in both English and Spanish in 1980, sold out its entire advertising space to Burger King.

Other LO programming varies from commercially imitative items – pop music, quiz shows, health programmes, etc. – to ones of direct relevance to the community, such as interviews with candidates for local government office. In Syracuse between five and ten hours of original material are produced every week and three to four repeats of each programme bring the total weekly output to some forty to fifty hours. A full-time programme staff of fifteen assists community groups and other volunteers making LO programmes, with the resultant quality variable but occasionally matching broadcast stations' local output. Rogers' belief in the need for a certain minimum standard and amount of LO programming, if it is to have a reasonable appeal, is reflected by the fact that it is spending up to two-thirds as much again on LO and access as is required under the franchise agreement, amounting to about fifty cents a month for each cable subscriber. Table IX gives examples of typical local-origination programmes.

In Columbus and its other franchises Warner Amex, not surpri-

TABLE IX

Typical local-origination programmes, Syracuse Cablesystems, 1982

Title	Frequency	Local bodies involved	Character
Cable Sports	Weekly	Local high schools, colleges	High-school, college and university sports (two hrs)
Doug Brode Review	Bi-monthly	–	Reviews of HBO/Cinemax films by local critic (thirty mins)
Silver Threads	Monthly	Metropolitan Commission on Ageing	Phone-in show on issues of senior-citizen concern (thirty mins)
Musicuse	Weekly	Local DJ	Local contemporary music, news and events
Syracuse Common Council Meetings	Bi-weekly	Syracuse Council	Complete coverage of Syracuse Common Council Meetings (two hrs)
For Medicinal Purposes Only	Monthly	Onondaga County Council on Alcoholism	Anonymous phone-in programme on drink and drug abuse
Educational Options	Six progs.	Regional Learning Service	Explaining adult-education opportunities in Syracuse
The Good News	Special	Holy Cross Church	Thanksgiving message from local church (thirty mins)
Choosing Child Care	Special	Onondaga County Child Care Council	A look at home day care (thirty mins)
The Second Annual Westcott Jazz Festival	Special	YMCA Media Unit	Two-hour coverage of local performers
805:Live	Special	Syracuse-Cablesystems initiated	Local band (sixty mins)

singly, sees Qube's interactivity as having considerable community potential. Qube enables viewers to certain programmes to respond to multiple option questions and to express preferences. In this way, Warner Amex argues, subscribers will more actively involve themselves in television, with viewing becoming more than a passive experience. The result will be a more direct identification between the community and its cable operator and also between different members of the community. The interactive facility can be employed for both serious and entertaining purposes, and on the government access channel it has even been used to determine the views of Qube subscribers (not, of course, representative of Columbus's population as a whole) on local-government issues. The concept of electronic polling by television, though much discussed, remains highly suspect as Warner Amex acknowledges, since it disenfranchises all non-cable subscribers.

As for interactive LO entertainment, the Columbus system produces about fifteen hours of original programmes each week, of which perhaps a third have an interactive element. Most of the latter have nothing intrinsically local about them and Warner Amex is now distributing such shows to its other Qube systems, thereby reducing its overall production costs. Subscribers in each city are able to make their own interactive response. Thus 'The Magic Touch' is a quiz show which allows viewers to compete against each other for prizes, while the daily 'Soap Scoop' recaps the events of television soap operas for those who missed an episode, then polls viewers on what they think will happen next or on who is the most popular character. Similarly 'Qube Games' allows viewers to play games ranging from poker to chess with its presenter, Flippo the Clown, while 'Qube Football Review' polls them on who is likely to win the following week's game.

Warner Amex's commitment both to Qube's potential and to LO programming of this kind is obvious, not least from its large programming staff of forty in Columbus and four advertising executives to sell space on the LO channel, ESPN, CNN and MTV. Nevertheless its LO operation continues to lose money, while the real value of interactive entertainment programmes remains at best unproven. A survey of Qube subscribers in 1982 showed that only 16 per cent of respondents used the interactive facility very or fairly often, 55 per cent 'not too often' and 29 per cent never. On the other hand, the local-origination channel as a whole, including sports coverage and the 'Columbus Alive' local affairs show transmitted four times a week, is watched regularly by 59 per cent, indicating a respectable degree of interest in such local programmes. This matches Syracuse Cablesystems' findings that 60 per cent of subscribers use its LO channel, with 15.3 per cent stating that they do so at least once a

206

week. Of the non-broadcast basic cable channels only CNN and ESPN have a wider usage (84 per cent and 70 per cent respectively). Most remarkably in Jacksonville, Florida, Area Cablevision claims that its local origination channel achieves a 6 per cent overall share of its 62,000 subscribers. This figure should, perhaps, be treated with caution; if accurate, however, it suggests an interest in local programming which few even of LO's advocates would have suspected.

These examples do suggest that there is a demand for at least certain types of community programme and that in larger systems of over 50,000 subscribers some items – local news and sports coverage – could even be financially self-supporting from advertising sales (although a high number of advertising minutes per hour are likely to be necessary). The question arises as to whether system operators should in fact attempt to finance their LO channels entirely from advertising. There is a danger that if the need to cover costs becomes an absolute requirement this will have a major limiting effect upon the types of programme it is possible to produce. Even at this level, where a programme can be made for $1-200, the problem of a minimum audience applies. A local sports game, a news bulletin or even a local quiz show or pop group may draw a sufficient audience to attract advertisers at adequate advertising rates, but a programme on library services or childcare in a particular part of the system area is much less likely to do so. At this low level, moreover, the costs and likelihood of statistical error in calculating audience sizes and hence advertising rates make the attempt to do so doubtful, although this problem would be eliminated in an interactive system where the operator could discover exactly how many homes were switched to each channel at any one moment.

Even at a local level, therefore, it is possible for the spectre of audience maximisation to arise, with the LO channel attempting more to emulate a local commercial radio or television station than to serve small groups within the community. The fear is that, as making money becomes more important to the LO operation, so much of the creativity and freedom and sheer fun that now exists will disappear. This is why many LO advocates, and even a few cable operators themselves, do not believe such a channel should carry advertising or, if it does so, be expected to rely entirely upon it for revenue. Most local programming is still financed from the basic cable subscription. A standing commitment by the operator to put a certain amount of that subscription into LO programmes can help to ensure that programme decisions continue to be made on criteria other than whether they can be self-supporting. At the same time, an element of truly local advertising could itself be regarded as a useful community service.

The lesson seems to be that if too much is not expected of a locally originated community channel then it can fulfil a worthwhile function for which there does seem to be a reasonable demand. Indeed, only a few hours of original programming each week can produce a valuable service. While an LO programme may not be attractive enough for people to make a premeditated decision to watch at a particular time, in preference to the richer fare on other channels, multiple repeats can build a respectable cumulative audience. Indeed, LO is one area where an established schedule of repeats is both accepted and welcomed by the viewer. Moreover, where the 'facilitator' approach is used – in other words where a relatively small LO staff of five to fifteen is employed to facilitate or help the community in producing programmes itself – the cost to the operator can be kept relatively low. The operating costs of Syracuse Cablesystems' local origination and access programming combined was $177,000 in 1982 and about $205,000 in 1983.

In any consideration of community channels, however, one point must be kept in mind: not even in the most mature system does cable reach every member of the community. In most barely half are connected. An LO cable channel can only serve the *cabled* community; it is a sad irony therefore that many of those who would benefit most from such a service – the old, the less well off, the socially disadvantaged and the 'information-poor' – are just those who are least likely to receive it.

ACCESS CHANNELS

The objectives which lie behind local origination date back to early FCC policy on localism in broadcasting. Those at the heart of access find their origin in the First Amendment to the American Constitution, the concept of the citizen's right freely to address his fellow men. Before the plethora of satellite services appeared, most cable systems, even those with limited capacity, had spare channel space. As we saw earlier, this opportunity to give the individual access to the airwaves was taken up by the FCC in 1972, when it made such channels a statutory requirement for systems above a certain size. Subsequently, access requirements exceeding even the FCC's stipulated minimum became a common feature of franchise contests and today some of the largest systems are offering up to thirty access channels of various kinds.

As with local origination such extensive allocation of system capacity (over 20 per cent of subscriber channels, in Boston's case) does not necessarily indicate a strong belief in the citizen's right to be heard. Once again, winning the franchise is all-important, and it remains relatively inexpensive to give away twenty channels as part of a franchise requirement when over eighty remain, channels for

208

which in any case there is no other programming. For the slightly older thirty to thirty-five channel systems, however, the loss of two or three for access purposes is rather more of an irritation, particularly where the public does not use them. The idea of renouncing all claim to or control of what is in essence their physical property – some fifteen to thirty megaherz of cable capacity – is anathema to many operators. Access requirements, they argue, are tantamount to government regulation of programme content and hence violate their own property and First Amendment rights as electronic publishers. Such reasoning was successful in overturning the FCC's access rules in 1979, although local and state powers to impose such requirements remain.

Broadly speaking, there are three categories of access channel – public, dedicated (government, education, etc.) and leased access. Public gives anyone the opportunity to appear and speak their mind or 'do their own thing', at no charge other than a possible low rental of studio time. Advertising, or any such attempt by the programme maker or operator to make money on this channel, is forbidden. With leased access, on the other hand, the cable operator is permitted to sell channel space on a commercial, but still on a first-come-first-served basis. In New York costs are about $75-100 an hour. The user is then allowed to sell advertising spots during the course of the programme in order to try to recoup costs. The objective of leased access is to ensure that the system operator cannot use his monopoly power to deprive a programme producer of all access to his market. Many within the industry, however, see it as the thin end of the common-carrier wedge, challenging their right to determine the messages transmitted on their systems and so threatening to remove the crucial distinction between themselves and the telephone companies. They argue that DBS, MDS and other technologies will shortly be competing with them and providing alternative outlets for programming, so making compulsory leased access unnecessary. In any case the idea has so far had little success. Advertisers are reluctant enough to advertise on the mainstream cable services, so that the occasional programme which appears on leased access receives little support. Only in Manhattan is the leased access channel much used, and then largely for late-night pornographic shows such as 'Ugly George' and 'Video Blue', supported by advertising for porn shops, massage parlours, sex clubs and escort agencies.

The two most common dedicated access channels are for local government and educational programming. The government channel can be used for both internal and external communication – between government and citizens, or between different local government departments. Council meetings can be televised, public announcements on road alterations, health care and other local government issues made – usually on a rolling-text 'bulletin board' – and interviews held with local politicians. In Columbus several municipalities do regular monthly programmes for their own area, such as 'Upper Arlington Today' and 'The Gehana Town Meeting'. For internal use, municipal training programmes can be televised. Firemen can watch nationally produced firefighter-training films which can be shown repeatedly for different shifts, new recruits and refresher courses, although only where a programme can be addressed to specific buildings such as fire stations can sensitive material be transmitted. A video recorder and videotape library in each training centre might do the same job, but, given the existence of government channels in many systems, it makes more sense to use what is essentially a centralised audio-visual facility.

Educational channels have similar functions, although in practice external use predominates over internal or inter-school programmes. Education channels are used for everything from further education courses to televised school board and parent association meetings. Where a system serves a university town, however, the education channel has also been used to extend the reach of the university's own closed-circuit television and audio-visual system. Indeed, in some areas more than one education channel has proved necessary. Portland has two from the outset, with provision for a further two when needed.

Some new systems have a wide spectrum of dedicated access services, in addition to education and local government, offering many of the same benefits as Portland's theme channels. Thus the elderly know that there is a senior citizens' access channel which they can appear on and watch, while the black community is able to programme a channel to suit itself. In Boston programmes from Italy may be provided in this way to serve the Italian community. In Manhattan two or three hours each evening is given over to the Chinese community and is programmed by a group called Asian Cine-vision, partly with locally produced items but largely with material bought in from Hong Kong. Similarly, Puerto Rican and Japanese programmes are shown occasionally. To many Chinese-Americans and others who do not speak English this is the only television service of any value, while for the cable operator it means additional subscribers, despite the fact that it is not profitable for him to bother to provide programmes himself. For a minority group which can afford to buy or produce material, free access of this kind provides the one opportunity to organise a service for itself, albeit on a tiny scale. On the other hand, there is a danger that such opportunities will only further promote the fragmentation of society and reduce any incentive amongst ethnic minorities to learn English. If used in this way access, and particularly dedicated access channels, can lead to ghetto broadcasting. This is the very opposite of what many see as a primary objective of public access, namely to bring together on one channel the multifarious minority groups and opinionated individuals who between them constitute one community.

210

In many systems the parallel aims of access and local origination have resulted in the practical distinction between them becoming decidedly blurred. To operators seeking to provide LO programmes of real interest to the community, and to do so as cheaply as possible, it is an obvious move to tap the interest and talent of local volunteers who might otherwise have turned their attention to public access. Many LO channels also cover local government meetings (as in Syracuse), thereby removing a primary function of any government access channel. In some cases the operator even relinquishes his responsibility over local origination and allows the community to run the channel itself. Conversely, most operators are required by their franchise terms to facilitate the production of access programmes by providing studios, equipment, training courses and technical assistance. Again, some actually manage the public access channels themselves; others hand this task over either to the city authorities or to a non-profitmaking access and community foundation, as in Boston.

Such a close relationship between LO and access means that on occasion the latter can become something of an overflow channel. What distinguishes it, however, is the right of anyone to appear, unconstrained by any form of editorial policy or censorship by the system operator. Moreover, public access, unlike local origination, is not bound by the FCC's fairness and equal opportunity rules, so that there is no need for political statements to be balanced against each other. The only restrictions are the State laws on slander and obscenity, and even here State definitions of obscenity vary widely. The result is that in some states and cities, particularly New York, access has gained a bad reputation as the 'anything-goes' channel. Even where exhibitionism takes forms other than pornographic, it can result in the most unwatchable programmes being shown, as individuals with little or no talent play at being a chat-show host, singer, phone-in compere, or homespun philosopher. Access means access to all, and it is not for one member of the community to determine whether or not another should appear.

Consequently, public access by its very nature is a lucky dip of worthless and worthwhile, interesting and excruciating and occasionally pornographic. New York's experience in this last respect, it should be said, is somewhat out of the ordinary, just as is New York itself. Naturally, many subscribers regard items as obscene or objectionable. Others consider many of the individual efforts at emulating network television to be cases of 'video vanity'. More of a problem is the danger that access may come to be dominated not just by a few exhibitionists but by one or two particularly vociferous minorities, whose regular appearance is out of all proportion to their position within the community. Without imposing censorship, it is evidently essential to encourage as much diversity of use as possible.

211

Developed with care, access can undoubtedly become a service of value. That value cannot, however, be judged purely in terms of its audience. Several years of experience in the United States has only confirmed that fact that audiences are for the most part minimal, with familiarity yet to breed interest. Rather, the value of access lies in the experiences it gives those who make access programmes. The very considerable effort required to plan, prepare and work together to produce a programme on an issue of shared concern can be and has proved immensely rewarding. For some it arouses a new sense of commitment and fellowship, while for others it can stimulate a reassessment of previously held assumptions. It can also end in frustration, exasperation and failure, for like any attempt at teamwork the experience can be either beneficial or disastrous. Equally, the end result can vary from the mediocre to the semi-professional. Much is simply dreadful, but it would be wrong because of the dismal efforts of some untrained access users to be dismissive of the whole.

Access also provides a useful outlet for student film-makers, amateur film societies and video artists whose work makes up in effort and in some cases craftmanship what it lacks in costly professional polish. For such groups and individuals, as for other minorities, it is only because there is a channel whose content is not governed by the operator's need to make a profit, only because there is an outlet through which to feed material, that they are able to offer their work to a wider audience. Access, perhaps, is where true narrowcasting becomes possible, as minority groups and individuals are given the opportunity to create or buy and transmit programmes in which they are interested.

None of this, however, is possible without money or efficient organisation. Access studios have to be equipped and maintained, tapes bought, staff paid for. It costs money to operate a channel, even if most of the programming is produced on a shoestring and financed by the makers. Nor can the system operator be expected to bear more than a proportion of the costs of access. Where he is expected to do so and where a fixed sum is not agreed, the natural tendency on his part is to discourage access in order to minimise his costs and responsibilities. It has therefore become normal practice for a proportion of the franchise fee, which most local authorities charge operators, to be allocated to access operating costs. Indeed, in recent franchise contests there has also been a tendency for the competing applicants to offer a further access fee – in Boston's case 5 per cent of gross annual revenue – as an additional lure to gain the franchise. An element of this is sometimes set aside as a materials and programme support fund, to provide small grants ($50-100) to access users who can demonstrate a need for such assistance.

Most public access, therefore, is actually paid for by subscribers, although this is preferable to relying upon local authority grants. There

212

the danger is of political influence by local politicians through financial control. Educational and government channels, however, are commonly financed from the educational authority and local government purses. As a result, many channels allocated for government and educational use remain unused, as the relevant authority cannot afford the capital costs of equipping studios in schools or government buildings (these being generally regarded as not the system operator's responsibility). A survey in 1980 discovered that where government channels were in use they required an annual budget of anywhere from $18,000 (in East Lansing, Michigan) to $130,000 (in Tulsa, Oklahoma), some of which did come from franchise fees. Equally, they needed between two and four full-time staff, employed by the local authority itself, although programming for most of the day consisted of a rolling-text bulletin board, with only two to three hours of live or video material each night.

As for public access, what is essential in all cases, if it is to work properly, is someone to co-ordinate the channel's use and to encourage and assist those who would not normally consider using it. Experience has shown that a high proportion of individuals and groups are dissuaded by the apparent complexity of making a programme themselves. A continuing failure to regard television as a tool for public communication, a lack of planning skills or dedication in preparing items, and above all a simple ignorance about public access rights have all been reasons why in many systems these channels have not been used as much as was hoped. In particular, studies in both the USA and Canada, whose experience in this respect are similar, have revealed the real importance of a full-time access co-ordinator and ideally a dedicated 'facilitator' group, comprising cable staff and trained volunteers. A survey in Toronto in 1977 demonstrated that quite the most important factors in persuading groups and individuals to make a programme were personal contact with those who had already done so and direct influence by members of the cable company's community programming staff. It is this face-to-face community relations work which is essential; indeed, other promotional devices such as advertising and leaflets are much less successful at breaking down traditional caution and doubts.

This same study and another by the CRTC in 1978 also discovered a heavy reliance upon the cable operator or facilitator group for both equipment and production assistance, a reliance which, perhaps surprisingly, did not decline as people became more used to programme making. It would seem that, contrary to the belief that most access users are primarily interested in showing off or in playing at being television producers or personalities, the majority wish to use it as any other medium, to put across a message. It is that which draws them rather than the mechanics of programme making. Not surprisingly, therefore, the most widely acclaimed access and community efforts are those which bring together people trained or interested in the mechanics of production with others who simply wish to use television to make a point. One such is in Reading, Pennsylvania, where the system operator, ATC, has handed the access channel over to the non-profitmaking Berks Community TV group. Drawing on funds from the city, county, local foundations, private corporations (which receive tax relief) and individual donations, the group contains both full-time and voluntary technical and co-ordinating staff. As a result, it is able to produce several hours of programming every day, with a particular emphasis on the elderly of the community.

Access, like community channels, can fulfil a useful purpose, although not necessarily in the traditional sense of television entertainment or information. The value of public access in particular lies in the opportunities it gives programme makers and in its impact on individuals and groups as much as on the community. For minorities not otherwise served by television, it can provide the one real opportunity for true narrowcast programming, even if on a very small scale. Not least simply the fact that such a channel is available is important. It can be a melting pot in which all the ideas, viewpoints and reactive elements within the community can be brought together and a safety valve by which individuals are able to let off steam. But if the concept of access is to be successfully realised, then much more than just channel space, studios and video equipment are needed. To work well it requires an assured source of finance, a co-ordinating body and above all a long-term commitment by both the operator and the community. Where that exists the access channel can discover an identity of its own and a worthwhile role. Where it is absent the end result is likely only to provide further fuel for critics who consider the whole idea a wasteful and pointless exercise.

12 Enhanced and Business Uses

Technically there is no question that two-way cable can provide a whole host of non-video services, some requiring an active response from the cable subscriber, others passively monitoring certain functions within the subscriber's home. Of the latter perhaps the most talked about is cable's ability to provide an advanced form of emergency and security service. Burglar and fire-alarm sensors in the house can be monitored every few seconds by the cable operator's headend computer, which automatically alerts the relevant emergency service if it observes anything wrong. A third element to this alarm system is a medical alert button, which can be used to summon immediate assistance if required. In a similar fashion, two-way cable can be used by the local utility companies to read and monitor gas, water and electricity meters automatically, as well as general energy consumption within an area, allowing production of electricity in particular to be matched to its use much more accurately than hitherto, with potentially enormous savings.

Among the two-way services in which the subscriber is actively involved are teleshopping and telebanking. Teleshopping allows the customer to request information on a variety of products and potentially to view certain items on the screen. In some cases it may even be possible to have them demonstrated. Goods can then be ordered via a direct-response keypad, with the entry of an access or code number allowing the transaction to be directly debited from the purchaser's bank account. Similarly, telebanking, or 'electronic funds transfer', allows the subscriber to check his or her bank balance, pay bills and transfer money between accounts, all via cable. A number of security devices are being developed to prevent unauthorised access to personal accounts.

Such uses for cable are essentially specific applications of videotex or viewdata technology, which allows the subscriber to call up information from one or a variety of databases. A number of companies, particularly the large publishing houses, are now developing large databases for use via cable or telephone line, just as Prestel and other videotex services now operate in Britain. By this means, a wealth of information becomes available to subscribers, including such immediately useful details as train times, aeroplane seat availability, theatre bookings and the daily news, with the possibility of a hard-copy printer in the home to copy items which the subscriber wishes to peruse at greater length or leisure. The simpler one-way technology of broadcast teletext is similarly just being introduced in the United States, and a few companies are extending its application to cable where the space available. makes possible a much larger information capacity and a quicker average response rate than can be achieved over the air. Meanwhile, the videogame boom is also to be tapped, with various companies developing cabled videogame systems. Turning to business and institutional use, many systems now include institutional networks to interconnect private businesses, separate units of individual companies, public buildings, schools, government offices, hospitals and other institutions, allowing data transfer, electronic mail, teleconferencing and even remote 'tele-medicine diagnosis'.

All this and more is now possible. Yet it does not mean, because the technology and system capacity exists, that every one of these services is readily available, worth having, economically viable or wanted. Although the construction of new systems will increase their availability, or at least the proportion of systems technically capable of offering them (an important distinction), the same proviso must be made here as earlier. Some 40 per cent of cable subscribers still have access to only twenty channels or fewer. Barely 3 per cent are on even one-way addressable systems and fewer than 1 per cent on fully interactive, two-way addressable. It is still early days and few companies have any hard evidence as to the likely interest in or prospects for the majority of such offerings. Major teething problems remain, while only in a few cases has development got beyond the experimental stage. As with access channels, an operator's commitment to provide teleshopping or information services may still owe as much to the pressures of the franchise contest as to any real certainty about their viability in the short or medium term. If any become more of a long-term liability than a reasonable prospect, there is every likelihood that cable companies will abandon them until a more propitious time. Even Warner Amex, the company most firmly committed to interactivity, is keenly aware of its high cost. In an ominous statement in May 1983, Warner Amex's chief executive, Drew Lewis, announced that the company could not recoup its costs in the new and most advanced Pittsburgh system, even in the course of the full fifteen-year franchise: 'We've got to get costs down and get rid of things that have no economic value' (Quoted in *Screen International*, 6 June 1983, p. 15). Already a number of surveys have revealed a continuing lack of consumer interest in videotex and other facilities, although this must reflect in part an ignorance of what is involved and a resistance to the new and unknown.

What is clear is that the capital cost involved in the headend, distribution system and home terminal for most of these services is such that for some at least it may be a case of succeeding together or not at all: costs for the interactive technology, which would be prohibitive if only one service were involved, become more acceptable if they are shared across several, including pay-per-view. Since it is unlikely that many subscribers will take every available enhanced facility, what is required is a relatively large total subscriber count, so that limited consumer demand for each may in the aggregate justify the installation of interactive plant.

The one interactive service which is undoubtedly on the verge of becoming a profitable and fully commercial business in the United States is the emergency alarm system. By April 1983 over seventy cable systems offered security, fire and medical alert services, although the total national take-up was probably still under 20,000 homes. Nevertheless, the potential market is immense and the need increasingly apparent to the average home-owner. According to the FBI, there is now a burglary every seven seconds in the USA. In 90 per cent of these entry is gained through a door and in 8 per cent through a ground-floor window. Consequently, security protection of such entrances, or a sensor which detects unexpected movement and reports it to a central monitoring station, could be of considerable value. Such devices have, of course, long been available from private security companies, using the telephone line to alert the relevant service. Nevertheless, these companies still protect only 2 per cent of all residential properties, concentrating predominantly on the industrial and business market. The high cost of installation ($1,000-3,000) and monthly charges of $17-35 have naturally been offputting to all but the wealthiest households.

Cable companies, by contrast, should be able to offer a cheaper service because they do not pay high phone-line tariffs. By offering installation charges at or below cost they can undercut conventional alarm systems, while in most cases also offering a superior service. For, unless the conventional security companies use an even more expensive dedicated telephone line system, they are unable to offer the constant central monitoring facility. A cut telephone line effectively disarms them. By contrast, a cable system monitors each home terminal every four to six seconds. Advanced systems such as that in Syracuse have an automatic telephone check procedure, ringing the home where an alarm has sounded to confirm that there is a genuine emergency. If it is a false alarm, this saves a wasted visit by the emergency services. If there is no response to this check, they are despatched immediately. Such systems can also provide the relevant emergency service instantly with essential information about a house where an alarm has just been recorded. Its central computer can hold details of number of occupants, medical

217

history (where appropriate), house plan, location of nearest fire hydrants, telephone numbers of friends and relatives and any other information which the subscriber is prepared to give in advance. (The possible threat to personal privacy involved is the other side to this coin.) But perhaps the cable operator's biggest advantage is the contact he already has with his subscribers, who are in any case already used to the idea of paying monthly subscriptions for cable services. Emergency alarms become just another tier of service, rather than a totally new financial commitment.

At present opinion is divided as to whether financially it is more sensible for a system operator to develop and market alarm systems himself or to collaborate with a specialist cable security company. Smaller operators, or those already fully occupied in developing the more traditional cable services, may well find it easier to hand the management and marketing of alarm systems over to a separate entity such as Smith Cable Security or the leading security hardware and service company Tocom. Warner Amex, however, have established a separate business, Warner Amex Security Systems, to run the service, while Syracuse Cablesystems are keeping it in-house.

Cable security is still a young business and early systems have had serious technical problems. Indeed, many have had to use telephone lines for the return signal until the problems can be solved. False alarms caused by anything from signal noise to ants crawling into sensors are an inevitable concern and have led to some reluctance on the part of police and fire officials to support devices which might make enormous extra demands on their manpower. Many consider the false alarm problem as too high a price for the emergency services (and therefore the local tax-paying community) to pay, and some cable engineers have even questioned whether it will ever be possible to overcome noise interference economically. However, as cable security matures, so more evidence is becoming available; in particular a number of surveys in The Woodlands (Texas), Columbus and Syracuse are beginning to provide positive information as to the business's problems and potential.

In The Woodlands a new housing development was completely cabled in the mid-70s, with Tocom fire sensors, security and medical buttons being installed as standard. After three years no cabled home had suffered fire damage in excess of $10,000, while in 1977 the total cost of fires in the development was only $40,000, certainly significantly lower than normal for a community of some 4,500 homes, Moreover, there were no successful burglaries from subscribing homes during the first two years, while there were twelve in ones which did not subscribe. Perhaps most significant of all, insurance companies have accepted the advantages of the system by giving reductions on insurance premiums of between 15 and 36 per cent. Since this saving is close to the monthly charge for taking the service there is clearly a strong incentive to do so.

218

Warner Amex have also been offering alarm services in Columbus since December 1979 and claimed over 5,000 subscribers by the beginning of 1983. Rather interestingly, the security service, being a separate operation, is marketed outside the franchise also, and over half of its subscribers are beyond the Qube area, being served by telephone line. These figures therefore indicate that after three years it had attracted about 2 per cent of the 120,000 homes within the system area, or 4 per cent of cable subscribers (there is, of course, no reason why a home which takes alarm services should necessarily be interested in cable television, and even in the cabled area they are sold separately).

This apparently low interest in cable security reflects the fact that, despite being less expensive than conventional security systems, it is still not cheap. The average installation cost is $1,250 and the monthly charge $16.50-$18.50. The service is still far from being one for the average home, although once again insurance companies give reductions on home insurance of 12-37 per cent for security subscribers. Interestingly, the service once taken is highly valued, and has a churn rate of under 1 per cent a month.

Even though the subscription level is still low, the operation is almost certainly profitable. As a fixed-cost business, cable security depends less on percentage penetration than on absolute numbers, with 2-3,000 generally regarded as the break-even point. Once that has been reached, profit on subsequent revenues is probably above 50 per cent. What this means, however, is that Columbus would still not be profitable if Warner Amex had not been able to poach on its neighbours' territory. In general, systems will either have to be larger or the percentage penetration higher if cable alarm services are to make money. Yet according to industry analyst Paul Kagan, only Columbus had more than 1,500 security subscribers by July 1982 and only Park Cities in Texas had reached a 5 per cent penetration (730 out of 13,500 homes passed).

Again it must be emphasised that all these operations are in their early stages and few would have expected to break even within three years of starting. At Syracuse, however, a different approach is being taken which may encourage wider interest. With the conscious objective of marketing a low-cost system, Syracuse Cablesystems are offering fire, medical and burglar alarms separately. Consequently, installation costs for fire or medical alerts alone begin at the not unreasonable level of $130, with a monthly charge of $7.95. The two together still cost only $169 and $8.95 monthly. The inclusion of intrusion sensors brings the total price to $550 installation and $15 a month, still well below the cost of systems elsewhere. Annual operating costs for the service are some $450,000, requiring about 3,500 subscribers to the various tiers in order to break even (most subscribers to alarm services, it is anticipated, will take fire and medical alert only, at least initially). The company expects to reach this figure, amounting to 5 per cent of the 68,000 homes passed, by the fifth year of operation, and to retire its accumulated deficit in the sixth.

As a preliminary to this full-scale commitment, a 1,000-home experiment was conducted during 1981 and 1982. In one year the Syracuse fire department received 1,705 alarm calls via the system, of which 86 per cent were discovered immediately to be false by the automatic procedure of ringing the house in question. In 14 per cent of cases fire vehicles were despatched and 5 per cent (eighty-five) were found to be genuine fires. The fire service agreed that because of the latter lives were saved and damage minimised. Indeed, there were no major losses in protected homes while several unprotected ones were destroyed. The police department similarly received 464 alarm calls of which eighty-four were genuine. In the majority of false alarms a telephone call prevented the need to send a police car itself. Appendix II contains two examples of the system in operation.

The 95 per cent false fire alarm rate would seem to confirm initial fears about the new demands on manpower. According to an independent study of the experiment, however, no extra equipment or manpower would be required even when the system was offered throughout the city. Existing emergency services could cope even with increased demand as early response to fires would make it very much easier, quicker and cheaper to deal with each. Indeed, for most incidents, small, two-man fire crews might be sufficient. As in The Woodlands and Columbus, insurance companies are already offering lower premiums to protected houses.

As an additional business for larger cable systems, the prospects for alarm services seem fair, justifying the capital costs involved. Nor does evidence so far suggest that the result will be an unacceptable burden upon the emergency services. Firstly, early response to emergencies might allow a restructuring of the fire service, for example, into smaller units spread evenly throughout the community. Secondly, even at the prices being offered in Syracuse, it is too early to suggest that alarm services could become a standard utility in every home. Even Cablevision in Boston do not believe that more than 7 per cent of homes passed will take it in 1993, ten years after it is first offered. At this level it is likely to contribute some $3.5 million to the system's revenue, a small but useful 4 per cent of the total. The worth of the service in terms of lives and property saved is clear, and once installed insurance savings should largely compensate for the cost. Nevertheless, for the time being it remains a service for those more wealthy subscribers who can pay, despite the fact that by far the majority of fires and burglaries occur in low-income housing, with the medical alert button being most needed by the elderly who are least able to afford it. If in the long term cable alarms actually reduce the burden on the community's emergency services, it may prove economically sensible as well as socially commendable for the community itself to pay for universal connection, even amongst its poorest members. That, however, is still a very distant and unlikely prospect.

With videogames a $5.6 billion industry in the United States in 1981, including $600 million in home games, it was inevitable that games companies should seek to exploit this market further via cable. Playcable, a joint venture between the videogames company Mattel and General Instrument, is now available to 650,000 cable subscribers on thirteen systems, being transmitted as a one-way service via a small portion of each system's FM radio spectrum. It provides twenty games a month in rotation for about $12, and an annual total of forty, the signal being picked up by a Mattel Intellivision games console which the subscriber has to purchase in advance. Mattel currently has about 17 per cent of the videogames market in the USA, so that many homes already possess this unit. Nevertheless, its high cost of about $200 has been blamed for the very low response since the service started in 1981. About 3 per cent of homes to which the service is available actually took it by March 1983, less than 20,000 in all.

A rival service called The Games Network avoids this problem by leasing its console to the subscriber. Even so a modem to connect it to the cable costs the subscriber $50, while the monthly charge is a hefty $14. To succeed The Games Network is said to require at least 500,000 subscribers, or 10 per cent of the 5 million connected to systems which have agreed so far to carry it. Its console, like Mattel's, can be upgraded to a more complex home computer with a larger memory, allowing additional services to be offered in due course. Moreover, it hopes to offer games by a wide variety of manufacturers, so that individuals are more likely to take the cable service than to buy a particular console which can only accept the cartridges of one company.

At present the economics of cabled videogames seem dubious. The logic behind them is that, with games cartridges costing at least $28, videogame addicts will do better to pay $12-14 each month for a wider selection than they could otherwise afford. The well-developed practices of cartridge swapping and duplicating are not, however, taken into account; nor are suggestions that the videogames boom may be past its peak, with Atari's sales dropping drastically in 1982. To the cable operator such a service has the benefits that it does not occupy a full channel nor require expensive two-way technology. As such, therefore, it may be worthwhile as an additional attraction to draw new subscribers. Indeed, a survey done by Cable Marketing Management in 1981 suggested that 9 per cent of passed homes which did not subscribe to cable might do so if a games channel were available. In practice, however, Playcable has failed to meet such expectations, while it is too early to judge how The Games Channel, which has only just started, has been received.

Despite the fact that Warner owns Atari, Warner Amex does not yet offer a videogames channel. As part of a complete videotex service on two-way cable, however, videogames do have additional potential. Interactivity allows subscribers to compete with each other and some games are even being devised which involve up to 100 participants at the same time. Co-ordinated by the headend computer and utilising far better graphics than are currently possible in home videogames, the overall effect should be stunning. Equally, so should be such a service's costs and complexities, so that for most it seems likely to remain part of a broader videotex package.

CABLE VIDEOTEX, SHOPPING AND BANKING

Any discussion of videotex needs to start with a definition. Videotex or viewdata is a fully interactive, wired system for obtaining information from or feeding it to a remote database, usually using either a domestic computer or a television set and keypad as the home terminal. The central database in such a system can in its turn be connected to other computers, allowing subscribers to 'talk' with, gather data from and give instructions to a whole host of services, including general and specialised information providers (newspapers, press agencies, stockbrokers, publishers, libraries, etc.), banks, mail order companies, other retail outlets, theatre booking offices, travel agents, estate agents and many more. The first and best known videotex service was British Telecom's Prestel, and, with France, Canada and Japan introducing their own Télétel, Telidon and Captain systems, the USA has until recently appeared to lag behind. Almost all of the current American experiments employ one or other of these foreign systems.

Consequently, the prospects for videotex are as uncertain in the United States as they are in the UK and elsewhere. Indeed, the failure of Prestel to attract significant domestic interest in Britain is commonly cited in America as an example of the likely problems. The continuing indecision over an agreed technical standard has also led both hardware and service providers to hesitate before committing the enormous sums involved. Nevertheless, the number of major corporations investigating and experimenting with videotex now matches those who have gone into cable itself. So far the majority of such services and experiments have been undertaken using the telephone line as the carrier, while almost all those which are working on a fully commercial basis are aimed primarily at business users. Naturally AT & T is heavily involved and has been conducting a videotex pilot scheme for 150 domestic consumers in Coral Gables, Florida, since 1980, in conjunction with the major publishing house Knight Ridder. The latter alone has put some $34 million into the scheme in four years and is now expanding it into a commercial service to reach 5,000 homes. AT & T is involved in a similar experiment with CBS in Ridgewood, New Jersey, although in neither this nor the earlier project has any charge been made for the service. Other experiments in information, home banking and shopping using the telephone line are being conducted by the Chase Manhattan Bank, Citibank, First Interstate Bank, Times Mirror and many others. Meanwhile, the various commercial databases available nationally, again via the telephone line, include Dow Jones News Retrieval, CompuServe (owned by the Chicago Tribune company of H. & R. Block), The Source (Readers Digest) and several hundred much smaller and more specialised services. Of the latter one of the best known is Lexis, by Mead Data Central, an invaluable case-reference source for the legal profession. All the major publishing houses are looking to see how they can become involved in a technology which seems certain to have profound implications for the gathering and distribution of information and hence for newspapers and publishing generally. The Hearst organisation, slow off the mark by comparison with Time Inc., Dow Jones and others, is analysing the enormous information resources of its army of over 100 publications, with the intention of creating and marketing two or three broad and specialised databanks. Dow Jones alone already offers over a dozen specialised databases directed to particular target users and intends to add a further fifty over the next two or three years

None of these services is cheap. CompuServe and Readers Digest's The Source charge by time used, at about $20-22 an hour during business hours and $5 an hour (8 cents a minute) in the evenings and at weekends. This is in addition to any telephone charges. The Dow Jones News Retrieval costs $22-60 a month depending on the level of service taken. The rates for the expanded AT & T/Knight Ridder project in Florida are likely to be set at a minimum of $25 a month to the subscriber, although to be profitable the cost has been estimated at between $35 and $60 each. The difference, therefore, will have to be found from sales of advertising and charges to service providers such as banks, travel agents and retailers. To receive the service in the first place, moreover, a subscriber will have to buy a terminal and modem, expected to cost about $600. Similarly, the CBS/AT & T experiment anticipates a subscriber charge of $20-30 a month if and when it becomes a commercial operation, with a further $20-30 for each subscriber from advertising and payments by transactional service providers.

To the cable industry an important question is what part it can play, competing as it would be with telephone delivered videotex. To the videotex operator and connected database providers the telephone's big advantage is its high penetration of homes, particularly in comparison to the still negligible reach of two-way cable and its much lower penetration even in areas where it is available. The switched structure and dedicated character of the telephone line is also potentially better suited to personal videotex services and more secure than the tree and branch structure used in almost all American cable systems. This is certainly an important consideration for banking services. It is already apparent that the telephone-based/videotex experiments are quite well advanced, while there is very little experience of cabled videotex. At present, therefore, telephone-based systems appear to have significant advantages.

On the other hand, cable's much greater bandwidth enables more information to be transmitted in a shorter time. In theory, at least, it could also be cheaper because of the lower regulatory constraints upon it. Moreover, it allows both better-quality graphics and potentially full-motion video, although this would require at least one video channel to be allocated to the service. By contrast, telephone-delivered information is limited to more slowly delivered still pictures or relatively crude graphic representations. For certain services, particularly home shopping, this could make a major difference, since the number of items which a consumer is prepared to buy sight unseen is limited to those whose nature is already known. Only cable could provide some of the more advanced services talked about, such as videotex details of houses for sale in a particular area, followed by a full video tour of ones in which the subscriber is interested.

Equally important is the fact that videotex completely ties up a telephone line while it is in use and if used by large numbers simultaneously could clog the entire telephone system. Unless the subscriber pays yet more for a second line to be brought in, he is effectively cut off from outside callers while using it. A videotex experiment in Columbus in 1980 discovered that over half of those involved disliked this tying up of their phone, whilst only 11 per cent objected to its also using the television. A television programme lost was 'just television', and a conscious consumer decision. In any case, the increasing incidence of multiple-TV-set homes made such a loss less likely. A missed incoming phone call, however, was a more personal loss and an irritation.

The potential of cable for videotex use is being seriously investigated by a number of companies, most of whom are also preparing to offer it on a commercial basis in various new cable systems. Once again it must be said that such a commitment reflects more the competitiveness of franchise bidding than a belief in videotex's short- or medium-term profitability. Warner Amex, perhaps surprisingly, has not so far put much emphasis on these aspects of its two-way technology. Only since December 1980 has it provided the CompuServe service to a very small experimental group of about twenty households in Columbus, each provided with an Atari home-computer terminal. It may be significant that in its latest franchise agreement for the Brooklyn system in New York it promises to provide Qube and security, but only to install other videotex services once they have passed the experimental stage. Warner Amex is, however, now developing a home-shopping experiment and has already tried direct-response advertising on its local origination channel in Columbus. Meanwhile, Dow Jones is offering its News Retrieval service to cable operators and as of May 1983 had installed it in four systems, including The Woodlands and Park Cities mentioned earlier. Times Mirror is conducting a side-by-side experiment between telephone and cable-delivered services in 350 homes in Orange County, California, whilst Cox Cable has developed its own Index videotex service in San Diego and Omaha, providing banking, shopping, local databases and access to The Source on an experimental basis. More importantly, it has agreed to provide Index commercially in the franchises it has won in New Orleans, Tucson, Vancouver (Washington) and New York. Cablevision has similarly promised banking, shopping and information services in its Boston and New York franchises. Needless to say, however, the results of the various experimental projects so far are a closely guarded secret.

Two aspects of videotex which have aroused particular interest as a means of attracting the domestic consumer are telebanking and teleshopping, and it seems certain that any commercially viable domestic videotex service will include these as standard. Among the potential benefits to the consumer of shopping from home are saving fuel and time on visits to shops for standard items, possible demonstrations of rival products and even cost comparisons. Goods could either be delivered or else picked up at a local collection point. Such a service would be combined with 'electronic funds transfer' (EFT), allowing the cost of items purchased to be automatically debited from and credited to the relevant accounts. As for the other aspects of home-banking services, there can be little doubt of the value to subscribers of having bank account, mortgage, tax and other personal financial details readily to hand, all updated electronically and with the minimum delay.

From the service provider's viewpoint there are similar advantages. Both for mail order companies, such as Sears and American Express, and for mass merchandise outlets (store chains, hypermarkets, packaged product retailers, etc.) direct-response home shopping has obvious attractions, as well as such less apparent ones as closer monitoring of consumer demand and easier and more economical stock control. Already mail order and freephone purchase of products advertised on television are the fastest growing areas of retail sales. The banks are also keen on teleshopping since they see an opportunity to make a profit by charging for each EFT transaction. Meanwhile, they have been taking a lead in videotex because of the ever-increasing cost of maintaining large networks of branch offices and of processing cheques and carrying out other 'paper-pushing' tasks. According to the Electronic Funds Transfer Institute, it costs the banks forty-one cents to process a cheque by conventional means, but only seven cents to make a similar transaction electronically. To reduce such costs by a factor of six would make a quite dramatic difference, so much so that a stage could eventually be reached where banks would subsidise the installation of domestic videotex terminals and require as many transactions as possible to be done electronically.

Such speculation, however, cannot ignore the innumerable problems which need to be solved before such large-scale changes can take place. Cash will continue to be an essential requirement for many purchases, so that electronic funds transfer will not obviate the need to visit a bank. EFT will similarly not be possible, or at least be more difficult, when one party does not have an account or for some reason is not connected to a videotex system. That will include the majority for some time to come, since even the most optimistic projections do not anticipate a videotex penetration of more than 15-20 per cent by 1990, while most consider the probable figure to be significantly lower. The normally optimistic advertising agency, Doyle Dane Bernbach, forecasts that by 1990 only 7 per cent of American homes will have either videotex or the simpler one-way teletext information service.

Meanwhile, although some of the cost of teleshopping and banking will be absorbed by retailers and banks, a cable subscriber will still have to pay an additional monthly charge on top of that for access to the interactive tier. One report on home banking estimates such a fee for the latter service to be at least $15 initially, although this might fall if charges for EFT prove particularly profitable. The savings to subscribers may, of course, outweigh the costs, but a high proportion of goods will still require regular shopping trips, while for the many who do not possess home-shopping services shops will continue to be as necessary as ever. Such individuals could also suffer from having the cost to the retailer of a service they cannot enjoy added indirectly to the price of goods purchased, unless items bought electronically have an additional tariff placed on them. 'Enjoyment' of such a service is in any case a relative term; its convenience could for many be offset by the loss of more traditional conveniences, such as the pleasure and benefit to be gained from browsing and physically handling a product before purchase. As the amount of time which the average individual spends working declines, so the simple pleasures such as shopping trips and browsing may become more important. Browsing of a kind would be possible on videotex, but even for the retailer a major disadvantage could be significantly reduced impulse buying, buying which normally results from point-of-sale advertising, appealing packaging and careful juxtaposition of products or groups of products on the shelf or on the most commonly taken routes through a store. Information videotex services are already stimulating a new research industry to determine the most convenient and common user strategies for gaining access to information. Similar research will be required by retailers to analyse the routes an electronic shopper takes and the most appropriate marketing responses.

If teleshopping and telebanking are successful, they will obviously have a major effect upon the way in which people organise their lives, upon the size and organisation of retail business, the amount of money in circulation, even upon the financial structures and processes which underpin the economy. The electronic publishing aspects of videotex have similar implications for reading habits, television viewing and possibly the very character of the language. The emphasis in the new information society upon information as a commodity rather than a right may challenge fundamental assumptions about the workings of democracy, as well as widening still further the gap between the information-rich and information-poor. Concentration of ownership in electronic publishing seems likely also to become an issue if the large national media conglomerates, such as Dow Jones and Time Inc., continue to demonstrate their dominance in the new medium. Where they also own the means of delivery of electronic information – the cable system – questions of vertical cross-ownership will also arise, as will the political issues of balance and equal access. As the boundaries between television and publishing become more and more blurred, so the differing regulatory constraints over the two media, particularly with regard to First Amendment rights on freedom of speech, will be challenged and will have to be reassessed. While the immediate concern is with the technical and economic practicalities of videotex, many broader issues are also becoming apparent.

How are the various videotex services to be financed? Access to the interactive tier on both Qube and Index costs the subscriber an additional $6 or so each month on top of basic cable subscription. This makes it possible to use or order a number of interactive services including pay-per-view, emergency alarms and, on Index, videotex information, videogames and some banking and shopping services. In each instance, however, there is either an additional monthly charge or a per-use fee, and in some cases both. Index, when it is fully commercial, will probably provide some of the most elementary information services – news, weather, film listings, etc. – for the basic Index tier price, but charge extra for access to the more specialised services of The Source and to telebanking and teleshopping services. Each could cost a further $10 a month or more. In other systems, such as the Telidon information service offered by Cablesystems in Portland, there may be charges per page of information used or for time taken.

Such monthly costs for access to these services, plus possible page charges, could be a serious hindrance to their use. Consequently, it is generally agreed that advertising sales must contribute significantly to videotex revenue, allowing pages to be offered free. In this respect classified advertising on two-way cable could play a valuable role. Newspaper classified advertising earns some $5 billion each year in the United States. The electronic sorting, instant-response purchase of goods and immediate updating of information (adding new advertisements continually and removing those for sold items), to which videotex is well suited, could prove a major advantage for classified advertising making the process more efficient and cheaper than for newspapers.

Two-way text advertising has crucial advantages which one-way text, discussed earlier, lacks. Further revenues, as already mentioned, will have to come from transactional service providers such as banks and retailers, and from users, possibly on a per-transaction basis. Indeed, Times Mirror believe that up to 70 per cent of revenue will have to come from sources other than subscription if the latter is to be kept acceptably low. Full videotex service is unlikely to be cheap either to get access to or to use, while to the cable operator the capital costs of two-way equipment will be high. The Indax box which goes in each subscribing home is said to cost double the $150 of a one-way addressable converter. Not surprisingly, therefore, a number of cheaper systems have been developed, offering to do as much as most subscribers are likely to want. The Portland operation, for example, calls its information service 'Time-Shared Telidon', since the decoding equipment normally placed within each home has been located earlier in the distribution system, with two videotex terminals serving a potential 300 homes. The concept is equivalent to a shared telephone line, cheaper to offer but with the same problems of reduced privacy (making telebanking more difficult) and a higher probability of the service being engaged when it is wanted.

Meanwhile, a completely different approach has been taken by Time Inc. which has gone right to the heart of the matter – the high cost and low proportion of interactive cable – and rejected the very concept of true two-way cable information. Pilot trials have been conducted by its subsidiary, Time Video Information Services, with full-channel teletext. Unlike the limited capacity of teletext services, which use only a few lines in the vertical blanking interval of a broadcast service – such as the BBC's Ceefax and ITV's Oracle – full-channel teletext utilises an entire video channel capacity. Far from being restricted to a hundred to two hundred pages of text, with a possible retrieval delay of up to thirty seconds, Time Teletext has a 5,000 page capacity and a recall time not exceeding ten seconds. There is also the capability to download information into home terminals, computers and even on to hard-copy printers. By this means it might eventually be possible to supply relatively complex videogames, educational services and other computer programmes.

The results of the pilot trials in Orlando, Florida, and San Diego have been less encouraging than Time Inc. had hoped, largely because of the high cost of the home terminal involved. At the time of writing the signs are that the scheme may temporarily be shelved. If it does go ahead, however, Time Teletext will be distributed nationally by satellite to cable systems and offered to subscribers simply as another pay service, although they will require a more complex decoder than normal. Monthly charges would be about $7-10, with advertising contributing a similar amount. Additional payments would be made for downloaded videogames and computer programmes, and revenues would be shared between Time Inc., a local newspaper which would provide local information pages, and the cable operator.

A relatively limited service of this kind is intended more for the general domestic user than for someone seeking specialist information. Nor does it allow true interactivity, either in supplying or seeking information or in making transactions. It is, however, likely to be much cheaper than full videotex, to avoid the offputting per-page charges which have proved such a disincentive to domestic Prestel users, and to reach a very much wider market more quickly than cabled videotex. Indeed, the potential may well exist to develop an interactive element by combining it with a return line via the telephone system, whose reach would more closely match that of Time Teletext than would two-way cable systems. For the time being, a more limited service of this kind at a lower price than full telephone or cable videotex may well prove a more attractive and practicable option.

The question remains to what extent there is a real consumer demand or need for videotex services; neither Prestel nor the French Télétel systems have yet demonstrated any large-scale domestic interest. Nor is it clear what kinds of information people would be prepared to pay for. Videogame services were initially used extensively by homes subscribing to Prestel in Britain, but have now dropped back behind travel timetables, restaurant and entertainment listings, business news, financial data and weather reports. By contrast, a CompuServe trial in the United States discovered that news and information services were more popular at first but eventually become the least frequently consulted part of the service, with videogames establishing themselves as the most often used. In these early years such factors as system design, indexing structure, page layout and general ease of use will inevitably be important factors in determining how popular the various videotex services are. But in some cases it may be that the information provided simply is not wanted. In the Knight Ridder/AT & T Viewtron experiment, it was discovered that fully 65 per cent of all the news and information pages provided by the contributing press agency, Associated Press, were never consulted by anyone. Similarly, a home banking study by CSP International has concluded that such service appeals to no more than 15-20 per cent of a bank's customers. Additional unresolved questions concern the maximum tolerable viewing time for electronic text, and subscribers' readiness to accept advertising pages. Most importantly, just how much will they pay?

Perhaps one of the most encouraging signs is the quite separate but tremendous growth in the domestic computer market. By 1985 there should be at least 16 million home computers installed, although many will be for office use. About 3 million of those in homes will also have the telephone modem necessary to connect them to a videotex provider. Indeed by 1990, according to the Videotex Industry Association, home computers should be in some 30 million households, with perhaps 10 million taking a videotex service. To homes with such a domestic terminal already in place the added benefits of connection to the very much greater information capacity and software library provided by a videotex system could help to compensate for the cost. Homes with a videogame console which can be upgraded to a domestic computer should add to this market. Major compatibility problems exist between cable or telephone videotex systems and a multiplicity of domestic computers of differing standards, but already CompuServe has found that many of its domestic subscribers are amongst this ever-growing category.

Like cable itself, cabled videotex seems likely to succeed only if it can rely on a number of different sources of revenue and offer a package of services. Nor will it develop in isolation; telephone-delivered videotex and perhaps full-channel teletext will take much of whatever market there is. Where they have been promised as a franchise commitment, cable operators will provide a number of videotex services; but even optimistic projections do not envisage more than 10-15 per cent of TV households being connected to two-way cable systems by 1990, with the proportion taking videotex much lower.

What does seem probable is that without a major collaborative effort between videotex packagers, banks, retailers and other service providers to reduce direct subscriber costs by transactional payments, and without a tremendous reallocation of advertising resources by advertisers, videotex will for many years remain the education and information tool, convenience service and plaything of the more affluent. Perhaps this is particularly true of telephone-delivered videotex, which it is generally agreed will cost some $25-40 monthly as an independent service, plus possible time and transactional tariffs. Where cabled videotex is available, it may succeed in reaching somewhat further down the economic scale, particularly if it is marketed as just one feature of a generally attractive package of entertainment and information services. By separating out some or all of the cost of interactivity from the individual charges for each interactive service, and by including within the same tier access to such potentially attractive services as pay-per-view and additional basic and pay channels, cable operators

230

may at least entice subscribers up to a tier level where they can take any of the individually charged interactive services should they wish to do so. Having reached that level, further subscription to each new service becomes slightly less of a financial shock than it would otherwise have been. A number of companies are developing videotex services for mass domestic use rather than just specialised business, while the franchise commitments of cable operators such as Cox and Cablesystems will certainly lead to aggressive marketing. But just how many subscribers, having reached the interactive tier, will then go on to use the various videotex information and transactional facilities, which they will choose, whether the use of any individually will prove too low for it to be viable, and whether aggregate use will be enough to support the whole, are questions which still cannot be answered. The concept of videotex as a mass medium has received a poor press in Britain because of the problems encountered by Prestel. In America the real test of consumer acceptance will come over the next ten years and on interactive cable systems.

INSTITUTIONAL NETWORKS AND BUSINESS SERVICES

If the future of domestic videotex services is uncertain, that of business videotex and the other business services which cable and telephone can provide is assured. Business information, funds transfer, electronic mail, data and voice carriage and teleconferencing are all tremendous growth areas, and almost all the major urban system operators are now seeking to tap this lucrative market, currently dominated though it is by the telephone companies of AT & T. To do so, however, they must appeal to a very different type of user than hitherto and demonsrate cable's advantages to business. Although they have had the technical capability to offer such services for some time, therefore, it is only recently that they have begun seriously to address themselves to this new opportunity.

Both the potential opportunities and the power of the competition can be seen from the figures for data transmission. By 1981 revenues for local data transmission in the USA totalled $1 billion. Of this fully 89.8 per cent went to AT & T-owned companies, 9 per cent to independent telephone companies, 1.05 per cent to private services such as Shell Oil and United Airlines who have their own microwave systems, and a bare 0.15 per cent to cable companies. In 1983 all of Bell's 6,874 local telephone exchanges (providing 80 per cent of all local telephone services), and most of the remaining independent telephone companies in urban areas, offered data transmission services. By contrast, only 139 cable systems were capable of doing so as of May 1983 and no more than eight actually did.

Yet, although cable data transmission is currently of little importance, every new urban franchise is now being supplied with a high-capacity 'institutional network' for public and private institutional use. An institutional network or loop is a broadband cable connection linking offices and organisations and capable of providing a range of facilities, including one-way or two-way data, voice or full television transmission. It can provide high- or low-speed data distribution and can connect two or more teleconferencing rooms with audio and freeze-frame or full moving video links. Different organisations or departments within the same organisation can be interconnected, with the video, voice and data communication needs of each all being handled by one cable rather than by a number of individual systems.

In some instances the same trunk cable is used as for the domestic subscriber entertainment system, with a certain bandwidth being set aside for institutional use. In the larger and more recent franchises, however, operators have more normally offered a separate, single- or dual-cable 'loop' passing through all the major business areas and reaching out to public institutional buildings such as schools, fire stations, libraries, hospitals and local government offices. Such networks are fully two-way, with almost as much upstream capacity as down, unlike the more limited return capabilities of most domestic two-way cable systems. The institutional loop is also used as a feeder network to the larger domestic distribution system, so that the educational and government channels on the latter, and in some cases the videotex information services, can have material fed directly on to them from the originating institution. Thus a school meeting, parents' evening, lesson or a school play can be televised from the school itself, which is wired into the institutional network, fed to the system headend and either back on the loop to other schools or out on the educational or community channel to all subscribers. The franchise itself generally stipulates which public institutions will be connected free by the operator and which will have to pay a connection charge.

For many years the non-profitmaking public institutional network has been accepted as a requirement of many cable franchises. Perhaps the best known is in Reading, Pennsylvania, where part of the public access programme mentioned earlier has involved a two-way videoconferencing facility for the elderly. Connecting four Neighbourhood Communications Centres, it allows senior citizens in each to see and hear one another, to discuss issues, produce programmes jointly and, using a split screen, transmit such material to every subscribing home. As a device for giving those involved a renewed interest and sense of purpose, it has proved very successful, while a survey in 1977 revealed that fully 61 per cent of subscribing senior citizens watched the daily two-hour programme at least twice a week.

The institutional network has also begun to show its potential as a way of saving on local government expenditure. The training and educational possibilities of local government and educational channels were discussed earlier, but the restricted access and two-way character of an institutional network may make this even more appropriate for training and discussion sessions for firemen, policemen, medical students and many other such groups in the public and social services. A study in 1978 by Michigan State University of interactive cable training for firemen in Rockford demonstrated that such methods could be significantly cheaper than lecture courses, where the lecturer had to travel around a number of fire stations and address various shifts. That this was so for a relatively small fire department suggests that the advantages both financially and in terms of standardised teaching (important, for example, in firefighting or medicine) could be considerable for a larger one, or for other and even bigger or more dispersed groups of public workers. Nor did this experiment discover any major hindrances to learning and appreciation from such an apparently dehumanising and depersonalising trend in the educational process. Interactive programmes with regular questions and tests built into them could hold the attention quite effectively and even aid retention (Michigan State University, *Rockford Two-Way Cable Project*, 1978, Vol. I, pp. 17-20).

In Manhattan too the city authorities have discovered the advantages of the cable system for data communications. Since 1981 data traffic between the city's uptown computer centre and its downtown municipal building has been carried on Manhattan Cable's institutional loop. This could save the city considerable amounts on its annual communications bill of some $6 million, since a clause in the cable franchise requires the operator to provide such services to the city at two-thirds the rate charged by the New York Telephone Company.

Until the latest franchising boom, the institutional network was regarded rather as a loss-leader primarily for public use, part of the price an operator paid for his franchise. Only in New York was a serious attempt made to finance it by selling data communications services to business as well. In the somewhat special circumstances of Manhattan the cable company in 1974 began offering a data link between the mid-town and downtown business centres, a service which has been taken up by several of the major banks and financial institutions on Wall Street. Now some twenty-five businesses use it, including Citibank, Chase Manhattan and Bankers Trust. By 1980 Manhattan Cable's institutional network revenue had reached $1 million, rising to $1.6 million in 1981 and earning it a profitable return on investment after tax of over 10 per cent.

Not surprisingly, therefore, the growing demand for data communications services in the major cities now being cabled and the ever-rising cost of building such systems have all induced other cable operators to consider more seriously the revenue potential of the institutional networks and to sell such services more aggressively than before. Although the public institutional aspect is as important a franchise requirement as ever, it is increasingly the business user which cable operators are seeking. To succeed, however, they must persuade such potential clients that the service they can offer has major advantages over the far more experienced and ubiquitous telephone company. The signs are that they may be able to do so, but that competition will be intense and the rewards relatively modest.

To start with, broadband cable's capacity is currently much greater than that of a standard-pair telephone line, allowing it to transmit data at computer speeds. Moreover, if Manhattan Cable's experience is anything to go by, cable can offer a consistently more reliable service than the older telephone lines, with a reduced error rate and quicker response to faults. The increasing congestion of the telephone service also means that at present it can take some time for a business to get new lines installed. For many businesses cable's current availability is a strong inducement. Not least important is the fact that, with its business service rates unregulated, cable can provide a service significantly less expensive than the telephone company, although current legislative proposals seem likely to put the two on a more equal footing.

One of the new areas to which cable is particularly well suited is teleconferencing, or more specifically full-motion videoconferencing. Many major corporations are now finding that great savings in time and travelling costs can be made by means of a personal video link between distant executives. Indeed, the faster exchange of information which such services allow may make possible more rapid decision-taking and overall improvements in productivity. Examples range from a sales director addressing his widely dispersed and very large sales force, situated in twenty to thirty separate locations, to a dedicated two-way video link between senior executive offices in buildings ten miles apart. Another major application which has been discovered is in public relations work, enabling executives and others to hold continent-wide press conferences or shareholders' meetings, with audiences of several thousands.

Some businesses such as Aetna Life are already building their own teleconferencing rooms, although the cost is high. Allstate Life Insurance is creating a network of twenty videoconferencing studios across the USA, but will also make them available to other users. The tremendous advantage to executives in being able to see and hear each other in several locations and usually in groups, allowing general discussion, far outweighs the costs which for a large multi-location videoconference can reach $300,000. Intercontinental videoconferencing not only offers savings of time and money but also avoids such problems as jet lag. A number of estimates suggest that between 30 per cent and 60 per cent of all executive international travel, which was a $7-billion business in 1980, could be rendered unnecessary by the wide-scale development of effective tele-and videoconference facilities.

Where such opportunities exist, it is not surprising to find many different businesses jumping in with their own special expertise and facilities. Many hotel chains, including Holiday Inn, Hilton and Intercontinental, are building teleconferencing facilities in all their major hotels. The Holiday Inn Video Network (HI-NET) already has 350 videoconferencing sites interconnected by its own satellite transponder, and naturally provides accommodation and catering for attending executives. A number of broadcasting stations are also using their studio facilities and satellite dishes to provide videoconferencing services. Meanwhile, where short distances are involved the institutional networks of cable systems can offer a full video service on the same cable that carries a company's data and voice traffic. In Dearborn, Michigan, for example, Ford Motors is considering interconnecting its various local plants with two-way video via a Group W cable system. For long distances cable operators can increasingly provide the costly down- and uplink satellite facilities to any company wanting to use them, saving the latter the expense of installing their own. Cable operators with institutional loops seem to have a good opportunity of getting into the office-to-office end of the videoconferencing business.

One recent development, however, may limit their chances. Until now telephone companies have been restricted to audio-only teleconferencing or at best 'slow-scan' or freeze-frame pictures, because of their narrow bandwidth availabilities. Now the new technology of picture 'compression' may alter that. 'Compression' works by eliminating all unnecessary information from the video signal, concentrating on the differences between each frame transmitted and ignoring information which does not change. Thus the relatively static picture of most videoconferences, with only facial and occasional arm movements, can be compressed and transmitted down a comparatively narrow bandwidth line. Only when the screen is too crowded with movement do the system's limitations become apparent. Clearly this new development could be of major importance and remove some of the undoubted advantages which the wideband institutional loops of cable systems currently enjoy.

Cable operators face intense competition in the business market, one which is in any case very different from their traditional arena. Nevertheless, many urban system operators are increasingly optimistic that they can win themselves a piece of the business service pie. In the latest franchising round institutional loops offered have greatly exceeded the minimum specified requirements. Warner Amex, Cox, Storer, Cablevision, Rogers, Viacom, ATC, Daniels and many others are all providing them in their new systems, and some even see the business services supporting the public institutional network. In Montgomery County, Maryland, for example, Times Mirror's franchise proposal (eventually unsuccessful) offered a dual-cable residential network some

1,700 miles long and a separate dual-cable institutional network of similar length. A further high-traffic cable was offered to serve businesses in the particularly important Bethesda–Silver Spring area. Not surprisingly Times Mirror saw such an enterprise as a separate business in its own right, with its own institutional network staff. It also predicted that the service would break even in the sixth year and by the tenth net $2.2 million on gross revenues of $7.7 million.

With such proposals, institutional networks are becoming cable systems within cable systems, and cable operators are moving even further into the telecommunications industry. Indeed, as AT & T's local telephone companies are split off from its long-distance business and as other long-distance carriers spring up using satellites and microwave trunks as their links, so the opportunity is gradually appearing for cable to become the local distribution network for an alternative communications service, at least for business use. In 1981 Manhattan Cable and Viacom in San Francisco tested the feasibility of such an intercity data transmission service using cable for the local link. The long-distance carrier in this test, Satellite Business Systems, is also contemplating using local cable for final distribution. Perhaps most significantly Cox Cable and long-distance service MCI are carrying out a joint experiment whereby the former's system in Omaha is being used to distribute not just data but also voice services for MCI.

Cable as a business telecommunications service, however, is still very much in its infancy, and it will have to pit itself against an experienced and tremendously powerful adversary. AT & T and its local companies are certainly not sitting still. Already they are upgrading their trunk networks in a number of cities to allow much faster digital services and are installing advanced electronic switching systems which should also make possible more competitive rates. Such developments, together with compressed video, will allow both teleconferencing and data transmission at computer speeds. Moreover, for many teleconferencing needs the full audio and 'slow-scan' service which is already possible via the telephone may well be quite adequate, as well as very much cheaper. AT & T itself plans to have public teleconferencing centres operating in forty-two American cities by the end of 1983. Indeed, as they gradually upgrade their trunk lines to optic fibre, AT & T and the local telephone companies will be able to provide the same bandwidth as cable. Perhaps the telephone companies' biggest advantage, however, is psychological. Businesses are used to using the telephone for their communication needs and equally used to regarding cable as entertainment. Even cable operators are only now beginning to regard themselves seriously as telecommunications carriers. Such preconceptions can be a major barrier to entry into a new field.

Meanwhile, other wholly dedicated telecommunications companies are moving in to provide both data and videoconferencing services by other means, potentially even more cost-effective that cable. Long-distance carriers such as MCI, Tymnet and Satellite Business Systems, frustrated at having to use the telephone companies' lines for the local link, are not only investigating partnership with cable systems but also actively developing their own microwave links, known as Digital Termination Service (DTS). The FCC is authorising up to thirteen DTS licences in every major metropolitan area, and MCI, SBS and others have already been awarded the right to offer it in at least thirty cities each. Even Cox Cable has recognised the capital-cost advantages of DTS and has applied for a licence to offer the service in several of its franchise areas. Since many cable operators already use microwave links between their headend and local distribution hubs, they are in a good position to exploit this alternative technology themselves. DTS should certainly be competitive as a data and teleconferencing business service, although it does suffer from line-of-sight problems in built-up city areas, as well as possible radio interference. Meanwhile, in Minneapolis long-distance carrier ShareCom is actually wiring its customers directly to its uplink facility and offering a 20 per cent discount on long-distance calls. Indeed, given the right regulatory conditions, there is no real reason why the cable and local telephone companies should be the only ones allowed to provide a fully wired institutional network. Equally possible are independent networks or joint ventures between cable operators, long-distance carriers, independent service companies and perhaps even local telephone companies themselves.

Cable's potential problems do not stop with its competitors. While the tree-and-branch layout of American systems does allow a number of dedicated links between specific locations, it is certainly not sufficiently flexible to offer the equivalent of a true telephone service. Its non-switched character may give initial cost and rate advantages, but as a result it will never be able to provide a comprehensive telecommunications service, nor tap a principal element of the telephone companies' revenues. Another problem that certainly must be resolved is that of technical incompatibility between systems. As exchange of information grows, there is a vital need to establish consistent intersystem standards. One of the biggest problems, however, is the regulatory situation. Once cable begins to act as a common carrier, there ceases to be any good reason why in that aspect of its operations it should not be treated as one and regulated accordingly. Certainly, in the one or two instances where cable is to offer voice services, it could well be challenged and brought under state and local utility commission control. Even unregulated data services may be on shaky legal ground. Clearly, it will be in the interests of regulated telephone companies to challenge the status of cable at every opportunity, and in current legislative battles they are already doing so. Cable operators are certainly worried lest in entering the common-carriage business they open the door to wider restrictions.

At this moment cable operators with institutional networks in place or being built do seem to have an opportunity to demonstrate significant benefits for businesses thinking of using them. Those advantages will not necessarily last, while in the long term cable's entry into business carriage seems certain to affect the regulatory position. Like other enhanced services, it is also highly unlikely that the institutional network will do more than play a supportive role to the main business of entertainment for the foreseeable future. Once again the projections for Boston provide a useful example; there Cablevision, which is providing a high-capacity dual-cable public and business institutional network, anticipates that revenues from it will reach $3 million by the eighth year of operation, but that it will not provide more than 3.6 per cent of the company's revenue even by the tenth. If a cable company in a major urban franchise addresses business services as a separate operation and markets them aggressively, then there seems a good chance that it will win at least a sufficient share of a growing market to make the effort worthwhile. What it will never be, however, is more than just one among many competitors.

Business services, cabled videotex, videogames, security and pay-per-view – all have been suggested as significant revenue earners, yet none by itself seems likely at present to provide a rapid solution to the cable industry's financial problems. Nor for several years will many operators find it worth the effort to provide them. For a large proportion of the subscribers to whom such services are available, they will have little practical value in view of their cost. Yet the considerable public attention which the various enhanced services have attracted has also obscured the fact that few cable operators have actually based their system's financial calculations on the expectation that any would earn significant revenue before the system as a whole had broken even. The same comment applies to local advertising revenue. Basic and pay subscriptions for entertainment services remain, with few exceptions, the heart of cable financing.

The immediate drive to develop additional services and revenue sources undoubtedly owes much to the competitiveness of the American franchising process. Yet, even had this not been the case, the industry would still have had to expand and innovate in this way. Only experience can reveal the true potential of one service or the non-viability of another. Only experience will uncover yet new directions for an industry to take. Cable may be equal or superior to its competitors in the various fields in which it is active – entertainment, information, data carriage, teleconferencing, security, etc. – but it will not remain so if it does not continually investigate every possible option. These enhanced and business services, therefore, are opportunities, not certainties and, like all opportunities, once taken may prove also to be a heavy burden.

238

13　Cable and the American Consumer

The development of cable, of television which has to be paid for and of programmes which are not universally and freely available, undoubtedly holds major implications for the role which television has traditionally played as a socially cohesive force. For all, it will mean changes to the information and entertainment available. To those who embrace and can afford cable in its various forms, the choice may well improve; for those who do not or cannot, the character of broadcast services will at least be altered, in some cases for the worse, but occasionally also for the better. Who are the cable subscribers, why do they subscribe and how does it affect their use of other media? Who, more importantly, are the non-subscribers? Cable seems certain to create a new division between haves and have-nots where none existed before. Who will be on either side of it and will it matter? Or will it become simply another and individually insignificant division amongst the multiplicity which, by definition, exist within a capitalist economy and are the manifestations of consumer choice?

Any attempt to define the typical characteristics of the American cable subscriber must take account of diverse conditions and changing circumstances. Ten years ago subscribers were predominantly small-town dwellers with a higher-than-average median age and lower-than-average income. Now the story is very different. Nor has the USA reached cable maturity; at present, for example, pay-cable subscribers include a high proportion of videophiles, people who are always eager to innovate, to try new technologies, who enjoy gadgetry and frequently have also invested in other examples of the new media, such as video-cassette recorders and videogames. Inevitably such videophiles tend to be in the higher socioeconomic groups and to have more money available to experiment in this way. Yet, as cable establishes itself and demonstrates its value, so the more cautious, prudent and 'average' television consumers will assert their natural dominance in the statistics, so that many of the present differences between subscribers and non-subscribers will diminish.

Although there is certainly no such thing as a typical cable sub-

239

scriber, we can reach a number of general conclusions. In absolute terms the highest proportion are twenty-five to forty-five years old, educated to high-school level, skilled or unskilled workers and have total household incomes of over $20,000. But in relating subscriber characteristics to those of the population as a whole there are a number of interesting variations. For example, using an average index of 100 it can be seen from Table x that age is a significant factor in subscription:

TABLE X

Comparison of pay, basic and uncabled homes by age of household head
Source: A.C. Nielsen, Nielsen Television Index, June 1982

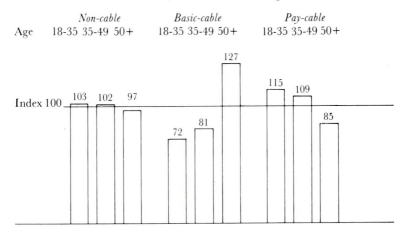

Non-cable subscribers are spread across the age range more or less equally; basic are much more likely to have household heads over fifty whilst pay subscribers are biased in the opposite direction. The high proportion of basic subscribers aged over fifty indicates an interest in television and in good reception but less so in films and a lower than average readiness to innovate. As present pay subscribers age, however, these differences will surely become less apparent.

A similar relationship can be seen between subscription and household size, with pay households, in particular, likely to contain larger families, as is shown in Table XI.

TABLE XI

Comparison of pay, basic and uncabled homes by household size
Source: A.C. Nielsen, Nielsen Television Index, June 1982

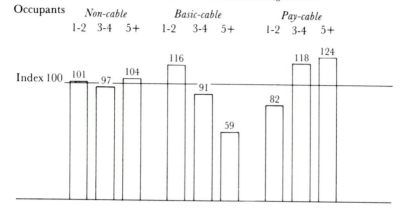

Finally, as might have been predicted, pay-cable subscribers are much more likely than basic or non-subscribers to be relatively affluent:

TABLE XII

Comparison of pay, basic and uncabled homes by household income
Source: A.C. Nielsen, Nielsen Television Index, June 1982

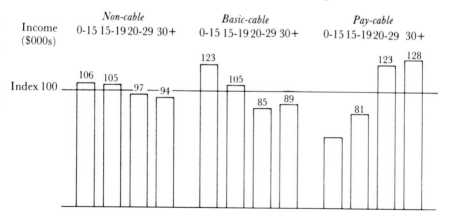

Here, as in the previous tables, the characteristics of pay and basic subscribers are in inverse proportion to one another. In other words, the smaller and poorer families tend to take the lower level of service, although this also demonstrates the continuing impact on

241

the statistics of older cable systems with a high proportion of basic subscribers. Furthermore, an analysis of multi-pay subscribers and of households taking the various enhanced services shows a quite extreme disparity from the norm. At present these additional levels are very much the preserve of the better off.

Pay-cable homes, both single and multi-pay, are therefore more likely than normal to have household heads under fifty, one or more children and an annual family income of over $20,000. They are also much more permissive about sex on television; indeed, in one survey of four cable systems it was discovered that while 1 per cent of basic households also subscribed to *Penthouse* magazine and 7 per cent to *Playboy*, for pay households the figures were 6 per cent and 13 per cent respectively. Cable subscribers as a whole tend to be younger, married with children, employed, home-owning and more affluent than average. The proportion of households with incomes under $10,000 which are cabled is only 76 per cent of their national average. Similarly the number of blacks who are subscribers is only 58 per cent of what it should be if it matched their proportion in the population as a whole. However, in both cases this is at least partly because the major cities which have high black and poor populations are only now being wired up.

Indeed, despite such trends it must be emphasised that these are not immutable laws; not all affluent households subscribe, while the proportion of low-income households which do is perhaps higher than might have been expected. Factors for and against subscription frequently counteract, so that the more highly educated tend also to be light television users with full-time jobs, making cable less attractive. The elderly, on the other hand, are more likely to be home-owners, stable members of the community and heavy television users, while ethnic communities and poorer households also use television extensively and typically have larger than average families. All these are factors favouring subscription. A survey of low-income families in Syracuse during 1982 revealed that poorer black and other ethnic-minority households were actually far more likely than average to subscribe, and this finding has been repeated elsewhere. Those least likely to subscribe are the single elderly, with a high proportion in the low-income category. Thus although income is necessarily a factor in whether people subscribe, particularly to pay, other influences such as household character, perceived need and how much the television is used are extremely important also.

Non-subscribers, almost by definition, do not easily fit into identifiable groups to which cable operators can readily appeal. Nevertheless market research suggests that such people are more likely to take at least basic if it offers categories of programme which are not available on broadcast television. (This is not as obvious as it seems;

many subscribers to basic do so to receive more of the same types of programme from distant stations.) Consequently a number of reports conclude, perhaps surprisingly, that truly local programming, news, religion and even educational channels are considered of above average interest by such groups, particularly the elderly and light TV users. Indeed system operators who offer these services on their basic tier sometimes advertise cable as 'television for people who don't watch television'.

Subscribers who take basic services but not pay do so primarily to improve reception and add some programme diversity. Yet although they have more channels available than non-subscribers they tend not to watch significantly more television – a marginal increase at most. Consequently some of the time spent watching basic cable services and distant signals has to be diverted away from that previously given to the broadcast networks and local independent stations.

The biggest difference in viewing habits is not between non-subscribers and basic subscribers but between the latter and those who take pay. Undoubtedly the principal reason for subscribing to pay cable is to receive recent films. According to one survey, 76.6 per cent of pay-TV subscribers take it for films not shown on broadcast television, 73.2 per cent also for the fact that they are uninterrupted, 60.5 per cent for its convenience, 60.1 per cent for the lack of commercials, 59.5 per cent for films missed in their cinema run, 59.1 per cent for unedited films, 48.9 per cent for the entertainment specials, 48.4 per cent for the economy of viewing films at home, 45.2 per cent for the greater programme choice offered, 43.9 per cent for adult films, 36.7 per cent for sports and 4.6 per cent for educational, cultural and other programmes. Returning to the idea of the videophile, people with home computers, videogames and video recorders are more likely than others to be pay subscribers. Fully 31 per cent of the 5 per cent of video recorder owners in the United States in 1982 took pay, an indication that the two are used in combination. Clearly this is of considerable significance for Britain with its high video population. Videophiles are also heavy media users generally, and pay-cable subscribers watch about a quarter as much television again as non-subscribers, both because they were heavier users before and because they have increased the time they spend viewing. Interestingly, the extent of the increase is closely related to educational levels, with the better-educated subscriber extending his or her viewing only slightly and the less well-educated very significantly. Household as opposed to individual viewing may be even higher; with the larger families in pay-TV homes it is more likely that at any moment one member will have the television switched on. In addition, not only are cabled homes more likely to have two or more television sets, but they are also increasingly taking advantage of them. Viewing within the family, in other words, is beginning to fragment, although there is still much joint viewing.

Actual use of the various cable services closely matches the reasons why people say they subscribe. Pay-film channels are the most used cable service, with specials and sports events also proving popular. More unexpected is the high use of the text weather and news bulletins – in Columbus almost 80 per cent of subscribers use these facilities, albeit for only a few minutes at a time. Equally unexpected is the fact that although the highly mobile, young, single flat-renters are among the lowest subscribers, those who do are amongst the highest users of films services. More predictably, the largest pay-cable audiences are to be found in primetime and the later evening. Overall, therefore, it would appear that most cable use is to obtain material not available on broadcast television, namely premium and uncensored films, some more sports and instant news and weather reports.

Although many subscribers have over thirty channels available, few make any attempt to use them all. Indeed, as Table XIII shows, the proportion used actually declines as the number available increases:

TABLE XIII

Number of channels a household views to channels received. (Minimum viewing period = ten minutes per week.)
(Source: Nielsen Television Index, May 1982)

Channels receivable	1-4	9-10	16-20	21-25	26+
Average number viewed	2.6	5.1	7.6	8.5	10.0
Percentage viewed to received	72%	54%	44%	36%	34%

If a more stringent definition of viewing, one hour a week, is applied, the number of channels used drops even more, as it does also if individual as opposed to household viewing is being measured. Other surveys indicate that in cable systems with over thirty channels the average individual viewer uses seven only. Since these will include the three networks, PBS, major independents and usually a pay channel, it would appear that all the basic cable services are competing for no more than one to three places in each viewer's normal selection.

Most households' needs, therefore, can be satisfied by a relatively small number of channels, although which these are will vary from family to family. Subscribers do not take full advantage of the range available, nor is there any reason why they should be expected to do so. Indeed, since less than half of all viewing is planned in advance using channel guides, it may be that cable has made viewers 'channel-selective' rather than 'programme-selective', choosing a service because of its known character and depending on the programme of the moment being interesting. Such viewing habits will be a further inducement to cable-service providers to develop regular and easily memorable evening schedules, pushing them back into the straight-jacket of standardised programme lengths from which some claim to have escaped. Yet at the same time subscribers are reacting to the greater choice available by becoming more discriminating about what they watch than previously. Certainly programme loyalty in cabled homes is much lower than in uncabled; subscribers switch channels far more frequently in search of more satisfying items, with pay-TV homes in particular watching a different channel almost hourly. Moreover, only one-third of the audience of a series return to watch the next episode the following week. From the advertisers' and broadcasters' point of view, an even more worrying fact is that almost 40 per cent of cable subscribers admit to changing channels 'always' or 'often' during commercials as opposed to 15 per cent of non-subscribers, a statistic which if true is disastrous news for commercial television. This trend is exacerbated by the growing number of TV sets with remote controls, of which there are a higher proportion in cabled homes.

Yet channel hopping during commercials may turn out to be one of the strongest cards which narrowcast basic services hold. A viewer's readiness to search elsewhere for entertainment when his or her attention is interrupted depends crucially on the degree of satisfaction with or interest in what is being watched. Programmes with high appreciation ratings are more likely than those with low to gain viewers' undivided attention and to hold on to them during the commercials. The result is that programmes with smaller audiences but greater audience appreciation may well be a better buy for the advertiser, which is exactly the argument which the narrowcast basic services such as Cable Health Network have been using.

Cable subscribers generally express greater satisfaction with television than do non-subscribers, and in terms of programme appreciation actually rate certain basic services above the pay-film channels, although the latter receive much higher viewing figures. The Christian Broadcasting Network, for example, has a small but highly appreciative audience. On the other hand, the considerable expectations which new subscribers have of cable are rarely sustained, hence the high churn rate. Cable services may be an improvement on broadcast, but for many they nonetheless turn out to be a disappointment. For system operators the problem now is to prevent that initial disappointment turning into a positive reaction.

Most people have only limited amounts of disposable income and leisure time. Yet cable and pay-TV in particular eat into both, impinging upon already allocated resources. They may take time and money previously devoted to other media, or they may increase total media use at the expense of non-media activities such as playing a sport, talking or sleeping. Alternatively, they may encourage people to use their time more efficiently and to undertake an increasing number of activities simultaneously, for example, eating while watching television, or watching TV and reading the newspaper. A number of studies suggest that all of these solutions are playing a part.

Looking first at how spare time is allocated, it is not surprising to find that watching television is and has long been the most common leisure activity, although it comes well below participatory sports, reading and other activities in terms of enjoyment derived, as can be seen from Table XIV opposite.

Between 1970 and 1981 the amount of time which each adult spent on passive leisure activities increased by some 25 per cent to sixty-five hours a week. This total includes as separate items leisure activities carried out simultaneously as well as time spent on leisure while also undertaking routine tasks (such as listening to the radio when driving to work or doing housework). The growth in leisure time, therefore, has come partly from decreases in such other non-leisure activities as work, housework, shopping and visiting, and partly from increased doubling up of activity. Looking at how leisure time is distributed, it can be seen that newspaper and magazine reading have both fallen slightly in absolute as well as percentage terms, while use of radio, records and tapes has grown proportionately. Television use has increased most, but proportionately remained relatively stable. Indeed, what is most noticeable is just how small many of the changes are; both this and other studies seem to indicate that although TV watching has eaten into other activities, an important trend has been to the more efficient use of time and to simultaneous multiple activity. Just how much further such a tendency can be taken, however, seems doubtful. Even now the natural corollary is that each activity receives a smaller share of attention while it is taking place than previously.

This table does not, of course, give a useful picture of cable's impact on leisure time in cabled homes. There the evidence remains ambiguous. A survey in Columbus during 1981 revealed little difference between subscribers and non-subscribers in their other media and recreational habits. They spend the same amount of time attending live sports events and in individual hobbies. Subscribers even tend to be slightly heavier cinemagoers and newspaper readers than non-subscribers. Subscribers are generally heavy media users, watching more television and reading more; it may be, therefore, that they have managed to integrate cable into their lives without

246

TABLE XIV
Time spent per person with selected leisure activities
(Source: Economics and Research (CER), Office of Economic Analysis, July 1982)

Leisure activity	Hours per Person per year		Percentage of total time accounted for by each activity	
	1970	1981	1970	1981
Television	1,226	1,511	46.5%	45.1%
Network and affiliated stations		1,131		33.8
Independent stations		334		10.0
Basic cable programmes*		17		0.5
Pay-cable programmes*		29		0.9
Radio	872	1,196	33.1	35.7
Home		754		22.5
Out of home		442		13.2
Newspapers	218	200	8.3	6.0
Records and tapes	68	190	2.6	5.7
Magazines	170	135	6.5	4.0
Books	65	70	2.5	2.1
Videogames: home	–	15	–	0.4
Movies	10	11	0.4	0.3
Spectator sports	3	10	0.1	0.3
Video-cassette recorder	–	6	–	0.2
Videogames: arcade	–	5	–	0.1
Cultural events	3	4	0.1	0.1
Total	2,635	3,352		
Hours per person per week	50.7	64.5		
Hours per person per day	7.2	9.2		

* These figures are national averages and so include uncabled homes.
Consequently they are of limited value.

significant disruption, making better and more creative use of their time than others. Many more activities may be undertaken simultaneously with attention swapping from one to another as required. Cynically one might say that many of the new cable services lend themselves to this kind of semi-attention, for example the continuous news channels, MTV, Nashville, the magazine formats of Daytime and CHN, and even 'adult' entertainment and repeats. In both format and use they are not dissimilar from breakfast television.

But even if cable subscribers do fit as many non-cable activities into their lives as non-subscribers, and so lead fuller lives overall, it may still be that cable has had a detrimental effect. They may, after all, have been even more active before they subscribed than they have been since, visiting the cinema even more often, reading more and attending more sporting events. Having previously been by nature the more active and constructive members of the community, they may now have been reduced by cable to the same level as the traditionally less active non-subscribers. Cable, in other words, may have equalised downwards in terms of non-cable activity. Unfortunately the evidence so far does not allow a conslusion either way. All we can say for certain is that those people who are cable subscribers do seem able, for one reason or another, to do more with their time than non-subscribers.

Turning to the question of how expenditure on the mass media is divided, one must immediately note an important constraint. A number of studies by C. E. Scripps, M. E. McCombs and others have demonstrated that, despite the rise of such new media as radio, television and now cable, the proportion of Gross National Product (GNP) and of consumer and advertiser spending devoted to mass communications has remained remarkably stable since records were first kept in 1929. Even when television was growing most rapidly, between 1948 and 1960, spending on mass communications remained proportionately steady. Total recreational expenditure has similarly altered little; in 1981 Americans devoted about 3 per cent of GNP to passive leisure activities (TV, newspapers, records, films, books, spectator sports, etc.), a percentage unchanged for over thirty years. Yet already some 18 million homes were spending $3.7 billion on cable and pay services and $5.6 billion was being devoted to an even newer activity, videogames. Together they accounted for nearly 12 per cent of all leisure spending.

Neither in the 50s nor today can such expenditure on new media be explained away by general economic growth. On the contrary, what seems to be taking place is a redivision of financial resources amongst the media, with each new means of communication or entertainment providing a functional alternative to an existing system and, if superior, drawing off a proportion of those resources. There is a direct relationship between the rise of some media and the proportionate (in some cases absolute) decline of others. Thus, as radio and television began to perform some of the news, information and entertainment functions of newspapers, so they attracted a share of the resources previously allocated to newspaper reading. As television grew, so admissions to the cinema fell. Given the relative constancy of the proportion of consumer and advertiser expenditure dedicated to the media, the conclusion is clear:

> Even in periods of rapid economic growth new media must battle some of the established media for a share of the market. It is unlikely that a new communication technology provides a totally new service. Rather such technologies are likely to be extensions

of existing services. These functional equivalents must battle for economic survival or economic accommodation in the marketplace (M. E. McCombs, *Mass Media in the Marketplace*, Lexington, 1972, p.47).

As cable and pay television grow, therefore, they will be competing against other media and leisure activities for a share of a limited and defined sum. Looking at how leisure expenditure has been distributed since 1950, it can be seen from Table xv that the greatest proportionate decline has been experienced by the cinema and newspaper industries, with radio also suffering. Growth in book and specialist magazine sales, however, means that the print media as a whole have maintained their general position surprisingly well. Expenditure on cinemagoing dropped throughout the period, but between 1970 and 1981 at a slower rate than previously. The greatest growth has been in the areas of videogames and broadcast and cable television combined. Total television expenditure in 1981 was about $22 billion, of which cable and pay accounted for some $2.5 billion and $1.2 billion respectively, or 4.6 per cent of all leisure spending. Separating cable from broadcast television expenditure is still somewhat difficult because of cable's broadcast relay function. Nevertheless, it is clear that by 1981 cable and pay were attracting expenditure as leisure activities in their own right and taking an increasing percentage of the combined television share. That percentage will continue to grow, and an RCA estimate sees cable and pay revenues (including cable advertising and pay-per-view) almost equalling those from broadcast television advertising by 1990.

If traditional patterns are repeated, therefore, cable's greatest impact should be felt by those media and leisure activities to which it provides the closest functional equivalent, most notably broadcast television and the cinema. Certainly this seems the obvious and likely trend. Yet cable cannot be so readily categorised by functional equivalents. Restricted as it still is to distinct geographical areas, for example, its equivalent from an advertiser's viewpoint is not so much the broadcast networks as the local broadcast stations or the local press. Reservations about the nature of narrowcasting notwithstanding, service providers would argue that the closest equivalents were specialist magazines, notably women's and sports. Pay-TV may appear to threaten the cinema, yet it cannot perform the latter's out-of-home function. Indeed the slowing of the cinema industry's decline during the 1970s and the relative resilience of other out-of-home activities, such as spectator sports and arcade video games, suggests that cinemagoing may not suffer as much as one might expect. Moreover the proportion of leisure spending gained by pay subscriptions on their own between 1970 and 1981 was nearly three times the loss suffered by the cinema during the same period. The implication is that

TABLE XV

Distribution of total expenditures on selected leisure activities in the USA 1950-81
(Percentage of total)
(Source: Economics and Research (CER), Office of Economic Analysis, July 1982)

Leisure activity	1950	1960	1970	1981
Cable (including pay)	–	0.2*	1.1*	4.6
Broadcast television	21.6	19.2	28.3	22.2
Radio	11.3	9.4	8.7	7.3
Newspapers	32.0	37.4	32.1	24.2
Records and tapes	4.1	7.2	7.9	8.6
Magazines	10.3	11.5	9.4	12.3
Books	2.1	2.9	3.8	5.1
Videogames: home	–	–	–	0.7
Cinema	14.4	7.2	4.2	3.7
Spectator sports	2.1	2.2	1.9	2.9
Video-cassette recorder	–	–	–	0.7
Videogames: arcade	–	–	–	6.2
Cultural events	2.1	2.9	2.6	1.6

* Estimate. In 1960 and 1970, of course, most cable was for broadcast relay purposes and so might legitimately be included in the television percentage. Most of the increase by 1981, however, was for cable and pay as leisure activities in their own right.

cable's impact was more broadly spread.

The theory that spending on mass communication and on leisure is constant has remained good for fifty years. Cable and pay as information and entertainment services should not alter the situation and their effect will certainly be felt to a greater or lesser degree by a wide range of services whose functions they at least challenge. Yet in due course cable's non-entertainment side may blur the distinction between spending on mass communication, on leisure and for other purposes. Cable's multi-function character may introduce an important new element into the calculations and force a redefinition of mass media expenditure. Almost certainly cable will have major consequences for the existing broadcasting and cinema industries, as well as for production. But just as it has proved difficult to judge the shape of cable services to come, so it is equally hard to assess what will be overturned as a result. Like many so-called revolutions this one is more of a prolonged transition, in which some existing forms and institutions will fall while others, perhaps changed beyond recognition, will adapt and survive. It is a transition in which some of the dire predictions made will prove unfounded and others all too true, in which many of the most far-reaching changes will emerge gradually and almost unforeseen. We exist at a time when, after a long gestation, the infant has just been born; what we are attempting is to assess from its first cries the nature of the adult and its place in the world.

250

14 Cable and Programme Production

One of the most severe charges made against cable is that it is essentially parasitic in character, living off films and programmes made for the cinema, foreign television or other media and producing little of note itself. Apart from such specialist channels as CNN and Cable Health Network, it is pointed out, relatively few of the films and programmes shown are originated entirely by cable. True or not, such a criticism fails to recognise the increasingly symbiotic character of the entertainment industry and its economy, in which much material is no longer produced for one single medium or with money from one central source, but depends for its profitability on a number of different outlets. In the past those outlets have been limited: a film would go from its cinema release and foreign exhibition into the networks and then to syndication, with the bulk of its revenue coming from the first. A television production's market was confined to networks, foreign television and syndication. Now, however, the new technologies have more than doubled the different ways in which a film or programme can be exhibited, even within the same market area, and each outlet has contributed at least something to a production's total revenue.

Perhaps ironically, one of the few places where the single-outlet programme survives is on the basic cable services. With their enormous demand for material but very low budgets, most depend on cheap programming produced in-house, by small independent producers or bought in from abroad or syndication. Where the broadcast networks pay $6-900,000 an hour for drama series, $3-500,000 for situation comedy, $200,000 for news and documentaries and down to $100,000 for cheaper programmes, basic cable services such as Nickelodeon and USA pay up to $65,000 an hour for original material and under $500 for acquired. According to Reaves Cable Productions, one of the leading independent production companies for basic cable programmes, its budgets in 1982 ranged from $10,000 to $50,000 per half hour. Moreover, whereas networks never show a programme more than twice, the cable services spread their already low costs over many repeats.

In a very few cases programmes shown on basic cable may have larger budgets in the hope that they can subsequently be syndicated or sold abroad. Nickelodeon has managed to sell to foreign broadcasting organisations, while the occasional original production on ARTS has a budget of up to $300,000 in order to give it an 'afterlife'. But invariably these will be co-financed, in some instances with the Public Broadcasting Service. As for the extensive and very cheap material produced by or for USA, Daytime, CHN, the religious channels or ESPN, very little indeed is expected to be saleable elsewhere.

However, it would be wrong to dismiss such services as contributing nothing to the production industry. Certainly they cannot afford programmes from the Hollywood majors or even the principal independent production houses. Nickelodeon may be part-owned by Warner, but the Warner studios simply would not be able to produce a programme for the money which this service could pay. Yet between them the basic cable companies do transmit several thousand hours of material each year, not including repeats or the live twenty-four-hour news channels. Together they probably spend over $200 million annually in licence payments and production costs and have created a market for a wide range of producers geared to their particular low-budget demands. In addition, the large amount of space available on cable has stimulated production among the many media interests who wish to use it to promote themselves or their products rather than to sell programmes at a profit. The most obvious examples of this are the video promotional tapes which record companies allow MTV to play free of charge. Together with a wider development of video promotion on broadcast television, cassette and laserdisc, this has formed the basis for a new production industry to produce music videos, often with high and expensive production values. In fact, by 1982 almost half of all new rock bands were introduced with the aid of a video promotion tape, and the proportion is increasing rapidly.

Another new source of programming for cable is the major magazine publishers. Hearst, predictably, is producing *Cosmopolitan* and *Good Housekeeping* segments for its Daytime service (now merged with Cable Health Network), using some personnel from the magazines' staffs. CBS Publications similarly owns *Woman's Day*, which has a regular video equivalent on USA Network, whilst the Cable Health Network has joined with such magazines as *American Health, Readers Digest, Prevention* and *Psychology Today* to produce health and science material. Meanwhile, on SPN, *American Baby* magazine has leased space to air twenty-six programmes on pregnancy and baby care, and is supported by advertising from Playtex and Fisher Price Toys. Such ventures help to give the newer and struggling cable services a certain recognition, borrowing a print magazine's reputation and seeking its readership. Similarly, they provide magazines with valuable promotion and an opportunity to experiment in the new medium. Following its series for

252

CHN, for example, *Readers Digest* has formed its own video entertainment subsidiary, although others have not found the prospects as attractive. The Meredith Corporation has ended its *Better Homes and Gardens* show on USA, following an unfavourable response from advertisers. Almost all these programmes are looking in the long term to paying their own way; if they fail to do so this boom in cable magazine ventures may prove short-lived.

The two types of programme which seem almost assured, even eternal, are those produced by religious groups and those sponsored entirely by advertisers and industry. The religious networks have already been mentioned as examples of 'free' programming, and on CBN, the Christian Broadcasting Network, God and Mammon are brought together three days a week in a cookery programme sponsored entirely by Proctor and Gamble. CBN has also adopted SPN's strategy of leasing space to anyone who wants it; each Sunday evening 'Travellers' World' comes to peripatetic Christians thanks to American Express and TWA. Devotees of culture have similarly received programmes on ARTS as a result of sponsorship from Mobil Oil, Exxon and Book of the Month Club – in fact, up to 15 per cent of revenue for both ARTS and Daytime comes from full programme sponsorship. Reports of cold weather on the Weather Channel are sponsored by Quaker Oats, those for holidays and resorts by Kodak. Several advertising agencies have stepped up their own production activities in order to create basic cable programmes tailored to their advertisers' needs. Most blatant of the entirely sponsored services is the Modern Satellite Network, all of whose programmes are financed and editorially controlled by advertisers and companies wishing to use a longer period than normally possible in advertising to explain a product or extol their own virtues. MSN is owned and operated by the Modern Talking Picture Service, the world's largest distributor of free-loan films, ranging from educational to industrial material, from a General Motors programme on the automobile industry to US army recruitment films.

The music trade, publishers, religious interests, industrial corporations and other advertisers – all are using cable to press home the message they wish, either sponsoring a cultural or sports event in order to project a corporate image or actually integrating editorial comment and programme content. Many of these programmes are crude and blatant plugs; others cannot be dismissed so easily. MTV's enthusiastic audience accepts video promotions as an entertaining extension of the record-touting radio stations, while the religious channels are merely following the long-established, accepted and respected tradition of evangelism. One may wince at some of the efforts on MSN, but enjoy the sponsored golf on ESPN. Whatever the ethics of sponsorship, it was Mobil Oil which financed the ad-hoc satellite network showing of the Royal Shakespeare Company's *Nicholas Nickleby* in 1983. The concept of sponsored programming in its various forms is undoubtedly ambiguous in its objectives and raises questions about artistic integrity; yet handled properly and recognised for what it is, the end result can be increased production and additional consumer services.

Turning to the pay channels, it is evident that a number are already bringing considerable sums to the production industry. HBO in particular is putting production money into both feature films and made-for-pay programmes, while the latter are also being produced by or for Showtime and smaller services such as the Disney and Playboy channels. Between them they also pay considerable sums for feature-film licences. The increasing importance of pay-TV (including STV) to the film industry, and the relative value of the various outlets in film-rental revenue can be seen in Table XVI:

TABLE XVI

Estimated total rentals by source for feature films of the seven Hollywood majors* 1978-82 (in $ million)
(Source: Wertheim & Co. Inc., 1983)

	1978	1979	1980	1981	1982	1983
US and Canadian cinema	1120	1075	1275	1210	1365	1430
Foreign cinema	750	775	765	750	625	600
Pay television	35	75	155	255	375	535
Network television	275	160	260	180	225	175
Domestic syndication	120	65	140	155	175	150
Foreign syndication	165	200	230	275	290	350
World video cassette and disc	2	25	55	115	200	240
Airline, hotel, etc	28	30	30	30	30	33
Total rentals	2495	2405	2910	2970	3285	3513

* The majors are the seven (formerly eight) principal companies: Warner Bros, Columbia, Paramount, 20th Century-Fox, Disney, MGM/UA and Universal.

The speed with which pay is growing is obvious; already it has overtaken network licences as a source of revenue and is well on the way to matching foreign cinema rentals. HBO alone expects to spend over $500 million on film licences in 1984. According to RCA's estimates, total domestic cinema box-office receipts should reach some $5.6 billion by 1990, of which about $2.4 billion should come back to the distributors in rentals. By then, however, pay and pay-per-view could be reaping $16.3 billion. This would include sporting pay-per-view events and items by companies other than the majors; yet the latters' revenue from pay would still probably equal or exceed that from the box office. Indeed, the

254

studios are annoyed that their share of the pay-TV gross will not be even higher; hence their efforts, as noted earlier, to buy themselves into the principal pay services, and hence a preference for a pay-per-view system in which their return per consumer dollar could match that from the cinema box office.

Against this new source of revenue must be set reduced licence payments from the broadcast networks and from syndication, as well as the probability of a lower cinema box-office take. The latter, however, is more than balanced by pay-TV's appeal not only to normal cinemagoers but also to the thirty-plus age group which rarely goes out to see a film. Consequently, no one really questions that pay-television will greatly increase the production industry's revenues. Indeed, the President of MCA, Universal's parent company, has stated that already, 'If you took away the extra revenues we get from cable, no one would make any movies' (S.J. Sheinberg, President of MCA Inc., quoted by the *New York Times Magazine*, 28 March 1982).

Additional revenues, however, do not necessarily mean either that profit will be higher or that more films will be made. Pay-TV has so far largely involved distributing the same amount of material through an increasing number of outlets, so that it could be viewed by ever larger audiences more times. Similarly, profit depends on interest rates, exchange rates and production costs. The latter in particular have risen sharply since 1978, far outstripping revenue growth and reducing overall profitability. Fees to stars have soared, while such blockbuster disasters as *1941* and *Heaven's Gate* marked the studios' temporary loss of control over their top producers. Even disregarding blockbusters, the average negative costs for a typical film by one of the major studios rose from $9.4 million to about $12 million between 1980 and 1982. With promotional costs of $6-7 million, it can take $18 million to launch even a relatively modest feature.

The traditional industry response in such circumstances is to cut back the number of films produced, placing the studios in a better position to negotiate favourable terms both with the talent involved in production (authors, stars, directors, etc.) and with the exhibitors. Certainly the number of blockbusters in production was reduced in 1982-3. But at the same time it would seem that a number of factors, including growing optimism as to the opportunities to be found in the new technologies, has stimulated a steady increase in the number of films released, as can be seen from Table XVII.

Again, however, more releases do not mean greater profits. The growing demand for films for pay-TV has not been matched by a significantly increased demand from the cinema audience which remains the industry's principal revenue source. Consequently, a higher number of releases can actually depress profits while increasing aggregate film costs. This problem will only gradually be solved as

TABLE XVII

Number of films released by the seven major Hollywood studios, 1977-82*
(Source: Wertheim & Co. Inc.; 1982 MPAA Statistics 1983)

	New releases	Reissues	Total
1977	89	22	111
1978	98	14	112
1979	112	14	126
1980	115	28	143
1981	123	28	151
1982	171	22	193

* These figures include independently produced films released through the majors. Conseqently, the 1981 figure is boosted by the inclusion of eight to ten films from AFD, previously distributed independently, and the 1982 by twenty to thirty of AFD, Embassy and Filmways. In each year the underlying trend remains upward.

pay-TV licences contribute an ever larger share to total revenue. Left to themselves, the majors would probably reduce their output rather than increase it. There has already been some evidence of an industry contraction during the last two years, with MGM taking over United Artists and, amongst the independents, Time-Life Films closing down, Associated Film Distributors effectively ceasing production, others such as Lorimar and Polygram cutting back on features in 1982, and the CBS film division temporarily moderating its plans and being absorbed into the broadcasting group.

Despite the upward trend, therefore, it is still too early to conclude that pay-TV licence payments are having a positive effect on feature-film production. Perhaps more important at present is the general perception of new opportunities and needs, as well as the more practical and active encouragement which Home Box Office is now giving in the way of pre-production financing. Since 1981, HBO has made an increasing number of agreements to put up production money in exchange for exclusive pay and occasionally some ancillary rights to films. It can justifiably argue that already several films would not have been completed without its assistance, including the highly successful and Oscar-winning *On Golden Pond* and *Sophie's Choice*. Its deal with Columbia has already been mentioned; in addition, it has invested heavily in the major independent company Orion, allowing the latter to take over Filmways in 1982, and has offered pre-production financing to New World Pictures, Polygram, EMI, Cannon and others, again in exchange for exclusive pay-TV rights. In the case of Orion and New World, it is said that HBO provides 24-40 per cent of the finance for every film produced, with typical budgets in the lower range by today's standards, i.e. at between $5 million and $10 million. HBO has also helped to form Silver Screen Partners which intends to produce ten to twelve films each year at an average cost of $10 million, with the pay-TV company paying 50 per cent. Most important of all is its entry into partnership with Columbia and CBS to create a new major studio, called Tri-Star, intended to produce twelve to eighteen films between 1983 and 1985.

By April 1983 HBO had made pre-financing deals which gave it exclusive rights to at least sixty-two films during the next two years, in addition to those produced by Tri-Star and Silver Screen. Its objectives in doing so are both to increase the amount of product available and to create a largely exclusive service in order to reduce churn. Many of the films it helps finance may prove unsuccessful at the box office. But this ploy also gives it the chance to scoop the really popular films, bar blockbusters, for which cable subscribers buy a pay service.

Meanwhile, both HBO and Showtime are also putting money into non-theatrical films, specials and series, while a side effect of pay has been to stimulate broadcast network production, as we shall see later. During 1983 and the first half of 1984 HBO will have a hand in twenty-four made-for-pay films, including *The Terry Fox Story*, co-financed with the Canadian pay service First Choice. Indeed, it is a constant feature of such films and other made-for-pay ventures that they are co-financed either with independent broadcasting companies or with overseas partners. HBO and Metromedia are co-financing made-for-pay films for release on pay and independent TV stations, while international co-productions for HBO include *Intimate Strangers*, again with a Canadian pay service, and the *Marlowe Private-Eye* series with London Weekend Television. Like the broadcast networks, both HBO and Showtime are also moving into mini-series, the former with the Australian-co-financed *All the Rivers Run* and the Goldcrest-produced *The Far Pavilions* from Britain. Showtime has similarly co-financed films with Goldcrest, including a new version of Robin Hood.

The extent of the pay services' involvement in financing varies from project to project. In its series *The Paper Chase* Showtime has effectively taken the broadcast networks' place as principal licensee, paying most of the production costs for the pay rights and leaving the producers, 20th Century-Fox Television, with subsequent overseas and syndication sales. Elsewhere, the pay services have also bought some of the subsequent rights; HBO, for example, paid $2.4 million for the pay and domestic syndication rights to the made-for-pay film *Right of Way*, which stars James Stewart and Bette Davis and was budgeted at $2.7 million in all. This is an example of programming which could only have been done on pay, having been rejected by the broadcast networks because of its story about an elderly couple who decide to commit joint suicide when one contracts cancer. Interestingly, Showtime has also joined with the

Public Broadcasting Service in filming stage plays, as did CBS Cable and the Entertainment Channel before they collapsed. The idea is to run the production first on cable and later on PBS, a strategy which once again demonstrates that cable's impact is never straightforward. In some instances this joint venture may lead to an item's delayed appearance on PBS; in others the public service will now get a programme which it could not have afforded to finance by itself. In 1982 HBO also moved into the filming of stage shows and plays, with an emphasis on musicals and comedies such as *Camelot, Bus Stop* and *Groucho*. However, both Showtime and HBO have found audience response to such ventures lower than expected and may well tone down the ambitious plans for monthly theatrical events which were initially planned.

With HBO and Showtime both expanding their made-for-pay series, films and specials, and with the Playboy and Disney Channels also producing their own particular brand of programme, pay is certainly beginning to make an impact on production, although still on a small scale by comparison with the broadcast networks. Other pay services remain unable to do anything other than license existing material, while some of the series which are produced for pay are still low-budget ventures. Showtime's Canadian co-produced 'adult' soaps, for example, cost it about $60,000 for a half-hour episode, as do Playboy's original productions. Outdoor shots are kept to a minimum, while the story-line progresses at a snail's pace in order to economise on sets and actors.

But in recent deals both HBO and Showtime have shown themselves able to buy up or create drama and comedy series at prices almost comparable to those paid by the broadcast networks. Although HBO failed in a bid for *Taxi*, it is said to have offered $460,000 for each half-hour episode, a price equivalent to that which it would pay (multiplied up for increased length) for a moderately successful feature film. *Fraggle Rock* is similarly said to have cost it $300,000 an episode, while Showtime probably paid $4-500,000 for each of seven episodes of *The Paper Chase*. Even so, the production company involved, 20th Century-Fox Television, regarded this as a cost-cutting exercise, filming on 16 mm., editing on videotape and paying lower than normal salaries to the cast. As for the made-for-pay films in which both HBO and Showtime are investing, the budgets vary from $2 million to $5 million, cheap by theatrical standards but more than many made-for-TV films. In each case, of course, the pay services' proportion will depend on what ancillary rights they buy; Showtime still cannot afford more than about $5-600,000 per project and so requires co-financed ventures in which each partner will take the rights of particular interest to them. Given the increasing amount of quality original material they need, both HBO and Showtime see co-financing as an essential and permanent feature of the pay-TV scene, while both are also seeking to escape the traditional

258

production inefficiencies of the major studios by looking to foreign and independent producers.

For the major studios prospects look mixed. Over the past thirty years they have remained powerful because of their position as film financiers and their control over film distribution. Similarly, they have come to dominate broadcast drama production. Now, however, other bodies are moving into film financing, new forms of joint venture are being devised and many independent production companies are appearing. Moreover, as pay-TV develops, so the cinema will become proportionately less significant as a means of distribution (although still playing an important role), so that the studios' massive apparatus of print laboratories and distribution offices will appear decreasingly cost-efficient. Co-financing and pre-buys will also deprive them of the opportunity to exploit the ancillary rights, including pay itself. In this way the studios could become less important in film financing, receive a lower share of revenues, yet remain responsible for the most costly form of distribution. In a better position will be the larger independents which use the majors for theatrical distribution but dispose of the ancillary rights themselves. These should also be better able to adapt to the new forms and lower costs of production required by the pay-TV services.

Yet it would be mistaken to conclude that there is no future for the production giants of Hollywood. They are still by far the most important financing and distributing entities for feature films as well as major producers for broadcast television. It would be absurd to suggest that they cannot and will not adapt to changing circumstances, and indeed in doing so they already have an enormous advantage over newer entrants in the shape of their very considerable film libraries. These are becoming increasingly valuable as cable services seek ever more programming.

The traditional production industry is clearly on the brink of major changes from which not everyone will emerge unscathed. Cable will alter the ways in which films and programmes are financed, how they are produced, who produces them and how they are exhibited. HBO's entry into feature film co-financing will equally importantly give it a major say in the types of film which are made, the storylines which are considered attractive for theatrical and pay release and even the way in which they are shot. Wide-screen television is still some way off; in the meantime the growing financial importance of pay-TV in the life of a film will inevitably force certain artistic concessions to the dimensions of existing television sets. It may even be that the current trend towards films of extreme violence will be reversed as the mainstream and middle-aged audience which makes up a major proportion of HBO's subscribers makes its preferences known.

Cable means more than a new distribution technology. It means a new audience, new conditions in which recent films are watched, new social groupings to watch them, new pricing structures and perceptions of their value. Cable means a further blurring of divisions between film and television programming and between entertainment and advertisement. In the past the character of a programme has been determined not only by audience preferences or artistic considerations but by the source and type of finance for it. Perhaps the biggest impact on production will be from the coming together of different forms of finance and different sources, to produce programmes and films which serve all their different objectives and needs and are released progressively through a wide range of distribution systems. Whether the end result will be a complementarity of interests or a conflict, a narrowing of range or a growth both in quantity and in content, it is still too early to say.

15 Cable, Broadcasting and the Cinema

Cable was described earlier as an infant, but it is quickly showing itself to be a precocious child. Already its many channels or fingers are reaching out to and grabbing the audience which nourishes the broadcast networks and in some cases the films and programmes which clothe both the latter and the cinema industry. Like all inquisitive and acquisitive children it is exploring every nook and cranny open to it, every business from which it might profit, every new programme source to serve its growing needs. Like or loathe it neither the broadcsters nor the cinema exhibitors can ignore this new force.

Already the three broadcast networks are feeling the effect of the new viewing alternatives. Barely ten years ago they could confidently expect to share between themselves up to 95 per cent of the viewing audience each evening. Yet now that proportion is exhibiting a steady decline:

TABLE XVIII

Broadcasting Network Audience Share (%) in the USA, 1976-82
(Source: A. C. Nielsen, Nielsen Television Index, November 1982)

	Primetime	Daytime
1976	90.3	81.8
1977	91.0	79.3
1978	90.3	77.2
1979	89.1	76.2
1980	85.2	74.4
1981	82.3	72.1
1982 (estimate)	78.6	68.5

These national viewing figures include areas where cable is not yet available, so that as its universe grows the networks' national share will continue to fall. Already it can be seen that they have lost 3-4 per cent of the primetime audience each year since 1979 and most estimates agree that by 1990 their share should reach 50-60 per cent. Indeed, in Columbus it has already fallen to 70 per cent and in Wilkes Barre, ten years after it became the guinea-pig town for HBO, to 60 per cent. Nationally, the summer figures are particularly poor, with only a 72 per cent primetime share in mid-1982, while those for pay services grew significantly. This seasonal shift is explained by the networks' long-standing policy of using the summer to repeat their winter fare. Disenchantment with such rapid re-runs has led viewers to look elsewhere, and particularly to the pay channels which continue to provide new films.

This declining share need not necessarily indicate a drop in absolute audience numbers. Pay-cable subscribers in particular do increase somewhat the time they spend watching television so that the actual amount, the hours and minutes they give to the broadcast networks, may not drop by much. Meanwhile, the total number of television households in the United States is rising as the population grows, so that estimates suggest usage of the networks could rise by 1 per cent annually to 1990. On the other hand, increases in viewing hours and in the television population are barely keeping pace with the declining share at present, so that both the networks' audience ratings and, for the first time in 1982, their absolute audience numbers, have also dropped.

TABLE XIX

Household rating and viewing of three networks in primetime 1977-81
(Source: A.C. Nielsen, Nielsen Television Index)

Season	Rating	Viewing (in 1,000s)
1977-78	52.3	38,100
1978-79	51.6	38,400
1979-80	50.9	38,800
1980-81	49.3	39,400
1981-82	46.6 (estimate)	37,400 (estimate)

Of course, the networks can still point to the fact that each continues easily to outstrip any single non-network rival. In June 1982 the average network primetime rating nationally was 12.9 per cent, while those for HBO and WTBS were only 2.2 per cent and 1.1 per cent respectively. But looking only at areas where the latter services were available, HBO's rating rose to 12.2 per cent of subscribing homes and WTBS's to 4.1 per cent. Most interesting is a comparison of audience shares in non-cable, basic-cable and pay-cable homes. As Table XX shows, the difference is remarkable.

Particular films on pay services can draw still larger shares; the first showing of R-rated *Saturday Night Fever* was watched by 54 per cent of HBO homes. *Star Wars* was similarly seen by 34 per cent of HBO subscribers, which means that even at a national level it received 8 per

TABLE XX

Primetime audiences by type of household, May 1980, 81, 82
(Source: A.C. Nielsen, Nielsen Television Index, May 1982)

	Network share	Network rating	Rating of other broadcast stations	Basic-cable channel rating	Pay-channel rating
Non-cable homes					
1980	87	47.7	8.4	–	–
1981	85	48.6	9.3	–	–
1982	84	45.9	9.5	–	–
Basic-cable homes					
1980	79	46.1	11.6	1.7	–
1981	78	44.5	12.1	2.2	–
1982	74	40.0	12.1	2.9	–
Pay-cable homes					
1980	61	38.9	14.7	1.9	12.4
1981	61	39.2	12.6	2.8	12.7
1982	58	38.5	13.6	4.3	14.5

cent of all viewers, plus those who were watching a similar showing on Showtime.

A number of points can be made about the above table. Firstly, not all network erosion can be ascribed to cable. Network shares in non-cabled homes have also declined since 1980, reflecting to some extent the separate growth of independent broadcast stations. However, the reach of the latter has been extended by cable, so that in cabled homes they are together responsible for some of the network fall. On the other hand, the higher ratings for independent broadcast stations in cabled homes do not necessarily indicate that people watch them more because of cable. Rather, it reflects the fact that heavy users of television are more likely to take cable, and particularly pay cable, than are light users. At the same time it is clear that television viewing does increase as a result of subscribing, and the stable network rating but declining network share in pay-cable households between 1980 and 1982 indicates that most of that increase is going to the pay and basic-cable channels, with particular gains in the later evening when the more risqué films and programmes on pay form a powerful attraction. Various estimates, including one by ABC, put the three networks' share of the primetime audience in homes with pay-TV at only 46-7 per cent by 1990.

Of equal interest to the networks are the questions of exactly who is being lost to cable and from what programmes. As we have seen, pay-cable subscribers tend to be in the younger and more affluent demographic groups and are more likely than average to have children. Consequently they are prime consumers whose loss is of great concern to the broadcast networks and their clients, the advertisers. Inevitably the former are seeking to minimise the problem, and a recent study by CBS emphasised that although this category of its audience was suffering some erosion the greatest loss is from the still younger and, to the advertiser, less desirable eighteen to twenty-four age group. Even this, however, is a major consumer group.

Meanwhile, one of the categories of programme to lose audiences most heavily is public affairs. Perhaps not surprisingly the networks' coverage of the 1980 Republican convention caused the pay channels' primetime share to jump by half. National news bulletins have so far held their own, but heavyweight current affairs programmes are doing less well. It is a widely catalogued experience that viewers in a multi-channel environment tend to choose the lighter and less mentally taxing fare, a tendency which clearly works to the detriment of documentaries, current affairs, cultural programmes and serious drama. Yet, although this is potentially a major problem, it is countered to some extent by two other factors. Firstly, the appreciation rating and audience loyalty of such programmes is relatively high, giving them continued advertiser appeal despite smaller audiences. Secondly, serious programmes benefit proportionately more from being repeated than do light entertainment. Viewing in order to be entertained tends to be 'time-period-oriented', i.e. people accept whatever entertainment programming is available at the time when they want to watch. By contrast, viewers decide to watch serious programmes less often, but are more conscious in their decision to do so. The viewing of serious material, therefore, is more 'content or programme oriented'. Consequently, if serious programmes are repeated, particularly at times more convenient to viewers than their normal late-night position, they pick up proportionately more than do lighter shows. If they are available on those rare occasions when viewers have the time and are in the right mood, then they are obviously more likely to be watched. Thus it is within cable's scope, by allowing for multiple repeats of serious material during primetime, to compensate for the losses it causes as a result of its multi-channel character. It may be that the programming on C-Span, the various news channels and ARTS will benefit as a result.

The Public Broadcasting Service provides a similar example of cable's 'swings and roundabouts'. Like other independent stations, those carrying PBS have benefited from being imported by cable into new areas. Again, however, there is a danger that its more serious programmes will suffer in a multi-channel environment, not least because they now also have to compete with ARTS and other highbrow offerings. Meanwhile, the service has been besieged on another front by ARTS, the now defunct Entertainment Channel, and even USA (the

264

English Channel) and HBO, all bidding for or siphoning off the British, European and other culturally upmarket programmes and films which it has traditionally shown. Although it was the first broadcast television network to use satellites to deliver its entire schedule to its affiliates, PBS has found the new technologies a mixed blessing, particularly since it is now threatened with major reductions to its annual budget by a Republican administration which favours cable's free enterprise philosophy.

For both the networks and the independent stations one of the most serious losses is to the audience for feature films. In homes where a film has already been available on a pay service the audience for its network showing can be more than halved. Overall, this may mean an audience reduction of 10 per cent or more. As a result the networks are less keen to show films which have been aired already on pay and are not prepared to pay the distributors as much for them, although the reduction does not match the profit to the film distributor from a pay showing. Similarly, the independent broadcasting stations who rely heavily on older syndicated films find them drawing much smaller audiences than before. Yet distributors who can earn more from a film in six to twelve months from pay than in ten years from syndication are naturally only too eager to do so.

There are two interpretations of how the pay market affects the time it takes a film to arrive on network or independent television, in other words to what extent it deprives those who do not have or cannot afford pay-TV of a feature they would previously have received shortly after its theatrical run. According to the first, the multi-tiered release cycle for films which is now developing – theatrical, video, pay-per-view, pay (exclusive and general), broadcast network and syndication – could actually hasten their arrival on free television. The argument is presumably that the first four stages would all occur within two years of a film's release and each be of relatively short duration, as the distributors sought to exploit several markets in turn. The useful life of a film, during which it earned most of its return, would thus be compressed into the earlier stages, leaving only the by now less important and less lucrative broadcast markets to be tapped. By the same argument, however, broadcasters would be less keen to show such an overexposed film immediately, preferring to hold it back until a reasonable interval had passed. The second interpretation in any case sees the earlier release stages holding on to a film almost indefinitely. A successful blockbuster, for example, could even stay at the pay-per-view stage, being 're-released' for one-night showings every few years in order to catch a new generation. It is by such means, after all, that the Walt Disney organisation has kept its feature cartoons fresh and earning money for over thirty years. Similarly, a one-year exclusive pay-channel licence could delay a film's release to broadcast television still further. In practice, the less popular films seem likely to be delayed little in their passage through to the networks, while for those which are successful the restricted release period will become even longer.

Another almost inevitable consequence of the increased number of programme outlets is a further bidding-up of programme costs. Already the networks are experiencing a serious rise in the amount they are having to pay programme producers, and as the pay services begin to compete for material this trend will increase. In 1982 HBO made its unsuccessful bid for the comedy series *Taxi*, previously aired on ABC, and this competition will undoubtedly have raised the price eventually paid by NBC. Similarly aggressive bidding by STV operator ONTV may have forced ABC to pay over the odds for coverage of the 1984 Olympics. In 1982 Showtime picked up the ex-network series *The Paper Chase* and in 1983 Cinemax actually pirated the satire *SCTV Network* away from NBC while it was still running, although NBC did not try to retain it, in view of its only moderate success in the ratings. Certainly both HBO and Showtime are now sufficiently powerful to bid for series against the networks and it seems inevitable that they will do so, though on a limited scale, given their different needs. Indeed, it is exactly in their need to provide consistently entertaining and high-quality material that the pay services will prove most dangerous, siphoning off, if they are able to do so, the critically acclaimed but popular network successes such as *Soap*, *All in the Family* (the American version of *Till Death Us Do Part*) and *M*A*S*H*. Entertainment specials, such as Paramount's recording of a Frank Sinatra concert in 1982, will also tend increasingly to appear first on pay, as is already happening, with possible subsequent sales to the networks or even to basic cable, DBS or straight into syndication. The ability of pay services to commission series and specials will at the least siphon off 'talent' – stars who would otherwise have appeared on network shows.

According to an RCA estimate, the pay and pay-per-view industries could be earning some $16.3 billion by 1990, compared to the networks' $13 billion, giving the former enormous buying power. Already the networks have lost certain sporting events to HBO and pay-per-view, principally boxing contests. They are unlikely, however, to lose their national football and baseball tournaments, as the sports industry will recognise the promotional value of such national coverage. But the emerging tendency for local teams to move to regional pay channels will certainly hit local broadcast stations, who have traditionally relied heavily on such games to win an audience. For independent broadcast stations, as for PBS, cable cuts both ways.

The audience shares of the networks may be falling but they remain the most heavily watched television channels. CBS alone had an average audience of 14.3 million per primetime minute in 1981. To advertisers, therefore, they are still by far the best way to reach a mass audience, and for many products that is exactly what is wanted. For this reason, and also because in absolute numbers their audience probably will remain relatively stable, most observers do not doubt that network revenue will continue to rise by a respectable 10-12 per cent each year. Central to their success are the concepts of the weekly series to hold an audience, the nightly schedule which viewers know and can rely upon, and the link with local stations to allow local news and items to be inserted into a national broadcast.

Nevertheless, the drop in their popularity remains a very considerable worry. Reduced shares mean lower revenue growth, with the loss of only one daytime rating point over the year costing a network some $60 million. To companies accustomed to a three-way share-out of 90 per cent of the audience it is a sorry prospect to have to make do with only 60 per cent. The demise of one of the three is even being talked about. Equally possible is a break-up of the entire network affiliate system. Satellites give broadcast stations access to a vast new range of material, as those which carry CNN Headline News have already discovered. Independent and PBS stations already receive many programmes in this way, and from 1985 NBC plans to transmit its entire schedule on one of parent company RCA's own satellites. No doubt the other networks will follow. But if network material finds it difficult to pull in the audiences, or if a certain programme proves unpopular in a particular market, there will be little to prevent the affiliates replacing it with another more popular show. Already this is happening on an ad hoc basis and could also prove attractive to programme distributors who, by distributing direct to stations, effectively cut out the network middleman. Although moves in this direction are still tentative and will certainly encounter many obstacles, the time may come when stations can earn more in this way than they do from the affiliate compensation they are currently paid for carrying network programmes.

Conversely, it might eventually be to the networks' advantage to drop their affiliates. By the mid-90s they might be able to reach the same sized audience as at present by a combination of satellite distribution direct to cable systems, DBS direct to uncabled homes and their own owned and operated broadcast stations. Ted Turner's WTBS superstation would effectively have shown them the way, with savings both in transmission costs and in the need to pay affiliate compensation. Thus, to the cable subscriber, the increasingly artificial distinction between cable and broadcast networks may vanish completely; indeed, already the other two particular characteristics of the broadcast networks – series and nightly schedules – are being adopted by cable services, as noted earlier. In due course the pay channels, 'broadcast' networks and basic cable services may be differentiated solely by the character and cost of their programmes.

Such extreme consequences of the coming of cable and satellites are still some way off. Yet already a growing together, even integration, is happening at a corporate level. The three network corporations are guarding their future by moving into the new technologies, diversifying and adapting to the new conditions, and this is certain to continue and intensify. From a programme standpoint, ABC appears the most aggressive, with interests in ARTS, Daytime, the ill-fated SNC, ESPN and a pay-per-view scheme with Cox. It is also developing TeleFirst Entertainment Recording Services, a system for broadcasting premium films on a pay basis overnight, for recording on subscribers' video-cassette machines. ABC Video Enterprises has been created to co-ordinate both these operations and the Corporation's expanding film and programme production business, as well as its sales of product to the overseas and domestic video markets. CBS, likewise, is entering new fields, including cable-system ownership, film production (for example, Jon Voight's *Table for Five*), multi-channel MDS, DBS-delivered high-definition television, videotex, other electronic publishing ventures and cable services through the short-lived CBS Cable. In the search for new sources of revenue, CBS is suffcently strong to absorb the latter's failure, just as NBC's parent RCA can write off the loss from its Entertainment Channel. Elsewhere, its involvement in the new technologies ranges from production to video cassettes and discs, domestic hardware (VCRs, videodisc players, televisions) and, particularly valuable, satellite ownership and operation.

In their broadcast operations, meanwhile, all three networks are reacting in various ways to the immediate threat of declining audience shares. In a clear response to Ted Turner's twenty-four-hour news channels and to his offer to provide news segments for network affiliate use, all three have extended their schedules and greatly increased their late-night and early-morning news and information programming. With news being one of only two areas where the networks are allowed to produce significant amounts of programming themselves (the other being sport), they are clearly concerned that neither the affiliates nor the audience should look elsewhere for it. In an effort to ensure viewers are tuned in both when they go to bed and when they get up, therefore, ABC has added news programmes from 12.00-1.00 a.m. and 6.00-7.00 a.m. NBC has similarly extended its late-night schedule to 2.30 a.m. with start-up at 6.00 a.m., while CBS, most significantly, has effectively gone to a twenty-four-hour schedule with news overnight from 2.00 through to 6.00 a.m.

The problem of particularly severe audience erosion during the summer has also led to an improvement in the service to consumers. Traditionally, network series have been in twenty-two episode runs, starting in the autumn with a repeat showing during the summer. There has been a mutually agreed non-competitive period in June, July and August. Now all three networks have begun to bring out new

268

programmes during the summer also and to reduce the number of repeats. CBS, for example, showed twenty-eight original episodes of *Dallas* in the 1982-3 season, rather than the normal twenty-two. Shows which have failed in the ratings in their first weeks may be given longer to prove themselves, instead of being withdrawn immediately. More interestingly from the producer's point of view, ABC and NBC have both expressed a determination to use the summer for more 'innovative and experimental' programming, although with an emphasis on low-budget production. The level of experimentation is revealed by ABC's decision to try in primetime a five-day-a-week soap opera of the kind normally shown during the day. Nevertheless, more original material can only be good news for producers and viewers alike.

Another programme trend which may or may not prove important in the long term is the increased use of mini-series and long-form programmes shown over two or more consecutive nights. During 1982-3 dramatised versions of bestsellers *The Thorn Birds* and *The Winds of War*, lasting ten and eighteen hours respectively, received huge audiences, effectively wiping out the non-network competition. *Winds of War*, shown over six evenings and given a massive promotional campaign beforehand, earned ABC audience shares of between 49 per cent and 56 per cent, amounting to some 140 million viewers. During 1983 all the networks showed between four and six such made-for-television blockbusters, in addition to a number of smaller two-part stories of the 'bestseller' variety. However, it is still too early to say that such material will become a larger and more permanent feature of the networks – a similar boom in mini-series between 1977 and 1979, following the success of *Roots*, proved disastrous. With up to fifteen such series being shown in a season, each demanding the viewer's attention for several consecutive nights, audience loyalty will be tested to the limits. In any case, these are essentially occasional and special events and cannot solve the audience loss by themselves.

Winds of War is said to have cost $40 million to make and $23 million to promote. Apart from such blockbusters, however, the networks seem certain to try to slow down spiralling production costs. Already there are signs that they are beginning to increase the number of co-production ventures they undertake with foreign companies and to reduce the licence payments they are prepared to make for the average studio-produced television series. At the same time made-for-TV films of standard length seem to be on the increase, as networks find that they can get as good an audience for such relatively inexpensive features as for theatrical films which have already appeared on pay. Instead of paying possibly $4-5 million for two showings of a theatrical film, a network can gain equal or better audience figures for a made-for-TV film costing $3-4 million. And at the same time the trend towards made-for-TV and away from films already shown on pay is very much a reassertion by the networks of the traditional exclusivity of their material. Finally the networks have for many years now been fighting to regain the right to take a financial interest in any programme they show and to own domestic syndication rights. Prohibited from doing so since the early 1970s because of their monopoly powers, they are now arguing that the new competition from HBO and others has left them in a disadvantageous position in their negotiations with producers. The FCC's widely expected repeal of this 'financial interest' rule, allowing them back into production in a big way, could be worth some $600 million-$1 billion a year.

In the long run the networks must accept that, skilled as they are in drawing a mass audience, the increased number of channels will of its very nature fragment the viewing public. Cable is all about fragmentation, cutting the cake into smaller slices. The networks will continue to broadcast programmes with the same mass appeal as before, and consequently to get the lion's share of that cake. They are and will remain in the mass audience business. But they will have to fight ever harder against a number of not dissimilar general entertainment and some specialist services. To do so they will have to keep on producing new but popular formats such as mini-series to differentiate themselves, and to promote programmes more heavily in advance and in other media. In the face of such competition and of such an inexorable ratings decline it may well be that many aspects of their service will improve, with fewer repeats and longer hours. What is certain is that in their search for the mass audience they will become more aggressively competitive than ever before.

Meanwhile the cinema industry has for several years now been seen as an inevitable victim of the new media, which it is supposed will complete the audience erosion begun by broadcast television. Cinemas, it is suggested, may become merely a means of promoting films in order to stimulate interest in them for their pay-per-view, video and pay-TV releases. Yet despite such dire predictions the traditional forms of distribution appear at present to be holding their own. In fact not only are box-office revenues growing slowly, but so too and more interestingly are cinema admissions. In 1982, a year in which pay-TV reached 15-16 million homes, cinema attendance actually increased slightly to 1.18 billion people, the highest since 1966. A continuing rise in the number of single people in the population should give a further boost, since these are amongst the most frequent cinemagoers. Far from directly competing with the cinema, pay-TV in its presently dominant per-channel form may even stimulate interest in filmgoing. Although it offers recent features it does not yet carry the very latest releases; nor can it yet provide the atmosphere, the excitement, on occasion the overwhelming emotional experience which the cinema is able to do. Until high definition television with a large wall-screen and altered picture ratio is developed, and in an economic form, the cinema's dominating screen size, its ever more complex sound systems and not least the sense of communal experience it provides, will remain a potent attraction, both for those seeking a special occasion and for the younger age group who wish simply to get out of the house. The present genre of special effects films only emphasises the difference.

The future of the cinema may become more fragile, however, as pay-per-view becomes an important option for film distributors. Then its prospects may come to depend crucially on the attitude of the studios themselves and the order of the film release strategy which emerges. Once the latest release is available on cable and video, how highly will viewers rate the cinema's unique qualities? If distributors continue to give films the current exclusive cinema release period of one year or longer then cinema prospects look fair. But if they find it more profitable to reduce that 'window', or even to remove it entirely and to release films almost simultaneously theatrically, on pay-per-view and on video, then it seems inevitable that the cinema's audience will decline. As yet such a strategy is simply not in a film distributor's interests. But if he could promote a film entirely on cable, dispense with the need to produce several hundred costly film prints, dismantle his physical distribution system and get the same return from one or two pay-per-view showings as from weeks and months of cinema exhibition, then it would obviously make economic sense to do so.

In these circumstances the only hope of the cinema owners might be themselves to adapt to the new technology. Already many have installed satellite receiver dishes and video projection systems in order to receive and exhibit the boxing championship fights which are the most popular pay-per-view events. They could equally use these systems to exhibit films released on a pay-per-view basis, thereby reducing (although not eliminating) the need for physical distribution. In the majority of areas, where addressable systems which allow pay-per-view remain a distant prospect, the way is open for cinema owners themselves to cash in on the very system which appears to threaten their existence. And even where cabled pay-per-view is possible, there may still remain a market for out-of-home viewing of films and other pay-per-view events. It will be an irony indeed if the cinema survives precisely as a venue for watching pay-per-view sporting events which only a few years before were available free and in the home on broadcast television.

That the broadcasting and cinema industries will survive the onslaught of cable there seems little doubt. In some respects the service they provide may even benefit. Broadcasters will have to react in new ways to new forms of competition, whilst cinema exhibitors will exploit the new potential of live pay-per-view programming. For neither do the prospects appear necessarily as grim as they have been painted. But equally the character of both will undergo significant changes so that the organisations and industries which eventually emerge will be very different from those which exist today.

PART FIVE
British Plans and Prospects

16 The Regulatory Environment

The American and Canadian experiences of cable clearly do not allow of simple or instant conclusions; nor can what has happened there be applied directly to Britain. Major differences exist in economic situation, cultural environment and (as between America and Britain) traditional political and social attitudes towards broadcasting. Nevertheless what has happened there does provide a standard or yardstick against which to gauge developments in Britain, as well as some valuable and salutary lessons. Moreover the conditions which exist in the USA or Canada do not all need to be replicated for at least some of what has happened in either to be repeated elsewhere. The differences of situation should not be allowed to obscure the similarities – notably the artificially constricted character of the industry until recently, the commercial, market approach which is now being taken, the early emphasis on entertainment services and the evident consumer interest in television, home entertainment and new technologies. On the last point the difference in disposable income between the USA and Britain is frequently mentioned as a reason for scepticism about the readiness of the latter to pay for cable; but it is worth noting that Britain has one of the highest annual expenditures on television, video entertainment and information sources per capita of all the developed nations, despite being now amongst the poorest. Disposable income, in other words, is a bad guide to media consumption.

Consequently we can and should attempt to learn from the experience of others, relating it to our own different circumstances, adopting and adapting where possible those aspects which have proved well judged and recognising where to take a different line when objectives have not been realised. To dismiss what is happening in North America as irrelevant is to deny the possibility of comparison – not of like with like but of one relatively well-advanced experience with another where the ground rules are only now being laid down.

In the year since Lord Hunt reported some thirty companies or consortia have declared their intention of bidding for between thirty and forty cable franchises, several system manufacturers have produced a variety of systems or components and up to twenty cable programming services have been announced. The tendency in all these ventures to share both expertise and the risks involved means that well over a hundred companies from Rediffusion to Ladbroke and W. H. Smith have by now declared an interest in system manufacture, construction or operation, or service and programme provision. For the most part such developments have taken place in the months since the cable White Paper was published in April 1983, for it is this document above all which has indicated how the Government intends to turn its general approach into practice.

The White Paper is an altogether more considered document than either ITAP or Hunt, as even the Shadow Home Secretary, Roy Hattersley, conceded during the Commons debate. Its policy proposals, now embodied in the Cable and Broadcasting Bill, are explained and justified in great detail, evidence of the problems which have been experienced in attempting to reconcile conflicting demands and of the inevitable compromises to which these have led. Moreover both it and the statements which followed its publication demonstrated a greater recognition than ITAP showed of the uncertainties involved, as Lord Whitelaw has admitted:

> What is certainly true is that cable systems will be expensive to provide and that if they are to have any chance of success the public will need to be convinced in significant numbers that it is worth paying extra for the service cable provides. To what extent, and how quickly, the country will be cabled is impossible to forecast. By the same token, the effects it will have cannot be known. . . What needs to be emphasised is that, just as I have expressed uncertainty about the way cable will develop and about how successful it will turn out to be, the Government's White Paper is not grounded in a total conviction that cable can achieve the potential which it undoubtedly holds (Lord Whitelaw, Debate on the Cable White Paper, House of Lords, 7 July 1983, col. 654).

This is not to say, however, that the White Paper is a cautious document or that the Government has in any significant sense retreated from its basic approach. On the contrary the latter remains extremely positive: 'The Government believes that the need to adapt to and harness the benefits of new technology is one of the greatest challenges facing our nation today . . . any attempt to disregard the technological revolution which is now upon us, or to embrace it half-heartedly, would be short-sighted . . . if the opportunities that arise are not taken, this country will run the risk of finding itself increasingly dependent on others, culturally as well as economically and industrially' (*The Development of Cable Systems and Services*, Cmnd 8866, April 1983, para 2).

Neither could the powerful warnings of cable's potentially dire consequences, nor the evidence of its shortcomings from North America, influence the fundamental political philosophy which has guided the Government in the policies it is following. Already its broader telecommunications policy is one of 'introducing and promoting competition so that both industry and the consumer can benefit from the resultant gains in efficiency' (Ibid, para. 174). Committed as it is to rolling back the frontiers of the state, to encouraging economic and industrial efficiency through the competitive process, to denationalising major industries and splitting them into smaller and more manageable units, it is hardly likely that it would take on board the state-financed national network which the Opposition has been advocating. Given its belief similarly in the verdict of the market, the very fact that cable's future is not assured could only reinforce Kenneth Baker's conviction that 'cable will flourish in this country only if it is funded and driven by the private sector. It is not for Government to invest in cable and dictate the pace at which it can be received' (Kenneth Baker, Debate on the Cable White Paper, House of Commons, 30 June 1983, col. 788-9).

Above all the Government's support for cable, privately funded and market led, is founded firmly on its dislike of regulatory constraint, particularly of the means of communication. The cable revolution is frequently criticised for being technology-inspired – for happening simply because the technology is now available which makes it possible, whether or not it is wanted or needed. Government policy meets this criticism head-on and asks why not? If a technology has within it the seeds of economic growth why should it be held back? Moreover, given the reality of the broadcasting duopoly – that whatever its advocates say it is the product of a technical limitation – why should not the removal of that limitation be pursued and welcomed? In its regulated character broadcasting has been an essentially abnormal development in the historical fight to reduce government involvement or intervention in communication; indeed the trend has already been towards a gradual increase in the number of broadcasting channels, a trend for which previous Conservative governments have been largely responsible. Now cable makes a major expansion possible, and the Government sees this as an opportunity to move for the first time some way from the traditional broadcast regulated model. Economic and communications policy reinforce each other in the Government's declaration of its 'duty to enable new technology to flourish and fulfil its potential unfettered by unnecessary restrictions' (Cable White Paper, para 87). Moreover the criticism of a technology-induced revolution carries within it a prima facie justification of the market approach. Where a new technology is involved for which the demand is unclear how else can it be determined whether or not the massive investment involved is justified, other than by allowing it to find its own level?

For the Opposition such a market and piecemeal approach is

short-sighted and inadequate. If cable has the potential which it is widely thought to have, if it is as important for the future telecommunications structure and hence economic benefit of the country as the Government insists, then surely its development should be planned, using a standard and British technology, constructed as a national network by a national carrier (BT) and regulated to ensure that its full potential is realised but without endangering the broadcast services supplied to non-subscribers. As Roy Hattersley stated during the Commons debate on the Hunt Report, 'We want to see a successful cable system. We want to see the jobs that it can create. We want to see the social and technical benefits that it can bring about. However we want all the benefits to be enjoyed by all the people, not to be exploited by a handful of foreign-based companies and not used to dilute the standards and content of British television' (House of Commons, 2 December 1982, col. 429).

The White Paper sets out the four elements which are at the heart of the Government's broad strategy. Firstly, cable investment should be privately financed and market led; secondly, regulation should be as light as possible so that investors are free to develop a wide range of services and facilities; thirdly, flexibility is necessary in the regulatory framework so that it can be continually adapted to meet changing conditions, as technology constantly changes what is practicable or economic; and fourthly, despite this light and flexible approach, a small number of key safeguards should be applied to guide cable development in certain desired directions, to ensure that existing broadcasting and telecommunications services are safeguarded and to take account of the fact that cable services will be directly available in the home. In its detailed policy proposals, therefore, the White Paper is an attempt to marry the first three elements with the last and to bring together and reconcile the various objectives of the cable revolution as originally proclaimed. That task has not been easy.

THE CABLE AUTHORITY AND THE FRANCHISING PROCESS

Although the Government has repeatedly emphasised that regulation should be as light as possible, it has nevertheless recognised that a degree of supervision is going to be necessary, both in awarding franchises and in overseeing system operation. Consequently, having accepted that the *de facto* local monopoly character of cable makes a formal franchising process essential, it has come down heavily in favour of a national cable authority as recommended by Lord Hunt, acknowledging in doing so the American and Canadian experience.

Furthermore, whilst the White Paper declares that companies should be free to carry on their business with the minimum of detailed supervision, it also emphasises that the Authority will have responsibility for 'monitoring the performance of cable operators to ensure that promises made are promises kept, and that the regulations for cable are observed and the public interest served' (White Paper, para. 43). Indeed the White Paper is peppered with such phrases, so that following its publication *The Times* even went so far as to describe it as a 'cautious and familiar framework' (28 April 1983). Some commentators have compared the new Cable Authority's potentially wide reserve powers and the flexible approach which it is intended to take with the position of the early ITA, and the *Guardian* concluded that 'the blithe vision of unregulated broadcasting, subject only to blessed market forces which infused Hunt, has grown much greyer. There is a lot more balance and public duty in this latest White Paper . . . the Home Office has been strong enough to bring cable within the existing ethos of British broadcasting but too weak to stop Industry and Downing Street getting, for heaven's sake, something *moving*' (*Guardian* 28 April 1983).

The new Authority is nevertheless designed to be a small body without direct day-to-day supervisory powers over cable operators, and its central task initially at least will be in awarding franchises. Following Hunt's analysis, the Government has accepted that there is no need to mandate separate cable system provision and operation, but also accepts that the two functions should be licensed separately. The central award is to be that of an eight-year franchise (twelve years for the initial award) by the Cable Authority to the operator, with the Department of Trade and Industry in turn granting a licence to the system provider after consultation with the new Office of Telecommunications (OFTEL).

Throughout the debate ministers have repeatedly emphasised that the underlying motivations for their encouragement of cable are firstly to provide a domestic demand for advanced technology, in order to stimulate the relevant British industries, and secondly to create an advanced broadband telecommunications system which would have an even more profound impact upon the economy. It would have been open to the Government therefore to stipulate as policy that only advanced fibre-optic and switched systems, in which Britain has considerable technical expertise, be used. That way, according to the *Guardian*, 'lies huge export potential and an adornment to our economic infrastructure' (28 April 1983).

Yet that route has not been taken. Indeed it is evident from the White Paper that the Government is extremely anxious to see rapid progress and fears that such technical restrictions could lead to unacceptable delay as well as creating further obstacles to the free workings of the market. As the White Paper points out, neither switched nor optic-fibre systems are yet fully field-proven; nor are they likely to be available on a production basis before 1985-6. Moreover their likely higher initial capital cost might, it is feared, dissuade some potential operators. In any case to specify a particular technology would be to exclude British industry from countries which did not go the same way, as well as to shut the door on possible technical developments in other directions. In this respect the White Paper notes the plans which Thorn-EMI announced during 1982 to develop an improved tree and branch system using teletext technology (in which Britain is again a world leader) for the interactive element. Restrictions and delays would therefore 'prevent UK industry from developing the production capacity in all the areas needed if it is to take advantage of the worldwide demand that is likely to develop' (White Paper, para. 27).

With these various considerations in mind, and determined as it is to maintain the impetus, the Government has therefore decided not to insist upon optic or switched technology, despite their apparent advantages, but to allow individual cable providers to decide. As expected it has rejected the idea that BT should be responsible for providing the entire physical network, although it will be able to provide individual systems and be a partner in cable consortia. This decision in itself has opened up the hardware market to a host of competing companies offering complete systems. The Government has also licensed eleven new systems under interim franchises in advance of the cable authority being established, so that construction work can begin during 1984. Each is to be limited initially to a maximum size of 100,000 homes.

Nevertheless one of the most important technical lessons from North America is the very evident need for flexibility and adaptability of design to meet future needs, and the long-term cost of taking too short-sighted an approach. Both use and technology are constantly evolving and the system architecture should be designed to allow for this. A number of steps have been taken, therefore, to encourage providers to offer the favoured switched systems or ones which at the very least are capable of being upgraded, and to adopt certain minimum standards which will allow some degree of interactivity. The underground ducts of all systems therefore, even tree and branch, must be laid out in a star configuration to allow eventual conversion to a switched-star network when the demand for interactive services warrants it. Moreover it has been specified that all systems must provide at least twenty-five downstream television channels with associated sound and teletext data channels, at least one return video channel, an adequate number of audio and two-way data channels (some of sufficient capacity for high speed data or voice telephony) and provision for several subscribers to have simultaneous access to the return video and two-way data channels. In addition (and in contrast to the United States) all systems must be compatible at their headends with the interconnecting networks of BT and Mercury, so that eventually they can be transformed from a collection of isolated cable systems into an integrated network capable of carrying most interactive services. As the White Paper seeks to emphasise, 'The Government is not prepared to see the introduction of

280

wideband cable systems solely in terms of the provision of more entertainment channels. The range of non-broadcasting services . . . which the new systems can support is seen as a crucial aspect in the development of these systems' (White Paper, para. 29). Finally, as an incentive to system providers to choose switched technology, the licences for the latter will run for twenty years as opposed to the less attractive period of only twelve for tree and branch systems. The character of the system proposed and the number of interactive services to be offered will also be taken into consideration in determining between competing bids at the franchising stage.

In considering how franchise areas will be chosen the Government has arrived at what could best be described as a negotiated compromise. Recognising that it will be very much for private companies to take the initiative, based on their analyses of market demand, it has been decided initially to allow the latter to propose areas for cabling rather than for the authority to divide the country into specific franchise 'plots'. Hunt's proposal that operators be required to take on less economic areas in return for the plum franchises has been toned down in view of the problems which many are likely to face in any case. However the Authority will be able to modify operators' proposals at the margins so that peripheral areas of less economic appeal can be covered. Moreover the Government has endorsed Hunt's view that franchises should not exceed 500,000 homes and that in general they should be much smaller, although the Cable Authority will have wide discretion on this point. Perhaps most important, however, the latter will have the duty in awarding franchises to take account of natural community groupings and to ensure that systems are not so large and amorphous as to lose their local identity. Cabling must also be comprehensive within a franchise area. In this way the dangers of 'cherry-picking' or 'creaming' – that is cabling only the roads or sections of a franchise where there are most likely to be potential subscribers – should be avoided. It is hardly surprising that in their bids for franchises most applicants have stressed the self-contained character of the area they are proposing to serve.

Despite these safeguards there must remain concern as to what extent this negotiated method of choosing franchise boundaries will in practice lead to the creation of uncabled areas which have few if any economic attractions from an operator's point of view. Perhaps this is unavoidable and certainly the Government has given the Cable Authority considerable freedom in developing its policy on this issue. Perhaps alternatively the economics of cable in Britain will surprise those who expect it to be essentially a largely urban phenomenon. Nevertheless the Government's decision not to impose upon the Cable Authority a duty from the beginning to encourage the complete cabling of the country may prove a handicap if this does eventually become a recognised objective. The

White Paper justifies the additional disparity in services between urban and rural areas which cable could create as 'one of those many qualitative differences between town and country life to which people attach more or less importance in relation to their personally held preferences' (White Paper, para. 6). The implication is that cable will only ever be regarded as a luxury and not as an essential service. Yet the same argument was being used in 1895 by the Liberal Postmaster General with regard to telephone companies: 'There is a great distinction between telephone companies and gas and water companies. Gas and water are requisites for every inhabitant in a district, but the telephone cannot, and never will be, an advantage which can be enjoyed by large masses of the working classes' (Quoted by *Screen Digest*, August 1983, p. 148). There are very few today who would argue that the telephone is not an important service which should be available to all who want it.

Predictably a number of restrictions have been placed upon cable system ownership and operation. Foreign companies may have a share in a system but not a controlling interest, whilst press, television and radio companies cannot control a cable operation in their own areas. Local authorities and religious and political groups can only participate in cable consortia in exceptional circumstances and if the Cable Authority is satisfied that their involvement is not against the public interest. In general the Cable Authority will therefore have a duty to prevent a concentration of media power within any single area, although minority interests by the local press or ITV/ILR franchisee in a cable company will be considered acceptable.

The nature of a company's ownership and the size of the area proposed are just two of the factors which the Authority will have to consider in awarding franchises. Others include whether an applicant's financial projections appear realistic, whether it will be able to provide all the services it promises within a reasonable period and the order and comprehensiveness of its cabling. The range and diversity of the entertainment services, the proposals for community, access and leased access channels, the provision of interactive services and the proportion of British and European programming to be used are also to be major criteria. The Authority will consult with local opinion in reaching its decisions, although the final decision will be its alone.

THE REGULATION OF CABLE SERVICES

Although the precise character of the services to be offered will be determined by individual system operators and by national service providers, the Government has nevertheless recognised that certain additional public considerations must be applied. Consequently it has set out a number of requirements for operators and guidelines for the cable authority to take into account both during franchising and in the day-to-day monitoring process.

Not surprisingly, for example, it has endorsed the 'must-carry' proposals of the Hunt Report, not only for existing broadcast services (including radio) but also, and more controversially, for future DBS channels, working on the principle that cable subscribers should have access to the same range of services as those equipped with individual aerials and receiving dishes. Nor has it thought it right for system operators to charge an additional subscription for DBS services which are free or advertiser-financed, although naturally they will be able to charge a premium for DBS pay services. Controversy has arisen over the large amount of a cable system's bandwidth which might be consumed by DBS services, not least because government policy on satellite technology might necessitate the duplication of DBS signals on two different transmission standards.

Beyond the must-carry rules there are no positive requirements upon operators as to the type of programming they should transmit. Indeed the White Paper even admits that there is no need to require operators to offer a varied and high quality service, since cable's success will depend on people's readiness to pay for it and recognition that it offers value for money. However the quality of service proposed will be a major consideration for the Cable Authority in awarding franchises and it will have a duty to monitor actual performance. One might question what this can mean in practice; even if an uncontested franchise application does not appear to offer the quality of service that might be wished for there will still be strong pressure upon the Authority to give its approval. Otherwise it would be restricting the growth of the industry as a whole and preventing an entire area from having the opportunity to receive cable. Since the majority of applications are at present uncontested the companies concerned are in a strong bargaining position. Government policy is based on the view that cable must succeed or fail and find its character through its interaction with the market and the general public and through the latter's perception of its value. It cannot have it both ways and, in the absence of competition between franchise applicants, impose additional values or criteria between cable and the market, in the shape of the Cable Authority. Nor will it subsequently find it easy to monitor performance.

This dilemma is evident in the approach which has been taken towards community and minority services. The Government has rejected the idea that operators should be specifically required to provide certain channels such as community, access, education and local government. In a rather weak justification of this decision the White Paper argues that 'to attempt to prescribe in advance those kinds of channels which all operators would have to provide would inevitably involve invidious and to some extent arbitrary distinctions between many intrinsically meretricious causes' (para. 131). Moreover, it suggests, cable operators will have plenty of space on their systems and so be very willing to accommodate such specialist programming. However in awarding franchises the Cable Authority will 'take account of the range and diversity of the services proposed and of the arrangements for community programmes and local access.' This should ensure, it concludes optimistically, 'that prospective cable operators take seriously the need to provide a programme package which will be in the best interests of the whole community' (Ibid). Certainly there are unlikely to be any prospective operators who do not recognise in this an expectation that community/access/minority needs will be met. Indeed it must be said that many are firmly committed to cable's community role, quite apart from recognising its marketing benefits. Nevertheless American experience has shown that community, access and educational facilities are amongst the areas which benefit most from the competitive franchising process, whereas in those franchises in Britain which are uncontested there is clearly an opportunity for any potential franchisee to define the community facilities to be provided as he wishes. Undoubtedly every system built in Britain will offer a channel for this type of use, as well as a studio, but many may be tempted to provide only the minimum in each case as well as only the basics of a production/community-training crew. It is all very well for an operator to state his intention to promote community use of cable by providing the facilities, but experience shows that a far more positive commitment and involvement by the operator together with an organised 'facilitator' or enabling group is really necessary if this type of service is to succeed.

The Government does not consider that it is for the cable authority to ensure a high standard of cable service; indeed it argues that diversity and quality of service will 'best be encouraged' by leaving such matters to the market. Nor are strict religious and political impartiality or balance essential, although there must be no bias across all the services of any system, news must be presented impartially and political and religious interests will not be allowed to control entire channels. But if in these matters the Government has shown a relatively liberal attitude, in the area of taste and decency it has taken a predictably conservative stance, accepting Lord Hunt's recommendation that operators should be subject to the same standards in both as are the BBC and IBA. This means that they will be required 'to ensure so far as is possible that nothing distributed offends against good taste and decency, or is likely to encourage crime or lead to disorder or to be offensive to public feeling; and to have special regard to programmes broadcast when large numbers of children and young persons are likely to be watching.' Moreover where Hunt suggested an exemption to this rule for electronically lockable pay channels, opening the way for 'X' (18) rated material, the Government has maintained a much stricter approach.

Recognising the view that violence and pornography are growing and excessive, it has ruled that the same standards should apply to all channels: 'So-called "adult channels" have no place on the sort of cable systems which the Government wishes to see develop' (para. 137). However ambiguity and compromise rear their heads in the very same paragraph when it is acknowledged that 'in certain carefully defined circumstances it will be acceptable for operators to show some material passed for public exhibition by the BBFC (British Board of Film Censors) which would not be appropriate on a generally available channel broadcast by the BBC and IBA.' Quite what this means will be for the Cable Authority to decide. Interpreted strictly it could result in a very severe restriction upon what films can be shown on cable and hence of its overall attractiveness and viability. Taken in the ambiguous sense in which it appears, it could merely mean that, whilst dedicated 'adult channels' are prohibited, more risqué (and violent) material could appear on a mixed film channel late at night – as on the earlier pay-cable trials. In the hard realities of the market the latter seems very much more likely.

As expected, the Government has also taken a different line from Hunt with regard to pay-per-view. Hunt had rejected pay-per-view on the grounds that it would be even more likely than pay-per-channel services to siphon major sporting events and other programmes away from broadcast television and so to deprive those who did not have cable. This decision was the subject of sustained pressure by the Cable Television Association and others, who argued that Hunt's other recommendations on non-exclusivity of major events would effectively prevent siphoning; such a ban would close the door on many other items which might have been shown on a pay-per-view basis, including events specially staged for cable, live coverage of sports, opera and theatre normally only broadcast in a recorded and edited form, local events not generally shown on television, newly released films and specialist programmes for a limited audience.

The Government has accepted this argument and that cable will need every available source of revenue if it is to succeed. In order further to ensure that siphoning does not take place, however, it has given the Cable Authority powers to prohibit the pay-per-view showing of any event or programme which has customarily been shown on broadcast television, if by doing so it would no longer be available on the latter. The White Paper acknowledges that detailed guidelines will be necessary, and these will obviously have to start by defining 'customarily' and 'available'. Does the successful and popular broadcast of a new sports tournament one year (such as the First World Athletic Championships in 1983) constitute custom? Equally, if a sports event has previously been shown live on broadcast television, is it still 'available' if the live showing is transferred to pay-per-view and a recording later shown off-air? Where potentially millions of pounds in extra revenue are involved these are likely to be highly contentious issues.

In three other particular areas the Government has considered or actually decided to impose additional regulations which have the specific objectives of protecting the existing broadcasting services and of promoting British programme production. These relate to programme exclusivity, advertising and the showing of foreign material. As far as programme exclusivity and siphoning are concerned it has been recognised that even without pay-per-view the time may come when cable generates sufficient revenue to be able to buy up a major event previously shown on broadcast television. It has also been accepted that certain steps at least should be taken to prevent siphoning of this kind. Accordingly the Cable Authority will be empowered to prevent the cable distribution of such major events as Wimbledon, the F.A. Cup Final and the Olympics unless the television rights have also been made available to broadcast television on comparable terms. However, quite what this means in practice is unclear, since the White Paper admits that 'the Government cannot guarantee that any particular event will continue to be available on public service television since the broadcasters may decide that the price demanded by the rights holder is too high' (White Paper, para. 108). The implication seems to be that, if a cable service provider can pay more than the broadcasters are prepared to do, he will get exclusive rights; all this safeguard really does is to ensure that negotiations on such matters cannot be carried out in secret. The position of the existing lists of major events which cannot be shown on an exclusive basis is not clarified either. Although the Home Secretary is to retain a reserve power to determine which events cannot be shown exclusively, it is not clear how this can be upheld in the face of a cable service provider's ability to pay significantly more than broadcast television. This is evidently going to be an area of dispute in future, although given the likely pace of cable's growth probably not for some considerable time to come.

One of the most important decisions which the Government has had to take has concerned advertising on cable. It has agreed with Lord Hunt that advertiser-supported services will be essential if cable is to attract a reasonable subscriber base. People may be ready to pay up to £10 for a film channel, but most want rather more for their cable subscription, yet without directly paying for it. Music, news, children's and similar channels all require advertising as a primary source of revenue. Moreover advertisers are very concerned that as the audience fragments so they should be able to follow it into new channels. The Hunt enquiry therefore concluded that, despite the long-term risk to ITV and ILR advertising revenue, no major restrictions should be imposed on the amount of advertising allowed, particularly since cable presented opportunities for new types, including classified and interactive advertisements and programme sponsorship. It did, however, suggest that the same advertising standards should be applied as for broadcast television.

Whilst agreeing with the last recommendation, the Government has responded to arguments from the IBA and ITV companies that it would be unreasonable if cable services were to have an unlimited opportunity to show the same type of national advertising as commercial television, while the latter remained restricted. Nevertheless it recognises both the continuing need to regulate advertising on ITV and the desirability of encouraging new forms of advertising on cable. Its solution is to restrict cable advertising but only at those points where it most closely resembles ITV and ILR advertising. Cable channels, whether general or specialised, which show programmes broadly similar to those on ITV (or in the case of cable radio which carry material similar to ILR stations), will be restricted to the same amounts of advertising, whilst classified channels, interactive and other new forms of service will be unlimited.

On the question of advertising standards a similarly sensible approach has been taken, with the recognition that the same basic core of standards should be applied, but with some leeway for cable where it differs significantly in its character from broadcast television – as in sponsored programmes and classified advertising. The Cable Authority will have the task of determining advertising standards and restrictions within these guidelines and working in close contact with the IBA (which regulates broadcast advertising). Further liaison between the Cable Authority, the IBA and the Independent Television Companies Association (ITCA) will be required to develop an efficient mechanism for the central pre-vetting and clearance of nationally distributed advertisements, although operators will probably be responsible for vetting locally originated advertising themselves, given the likely size of the task involved. The supervision of advertising standards and clearance of advertisements seems likely to be a major and continuing task for the Cable Authority, as will be the establishment of rules for programme sponsorship.

One of the most controversial of Lord Hunt's recommendations was that there should be no specific content quota for foreign programmes on cable, a decision which raised vehement protest from broadcasters, producers and unions alike. In its White Paper the Government similarly recognises that domestic production capacity will at first be inadequate to fill available space and that a higher proportion of American material will be necessary than has previously been the case for broadcast television. It further expresses its dislike of such artificial barriers to international trade, which interfere with the free workings of the market. Nevertheless it has been forced to acknowledge that, left to themselves, 'the economics of programme production will, unless there are some safeguards, militate for the maximum possible use of the sort of ready-made material of which there are vast archives in the United States available off the shelf at marginal cost' (para. 121). It also concedes that, although the Films Act Quota was never really successful in promoting British film production, the BBC and ITV quotas have proved extremely effective and have contributed significantly to the creation of the strong production base which is at the heart of the BBC's and ITV's success and quality. The quota has at least ensured that such programmes as are imported are the best of what is available.

Consequently it accepts that there is a strong case for going rather further than Hunt suggested in promoting British productions on cable: 'What is at stake is not simply jobs in the UK film and television industry, but the maintenance of the necessary sources of finance and corporate control which will enable it to continue to produce a wide range of high quality programme material with a distinctive national cultural identity. To move in one step from the stringent obligations which the broadcasters observe . . . to an entirely unregulated situation for cable could do irreparable harm' (para. 120). However, rather than impose a fixed quota which might turn out to be too rigid, it has been decided that the Cable Authority should require potential operators to specify in their franchise bids the proportion of British and European material, and particularly new productions, they intend to include in their services. The Authority will give particular weight to applicants who plan to use a high percentage of British or European material and to stimulate new domestic production. In addition it will be required to 'satisfy itself' that a 'proper proportion' of such material is shown on each channel, while taking account of each channel's character. Thus a sports or music channel would be expected to carry a high proportion of British items, but a film channel rather less so in view of American dominance of the film industry. The difficulties of applying such a requirement in the realities of the market are obvious. Without suggesting deliberate deception there can be all the world of difference between promise and performance; what is hoped for in terms of new revenue for production may not appear. In the absence of alternative material, what other course will there be than to buy off the shelf? To its credit the Government recognises these problems, accepts that heavy reliance on US imports will be necessary initially and emphasises that it will be the Authority's duty to ensure a continuing increase in the amount of British programming. But in everything it relies upon cable achieving a certain level of viability. Without that no amount of regulatory guidance can actually create programmes.

The final issue to which the White Paper pays specific attention is the question of the relationship between cable operators and the existing telecommunications carriers, BT and Mercury. At present only these two are legally able to provide the facility for switched interactive services to the public on a telecommunications system, a state of affairs which if continued would prevent cable operators from entering this field at all, or at best would require them merely to provide the facilities for BT or Mercury to operate over their systems. Concerned as the Government is to extend competition within telecommunications, this is not a solution which it finds acceptable. Nevertheless it has had to admit that direct competition, particularly for BT's main source of revenue – its voice telephony service – could endanger the latter's financial position, weakening its ability to provide a universal telephone service, particularly in loss-making areas. It has also recognised that even in certain major business centres, which produce significant revenue for BT from data transfer, competition for data and similar switched interactive services could be damaging.

Despite this concern the outcome remains highly satisfactory to cable operators and gives an additional incentive to provide such switched interactive facilities. For although it has been decided that only BT and Mercury should be allowed to offer voice services on cable systems, perhaps in partnership with a cable operator, no other restrictions on switched or unswitched services have been imposed. Only in Central London (the City of London, Westminster and Camden) and the business centres of Birmingham and Manchester will data services on cable systems also have to be provided in collaboration with BT or Mercury, and then only for the initial franchise period of twelve years. Thereafter cable operators in these areas will be free to supply such services by themselves if they wish.

Operators in all cases where collaboration is necessary can decide whether to do so with BT or with Mercury. In the longer term the way seems open for the creation of a second telephone network in many areas using Mercury as collaborator and feeding into its trunk lines. Meanwhile this decision breaks BT's control of local data transfer facilities, just as the 1981 Telecommunications Bill did of long distance lines. Only BT and Mercury, however, will be allowed to provide the links between individual cable systems and to provide the distribution system for national programming services.

The regulatory environment in which cable will grow, therefore, is one which in some respects offers a remarkable degree of freedom by comparison with traditional broadcasting services and which continues the break-up of BT's monopoly on telecommunications begun by Mercury. At the same time a number of important and specific constraints have been imposed and considerable emphasis placed on a range of undertakings to be made by the operator at the franchising stage. Like Hunt, the Government feels that the Cable Authority's approach to monitoring progress should be to react to perceived problems rather than to impose regulatory requirements in anticipation of them. The Authority, unlike the IBA, will have no ownership or control of the physical means of distribution, nor will it have significant regional representation. It is to be as small as possible consistent with carrying out its functions. Nevertheless, as the White Paper acknowledges, it will require both the means to monitor operators' performances and the necessary muscle to deal with those who are not meeting their statutory or franchise obligations. Supervision will take a number of forms, so that advertising will be dealt with in conjunction with the IBA and ITCA, whilst monitoring of proportions of British product may entail analysis of regular returns by operators to the Cable Authority. Similarly overall impartiality will be ensured by occasional spot checks, while taste and decency standards will be maintained by investigating and responding to public complaints made to the Authority. Cable operators will be required to keep video recordings of all programmes for three months after they are shown. The White Paper recommends that operators or service providers consult the Cable Authority in advance of transmitting material they are doubtful about; however it seems unlikely that many will be ready to relinquish their editorial control in this way. In addition the Authority will be able to monitor centrally the various nationally distributed cable services and to offer service providers guidance on the suitability of material in relation to the conditions set out in system operators' franchises.

The mainstay of the Cable Authority's power to ensure that an operator does not renege on his promises rests in its right to confer franchises and to renew or refuse to renew them. Indeed the ultimate sanction is to withdraw a franchise should an operator be in serious default of his obligations. This, however, is an extreme measure and the Government has agreed with Lord Hunt that some lesser power is needed to enable the Cable Authority to penalise an operator during the course of his franchise if he errs so far but not sufficiently to warrant disenfranchisement. Rejecting the system of financial penalties employed in the United States, it has decided to enable the Authority to forbid an operator from showing certain programmes and channels, and even to impose a much tighter degree of supervision over the whole operation. However it remains confident that such reserve powers should in themselves be sufficient to ensure that operators do not err, particularly given the ultimate sanction of withdrawing or not renewing a franchise. Moreover the Government has dismissed the suggestion that franchise renewal should be automatic if a franchisee has broadly met his original franchise obligations. The operation of a cable franchise, it argues, is a 'publicly conferred privilege', so that at its conclusion it should be readvertised to allow others to compete. This will 'act as a salutary reminder to operators that if they seek renewal they will need to be able to justify their stewardship of the privilege which has been conferred on them' (White Paper, paras. 74-5).

The Cable Authority has potentially wide powers to restrain and even to constrain errant operators, so that the interrelationship between the two will depend crucially on how the Authority interprets the objectives and criteria it has been given. Interpreted strictly it could impose considerable demands upon a profitable operator in terms of community services, British production and content and future system expansion, issues which all smack of public service. In that respect, therefore, it is not strictly accurate to say that cable is unrelated to traditional broadcasting and has no public service obligations. The very fact that there is public debate and legislation with major implications for two traditionally highly regulated areas of concern – broadcasting and telecommunications – demonstrates that inevitably cable is a public issue, requiring a regulatory policy wherever it touches the broader public interest. Indeed the more successful it is the more will be expected and demanded of it, as is the case with the present ITV companies. Conversely, however, the less successful it proves the less able will the Cable Authority be to impose conditions. The inevitable problem with this situation and with the flexible criteria set out in the White Paper is that minimum standards tend to be omitted. It is worth while asking just how unprofitable an operator will have to be before the Authority relaxes its content expectations, drops its community and access programming requirements and even lowers its taste and decency criteria. The Cable Authority may have wide reserve powers, but in a market economy it is ultimately the market which rules. Even more than broadcast television, cable's obligations to the community will be determined by its commercial success.

17 Cable Systems: Plans and Prospects

The policy proposals of the cable White Paper have now been translated into legislation which, at the time of writing, is expected to receive the royal assent in mid-1984. In the interim, however, approval has been given for eleven pilot franchises, several older systems are being modified (by providing existing subscribers with aerials to receive normal broadcast signals) and several new programme service providers have begun, or are about to begin, operating. A shadow cable authority has also been created, although it will have no formal statutory powers until the Cable Bill becomes law. In many respects the conditions for cable's growth are as favourable as they are ever likely to be. A sympathetic government is in power for another full term, a factor the importance of which can be gauged simply by comparing the speed of progress in Britain with that elsewhere in Europe. Partly as a consequence, Britain is rapidly coming to be regarded by interested companies as the major gateway into the potentially enormous European market, particularly for hardware manufacturers and programme/service providers. Certainly the early introduction of cable services in Britain has given an incentive to providers who are thinking in pan-European terms to concentrate their activities here. Within Britain itself the average consumer is already remarkably sophisticated and knowledgeable about new media and information technology opportunities thanks to video, home computers and teletext. Furthermore, a high quality programme production sector already exists and has been boosted by the recent creation of Channel Four. Finally, in the words of a recent report by the Economist Intelligence Unit, 'links with the United States in language, technical co-operation and the commercial organisation of the entertainment world' all provide significant advantages to the budding British industry (Economist Intelligence Unit, *Cable Television in Western Europe – a licence to print money?*, London 1983).

The conditions are as good as they are likely to be, but is that good enough? Major obstacles, both potential and real, remain. Will consumers double their annual expenditure on television? Can the hardware industry meet a sudden and new demand for equipment? Can arguments over royalty payments and international copyright issues be resolved in time? How significant will union resistance to this threat to public broadcasting and a national monopoly telecommunications system

292

prove to be? Most importantly, how much will it cost and how long will it all take? Is the return to investors worth the risk involved?

Clearly it is as difficult at this early stage to forecast how cable is likely to develop in Britain during the next few years as it is to predict a television play's conclusion from the opening music and titles. Nevertheless, the latter does set the mood of the piece and tells us the principal players. Similarly, the main features of the franchising and regulatory environment have now been set out in the White Paper; the degree of interest and general thinking of potential cable providers and operators have been indicated by the applications for interim franchises; numerous surveys have been undertaken to determine consumer reaction to cable; and several companies have declared their intention of providing a variety of programming services. Interest, intentions and promises are only crude guides to practice and performance, but, together with the evidence from the North American scene, perhaps we can use them to gain a few rough pointers.

WHO WANTS CABLE?

By all accounts the British are fond of their television and hooked on other new media technologies. At least 98 per cent of us have a television set, 36 per cent have two or more and over 80 per cent have colour. Perhaps most significantly, almost a quarter of homes now have a television with a remote control. We may each watch an hour less every day than American viewers, but we have the highest average adult viewing day in Europe at just over three hours. In general, viewers express a high degree of satisfaction with the services they receive and consider them value for money, although it is hard to say if this means they would like more or are happy with what they have got.

Nevertheless there has been much comment during the last eighteen months about declining audience figures, with dire warnings of falling interest in television either as a result of poor quality programmes or because other more attractive pursuits have appeared. The latest evidence suggests that in fact there has been little if any significant audience loss. But much of what has occurred can be traced to alternative use of the television set – to videogames, home computers and most importantly video recorders – both for time-shifting and playing pre-recorded cassettes. At the end of 1983 about 20 per cent of homes had a video recorder, a higher proportion than any other country in the world, with estimates varying from 35 per cent to over 50 per cent by the end of 1985. According to a British Market Research Bureau study, in September 1982 some five million people watched video for an average 1½ hours each evening, compared to 38.8 million watching television, although there was an overlap between the two groups. Other evidence by AGB indicates that 86 per cent of video time is spent watching time-shifted programmes and 14 per cent pre-recorded films. A rough calculation therefore suggests that by early 1983 some 700,000 people were watching a pre-recorded video-cassette each evening, compared to under 200,000 going to the cinema. Moreover, those cinema-goers were overwhelmingly between the ages of 18 and 35. The average adult over 35 visits the cinema just once a year. The implication is that many people have a strong interest in films but an equally strong dislike of having to go out to see them. Meanwhile interest in other forms of domestic information technology is indicated by the 1.5 million households which now have a home computer and the same number with a teletext television set, again higher proportionately than any other country, although this lead owes much to the fact that both teletext and the under-£100 computer are British inventions and have been marketed most successfully here.

How should all this be interpreted? Certainly those less optimistic about cable's chances have suggested that, in video, viewers have found an alternative distribution technology both to the cinema and to cable and one with its own unique advantages, whilst teletext, home-computers and videogames are providing all the text information and other enhanced services which most households are ever likely to use. The cost of renting or buying a television, a video recorder and occasional pre-recorded cassettes is already high, so that the amount available for further expenditure on television entertainment must be limited. On the other hand, as already mentioned, there does not appear to be a relationship between different national levels of disposable income and people's readiness to pay for television and information services. Predictably, therefore, potential cable operators interpret the evidence very differently. Detailed surveys of areas from Harrow to Preston and Aberdeen suggest that the same type of person is likely to be interested in cable as in video and that, more importantly, the two technologies are not mutually exclusive. Presumably such viewers are interested in the idea of more and different types of television – particularly recent films – and see both distribution systems as of value in this respect. Indeed initial surveys about people's interest in taking cable suggest that video homes are almost twice as likely to take cable as those without video, just as, incidentally, they are over twice as likely to have a videogames console, home computer and teletext set.

How such surveys will translate into practice, of course, is a very different matter. Cable operators will have to work even harder with video homes to persuade them that cable has something truly different to offer than they will with homes without video. The tape-renting habit is fast growing and by 1981 almost half of all video homes had at some stage rented or bought a pre-recorded tape. Indeed, a survey of one potential cable franchise area in 1983 found that over 60 per cent of video homes rented a pre-recorded feature film at least once a week, quite remarkable evidence of people's changing viewing habit if true. As a report by Euromonitor in September 1983 concluded: 'When you have a virtually unlimited choice of films to watch on VCR at the time that suits you, why subscribe as in the US to a cable system giving a weekly choice of only, say, a dozen films at times that may not suit?' (Euromonitor Publications, *Television: The New Era*, London 1983).

Turning to the question of who is likely to be interested in cable, we have already seen that in the USA subscribers include a wide mix, with a tendency towards the more affluent, young to middle-aged with children, but also with the less well-off and ethnic minorities with large families attracted where cable is available. The British pattern is in many ways likely to be very similar. Interest is highest amongst the 15-45 age group, particularly those with children, falling significantly for the over-55s. In general it is not the highest socio-economic groups who are most likely to take cable but the skilled office and manual workers in the C1 and C2 categories (55 per cent of the population), with the educated middle classes (14 per cent) and the traditionally heavy television watchers in the unskilled manual workers (17 per cent) following behind. As in the USA, factors such as large families or interest in ethnic minority programming can offset others militating against subscription, such as relatively low incomes. Already this has been shown by the unusually high take-up of video-recorders amongst the Asian and other ethnic groups in Britain who use them to show imported films. Indeed some potential cable operators see ethnic programming as a major factor in their success and have bid for areas with high ethnic minority populations.

Interest in cable, of course, is not the same as readiness or ability to pay. On the latter hangs the success or failure of the entire industry, but once again the evidence is anything but conclusive. Shortly before the Hunt Committee reported, a survey by CIT Research cast a wet blanket over the whole subject by announcing that whilst 30 per cent of people in Britain were 'very interested' in cable only 5 per cent would be prepared to pay up to £8 a month for it and 26 per cent only £5. Other surveys had similar findings and it appeared for a time that this might put an end to commercial interest. The thirteen pay trials described in Chapter 3 were generally agreed to have had extremely disappointing results and to have encountered major resistance to payment of more than £5-6 a month, although this was ascribed to the poor quality and high cost of the films on offer. In May 1983, however, AGB came out with the far more optimistic view that some 28 per cent of homes are prepared to pay at least £19 a month for a basic and pay service. Its conclusion was bright; 'Britain wants cable. Whereas previous research has been pessimistic, we found there is no real unwillingness for people to subscribe to cable' (Stephen Kirk, AGB, May 1983). Surveys by potential operators have had a mixed response, but the more optimistic appear to suggest that up to a quarter of households would be prepared to pay an economic subscription of up to £8 for a reasonable basic service, with only slightly fewer paying a further £8-10 for a pay film channel. Although such a level of interest is not economically viable as it stands, it has given many potential operators sufficient hope that with intensive marketing the demand can be pushed up to a reasonable level. Without a doubt, therefore, early take-up of cable in Britain will depend crucially on marketing ability and continued subscription on programme quality. For if American experience, particularly of churn, has shown anything it is that the consumer really is king.

TECHNOLOGY, EXPORTS AND JOBS

The attractiveness or otherwise of an area as a cable prospect is therefore related to a number of fairly standard factors, notably high housing density, availability of ducting (or ease of laying ducts) and such demographic considerations as a reasonable mix of homes in the B, C1, C2 and D groups, a relatively young population, a high proportion of families with children and an above-average take-up of video recorders. Areas which have a predominantly AB population or without a reasonable proportion of the relatively well-paid C2 skilled manual worker groups are less attractive as a cable prospect. A number of special characteristics can also be observed in certain areas for which franchises have already been sought. Notting Hill Gate has a high ethnic population, whilst in central London the hotel and business market has been a factor. Central London is also attractive because of the multiplicity of existing underground ducts, ranging from London Transport tunnels, Victorian utility walkways and the complex sewage system to the ducts of the London Hydraulic Power Company which used to supply hydraulic power to lifts in central London in the early years of the century. For Solent Cablevision the 'hi-tech' character of the area has been important, containing as it does the European headquarters of IBM as well as major research and production units of GEC, Plessey and Thorn-EMI. General awareness of new technology amongst the population is a significant consideration, while enthusiastic and high-technology oriented local authorities are a feature both of this area and elsewhere – for example the London Borough of Tower Hamlets where, rather remarkably, Western Union and the London Dockland Development Corporation together proposed a fully optic-fibre system at the time of the interim franchise contest.

A major question is the extent to which the technical requirements and incentives detailed in the White Paper will succeed in promoting switched systems. The *Financial Times* found the 20-year licence incentive 'unconvincing', while the *Guardian* (28 April 1983) thought the other specifications 'puny' and 'costless . . . a daft, deluded way to botch a revolution'. In the Commons, several opposition speakers have suggested that the Government is actually sacrificing Britain's technological lead in switches and optic fibres by not waiting until such systems are ready. 'Because it appears that a couple of bob can be made from existing cable systems, and because it appears that a few people wish to do a cheapie – for that is what we are talking about – on existing tree and branch networks . . . the Government are willing to sacrifice the development and export potential of British Industry just for the sake of two years' (Mr John McWilliam, House of Commons, 30 June 1983, cols. 753-4).

In the hardware industry, events have been moving rapidly for several months as companies such as GEC, Ferranti, Plessey, Thorn-EMI, Rediffusion, Philips and Wolsey have sought to develop either complete systems or major components to offer to the first system providers. GEC and BICC are now able to supply both coaxial and optic-fibre cable as needed and a number of smaller optic-fibre production units are also appearing. Line and subscriber equipment – amplifiers, taps, converters, decoders, etc. – are less readily available and more open to American imports or expertise. Consequently a number of systems propose to use some American supplied equipment. Although Thorn-EMI has now abandoned its plans, cited in the White Paper, for a tree and branch system using teletext technology, a variety of tree and branch systems are being offered including one from British Telecom. This latter design should be largely British developed and manufactured but may use American decoder technology, albeit produced in conjunction with BT and built under licence in Britain. Meanwhile, the major American manufacturer Jerrold (part of the General Instrument Corporation) has joined with the British GEC McMichael to adapt and market the former's tree and branch systems and decoders in Britain, whilst Racal and Oak Industries of California have also come together to market Oak's European designed encoders and decoders for use in tree and branch. In fact several of the leading British electronics companies have entered into partnerships with American system manufacturers in order to have hardware ready in time for an early start. In addition to GEC-Jerrold and Racal-Oak, Plessey and Scientific Atlanta have formed a joint venture, as have UEI and the American Times Fiber.

Not surprisingly the systems being offered by such partnerships invariably include a sizeable element either of US manufactured equipment (GEC-Jerrold, Plessey-Scientific Atlanta) or of American technology manufactured under licence (UEI-Times Fiber). This is not, however, to say that they are simply examples of what one cynic has nicknamed STOAT (Same Tired Old American Technology). For a start, much off-the-shelf American equipment is simply not appropriate to British conditions, because of the different transmission standards, climatic conditions, the much higher level of underground cabling necessary, stricter crosstalk and interference requirements and, most importantly, the very different system structure specified by the Government. Indeed the combination of these joint ventures and of the Government's star shape requirement and preference for switching has resulted in a number of hybrid systems which differ from American systems in several important respects and take a significant step in bridging the gap between the tree and branch and star configurations. Thus Plessey-Scientific Atlanta have developed a hybrid 'multi-star' system which incorporates traditional tree and branch trunk technology with a small British designed 20-way switching centre for the home drop, directing individual channels to homes as requested by subscribers. This switch obviates the need either for a decoder/converter in each home or for signals to be scrambled and descrambled. The tree and branch trunk equipment limits the capacity of the interactive return path, but does allow for subsequent upgrading with relatively little inconvenience. About 55 per cent of the value of the system lies in the British manufactured switches and other equipment, with 45 per cent being imported.

Not dissimilar is the system being offered by Cabletime, the UEI-Times Fiber venture, a modified version of the latter's entirely American switched system utilising optic fibres for the home drop. Although American, this system will be manufactured under licence in Britain by UEI companies. Meanwhile Philips have developed a 'mini-star' system which, whilst switchless and using essentially tree and branch techniques, does concentrate the home drops to a number of subscribers at one point, again reducing equipment in the home, simplifying the system, making interactivity easier, reducing the need to scramble signals and aiding maintenance. BT's tree and branch system also has a star-shaped home drop configuration and is designed in such a way that it can be upgraded to switched in due course without major reconstruction.

A number of companies such as Plessey-Scientific Atlanta are hedging their bets by developing systems which can either include switches or be built entirely as tree and branch with simple 'taps'. However, in addition to its tree and branch system BT is offering a fully switched system using a switch being produced for it by GEC McMichael. This will probably use an element of optic fibres in the trunk lines. BT is even planning to provide a video library system in which individual subscribers can request particular films, programmes or types of information from a central library, the signal being directed down a dedicated path to the relevant home. Unlike so much cable hype, this is a practical system which BT's broadband division is actively developing. GEC-Jerrold has also developed a switched system, while Thorn-EMI is trying to do so following its teletext tree and branch failure. Others such as Visionhire and Cablevision Scotland have devised their own switched systems, using components from a variety of sources. Finally Rediffusion, long an exponent of switching, has produced its own 'System Eight' fully interactive switched network. This system, like BT's, is almost entirely British developed and manufactured.

What is clear is that either on their own or through joint ventures the principal British hardware interests have built up a considerable momentum. Moreover, because of the obvious potential and of the Government's clear preference for switched systems, all are actively developing switched technology and in such a way that it can be offered at an early date. As the Technical Director of GEC-Jerrold stated in September 1983, 'it now seems that most equipment manufacturers will be launching their own particular switch equipment rather earlier than was first thought' *(Broadband, September 1983)*. At the research and development stage there will inevitably be hitches, as well as problems in moving to commercial production. It would be too much to expect the industry suddenly to be able to gear itself up from nothing to meet the potentially considerable demand; in the first few years equipment shortages and delays could present a major problem, as will shortage of skilled manpower actually to construct the systems in the field. Nevertheless it seems certain that a number of switched systems will be ready when system operators want them by the end of 1984 or early 1985, using predominantly British developed and manufactured switches. At the same time the Government's approach has encouraged the development of hybrid star-shaped tree and branch systems, certainly in some cases based on foreign technology but adapted to British requirements and designed to take switches either as soon as they are available or in due course. As one BT official has commented, these systems are becoming less of two truly distinct types, but instead represent different gradations or levels leading one into another.

In an international cable hardware market dominated by American companies, such joint ventures and hybrid systems may actually turn out to be the best way for British companies such as GEC and Plessey, with their considerable switching expertise but lack of cable system experience, to gain a foothold. Indeed Plessey even sees its partnership with Scientific Atlanta, and the development of a switch which can be used with tree and branch technology, as a major opportunity to enter the sizeable American market for upgrading systems. Moreover, Britain's early start by comparison with other European countries does give opportunities for exporting equipment to those which do not themselves have a domestic cable hardware industry, particularly where Britain's own PAL broadcast transmission standard is used. Certainly American companies such as Scientific Atlanta, Jerrold, Oak and Times Fiber are looking for partnerships or licensing ventures in each potential market – Times Fiber, for example, has made a licensing agreement with CIT Alcatel in France – and export opportunities to France and other countries which use the SECAM broadcast standard and to major nations such as West Germany, must be limited. Nevertheless American and other manufacturers do see Britain as a gateway to Europe, as well as a source of valuable expertise on the new breed of switched systems. British export and licensing opportunities may be limited by intense competition, but in a potentially enormous market the British companies and Anglo-American joint ventures do have distinctive products to offer and can expect at least a share.

As to the home market, it would appear from the thirty-seven bids made for interim franchises and the eleven chosen that in fact hybrid and fully switched systems will predominate from the very beginning. No fewer than nineteen applicants proposed fully switched systems from the outset, eight of which have been chosen. Others have expressed a firm intention to add switching at an early date. British Telecom has been involved with ten consortia, six intending to use its switched system, the remainder its upgradeable tree and branch. Of these, three switched-star and two tree and branch have been selected. Clearly many potential operators seem to have considered that the long term potential and lower operating costs of switched systems far outweigh the higher capital costs; indeed Plessey-Scientific Atlanta claims that its switched hybrid already costs no more than a one-way addressable tree and branch at 30 per cent penetration. Since few cable operators would even be considering the business if they anticipated penetration of under 30 per cent within a relatively short time of start-up, this does seem a particularly attractive proposition. Moreover, in competing for the first twelve franchises, many applicants obviously felt that only advanced switched systems would be successful. The expectation that switches will be available on a production basis only from early 1985 has also been accepted as unlikely to delay the construction timetable significantly

The earliest systems to be built will therefore include examples of fully switched, switched hybrid and hybrid without switches but upgradeable. Systems built from 1986 onwards will also include a growing proportion of optic fibres. Following the first flush of building it may be that cable providers will consider it uneconomic to build switched systems in more marginal areas and so propose switchless hybrid. But by then the price of switches may have fallen and the general impetus to switched systems grown sufficiently to ensure that they constitute a high proportion of those built in Britain.

Turning to the related question of industrial and job opportunities, the White Paper was noticeably more vague and less optimistic about cable's direct effects than earlier government statements had been. Whilst admitting that 'it is not possible to form a reliable estimate of the direct economic effects' of cable, since this will depend on the extent and pace of growth, its assessment of the likely growth of employment in cable research and programme production/provision shows that it does not expect many more than about 15,000 permanent jobs to be created

300

by 1990, with perhaps 2-5,000 temporary ones for system construction (White Paper, para. 35). Moreover, it accepts that 'none of these estimates takes into account possible off-setting reductions elsewhere in the economy' (para. 36).

It is interesting to note that such an estimate is very close to that produced in a politically critical report on cable by the Economic Policy Group of the Greater London Council. This suggests that, if half the country is cabled by 1990, an additional 8,500 could be employed in system operations, 8,500 in programme production, 1,000 in equipment manufacture and 5,000 temporary workers in system installation – a total of 18,000 permanent and 5,000 short-term jobs (Greater London Council, 'Cabling in London', December 1982, p. 68). Furthermore this report indicates areas which might well suffer job loss as a direct result of cable. Given a set proportion of consumer expenditure being spent on leisure, and continued slow economic growth, it seems likely that the movement of leisure expenditure to cable will hit other, probably more labour-intensive, leisure industries such as cinemas, restaurants and providers of different forms of home entertainment (hobbies, books, records etc.). The net effect of cable upon jobs in the entertainment industry, suggests the GLC report, could well be negative.

No one suggests that these various estimates are anything but very tentative, yet even on the White Paper's calculations it seems doubtful that cable will be a significant direct creator of jobs. More important in the long term, the Government remains convinced, will be the indirect effects of cable's interactive information and data transfer services. The White Paper cites the telephone as a good example of the massive indirect effects of new technology and argues that cable will have a similarly beneficial effect on the general growth in productivity. Yet once again it admits that this growth will be 'steady rather than explosive. . . . As in all cases of technological change, short term problems could occur, adversely affecting jobs in particular sectors, places and types of work. But, in the long run, such growth should have beneficial effects on employment: as productivity gains make lower unit costs possible, the economy should adjust to higher levels of output and activity' (White Paper, para. 38).

It is, of course, almost impossible to make any meaningful assessment of long-term and indirect job prospects as a result of cable development. One is tempted to suggest at a superficial level that, if telebanking and teleshopping prove successful, they will actually reduce the number of jobs in two relatively labour intensive industries. Cable, by making many journeys unnecessary, could also damage the motor, air and transport businesses. Yet, equally, what would be the cost of not keeping pace with such technological change? Productivity can only be improved by greater efficiency, and in a competitive world the country which lags behind must suffer. Inevitably conclusions must be tentative and

301

simplistic, and all one can really say is that what indirect effects there might be will remain long term while cable stays essentially an entertainment medium.

CABLE SYSTEM GROWTH

It is almost equally difficult to anticipate the speed and character of cable's growth in Britain, although a number of extremely vague estimates have suggested a penetration of television homes of anywhere from 10 per cent to 33 per cent by 1990. Certainly the demographic conditions appear quite favourable; compared to the United States and Canada, Britain's population is extremely concentrated, with over 70 per cent being classified by the Census Office as urban and with almost 60 urban communities exceeding 100,000 people in size (four over 500,000). A further 100 towns have populations of 50-100,000, although numbers of houses, at an average 2.8 individuals per household, are much smaller.

Looking to the immediate events and prospects, some thirty individual companies or consortia bid under the interim process for thirty-seven franchise areas of up to 100,000 homes in thirty towns, cities or London boroughs. Only in six areas was there competition between two or more contestants, and it this continues to be the pattern the Cable Authority will have a major duty to ensure that an applicant offering minimal standards does not gain a franchise 'cheaply'.

In addition existing cable operators have announced their intention to provide new cable services (up to the maximum allowed of four) on their old, limited-capacity systems. Telefusion, Rediffusion and Visionhire, for example, intend to do this on 42, 54 and 55 of their systems respectively. The licences for these older networks will be of limited duration only (or until someone proposes to build a new one in each area concerned), and it is unlikely in practice that they will all be converted to carry the new services. Nevertheless privately operated CATV systems do pass altogether some 3.5 million homes. Moreover they are likely to be of major importance in providing an already constructed market for the first programming services, whose existence will undoubtedly be precarious for several years until a reasonable subscriber base has been reached. This factor may also be important in bringing pressure to bear for the conversion even of some of the largest MATV systems so that they can receive satellite distributed services, although in many cases technical restrictions will prevent this.

Several other new entrants have declared their interest in building and operating cable systems but have decided to wait until the cable authority is fully established and a number of nationally distributed cable services are actually in operation before applying for franchises. Many of those who have been successful at the interim stage will also be requesting extensions to the original interim maximum of 100,000 homes. Interestingly several of the interim bids were not for the maximum permissible size, disproving earlier assertions that the economics of smaller systems do not make sense and matching American experience. The switched system which Rediffusion is proposing to build in Guildford, for example, is for only 22,000 homes, although the majority appear to be for 70,000-100,000. It is quite possible, of course, that the Cable Authority, once established, will reject a number of applications, whilst others will be withdrawn if early signs do not look good. Nevertheless it is reasonable to assume that by the end of 1986 some four or five million households (21-26 per cent of those with television) could have cable services available to them on new and old systems. By 1990 many more systems will have been built but will to some extent have been offset by the closure of old ones. Perhaps eight million households will have cable available, mostly on new systems. Under favourable conditions, and assuming that early systems rapidly demonstrate their viability through high penetration, then building will presumably accelerate from about 1988 onwards. If so one might hypothesise that by 1994 some 12-14 million homes (55-65 per cent of UK households) could have cable available and that at an optimistic 55 per cent penetration (the current American average) the number of homes connected might total 6.6-7.7 million. This, however, is the most optimistic of scenarios and, at ten years hence, very much a 'guesstimate'.

Coming back to the present, the towns and areas for which bids have already been made or where an interest has been declared are listed in Table XXI overleaf.

Although the White Paper specified that ITV and ILR franchise holders and local press interests should not be awarded cable franchises in the same area, in practice this has been taken to mean simply that such companies should not have a controlling interest in same-area cable operation, and not that they should be excluded altogether. Consequently a number of the earliest applicants for franchises include same-area ITV and ILR companies. (Yorkshire TV, Grampian, TV South, Ulster TV) and local newspaper groups (Portsmouth and Sunderland Newspapers, D. C. Thomson and Co.), sometimes in the same consortium. The advantages to a cable consortium of having the expertise and resources of the local television, radio and press are obvious, particularly in the area of community information and other programming and in the co-ordinating of local advertising. But the Cable Authority will no doubt be taking a particular interest in areas where such close liaison exists.

The two most notable features of the emerging pattern of ownership are the wide diversity of interests involved and, with relatively few exceptions, the tendency to favour consortia over single monopoly

TABLE XXI

Proposed new cable systems in Britain (in many cases only a part of the town or city names is to be cabled initially)

A) Successful franchise applications:

Town	Company	System
Aberdeen	Aberdeen Cable Services	Tree and branch – British Telecom
N. Glasgow	Clyde Cablevision	Switched-star – Plessey Scientific Atlanta
Belfast	Ulster Cablevision	Switched-star – British Telecom
S. Liverpool	Merseyside Cablevision	Switched-star – British Telecom
Coventry	Coventry Cable	Tree and branch – British Telecom
Windsor, Slough and Maidenhead	Windsor Television	Switched-star – GEC-Jerrold
Swindon	Thorn-EMI	Tree and branch – Thorn-EMI
Ealing	CableTel Communications	Switched-star – probably Plessey-SA
Croydon	Croydon Cable TV	Switched-star – Plessey-SA
Westminster	Westminster Cable	Switched-star – British Telecom
Guildford	Rediffusion	Switched-star – Rediffusion

B) Other towns bid for at interim franchise stage:

Barnsley/Dearne Valley
Basingstoke
Bolton
Cardiff
Cheltenham/Gloucester
Dudley
Edinburgh (West)

Leeds
Leicester
London:
    Bexley
    Notting Hill Gate/Queensway
    Tower Hamlets
    West End

Milton Keynes
Plymouth
Preston/Leyland/Chorley/S. Ribble
Southampton/Fareham/Portsmouth
Southend-on-Sea
Sunderland

C) Areas in which interest has been expressed:

Blackpool
Brighton/Hove/Worthing/
Bognor Regis/Littlehampton

Bristol
Kilmarnock/Ayr/Irvine
London – Camden/Hampstead

Manchester Central
Newcastle-upon-Tyne
Norwich

ownership. Nine of the eleven initial franchises have gone to consortia such as Merseyside Cablevision, which includes Pilkington Bros. (glass manufacturers), Virgin Records, Telefusion, Whitbread, BICC, Plessey, BT, Littlewoods, the Liverpool Post and ex-Beatle Ringo Starr. A number of consortia include an American interest, often providing valuable expertise or hardware. Examples include World Cable (50 per cent owned by Cox) with a 20 per cent interest in Cablevision Scotland, AT & C as part of Westminster Cable and Aberdeen Cable, and Racal-Oak in Croydon. Cablevision Scotland provides a good example of the coming together of companies which each provide a necessary element in the cable mix. Bidding for Edinburgh, South Glasgow and Aberdeen (the latter unsuccessfully), it includes the British Linen Bank to raise the necessary finance, Ferranti with its extensive electronics and engineering experience, Press Construction to lay the network, Grampian TV with its programming and advertising knowledge, D. C. Thomson with its local newspaper interests and the American World Cable.

The capital costs of the systems being proposed vary widely according to size, technical structure and character of the area, and for a 100,000 home system anywhere from £15 million to £30 million has been quoted by potential operators. One not untypical franchise applicant sees his initially switchless coaxial hybrid system costing almost £32,000 per mile. Elsewhere the cost per home passed has been quoted at anything from £300 to £500. At these levels a combination of equity and debt financing will probably be used. Several merchant banks are members of consortia, and certainly the larger part of the financing will have to be raised through the City from major investors such as insurance companies and pension funds. British Telecom is heavily involved in financing the systems it is building, as are other hardware manufacturers who see the need to invest early on in order to stimulate further demand for their systems. The role of large companies with profitable interests in other fields in financing cable has also been repeatedly emphasised; indeed the efficient utilisation of trading losses and of large capital allowances is seen in many cases as making the crucial difference in the possible post-tax rate of return. According to accountants Deloitte, Haskins and Sells, a cable operator who used group tax relief might expect a real annual return twice as high as one who did not – on their model 14 per cent or 7 per cent during the first franchise term. However studies by Pearson Longman and AGB in Harrow and Wandsworth respectively have been considerably less hopeful. Despite the apparent attractiveness of both areas to cable operators, Pearson Longman estimated that, even with an optimistic 55 per cent penetration of Harrow after 5 years, its rate of return would be minus 1 per cent in real terms. Meanwhile AGB's calculations suggested that the cost of running a 100,000 home franchise for a 12-year period (using an unswitched system) would be some £6-8 million a year, including interest and amortisation; even with 36 per cent of homes paying an average £14 a month, annual revenue would only reach £6.3 million, giving a marginal return of only 5 per cent before inflation. Only if additional revenue sources proved significant, such as advertising and teleshopping, would this be a viable prospect.

For potential operators and investors the lessons from North America are only too evident. The risks are high, the pay-back long and the return for many years low. The rate of return is crucially dependent on consumer interest and the movement of interest rates over many years – not at all an encouraging consideration. Capital costs appear almost as a matter of course to run well ahead of expectation, so that the very closest accounting must be done at the outset. In the absence of intense competition for franchise areas it may be that cautious investors will hold back for a while after the first round of franchising to watch consumer response and operators' competence at controlling costs, before committing themselves further.

As for the principal source of revenue in the first franchise term, it is evident that most potential operators are basing their calculations predominantly on basic and pay subscriptions. One potential operator who intends to offer two pay services, business facilities and pay-per-view, as well as standard services, sees basic subscriptions, connection charges, remote control handset rental, rental for connection to a second television set and income from a printed programme guide together bringing in some 46 per cent of his gross revenue over a twelve-year period. The first pay service should account for about 36 per cent of the remainder and the second for about 13 per cent. Pay-per-view and business services, offered from the third year of operation, are expected to rise less than 3 per cent and 2 per cent respectively, whilst local advertising has a low anticipated yield at under 1 per cent. Even in the twelth year, when the system has reached a reasonable maturity, the percentages are not expected to be significantly different.

These estimates are for a switchless system, with switches being added within five years, but there is no reason to suppose the initial estimates for switched systems will be very different. The market for interactive and business services is simply too unknown for major revenue from it to be taken into account in these early calculations as to viability, even though operators may have high hopes. Most systems, in other words, have been calculated on the assumption that they can be profitable as entertainment providers, with additional services a possible further source of revenue, although naturally in business centres such as central London the expectations for business revenue may be somewhat higher.

Most potential operators at present anticipate an operating profit within four years and profitability after depreciation, interest and tax (assuming tax relief) in six to eight. American experience suggests that this can be achieved but that escalating plant costs and interest rates could affect such estimates significantly. Above all, however, whether or not these projections are realised will depend crucially on the speed of take-up on the part of the public. Here estimates vary widely from 20 per cent to 38 per cent penetration in the first year and rising to 40-50 per cent and above after eight years. There is general agreement that in the areas proposed anywhere over 35 per cent would be viable, with from 50-90 per cent of basic subscribers taking a pay film service. The cost to the subscriber of the basic tier is expected to be about £5-9 a month (although some operators intend to offer two tiers of basic) and for each pay film channel about £8. At least one potential operator has proposed that the first premium film channel should be included in the basic service, for about £15 in all, since most potential subscribers are primarily interested in getting films. This may well be a good marketing ploy and successful in maximising revenue, but it must also reduce the total number of subscribers, as well as restricting the options for those who, in fact, do not want a film service. Such is the price one may have to pay for not regulating rates in a monopoly business.

If cable is available to five million households by 1987 then an economic penetration of 35 per cent could translate into 1.75 million subscribers, with the majority taking a pay channel. A 40 per cent penetration of eight million homes by 1990 would mean some 3.2 million subscribers. The most optimistic penetration figures suggested for 1987 and 1990 (40 per cent and 50 per cent) would be equivalent to 2 million and 4 million subscribers respectively. Our most favourable scenario for 1994 has a 55 per cent penetration of 14 million homes (65 per cent of those in Britain), or almost 8 million subscribers. This means a total penetration of British homes of some 37 per cent. It would be well, however, to compare this with the telephone, which only thirteen years ago in 1970/71 had still penetrated a mere 36.5 per cent of homes, after over 75 years of existence and although available to over 95 per cent of the population. Even today when it is almost universally available it is still in only about 75 per cent of households. On the other hand the British do seem eager for additions to home entertainment; colour television sets were in over half of all homes within ten years of first appearing, largely as a result of rental. Now video seems likely to do the same. Comparisons of this kind, therefore, are uncertain guides. In general even the most optimistic cable advocates do not believe that British construction and penetration rates will match or exceed American. Our most certain conclusion, therefore, is that the main determinant for some time to come of whether a consumer subscribes to cable will remain geographical location; for between 35 per cent and 50 per cent of British homes cable will almost certainly not be available within ten years.

18 Cable Services

The first subscriber to the first of the new cable systems approved under the interim franchises should be connected and receiving additional cable services by early 1985, although systems which are switched from the outset are unlikely to come on line before mid-year. Meanwhile a number of existing systems should be converted during early 1984 to carry up to four new services. Nevertheless the industry will for some time be faced with the problem of a cable market too small to be profitable to service providers, but needing an attractive variety of services from the very beginning if it is to grow. Certainly the eventual rewards could be considerable, especially for pay service providers and for those who look at the market in European terms; but the costs and likely losses involved in the early years will be equally huge, particularly for advertiser-supported services. At present there is no reason to suppose that in this respect British experience will be any different from American.

Not surprisingly, extensive research has been undertaken as to what is most likely to attract subscribers. Without doubt the greatest interest is shown in recent feature films, a fact confirmed by current video use. Over 70 per cent of off-air recording is of films, as is over 85 per cent of video tape rental. Of the latter thriller and horror films easily predominate, with science fiction and adult fare trailing some way behind. Sport, music, children's and educational videos make up a very small proportion of those bought or rented. Such evidence supports surveys of what people want from cable, with a channel showing recent film releases consistently topping the list by a large margin. This is followed by a news channel, sports, light entertainment and music, although few people would be prepared to pay individual subscriptions for any of these. Evidence of interest in children's programmes, science and wildlife documentaries, arts and local news/information channels varies widely, with the latter in particular finding strong support in some cable franchise surveys and only moderate interest in others. Stated interest in all such categories of programme, however, must be treated with caution, for social and educational aspirations are strong factors in leading people to express an interest which is not necessarily translated into viewing figures.

Conversely lack of interest in interactive services such as telebanking and teleshopping must to some extent reflect a lack of knowledge about them. Once again surveys by potential operators in different areas have had varied results, with home banking/shopping scoring well in the Solent area but less so in Scotland, and domestic alarm systems having the opposite result. Whilst there may well be differences in attitude to crime and security between Glasgow and Portsmouth, the overall impression is that very few people really have any idea of what these services involve and so cannot give an accurate idea of the absolute or comparative value they attach to them. Despite an early high take-up of domestic videogame consoles, however, a number of surveys do indicate a relative lack of interest in cabled videogames. Indeed a recent BARB survey added weight to this finding by concluding that the proportion of households with game consoles had actually dropped back from 12 per cent in 1982 to 10 per cent in 1983.

After all the hyperbole it is interesting to see the range of services which most system operators are proposing to carry or provide initially. There will be no 52-channel basic tiers in Britain for the foreseeable future; nor will any service be 24-hour from the outset, although several state this as an eventual aim. Present proposals commonly envisage between twelve and sixteen channels in a basic package, with at least five of these being relays of existing broadcast services (including one out-of-area ITV channel). Two of the remainder comprise an alpha-numeric channel guide and a combined alphanumeric local informa-tion/classified advertising service, possibly with some teletext news taken from Ceefax and Oracle. Most operators appear, as expected, to be offering only a single community/access channel, in some cases carrying educational programming as well. Out of a typical fourteen-channel basic tier this leaves space for only five or six new 'entertainment' services. The standard line-up includes music, sports, news, light entertainment/general and children's channels. Operators offering slightly more basic channels are proposing a wide variety of alternatives, including a second out-of-area ITV channel or Channel Four Wales, separate access or educational channels, women's/lifestyle, arts, classic films, ethnic and repeats of the previous evening's broadcast program-mes (although this is currently prohibited under copyright law). If any of the BBC's or IBA's DBS channels are offered free to viewers (an increasingly unlikely prospect), these also will have to be carried on the basic tier when they appear in 1986 or after. In addition operators will all carry national and local radio services and some are planning their own advertiser-supported music cable radio channels.

Turning to the premium services, most operators initially are thinking in terms of one or two film services only, plus the BBC and independent premium DBS channels (again when available). A number of additional services have been mentioned and could be offered if distributed on a national basis. They include the Disney Channel, an educational service, pay sports and a classic and foreign film channel. An ethnic film and programming service seems a likely prospect in relevant areas. In general new system operators will take most nationally offered pay services, although they will face the same law of diminishing returns on multipay which has been experienced in the United States. Given the Government's flat rejection of adult channels such as Playboy, the above pay services are the only ones likely for some time to come, although there is no reason why cable operators should not carry complete foreign-language broadcast or DBS channels on a pay basis, relayed from France, Germany, Italy or elsewhere, if a sufficiently large minority within the community justifies it. A system serving central London hotels, for example, could relay a variety of services from other countries on a pay-per-view basis. One system proposed for the West End of London is centred around channels for the large Arabic community living there, using programmes brought in from the Middle East.

In general it seems most likely that subscribers will be unwilling to take more than two pay channels, with the majority taking one only, as in the USA and Canada. With relatively few exceptions that one will be a premium film and entertainment channel. Indeed a proportion of those who take two pay services will choose a second film channel also, for although the various services of this kind being developed will not have exclusivity of the major films they show, they may well carry additional material exclusively – specials, HBO made-for-pay items, BBC program-mes (on its DBS service) and sports events. The result could be a very small market indeed for any more specialised pay services, except on a standalone basis where circumstances warrant it (such as a high ethnic population).

It is already evident that, as in the United States and Canada, the majority of cable entertainment services will be nationally packaged and distributed to individual operators. The major MSOS (Rediffusion, Visionhire, Thorn-EMI) will take advantage of their early control of access to the audience (on their existing systems) to market the particular services in which they have an interest. A number of franchise applicants have declared their intention of putting together specialist standalone channels or of taking only elements of national services which they will repackage to suit their particular community – rather similar to the approach being taken by Rogers in Portland. But in practice the cost and complexity of doing so in the early years when all systems will be running at a loss should prove a strong incentive to most to take nationally distributed feeds as they stand. The national service providers will in any case exert strong pressure upon operators to do so, not least by providing nationally oriented promotional literature and programme guides. Indeed the biggest problem is going to be a shortage of appropriate material, so that only the most local of programming will not be distributed and shown on several systems.

310

Inevitably, therefore, the entertainment channels being proposed by system operators reflect closely those on offer nationally. At present almost twenty national services are being planned by a variety of companies, yet competition means that they are of only eight or nine distinct types. At the time of writing four premium film services are being planned, two pop-music channels and two sports, while four separate companies have expressed interest in supplying a pan-European news service, although none have yet committed themselves to it. In addition there are a number of channels which aim to provide general entertainment, as well as individual children's, leisure, cultural, education and ethnic services. Those who have already definitely announced themselves aim to be operational during 1984. Table XXII lists the principal nationally distributed service providers who had declared themselves at the time of writing, followed by companies who are considering entering the field. (See overleaf.)

Several of these services are intended for a wider European audience (particularly news, music and general entertainment), but it seems clear that the economics are extremely dubious for anything more than one of each type to survive. Many observers are extremely sceptical about the prospects for a cultural or educational channel at all, following the failure of CBS Cable and C-Channel. Certainly several of those listed above will not even get off the drawing board. As it is, all the prospective providers recognise that the cable audience will take time to grow and that the business will be a long hard slog. All, as in the United States and Canada, will rely very heavily on multiple repeats, both of programmes and of blocks within each day.

The pattern emerging, therefore, is almost identical to that which exists in the USA, with a relatively small number of nationally distributed and predominantly broad appeal pay services; a rather higher number of national services supported by advertising and per-subscriber fees, generic in character but again for the most part seeking a comparatively broad audience; and locally generated community services. Pay-per-view, enhanced and business services are also likely to appear, particularly on switched systems, within three or four years of start-up, but only gradually will they assume significance.

THE NATIONAL PAY SERVICES

If HBO's experience can be repeated, the premium film services are certain to be the most financially attractive and rewarding prospects. By March 1984 there should be three in operation, and by 1987 four, including the BBC's DBS service if it goes ahead. The two principal consortia, United Cable Programmes (TEN) and The Entertainment Group (TEG), are notable not least for the presence of almost all the major American studio and distribution interests, demonstrating their

TABLE XXII

Organisations providing, planning or considering national cable programmes sevices in Britain, 1984.

Organisation	Title of Service	Nature/Description
BBC	—	First DBS service, originally planned as pay-film and premium programme service, starting in 1986 and relayed on Unisat 1. Plans currently being reconsidered.
	—	Second DBS service, originally planned as a 'Window on the World' service, showing top-quality programmes from Britain and abroad. Plans are now being reconsidered.
	—	Possible serious music and cultural service, transmitting live concerts on Pan-European basis. Feasibility study for pay-TV service relayed on low-power ECS transponder and commencing by 1986 now being undertaken with merchant banker Morgan Grenfell and concert manager Harold Holt.
		Possible 24-hour European news service. Feasibility study being undertaken with Visnews.
British Cable Programmes	—	British Arts channel, showing drama, concerts, jazz, starting 4 hours a day, possibly 1984. May carry advertising and sponsored programmes.

CSS Promotions & Fleet Holdings	Cable Sports & Leisure	Sports & Leisure channel, starting early 1984, initially 5 hours a day. Financed by per-subscriber fee, advertising and sponsorship. Promises 50% British content and to produce 1,800 hours of sport a year.
European Broadcasting Union	Eurikon	Pan-European high-quality prestige programming service using material supplied by EBU members (including the IBA). Supported by advertising mainly. May start in 1984, relayed on ECS 2.
IBA	—	Due to advertise two DBS franchises in 1984, for start in 1986-8. May be awarded to companies mentioned here already relaying service on low power satellite, or to new service providers.
ITN	—	Said to be considering a new channel, but still at preliminary stage.
Mirror Group	MirrorVision	An entertainment and information service, with music, sport, hobbies, advertising features and general entertainment. Starting in 1984 as a weekly two-hour programme only, but with bigger ambitions. Supported by advertising.
Rediffusion (see also UCP)	—	Planning a general entertainment channel of series, soaps and repeats, supported by advertising.
	—	A leisure interests channel, supported by advertising and sponsorship.

TABLE XXII – continued

Organisation	Title of Service	Nature/Description
Satellite Television	Sky	General pan-European entertainment channel already broadcasting 5 hours a night on ECS 1. Financed by advertising and per-subscriber fees. Controlled by Rupert Murdoch's News International, other investors include D. C. Thomson, Guinness Mahon and the Ladbroke Group
Screen Sport	Screen Sport	Sport and recreational service, operating 54 hours a week from early 1984. 20% British content. Supported by per-subscriber fees, advertising and sponsorship. Backers include Richard Price, Hill Samuel merchant bank and, with substantial minority holdings, ABC and ESPN. Relayed on Intelsat V.
SelecTV	—	Said to be planning a number of services, including a horse racing and betting channel.
Southall Cable	—	A national ethnic channel, starting with an Asian segment 4 hours a day, 3 days a week, but eager to encourage other minority communities to take space on service eg. Greek and Turkish. Programmes largely British produced, but at very low cost.
Television Entertainment Group	—	Premium films, specials, series. A 12-hour pay-TV service relayed on Intelsat V from early 1984. Investors include Goldcrest (51%) Home Box Office (12.25%), Columbia (12.25%), 20th Century-Fox (12.25%), and CBS (12.25%). Will probably seek IBA DBS franchises.

Thorn-EMI	Premiere	Premiere film channel. Pay service, about 6 hours nightly at first. Initially tape-delivered.
	Jack-in-the-Box	Children's service, per-subscriber and advertiser supported. About 4 hours a day and including some material from Nickelodeon.
	Music Box	Rock music service. Per-subscriber and advertiser supported. Starting early 1984.
United Cable Programmes	TEN	Premium films, specials, general entertainment. A pay-TV service, may also take advertising. 12 hours initially, relayed on Intelsat V and starting early 1984. Investors include Rediffusion (14%), Visionhire (14%), Rank Trident Satellite & Cable (14%), Plessey (13%), UIP (Paramount, Universal, MGM/UA) (45%).
Virgin Records/Yorkshire TV	The Music Channel	Rock music service now operating on Satellite Television. Supported by advertising, per-subscriber fees and sponsorship.
Visnews	—	Considering a pan-European news service, in conjunction with BBC. Undertaking programming experiments to assess feasibility.
Wyvern TV	Key Channel	Information, training and education channel, including much sponsored programming. Due to start towards end of 1984. Method of finance undisclosed at present.

determination not to allow a repetition in Britain of HBO's domination of American pay-TV. This, should, however, encourage a more realistic attitude on their part, through the MPEAA, towards the amounts charged to pay-TV programmers for films – a major problem during the earlier British pay-TV trials. Certainly the cost of programming will have to be reduced from the previous minimum level of £0.43 per film if a realistic wholesale price of £3.50-£4.00 is to be charged, allowing the system operator to ask £7-8 a month from subscribers for each premium service.

The two consortia differ in that one is dominated by production and distribution interests but has no assured system market, while the other has immediate access to Rediffusion and Visionhire systems through their involvement as partners in it. The Thorn-EMI 'Premiere' channel similarly has a guaranteed access to subscribers on Radio Rentals' systems. Both TEN and the TEG channel are starting on a limited twelve-hour basis, using BT or Mercury-owned transponders on Intelsat V. Each anticipates a necessary investment and peak operating deficit of some £15-20 million before breaking even after three or four years of operation, in about 1987. By that time each is hoping for some 1-1.5 million subscribers for an annual revenue of £42-63 million. Our earlier estimates of cable penetration suggest that such expectations may well prove optimistic with four national services in operation, although the advent of DBS will naturally widen the market considerably. Indeed it seems quite probable that, in addition to the BBC service, the Goldcrest/ HBO group will also seek a DBS transponder in order to compensate for their lack of access to older Visionhire and Rediffusion systems. Others may well follow suit. By 1990 the cable universe should be large enough to support two or three such premium film services, particularly since the growth of new systems will increase the number on which two or more pay channels are offered. However it may well be that, in the interim, progress will be slower than expected and even for some unacceptably slow, with the DBS market providing a lifesaver when it eventually arrives.

The general character of these channels will vary little from one to another. They will most closely resemble HBO as film centred services with a certain amount of additional programming – specials, concerts, cartoons, pop-videos, mini–series and even comedy and other series. Each will show ten to fifteen 'new' films (released within the previous nine to eighteen months) a month and depend heavily on repeat showings, although the likely very high video-recorder levels amongst cable subscribers must prove a problem in trying to sell repeats as a consumer convenience. At present there is little likelihood that the major features will be bought and shown on an exclusive basis, simply because all the services will be starting at about the same time and, immediate access to older systems aside, should have few advantages over each other. Unless one of them establishes a major dominance there will be

316

little incentive for film distributors – even those with an interest in a particular service – to sell films exclusively.

Nevertheless, each service will be seeking to differentiate itself and to demonstrate its individual attractiveness, particularly as multi-pay becomes a consideration. Consequently it is in the programming around films – in specials, series and 'fillers' – that exclusivity may well be sought and be affordable, as Showtime has discovered. This is particularly important from a British point of view since it is precisely in such material that the first opportunities will appear for new original production. All services have expressed their firm intention to provide as large an element of British and European programming as possible, in line with the Government's wishes. Nevertheless the majority of popular feature films are American, so that if they are to fulfil this pledge it seems likely to be reflected particularly in their non-film programming. None, however, intends to invest in new production from the start; rather, as in the early years of pay-TV in the United States, they will merely make licence payments for material, encouraging new programmes by creating an additional source of revenue but not by putting money 'up front'. Even as an additional revenue source their contribution will be pitifully small for several years.

This is not to say that individual partners within each consortium, such as Goldcrest, will not from an early stage take pay revenue into account and expand production accordingly; on the contrary, as we have already seen, the trend is to ever more international co-production and also to co-financing by companies or interests at different levels on the distribution chain. The BBC in particular seems certain increasingly to share its production costs both with international partners (such as HBO already) and between its DBS and broadcast services, with a programme's staged release reflecting these origins. Pay-TV in Britain will add several more layers of complexity to the already complex subject of international production financing. New British productions will be encouraged, but predominantly as part of a larger movement towards co-production and progressive release. The Government and Cable Authority should obviously look to the Canadian experience to consider ways in which Britain can take even greater advantage of these trends. As in Canada, however, questions will arise as to what really is 'British' and to what extent these developments will influence the character of programmes produced for more than a domestic audience. What is certain is that, given the structure of the film industry, these pay film services will continue to be dominated by American product; it would be naive to believe otherwise. For the last thirty years most British content in British cinemas has been filler material – newsreels, short documentaries before the main feature, children's matinée productions and the occasional low-quality film produced on the tightest of budgets. History doesn't entirely repeat itself, for Goldcrest in particular seem to have found an extremely successful formula for turning out tightly budgeted films of high quality. Nevertheless the British filler may become a common feature of these pay services in years to come.

Current plans for film services demonstrate the White Paper's ambiguities on taste and decency and the inevitable tendency to interpret its strictures on this subject liberally. Most services propose to show both '15' (AA) and '18' (X) rated films, albeit after 9 p.m. and 10 p.m. respectively. Until the Cable Authority clarifies the issue this will continue to be the case, and indeed it is difficult to see how it could be otherwise. In 1982 fully 36 per cent of films registered had an '18' rating and 39 per cent a '15', leaving only 25 per cent – a total of 52 films – rated U or PG. For a film service, and one which naturally wants to show the most popular films, this is a major problem. Yet, as the providers of such services argue, both BBC and ITV now carry scenes of nudity and violence in late-night films and are not bound by British Board of Film Censors' ratings. It would be difficult in the extreme for the Cable Authority to make a major stand on this issue, faced with commercial realities and evidence of consumer demand. Most likely is some token and self-imposed limitation on what can be shown. Some system operators have also expressed their intention to show '15' and '18' films in edited form only, as do BBC and ITV.

At present few people seem to believe that consumers will pay for anything other than a mainstream film service, although one or two system operators are considering a very cheap classic films and repeats channel. The possibility of a pan-European pay cultural service is also being investigated by the BBC and others. Finally Wyvern Television is planning a business and educational channel which it hopes will overcome consumer lack of interest by being made available for a low subscription of about £1 a month. Called Key Channel, it aims to be educational in the widest sense and thereby to have broad appeal, although naturally the core market will be schools, colleges, trainee schemes and industry. Operating for nine hours a day by 1985, it promises to be 80-90 per cent British and European in content, but will rely for much of its material on commercially sponsored films and programmes financed by large companies for in-house industrial and business training.

NATIONAL ADVERTISER-SUPPORTED SERVICES

As in the United States, the strong evidence of consumers' non-readiness to pay for more than one or two film channels has forced companies wishing to supply other services to look to advertising. Almost all, however, have learnt the American lesson about dual forms of finance and see a per-subscriber fee as crucial. One company, Music Vision, did initially intend to offer itself free to system operators, competing as it was against two other music channels being planned in this most fiercely fought over sector of the cable programming market. Even before starting, however, it recognised that three such services could not survive and so merged with one of its rivals, Cable Music, into The Music Channel. Both this and its remaining rival, Music Box, have aspirations to be pan-European services but see Britain as the earliest market; they both anticipate breaking even within about four years and with a subscriber base of perhaps 3-4 million. Although the per-subscriber fee, revenue from programme sponsorship and, hopefully, from programme sales will all contribute, such projections do seem extremely optimistic, particularly given that they will be competing with each other for access to systems. Few if any system operators will contemplate carrying more than one video music channel.

The interests behind these services include such doyens of the music pop video business as Virgin Records, Palace Video, Thorn-EMI, Ringo Starr and Tony Hemmings, just as major sports promoters are amongst those currently putting sports channels together – for example CSS Promotions, whose clients include the Football League. Like the music services, CSS's Cable Sports and Leisure channel and its rival Screen Sport are to begin as five- to seven-hour services, repeated once or twice each day, in early 1984. Both will seek a wide appeal by covering not only sport but other recreational activities and hobbies such as motoring and photography. Once again revenue is to come from advertising, per-subscriber fees, programme sales and, particularly significantly, sports sponsorship. As Barrie Gill of CSS states, 'We had so many clients who wanted to get sponsored events on television that a cable channel was a natural development' (quoted in *Television Weekly*, 23 September 1983).

Natural or not the problems remain enormous and costs will have to be kept to a minimum. Where sport costs ITV some £60,000 an hour to produce, both Cable Sports and Screen Sport are thinking in terms of £10-20,000 an hour and below, more in line with Channel Four's sports programme expenditure. Consequently a high proportion will at the outset have to be bought in; only 20 per cent of Screen Sport's material will be produced in the UK and, since it has the British rights to ABC, CBS and NBC sports coverage, it seems probable that much will come from the States, as well as Canada, Australia and Europe. Cable Sports and Leisure, however, claims that at least half its output will be British from the start, which if so would entail as much as 900 hours of new material – more than either the BBC or ITV produces each year. All coverage, moreover, should be exclusive to one service. There seems likely to be heavy coverage of horse racing in conjunction with the International Racing Bureau, which promotes coverage of the forty-three race courses in Britain not currently televised by the BBC or ITV.

A number of other sports promoters, including West Nally and Mark McCormack's Transworld International, are seeking to become wholesalers of televised sports events to cable and it seems probable that in due course one of the two sports channel contenders will similarly revert to a promotional and wholesale role, leaving a single sports service. Typically the channels are looking to cover both a wider range of minority sports and existing major events more fully – complete coverage of golf or smaller tennis tournaments, of football matches and Grand Prix race meetings. As such they argue that they will be serving a complementary role to BBC and ITV rather than competing with them. Indeed it is suggested that the broadcasters will welcome the selling of rights to extended coverage and even agree to reciprocal coverage of events to reduce costs. Naturally any suggestion that in time sports services could bid against the broadcasters for rights, or turn the tables and leave the preliminary rounds of tournaments to the BBC and take the finals for themselves, is hotly rejected. At present, in any case, BBC and ITV have a firm hold over sports coverage in Britain. Nevertheless if such a sports service does prove a success – and there certainly seems to be plenty of material and potential sponsors for it – then eventually such competitive bidding for new and previously untelevised events must become both possible and attractive.

For the present and for several years to come such questions will not arise. The principal task, as in the United States, will be to attract advertising and sponsorship while the subscriber base is still pitifully small. In 1988, a year commonly offered by service providers as the date by which they hope to break even, there may be 3 million cable subscribers in Britain. Both sports services intend to charge a per subscriber fee of £0.50 a month, giving a total annual income from this source of £18 million. It should be noted that such a fee is very high by American standards. If one assumes a comparable peak-time rating to that achieved by ESPN (2-3 in homes reached) that implies a maximum audience of only 60-90,000. When current audience research considers any programme which gets under 250,000 as 'zero-rated', it is clear that few national advertisers – even those attracted by the demographics of the audience – are going to make major advertising commitments to these services at such levels. Nevertheless if the channel providers charge advertisers the same cost per thousand homes as existing broadcasters (and American experience suggests that they will have difficulty in charging more), then by selling eight 30-second spots an hour for seven hours of original programming each night (leaving 2 minutes per hour for system operators to sell) they could gross about £7 million a year (this assumes a 3 rating and a cost per 1000 of £4.50 – comparable with ITV charges in August 1983 – less advertising agencies' standard 15 per cent commission). Leaving sponsorship and programme sales to one side for a moment, this suggests a possible total annual revenue for a seven-hour nightly service of this kind reaching 3 million households of about £25 million, or an hourly income of some £9,800.

320

Turning to the costs side of the equation, it is evident that budgets will have to be markedly lower than those for BBC and ITV. Channel Four has undoubtedly shown the way here, with American football, basketball and minority sports such as British cycling. Together with overheads, transponder costs and marketing, one might optimistically project an hourly service cost of £10-15,000, the cost of programming being kept low by sponsorship, rights sales and by purchase of at least half of all material from abroad. At £10,000 an hour the service would cost about £25.5 million, rising to £38.3 million at £15,000.

Inevitably there are many variables in such a calculation; service providers, for example, could attempt to justify higher advertising rates because of block repeats of the channel. Nevertheless the general conclusion to be drawn is that viability will only be reached with a subscriber base of about 3 million if costs are kept below £10,000 an hour. Crucial to success will be a high per-subscriber charge which will form the principal revenue stream for many years, sponsorship to reduce programme costs and a high proportion of bought-in programming. Equally evident is the fact that subscriber growth will be too slow to support two sports channels within a financially acceptable period.

System operators who recognise sports and music channels as important attractions for subscribers will be prepared to pay comparatively large per-subscriber fees to receive them. The same may be true of the news service which Visnews is currently planning. Nevertheless such programming costs are not expected to consume more than about 25 per cent of basic subscription – up to £2 a month at most. This means that with six or seven different types of basic service available (music, sports, news, children's, arts, general entertainment and possibly leisure/lifestyle) most will have to charge considerably less per subscriber to get into the basic line-up. The general entertainment service, Sky Channel, for example, will have a per-subscriber charge of £0.10 only. Advertising and sponsorship will therefore have to be major revenue sources from an early date. Sky does, however, see itself as a pan-European service and is already carried on cable systems in Finland, Norway, Switzerland and, from early 1984, Britain, reaching some 700,000 homes. The Visnews news channel similarly is envisaged as a European service, using a multi-language track audio facility to broaden its appeal for non-English speakers.

The question therefore remains to what extent advertisers will be prepared to put money quickly into a small and untried medium? Undoubtedly advertising agencies are in something of a dilemma as far as cable is concerned. They are keen to encourage such an expansion of TV advertising space, particularly as in recent years inflation in television advertising has risen faster than the national average, in part reflecting a growing demand for the medium. Yet they also have to recognise that for a long time to come the minuscule audiences involved will have few attractions to advertisers. As a report by Young and Rubicam concludes, 'It will be 1995 before cable's household penetration reaches 30 per cent, the level that American experience suggests is critical to any new electronic medium's chances of attracting serious consideration from national advertisers. Even at this level of penetration, cable TV's value to the advertiser will be limited unless provision is made for advertising to appear in pay-cable programming (mainly movies)' (Young and Rubicam, *Advertising on Cable in Britain and America*, May 1983, p. 28). This last suggestion is one which several agencies have made in an attempt to prevent the loss of access to the television audience which pay-TV has meant for advertisers in the United States. As a result TEN has announced that it will experiment to see if pay subscribers will accept advertising between films. The Entertainment Group have so far resisted the idea, arguing that it would alienate viewers and so actually reduce revenue.

Not only will the cable audience be physically limited for many years, but also its viewing habits will undergo major changes largely unrelated to cable. Video will be a particularly important alternative in cabled homes, Channel Four and breakfast television should gradually increase their audience share from present levels, remote controls will become the norm as will homes with several portable – and therefore uncabled – television sets in bedrooms and kitchens. All these factors will further limit the audience for cable advertising. At the same time the concept of narrowcasting, of appealing to a narrow market segment, only becomes really attractive to advertisers when the physical reach is as large as possible. Certainly individual cable systems can be used for local advertising and as test markets, but inevitably most advertising revenue for service providers will come from national advertisers seeking specific demographic groups.

Channel Four, with its specialised programming, provides a possible guide to how advertisers might react to new television opportunities. After a very slow start Channel Four's average 5 per cent audience share is beginning to attract advertisers, particularly those looking for younger and up-market demographic groups. Even so, many advertisers have decided not to take space on the new channel while the dispute continues with the actors' union Equity. As a result the independent television companies which sell advertising on Channel Four have been forced to reduce rates drastically, in some cases to less than half those for the main ITV channel. Partly as a consequence there has been a greater emphasis on local advertising than on ITV, this being the first time many local advertisers have been able to afford television space.

For a variety of reasons, therefore, and possibly temporarily, Channel Four and TV-AM have introduced cheap advertising to television and the result has been the appearance of advertisers and hence advertising money new to the medium. If cable were able to offer similarly cheap

322

rates then it too might be attractive. On the other hand it will lack Channel Four's and TV-AM's biggest advantage from a narrowcast viewpoint, namely almost universal reach, so that even more than for them its early appeal could largely be to local advertisers, benefiting system operators in offsetting the per-subscriber fee but not helping the service providers.

Channel Four by itself has already increased the amount of advertising space available on television by some 55 per cent from 90 to 140 minutes a day. TV-AM's additional 20 minutes means that in the space of one year advertising availability has grown by almost 80 per cent. Yet that is nothing compared to cable's impact. If one assumes that new cable systems carry an average of six of the advertiser-supported services (excluding classified advertising and shopping channels) and that on average each service consists of a six-hour block each day, possibly repeated, with ten hours daily at weekends, then at least 250 minutes of advertising space will be added, an increase from 1983 amounts of 256 per cent and from pre-C4/TV-AM figures of an enormous 455 per cent. Channels carrying nothing but advertisements – classified, infomercials, shopping channels – will add to this, while most importantly programme sponsorship will present major new opportunities for 'advertising' outlay. It seems impossible that there could be sufficient demand for such an increase.

In practice, of course, television advertising expenditure will be limited by the rate of cable system growth. If one assumes that American experience is repeated here, all basic services combined might be achieving a 5 rating in cabled homes within four years and an 8-10 rating by 1990. At 4 million subscribers in the latter year this suggests a possible hourly peak-time audience for all basic cable services of perhaps 320,000-400,000. If cable costs-per-thousand are comparable to those on broadcast television (in fact they are likely to be lower given the amount of competition) then we are looking for cable advertising revenue of between £44 million and £55 million, or about a third of that required by Channel Four. Ventures into sponsorship and dedicated advertising channels will no doubt increase this, as would a live 24-hour news channel. Sponsorship in particular may prove attractive as remote-control channel-switching and fast-forward wind through advertisements in video-recorded programmes reduce the efficacy of spot advertising.

Overall, therefore, one might be considering a maximum possible annual advertising expenditure increase by 1990 of some £50-80 million at 1983 prices. If each service gives two advertising minutes every hour to system operators, some £10-14 million of this would be local advertising. Since even £80 million amounts to barely 3 per cent of current total display advertising expenditure and since, according to the Institute of Practitioners in Advertising, display advertising revenue has grown by 25 per cent in real terms during the past ten years, this must be considered an attainable objective. Indeed one might also note that over the same period television has increased its share of display advertising revenue from 36 to 41 per cent, while advertising's share of Gross National Product is also rising. According to the Advertising Association, overall advertising expenditure increased by 3 per cent in real terms in 1982 alone. It would appear likely, therefore, that sufficient advertising resources will be available for the new services as systems grow, albeit on a limited scale and as just one, possibly subsidiary, revenue stream. Growth in GNP, in advertising's proportion of GNP, and in television's share of advertising revenue will all help, so that money new to advertising, advertising money new to television and reallocated television advertising budgets will all be used.

It must be emphasised that this is simply one scenario amongst many possible, and that if there prove to be more than about six basic cable services, or if each consists of significantly more than a limited six to seven-hour original programming block and relies on advertising as the principal revenue source, then it is most unlikely that total advertising revenue growth will meet requirements. Nor will it do so quickly enough. Even with the assumptions made, it is extremely doubtful that cable advertising revenue will meet the timetable anticipated by prospective service providers, nor be anything like sufficient for all the services currently proposed. Advertising expenditure will initially be spread far too thinly over too many services. Even once the latter have been reduced to sensible proportions it is most unlikely that advertisers will commit as much to them or as fast as they would like. Services will have to reduce rates and offer incentives just as Channel Four and TV-AM have had to do. Already Sky Channel has done just that, dropping its charges dramatically in an effort to interest advertisers.

Traditionally cautious about new media, advertising agencies will see cable as offering opportunities for experimentation, test-marketing, local advertising and sponsorship. They will also be used to reach the audience in cabled homes which almost inevitably will be watching less commercial broadcast television. International companies may use the pan-European services to develop unified international marketing campaigns. AGB is also developing an infomercial service for distribution on a number of cable systems. The narrowcast argument should have attractions for local specialist advertisers for whom 35-40 per cent penetration of an area would be acceptable, but carry less weight with national advertisers for whom a 20 per cent national penetration is of little interest. If the latter are to be drawn quickly it will be essential for a central cable advertising sales system to be established to avoid agencies having to deal with a multiplicity of system operators and service providers. Even more crucial will be reliable audience research information, the absence of which has been a major hindrance in the USA. If audience fragmentation is to be the way ahead, advertisers will want to know exactly how it divides. Cable will only suceed as an advertising medium if it can be proved to be a more efficient and precise allocation of advertising resources. As in the United States the one certainty, therefore, is that television advertising will become ever more complex as the audience divides geographically and demographically.

LOCAL, COMMUNITY AND ACCESS TELEVISION

Although the experience of community and access cable television in Britain over the past decade has not been altogether happy, the opportunities which they are seen to present remain a major attraction to those involved in local affairs, community activism, voluntary organisations, education, lobby groups and minorities without other access to the broadcast media. Indeed the Government has argued that it is exactly this multiplicity of interests which justifies its policy of not making specific community and access channel requirements of cable operators. In Chapter 16 it was questioned to what extent this decision, together with the present relative absence of competition for cable franchises, will allow potential operators to offer minimal facilities only. By recent American standards current proposals do indeed appear modest, particularly given the – again by American standards – comparatively large franchise areas concerned. In operators' defence it might be argued that even in the United States demand for large numbers of community and public access channels has yet to be proven and that, in line with the relatively moderate proposals and expectations for cable services in Britain, what is currently being suggested may actually be more realistic, effective and sensible. Nevertheless the Cable Authority might well consider a franchise clause requiring operators to increase the channels and facilities available for this type of use if and when the demand reveals itself – as is the case on Californian systems.

For the most part applicants for franchises have proposed a single combined community and access channel, some even seeing it as also fulfilling an educational channel role. A few have included separate access and educational services but these tend to be the exception. A similarly standard set of technical facilities include a colour-equipped studio, in many cases with ¾ inch U-matic video equipment, an outside broadcasting van and two or three sets of portapak video equipment. Production staff, including maintenance engineers, number between three and six for each system. In most cases the emphasis is very heavily on providing the facilities but depending upon and encouraging members of the community for actual production. Typical proposals envisage capital expenditure on local facilities of £100-250,000, depending on whether additional more commercial uses are planned, and annual operating expenses of £60,000 to over £100,000 including staff salaries. Subscribers to a typical 100,000 home system at 35 per cent penetration might, therefore, be paying up to £0.25 a month to finance this service.

The amalgamation of community and access channels into one may be convenient, but it carries with it potentially major problems in trying to determine whether or not any editorial control can or should be exercised, and if so by whom. The question of the operator's status as publisher will also have to be resolved; a number propose to retain the right of veto over programmes in order to prevent transmission if, in their opinion, any contravene the law or Cable Authority regulations. Such a legitimate concern could nevertheless be open to abuse – as indeed some community programme-makers claim happened occasionally during earlier community cable experiments when items were vetoed for reasons other than those stated.

In many cases the proposals made in the initial franchise applications are couched in terms too vague to give any clear idea of the operators' understanding of their role. This could vary from simply providing technical facilities and basic training advice to involvement in the organisation and management of a 'facilitator' group, or to active participation technically, administratively and, in some instances, editorially in the production of programmes. Inevitably each of these approaches has its advantages and drawbacks – few potential partici-pants would welcome operators having editorial control over all output, while the wholly passive concept of providing facilities as a neutral resource has been shown repeatedly not to work. Not only does it fail to stimulate and encourage participation from those traditionally less articulate or non-self-motivating groups within the community who might benefit most, but as a corollary it tends to become dominated by a number of already highly vociferous elements – categorised by one writer as 'middle-class radical chic'. If only the 'video vain' and the activists of already dominant social groups become involved then community/access cable will be of little true community value.

A closely related problem has been highlighted in a report for the Greater London Council on cable and the voluntary sector, published during 1983. This addresses the distinct possibility that cable, through sponsorship, leased access and public access, will allow well organised, wealthy and powerful voluntary interest groups of various kinds – industrial organisations, churches, political interests, large charities – much greater access to the public via television than hitherto, to the detriment of smaller and less powerful associations. Until now the absence of sponsorship or access has meant that broadcast coverage of an organisation's activities and objectives has depended on the decisions of programme producers, so that large and small, wealthy and poor bodies have usually benefited equally. Now new methods of finance and access could favour the wealthy, organised and media-wise. Large

326

national charities, for example, possibly with the resources to produce their own programmes and appeals, could via cable reach an audience in a much more professional and attractive way than small local charities would be able to afford. The problem closely resembles that experienced by some local churches in the United States, competing against national religious channels for the financial offerings of their congregations. Indeed the fundamentalist churches which dominate the religious channels in the USA are said already to be poised to enter the British market themselves. Advertising by charities, churches and similar voluntary organisations has always been prohibited on commercial television in Britain. Now the implications of sponsorship, access and leased access will have to be considered closely by the Cable Authority.

Without doubt one of the objectives for community cable most commonly mentioned by operators is a local news and information service. In some cases even this is seen as something which volunteer members of the community should put together themselves. In other areas, where a local radio or newspaper company is involved in the consortium, there are obvious advantages (and dangers) in making use of their news resources, as well as in selling joint newspaper, radio and cable advertising space. Indeed a few operators do believe that local news could be made to cover or contribute to its costs – the Advertising Association estimates that in 1983 over £800 million will have been spent on advertising in the local press, suggesting considerable potential. Local sports may also be a category for which operators will use their own staff – already Thorn-EMI's existing system in Swindon has covered events of local interest such as the 1983 NatWest Trophy cricket match between Wiltshire and Northamptonshire. With the sponsors only too happy to allow free television coverage, this event cost the company barely £400 for some six to seven hours.

Nevertheless, with one or two exceptions, the emphasis at present appears to be largely upon providing the facilities but depending upon members of the community for actual production. Essential to such an approach is a well devised training procedure and adequate technical support. For those who are not interested in the production aspects of programme-making there needs to be a professional crew or trained volunteers available to carry out such functions. But perhaps most crucial will be the overall organisational structure, the extent to which the operator, probably in conjunction with a community liaison group, actively encourages and promotes community involvement, makes the service and access to it known through cross-channel trailers, through addressing local groups, schools and clubs, and eases the passage of amateur programme-makers through the very considerable and daunting task of actually transferring their ideas and intentions to the screen. As the professional managers of the Swindon community cable experiment concluded in 1975, 'We have not sought volunteers to help shift a scene, twiddle the focus, or swivel a spotlight. We have encouraged, educated and enabled people to use the combination of video and cable as an effective means of communicating with others in their turn' (R. Dunn & M. Barrett, *Swindon Viewpoint: an experiment in community television*, 1975).

Local community cable will succeed where both the operator and the community are committed to the idea and work together to promote it, where the local authority, educational establishments, youth clubs, community centres and all the other elements – groups and individuals – who together make up a community are made aware of this new resource and are encouraged to use it. At least one writer has argued that it will prove most valuable not in areas with well established community identities but rather in new towns and estates and among highly mobile populations seeking a sense of belonging, 'where large numbers of people are strangers to a town and seek information about local networks of action, precisely where many of the traditional forms of direct information, the family, friends and neighbourhood information networks, will either be under-developed or completely absent' (M. Schacht, 'Community Broadcasting – Local Television as a Community Instrument', *Communication Studies Bulletin*, Autumn 1982, p. 9). As ever, too much should not be expected of local television; production values will inevitably fall short of broadcast standards – probably only a few hours a week will be possible for some time and audiences will be low. Nevertheless community television will be an immediate and permanent feature of the cable scene.

ENHANCED AND BUSINESS SERVICES

Throughout the cable industry in Britain the emphasis initially is very much upon the video entertainment services, such as film and music channels, which are considered most likely to attract subscribers and so to raise most revenue. As mentioned earlier, few operators are taking interactive and business services into account in their initial calculations. Most are proving cautious in the amount of money and effort they are currently ready to commit to services, the demand for which remains so uncertain.

Nevertheless the high priority which the Government has consistently given to cable's non-entertainment opportunities has been re-emphasised by the large number of switched systems chosen for the interim schemes. Consequently none of those bidding for franchises could afford to ignore the enhanced services completely. On the contrary the possibilities for home banking, teleshopping, security, information systems and business services are all spelt out in great detail, although the firm commitments are rather thinner on the ground. With some exceptions the general opinion seems to be that such services will make their appearance on a commercial scale perhaps three or four years after start-up – a usefully vague interval and probably a not unrealistic one.

As in the United States, most cable operators see themselves essentially as carriers of services, encouraging and participating in their development but not necessarily initiating. Cable space will be leased to videotex providers and to security service operators, to electricity boards for meter-reading and energy management and to business users for data transfer. The rate at which domestic enhanced and business services appear on cable will therefore very much depend on the interest and readiness of all these service providers as much as of cable operators themselves.

For this reason it may well be that information services will be amongst the first to appear, rather than security, as in the USA. After all, there are already three national text operations available, namely BT's Prestel and the BBC and ITV teletext services, Ceefax and Oracle. Prestel, despite its early problems, is a working videotex service with some five years of invaluable if hard-earned experience. Marketed originally as a broad-appeal database for both domestic and business users, carrying news, weather, travel, entertainment and a wide variety of other information, it rapidly discovered that its principal market was in the highly specialised business sector, with a number of diverse interest groups – travel agents, insurance companies, commodity brokers – each seeking a limited amount of extremely detailed and often private information. By the end of 1982 barely 3,000 of the disappointing low total of about 20,000 subscribers were domestic. As a result Prestel consciously turned its attention and structured itself towards serving business needs, while a number of other companies also saw the opportunities in supplying private videotex systems to individual users. These include Rediffusion Computers, Thorn, GEC and IBM. In particular Prestel has developed its 'gateway' service whereby subscribers can gain access not only to information on Prestel's own computer banks but also to third-party computers, allowing immediate transactions to take place – as in telebanking or the booking of seats on airline flights. The emphasis in the past two years has been on the concept of 'segmented market service', whereby specific potential user groups are identified and a package of services of particular value to them developed by Prestel in conjunction with a specific information provider.

With this experience gained, Prestel has now begun to re-attack the domestic market. In March 1983 it introduced 'Micronet 800', a service of some 30,000 pages of information specifically aimed at the budding microcomputer market. For the cost of a £50-80 modem (varying in cost according to type) to interconnect most makes of home computer with Prestel, a subscription of £1 a week, plus the cost of a phone call, domestic computer owners can gain access both to Micronet and to Prestel's other 250,000 or more pages (some 50,000 of which have additional charges of up to £0.50). Of particular appeal is the telesoftware facility which gives subscribers access to hundreds of individual computer programmes and videogames which can be downloaded on to their own domestic machines for use at their convenience. Since it was introduced, Micronet 800 has been attracting up to 1,000 new subscribers to Prestel each month and has become its most used service. As a result there are now almost 40,000 Prestel subscribers and this figure is growing by at least 1,000 a month – still slowly, but steadily upwards. Moreover, whereas in 1982 some 85 per cent of new subscribers were businesses, this has now dropped to under 70 per cent and seems still to be falling, with domestic users increasing proportionately. To emphasise Prestel's increasing success in identifying and satisfying consumer needs, it is also pointed out that annual churn of Prestel subscribers is a creditably low 12.5 per cent, although this naturally reflects the high proportion of businesses taking it.

Micronet 800 is a joint venture between Prestel and East Midlands Allied Press. A second new domestic service introduced during 1983, this time with Viewtel 202 (the viewdata arm of the Birmingham Post) and sponsored by the Department of Industry, is Club 403. This is a videotex service directed to the Solihull, Edgbaston and Sutton Coldfield areas and carrying local information, teleshopping, theatre/airline/hotel booking and an electronic local newspaper. Retail stores involved in the teleshopping experiment include Littledwoods, C&A, Debenhams and W. H. Smith. Groceries can also be ordered through the system and are delivered to the home twice a week.

Club 403 is a short-term sponsored and experimental venture aimed primarily at households in the A, B and C1 socio-economic categories in order to see how those most likely to take the service if offered commercially would use it. Interest so far seems to have been lower than hoped for and there were only 110 subscribers after five months of operation. It is still far from a commercial proposition. More significant, therefore, is 'Homelink', a scheme devised by the Nottingham Building Society and the Bank of Scotland, offered via Prestel and providing the first truly commercial attempt at a home banking service. Since September 1983 anyone with £1,000 deposited with the Nottingham Building Society can receive the service for about £40 a year, plus £20 subscription to Prestel. Savers with over £4,000 deposited pay only the Prestel annual subscription. For this they receive the loan of a keyboard terminal through which they can pay bills, transfer sums between bank and building society and check their accounts. As with Micronet and Club 403 they also have access to other services, including teleshopping from Trident, W. H. Smith and Telefusion, travel booking from Thomas Cook and all Prestel's information services.

This first nationally available home banking service is still in its early stages and its backers are naturally extremely reticent as to its anticipated and actual rate of growth. They describe the results so far as 'encouraging', but it is far too early to get a realistic picture. Currently some 35,000 of the Nottingham Building Society's savers have £1,000 or more invested and so are eligible. Nationally, at least 9 million people have building society accounts over this amount. Certainly the NBS is confident that by sponsoring the provision of the terminal they can attract sufficient business to cover costs. Already the project has been justified by the number of new accounts the NBS has gained. However the chief significance of Homelink lies simply in the fact that after a number of experiments telebanking has arrived as a commercial operation, and one which the major banks and building societies will surely follow. Not surprisingly Homelink has been approached by several potential cable operators with a view to supplying it on their systems. Prestel itself is also keen to be offered via cable as well as by telephone and BT is marketing it enthusiastically to potential operators. Indeed the successful applicant for the Westminster franchise, Westminster Cable, even intends to offer Prestel services on its basic tier, thereby making them available to all its subscribers. Valuable experience has already been gained in supplying Prestel to the eighteen homes involved in BT's optic-fibre experiment in Milton Keynes. BT has also established a special division, Cable Interactive Services, to market Prestel in a localised format, rather like Club 403, providing local information and services, videogames and access to national Prestel. Subscription, including rental of a Sinclair Spectrum computer for the home terminal, is expected to be under £10 a month, with certain services available through it also having a per-use fee, but most being offered free. Most importantly there would be no charge for the use of the cable, unlike telephone-delivered Prestel at present. As a result several other operators include the leasing of channel space to Prestel as an early, even immediate, aim.

Meanwhile at least two of the principal cable operators, Rediffusion and Radio Rentals, are considering the opportunities for local and full channel teletext and are negotiating for such services with Oracle, which again has set up a new division to market itself to cable. Indeed Rediffusion has devised a way of using teletext techniques for interactive services, including banking, shopping and even telebetting. Full channel teletext allows each subscriber to have personal teletext frames or pages which he or she can call up and use to enter data into the system – paying bills, buying items, purchasing access to pay-per-view events etc. Even without full channel teletext, each new cable channel could carry its own teletext service of equivalent capacity to ITV's Oracle – a potential capacity on fifteen activated channels of about 3,000 pages. In this way a sports channel could carry comprehensive teletext sports results, and a film channel credits, reviews and subtitles for the hard-of-hearing. With the broadcast audience already becoming attuned to the concept of teletext, the problem of 'techno-fear' on the part of potential users of enhanced cable services is being tackled even before they are available.

Predictably videogames are seen as an immediate opportunity and several potential system operators are proposing a subscription games channel from the start. Thorn-EMI is planning to supply videogames, as part of its teletext and telesoftware channel (downloading computer programmes on to domestic computers), on Radio Rentals systems and, possibly, nationally. BT Interactive Services is developing its own 'Game Star' videogames service, separate from Prestel. In addition W. H. Smith is to market the American Games Network in Britain, again potentially with broader videotex opportunities. Although it will simply distribute the American service in its entirety at first, W. H. Smith has said that it will produce its own software in due course. According to one spokesman, 'All the surveys show that what people want after a premium service for feature films is games' (Mr D. Ruffell, *Television Weekly*, 26 August 1983). As mentioned earlier, this bold statement is not entirely supported by the surveys of potential cable operators. Nevertheless BT, W. H. Smith and Thorn-EMI must have evidence to back their proposals, whilst the costs of operating such a videogame service are comparatively low.

The degree of interest in business services shown by potential operators naturally varies widely, depending on the character of the area. Particularly strong emphasis is placed on the opportunities in central London – in conjunction with BT and Mercury – but many of the other early franchise areas will also contain business centres whose broadband data custom can be sought. Indeed one or two franchises consider that business interest is already strong enough to justify building a separate business/institutional network. Thorn-EMI is certainly convinced that data transfer is a major market. Already it has joined with BT in an experiment to link offices in Swindon and Milton Keynes via BT's lines and its own business cable. It argues that data transfer on wideband cable will be significantly cheaper than on standard telephone lines. Several other operators also see potential in offering videoconferencing facilities; GEC McMichael's considerable interest and experience in this field make it a particularly likely service where they or BT are involved in a system.

Inevitably, switching will be a major incentive to operators to encourage business use, even though the response from the business community is likely to be initially cautious. In a number of cases, however, the scale of development and the long term telecommunications implications of cable will be radically affected by the involvement of BT's new rival, Mercury. One of Mercury's main problems until now has been to find an economical but reliable way of linking users to its trunk network. It would have been impossibly expensive to lay its own local lines from scratch, so that it has had to rely upon microwave relay and interconnection with the BT network. Now, however, cable systems offer Mercury an ideal alternative method of access both to smaller business users and even to domestic households, using either the same cable or a second one laid alongside in the same ducts. Indeed Mercury's estimates suggest that with the low incremental cost to system operators of providing such a service and, it believes, the high incremental revenue to be derived as a result, cable operations could break even much earlier than otherwise and could even derive up to half their net profits from this source after only ten years of operation. Consequently all the interim franchise consortia in which BT is not involved are talking with Mercury and four had already included voice services in their franchise applications.

The problems involved in providing a voice telephony service on a cable system remain considerable, not least in terms of the large-scale interconnection of BT and Mercury networks which would be necessary and the extreme union opposition which would certainly be encountered. BT itself argues that the economics of offering telephone services on cable still do not make sense; it is naturally worried that voice traffic on its local services could be eroded in the face of low-cost competition. The result of such a development, it fears, could be to step back to the era of a patchwork of separate local telephone companies dotted around the country. Nevertheless Mercury claims that it will be in a position to offer voice and data services whenever the first new systems are activated. Indeed, whatever the immediate rate of development, the construction of wideband switched networks must eventually and inevitably promote such an integration of television and telecommunications services, as BT itself recognises.

Despite the many futuristic predictions and confident assertions by potential cable operators, the prospects for enhanced and business services on cable remain unclear. Nevertheless it may be that their importance to operators will be increased precisely because so many of the traditional *raisons d'être* for cable as an entertainment service in the USA – bad reception, excessive advertising, lack of choice – do not exist in Britain. Operators may well discover that the concept of narrowcasting to different interest groups can be extended into the sphere of enhanced services. Full channel teletext and videotex might be marketed to those who have already discovered the benefits of Ceefax, Oracle and Prestel, as well as to home computer and videogame enthusiasts. Home banking services could be aimed primarily at subscribers who find it most convenient to deal with money matters out of working hours. Finally, if BT succeeds with its video library idea, pay-per-view cable could be sold as a very definite advantage to heavy renters of pre-recorded video cassettes. Other operators could develop a similar service by transmitting films overnight to pre-set video recorders in homes which had requested them, as ABC is planning to do with its TeleFirst service in the United States. Cable is just one of the burgeoning new technologies,

333

many of which have already found their way into the home. It may be that by showing the interrelationship of each and adding to their usefulness it can actually turn them to its advantage.

19 The Consequences for Broadcasting

As we approach the age of multi-channel cable, pay-TV, satellites and video it is only natural and sensible to look with concern at what these new technologies will mean for what has served until now. What will they do to our off-air broadcasting services and to the organisations which supply them? Cable will challenge many of the basic assumptions upon which broadcasting policy is founded; it is right to be wary of the consequences. Audience fragmentation, the end of the duopoly, competition for advertising, new levels of American imports, fewer constraints (whatever the White Paper says) on what may be shown, the end of the idea that all services should be universally available and fewer obligations in terms of public services – all this must surely have major implications for the broadcasters of tomorrow. Consequently the issue of cable's likely impact upon the British broadcasting system has been at the very centre of the present cable debate. There has been an implicit assumption throughout, even among cable's most ardent proponents, that the current public service system has been an outstanding success and deserves protecting. As a result the Hunt Inquiry proposed, and the Government has included in its legislation, the specific safeguards described earlier. In the White Paper the value of the public service broadcasting system is fully acknowledged, with the Government accepting its responsibilities towards it.

Nevertheless it is clear from the White Paper that the protection of public service broadcasting is only one among a list of equal priorities. Important it may be but sacrosanct it is not, and it too will have to be exposed and take its chance if the Government's objectives are to be attained. Broadcasting has only developed in its present limited form because of the finite nature of the frequency spectrum. Now cable promises to do away with such limitations. The White Paper stresses the Government's duty, side by side with that to public service broadcasting, to encourage new technology. It also quotes the verdict of the Annan Committee on broadcasting in 1977 that the BBC/ITV duopoly 'has already shown signs of becoming a strait-jacket and inhibiting the development of new services' (Annan Committee on the Future of Broadcasting, Cmnd 6753, 1977, p. 29, quoted in White paper, para. 87).

The overall thrust of the Government's argument, therefore, is that even though the existing system has been remarkably successful it should not be cosseted and over-protected at the expense of progress in technology and additional services. If these bring to an end some of the conditions which are thought to have been responsible for broadcasting's success, then so be it: 'The time has now come for a further step along the evolutionary path which was identified by the Annan Committee six years ago. The Government's desire to facilitate the development of multi-channel cable systems means that it is no longer possible to think in terms of providing different means of finance for the exclusive use of each programme-providing organisation . . . Audience fragmentation is one of the inevitable corollaries of moving from a limited number of channels to a multiplicity . . . Sources of finance will similarly be fragmented. In addition the broadcasters, who have up to now been able to exercise a powerful influence over the price paid for films, sporting events and other programme material, will no longer be alone in seeking to buy the rights. These developments will make the economics of broadcasting more complicated' (White Paper, para. 88).

Present evidence suggests that the new media must and will reduce the audience watching existing television channels. As new cable services arrive so those who watch them will take the time as much, and probably more, from current television as from previously non-viewing activities. The audience shares and absolute audience sizes of existing broadcast channels will fall. The crucial question is by how much? Evidently the larger the share captured by cable the more serious it is going to be. The BBC's two channels currently enjoy a weekly audience share of 45-50 per cent. In addition each week some 80-85 per cent of potential viewers do at some stage watch BBC. ITV and Channel Four together have a similar reach and slightly higher share. Both BBC and commercial television can therefore rightly claim a high degree of public support. The BBC is warranted in considering itself a national service appealing to almost all segments of the population through a variety of mass and minority interest programming. It is this concept, that it serves the entire nation and has universal appeal, which is used to justify the national licence fee. In turn it is the licence fee method of financing which gives the BBC a valuable degree of independence from political and economic pressure.

The BBC's idea of a service which is universally watched has always been so closely tied to that of the national licence fee that a threat to one is naturally taken to put the other at risk. If its audience share falls to 30-35 per cent then, it is feared, its reach would drop also, so that some viewers would never be using it or receiving anything for their money. Pressure to turn the licence into a discretionary subscription would mount as would resistance to raising the amount paid in line with inflation. Already the Corporation is in a dilemma. In the past, revenue growth came not only from licence fee increases but also from a steady rise in the

336

number of homes with televisions. The transition to colour also helped revenue. But with 98 per cent of households now paying some form of licence and over 80 per cent for colour the opportunities for further growth in this way are limited. Meanwhile no government is willing to increase the licence faster than inflation, although production costs generally are rising above this rate. Unless the BBC finds new sources of revenue it could gradually find itself being squeezed financially.

ITV's income could similarly be under pressure on two sides, from competition for advertising revenue and from lower audiences, producing lower returns. At present advertising space is sold to the highest bidder; whichever advertising agency bids most for a particular time slot gets it. Given a limited amount of space this has always tended to keep prices high. Now, it is argued, expansion of available space and competition from cable channels for advertising will pull down prices and hence revenue. Audience erosion will prove an even greater problem. According to London Weekend Television, a 2 per cent loss of ITV's audience would have the same effect on revenue; but an 8 per cent loss would pull down prices and so lead to a 13 per cent revenue loss. A 13 per cent fall in audiences could result in a 23 per cent decline in revenue. This, it predicts, will happen by 1992. The five largest companies which produce most of ITV's output would suffer most because it is the urban areas they serve that will be cabled first.

Naturally the effect of any major audience and revenue losses which occurred would be serious for the programmes of both BBC and ITV. Competing as the BBC would to retain its licence-justifying universal reach, the fear is that it could be forced to put ever more of its declining resources into popular programming at the expense of minority interest items and public service values. Similarly ITV might move low-audience programmes such as *World in Action* and *TV Eye* out of primetime, take money away from non-peak hour items and put it into the most popular shows, thereby maximising its audience. The public service requirements which the IBA imposes on ITV depend on the latter's profitability. If that profitability falls then it stands to reason that the IBA would be able to make fewer demands. The latter itself admits that 'in competition with a cable system able to buy in programmes cheaply from any available source, and with no similar obligations (to those of ITV) the range and quality of the public service side would come under severe strain' (IBA, 'More Channels–More Choice?', November 1982, pp. 4-5).

Already there are signs that the independent television companies are seeking a relaxation of their obligations. There have been calls for an increase in the 14 per cent foreign programme import quota, and in a significant move the IBA agreed in September 1983 to allow material from Commonwealth countries to rise by 1.5 per cent. This opens the way for more Australian and, particularly, Canadian programmes. In addition senior ITV executives are advocating an aggressive response to new competition. According to Muir Sutherland, Director of Programmes at Thames TV, 'As competition from unregulated television services increases, so in ITV must we be increasingly freed from regulations' (reported in *Television Weekly*, 29 July 1983). John Birt, Director of Programmes at London Weekend Television, has similarly suggested transferring minority interest programmes from ITV to Channel Four, putting more resources into peak-time and reducing local programming: 'I see no choice myself but to shift resources into network peak time away from other programme areas' (Reported in *Television Weekly*, 30 September 1983).

As in the United States, feature films seem likely to lose some of their value to broadcasters as pay services show them first. The BBC currently schedules about 600 films a year and ITV/Channel Four slightly fewer. In the week immediately before Christmas 1982 the four channels together showed over fifty films. Already videotape rental has reduced the viewing figures for blockbusters such as *Star Wars*, which were previously guaranteed huge audiences when they were broadcast. Indeed the result of this has been evident for some time, with ITV in particular but also BBC moving such films away from Christmas and other public holidays – when videotape rental is at its highest – and increasing the number of made-for-TV films which have not been previously released on video.

Both video and pay-TV (cable and DBS) will therefore almost certainly have an impact upon the showing of one of the broadcasters' most popular programming categories. Indeed pay-channels might even try to buy the exclusive rights to many classics – such as the Ealing comedies – thereby depriving broadcasting audiences of some of the best loved of films and the broadcasters of these always reliable hardy annuals. At the same time, however, and again as in the United States, the new competition will also lead to an extension of the hours actually broadcast. Already breakfast television has added three hours a day on two channels, and both BBC and ITV are actively planning to fill in the remaining morning and afternoon gaps in the schedules. Where one service goes its rivals must follow if they are to build and retain audiences and maintain their shares. Consequently if cable services begin an overnight service, the broadcasters will almost certainly do so too, with repeats, old films and Canadian and Australian soap operas providing the staple fare.

Just how serious is cable's erosion of broadcast audiences likely to be and how quickly will it happen? A large and rapid fall could obviously have profound consequences, particularly detrimental to the interests of those who do not or cannot subscribe to cable. But will such fears in the event prove groundless? Inevitably estimates vary enormously, with some of the most dire predictions coming from the ITV companies who believe their position to be particularly precarious. At the 1983

Edinburgh Television Festival, Brian Tesler, then London Weekend's Managing Director, forecast major changes by 1994 if cable proved popular: 'Despite the BBC's plans for a DBS movie channel, the BBC will have no movies at all – or only very old ones. They will have been pre-empted by the cable channels . . . The licence fee will not be increased in real terms and will probably be less. The BBC will have less money, much less, to spend on UK production. It will be on the brink of a vicious downward spiral. ITV audiences will also be eroded and losing out on advertising revenue. BBC 2 and Channel Four will either be wound up or very limited in the number of hours they will be able to broadcast' (B. Tesler speaking at the Edinburgh Television Festival, September 1983). Yet in the very same discussion James Lee, Chairman of Goldcrest Films and Television, put forward a much brighter future for the broadcasters ten years on: 'Broadcasters will be OK. They will inevitably lose a share of the audience, but will still have well in excess of three-quarters of the audience. ITV advertising will not be damaged by more than 10 per cent. The BBC licence will be higher in real terms than it is now. The content of broadcasting will not have changed dramatically. ITV will be making programmes for cable. The use of new channels will be limited.'

Once again we can make our own estimates on the basis of the figures for cable system growth suggested earlier. These were that by 1990 there will be between 3.2 million and 4 million cable subscribers in Britain, and that under the most favourable conditions there could be 8 million by 1994. Various additional assumptions need to be made regarding the proportions of pay and basic subscribers and the percentage that actually watch television in any day. Given that most will take cable for the film channels on offer, we may assume that some 80 per cent of subscribers will have pay. Given further that subscribers are certain to be heavier television watchers than non-subscribers, we will take an 85 per cent evening viewing figure as a reasonable estimate. (At present about 70 per cent of UK television households watch some television each day.) These figures suggest that by 1990 2.1-2.7 million pay cable homes and 0.6-0.7 million basic will be watching television – pay, basic and broadcast channels – each evening. This is out of a total estimated evening viewing audience of 14.5 million homes, or 70 per cent of the estimated 20.7 million TV households in 1990.

It is possible to break down the viewing habits of cable subscribers further, by adapting American figures for the relative audience shares of cable and broadcast channels to British circumstances. Table shows the relative primetime audience shares in American pay and basic cable homes, calculated from figures given in Chapter 15:

TABLE XXIII

US Primetime audience shares in pay and basic cable homes, 1982.

Channels	Share in Pay Homes (%)	Share in Basic Homes (%)
Broadcast Networks	58.0	74
Independent Broadcast Stations	17.7	21
Basic	5.5	5
Pay	18.8	–

In Britain there is no equivalent to the American independent broadcast stations, whose share would probably be largely retained by the broadcast networks, although a proportion would be taken by the new basic services, including the one or two out-of-area ITV channels relayed on each system. Given the generally high level of satisfaction with current British broadcasting services (compared to American) it is reasonable to assume that the shares gained by UK pay cable channels will not exceed those in the United States. In Britain, however, subscribers to basic cable only will mostly do so specifically to receive the new basic services, rather than to improve reception or get access to independent broadcast stations as in the USA. For this reason the basic service figures suggested in Table XXIV for British primetime audience shares in pay and basic cable homes are 5 per cent and 10 per cent higher respectively than their American equivalents:

TABLE XXIV

Estimated UK primetime audience shares in pay and basic cable homes, 1990-1994

Channels	Share in Pay Homes (%)	Share in Basic Homes (%)
Broadcast Networks	71	85
Pay	19	–
Basic	10	15

By 1990, therefore, between 700,000 and 900,000 cabled households would, on these estimates, be watching pay and basic cable services each evening. This means that out of a total national audience of 14.5 million some 4.8-6.2 per cent would have been lost from the four broadcast services to cable. The BBC's loss would be no greater than that already suffered at the hands of Channel Four. ITV's loss might be apparent but would yet hardly be sufficient to draw advertisers away or to reduce advertising rates, particularly since only 2.1-2.7 per cent of that loss would be to basic, advertiser-supported, services.

In 1990 it is most unlikely that cable will, by itself, have harmed existing broadcasting channels to any significant degree. Even if a further 1 million homes take a DBS pay-service via direct dish reception and watch in the same proportions as pay cable subscribers, the effect will be to reduce the evening broadcast audience share by only another 1 per cent. It is not until the relative shares are calculated for the 'most-favourable' cable scenario for 1994 that audience loss begins to look significant, with a total primetime defection to cable services of 1,776,000 households out of an estimated total TV audience of 14.7 million. This is equivalent to a 12.1 per cent share of which 5.1 per cent would be to advertiser-supported cable services. It is interesting to note that this estimate agrees with a number of others, including one by Professor James Ring, a member of the Hunt Committee. He has suggested a 12 per cent audience loss to cable and DBS combined by 1994, and argued that this would not be a significant threat to existing broadcast services.

The calculations made here have been consistently designed to take the best case for cable and realistic worst for broadcasting, so that audience loss from the latter to cable is most unlikely to exceed 12 per cent within the next decade. In addition DBS penetration of 2-3 million homes (excluding those receiving it via cable) could take a further 2-3 per cent and videotape rental 1-2 per cent. On these estimates the new technologies could together deprive broadcasting services of a maximum 15-16 per cent share of the primetime audience by 1994, although the actual figure is likely to be less. In all, ITV and Channel Four, currently with a 54-56 per cent share, might lose some 6-8 per cent, representing a fall in their audience of 11-14 per cent. On the figures produced by London Weekend Television and quoted earlier, this could mean a major drop in revenue of some 19-23 per cent, at least for ITV companies with significant cable penetration in their regions. In such circumstances it would be impossible to deny the threat to independent television's standards and, with companies already calling for regulatory relief, it is clear that pressure upon the IBA to relax its requirements will be steadily intensified.

Yet although revenue loss is certain it is by no means evident that it will be as serious as this. Even in such a 'worst case' estimate the audience loss to rival advertiser-supported channels would be no more than 5 per cent, while evidence in the last chapter suggested that advertising revenue growth could in fact be sufficient to meet the needs of the relatively limited number of new services which are likely to survive the initial surge of entrepreneurial activity. There has certainly been no sign of a fall in broadcast advertising rates in the United States since cable began to eat into network audiences. Furthermore, ITV companies have in the past ten years paid an average 14 per cent of their revenue to the Exchequer levy, so that there could be a considerable fall in income before ITV's profitability was damaged. The decline of the levy might, however, lead to an escalation of production costs – and hence of co-production – since companies would no longer be able to offset those costs against it, as they can at present.

Meanwhile the ITV networks, reaching the entire country and gaining 90 per cent of the audience for commercial, advertiser-supported television, will continue to hold most of the advantages for national advertisers. Nor will they remain passive in the face of revenue loss when the growth of the new technologies also means major new sources of income to be tapped. At present barely 2 per cent of ITV revenue comes from programme sales, yet as the demand for programming on cable increases so broadcasting companies such as Thames and Granada with major production facilities and extensive archives will seek to exploit these resources. Some will also extend their programme packaging role, as Yorkshire Television is doing with its involvement in the Music Channel. Others, including Yorkshire again, Granada, Central, TVS and Grampian, are planning to use their experience as regional television franchisees to involve themselves in cable system operation. None of them can afford not to meet the challenge by entering the new markets themselves. It will be for the IBA to ensure that in protecting their position either through retrenchment or through attack, the ITV companies do not themselves destroy the public service element of the independent broadcasting channels.

To the BBC, currently with a 45-50 per cent share for its two channels, the maximum likely fall by 1994 could be to 35 per cent. It has been suggested that it is at this point that its claim to be universally watched would begin to look dubious. Yet one of the features of a service offering varied programming is that its overall reach need not necessarily fall with its share of the audience. On the contrary, although the need to reach mass audiences is important, it is precisely in its programming policy of serving a wide span of minority tastes (often very large ones) that the BBC keeps its reach score high. In the last week of November 1983 ITV had a weekly share of 49 per cent compared to BBC1's 37 per cent. Yet the latter's reach was actually greater than ITV's at 82.5 per cent and 81.9 per cent respectively. The tendency for reach not to drop with share is supported by the experience of the American Public Broadcasting Service stations, mentioned earlier. There, the fact that cable subscribers are heavy but still fairly indiscriminate viewers and prone to channel-hopping has meant that although PBS's share has fallen in cabled homes its reach, rather remarkably, has risen.

Between different television programmes and channels there exists as much a law of functional equivalents as there is between different forms

342

of mass communication or leisure activity. Consequently it is where a new channel or programme serves a particular audience need as well as, or better than, an old one that the impact will be greatest – hence the early effect of film channels upon films on broadcast television. The new pop-music services will almost certainly hit the BBC's *Top of the Pops* hardest. Yet where cable fails to provide an equivalent service, or where what it does provide is either not as good as or strictly complementary to that already on offer, then the effect will be less severe. The broadcast networks' continued control of the rights to most major sporting events, for example, leaving mainly subsidiary tournaments and early rounds to cable, will ensure that they retain a significant sporting audience. Enthusiasts for a particular type of programme – sport, music, news – may certainly watch more of it if it is available, but few if any of us restrict our viewing to only one category. Still less does our desire for entertainment lead us to watch nothing but *Crossroads, Coronation Street* and wall-to-wall *Dallas*. Most people, irrespective of demographic classification, watch a wide variety of programmes including both those of general appeal and entertainment and others of a more specialised and demanding character, reflecting each person's individual range of interests. Indeed it is this second type of programme which is appreciated more. Yet early evidence suggests that the range of new programming offered on cable could be strictly limited for some time to come. The result may well be a defection to cable away from particular programmes, but with viewers returning to and making heavy use of the broadcast channels for the full variety and particular specialised items which they demand.

Moreover, as with ITV, the BBC starts from a very strong position, with enormous resources, vast experience in every aspect of television, national distribution, two channels to provide complementarity of service, vast programme archives and a largely appreciative audience well accustomed to turning to it for every kind of information, elucidation and entertainment. The Corporation has also shown itself very ready to react positively to the threat from the new technologies by making all the running with DBS and involving itself in the Visionhire pay-cable pilot scheme which pre-dated the ITAP report. Its entry into American cable via the now defunct Entertainment Channel was unfortunate but still showed a vital recognition of the need to develop overseas markets and to take advantage of cable's demand for programming. This has since been further demonstrated by the growing importance of BBC Enterprises, the Corporation's programme sales arm, the agreement with the entertainment unions for unrestricted release of BBC programmes on video and the agreement with HBO to co-finance up to six British feature films a year. The BBC has also announced its interest in being a partner in European Music Satellite, a pan-European pay cultural channel transmitted on a low-power satellite transponder. Such a service would not only have greater appeal, it believes, in Europe than in the United States, but equally importantly it would enable the Corporation to start offering new services even before its DBS satellite is launched. For this reason it is also involved in the Visnews project for a European news service.

A number of people are now beginning to suggest that the BBC should itself develop a complete range of specialised channels for cable, in addition to its DBS services. Aubrey Singer, Managing Director of BBC Television, has argued that 'the important thing in a 30-channel service is to get your name on as many channels as possible . . . I think of a news channel, a music channel, a sports channel, a children's channel. After all, if one can dominate six channels then there is more chance of the heartland of television remaining the base' (Speech to the Association of Directors and Producers, quoted in *Ariel*, 21 September 1983). Certainly in areas such as news and sport, where the resources which the BBC allocates necessarily exceed the amount of broadcast coverage given, there seems scope for extra coverage on additional channels. The BBC could either put together complete services, presumably on a pay basis, or provide regular programming or blocks of programmes for others. Indeed such a development could provide important new sources of revenue, thereby helping to resolve the problem mentioned earlier of sustaining financial growth without recourse to raising the licence fee above the rate of inflation. Already such thinking is behind the Corporation's plans for its subscription DBS channels.

Looking at the next ten years it does not seem likely that the BBC's position and its right to the national licence fee will be seriously threatened. Perhaps more of a danger would be if, as cable services matured and became themselves established features of the television scene, the audience mentally 'lost sight' of the BBC amongst the multitude of channels and ceased to differentiate it from the others. In an era of competition which will breed similarity the Corporation will have to work to retain a distinctive identity, a particular regard in the minds of viewers and a high profile. It may well expand and use its resources and economies of scale to become a major provider of programmes for cable. Meanwhile the IBA, if it does find ITV revenue seriously threatened, might in due course be forced to reduce the number of regional broadcasting franchises it offers, increase the overall size of each and accept that the local programming objective which it has always sought would gradually be taken over by the more truly local cable systems.

Change will undoubtedly come, but it will come more slowly than many expect. Certainly it could alter our broadcasting services out of all recognition, yet it need not necessarily be as damaging as some fear. Given the reality of the new technology and of the market approach which has been adopted, broadcasters cannot afford to be narrowly protectionist. The concept of public service broadcasting will have to grow and be as organic as its environment. Whether or not, therefore, it survives as a valid notion of how broadcasting should be organised and of its objectives, the White Paper is surely correct in arguing that 'public service broadcasting will best respond to the challenge of cable by drawing on its own capacities in order to participate in cable and, above all, by maintaining the quality of its own channels' (White Paper, para. 89).

20 The Cinema, Film and Production Industries

For many years now the British film, cinema and independent production industries have been in a state of apparently inexorable decline. In 1972 some 103 British films were registered for theatrical release.* Five years later the number had been halved to 51. By 1982 it had halved again, to only 24. English-language cinema is dominated by North America, in terms both of production and revenue. The films of the major Hollywood studios account for about 90 per cent of the American market, which in turn provides at least 60 per cent of the industry's income. In 1979 film rental in North America amounted to some $1,215 million compared to $750 million from the rest of the world. This situation is unlikely to change and will to a very large extent continue to determine the types of film, appealing to an American audience, which get made.

Meanwhile the British appear, quite simply, to have lost the habit of going to the cinema. In 1972 there were 163 million admissions to British cinemas, falling by 1978 to 127 million. Since then the decline has accelerated to over 10 per cent each year, and between 1981 and 1982 alone admissions fell by a disastrous 27 per cent to only 64 million, barely half what it was only five years before. As a result takings fell by 19 per cent. Since the early 1960s cinema admissions have dropped four times as quickly in Britain as in the United States, despite the fact that the films on offer were largely the same. Many in the industry hoped that 1982 was a fluke year with few blockbusters to draw audiences, and major distractions such as the Falklands conflict and the World Cup to keep them away. Yet in the first half of 1983 there was only a small improvement, with the underlying trend remaining downward. Today over half a million fewer seats are sold each week than in 1981, with the main audience losses being amongst the older occasional cinema goers rather than the regular 18-24 age group.

Not surprisingly cinemas have continued to close and the average number of seats available to fall. In 1981 there were 1,528 licensed screens, many in multiple cinemas, with an average 411 seats each; by the end of 1982 the figures were 1,439 cinema screens and an average 397

---

*I.e. films registered in UK over 52 minutes long, excluding films from outside UK.

346

seats. As a result some 1,800 jobs were lost, leaving only 5,324 full-time and 7,568 part-time employees in the industry. Such losses, however, must be set against the growth from nothing barely five years ago of the sizeable video rental business. Since November 1980 the latter has created some 12,000 full-time and 18,000 part-time jobs and now easily outdoes the cinema, with a total of about 32,000 employees in 6,500 primary video outlets. A further 9-10,000 stores deal in videotapes although their primary business ranges from stationery to groceries.

Cinemas now account for barely 3 per cent of all film viewing, with the remainder having been transferred to the home via broadcast television and video. The economics and convenience of broadcasting and videotape rental have proved conclusive and demonstrate clearly that, although people still like films, they prefer watching them in their own homes. Throughout the cable debate the Cinematograph Exhibitors' Association has tried to resist this trend by demanding a specific restriction on the showing of new films on television, giving the cinema at least a one-year exclusive 'window'. Yet, as both Lord Hunt and the Government have recognised, protection of the interests of one group must mean interference in the rights of others, in this case those of the film industry to sell its product to whichever outlets suit it best. Nor is there any obvious justification for penalising cable in this way when the principal culprit in recent years has been videotape rental. As the White Paper concludes, 'The Government's view . . . is that it is for the film industry itself to determine how best it wishes to promote and market its own product . . . The Government does not believe that it should intervene in the commercial judgements which the industry itself should take' (White Paper, para. 165).

Although the cinema industry appears to be holding its own against cable in the United States, its prospects in Britain, in the face of broadcast services and video rental, are already grim. The cinema's out-of-home function and its large-screen advantages appear to be significant factors for only a relatively small core of regular cinemagoers. Indeed the same is true of many of the traditional out-of-home entertainment services; attendances at theatres, football matches and even pubs have all been falling in recent years, while the move to in-home entertainment seems to be confirmed by the phenomenal growth not only of video and videogames but even of take-away food and canned beer.

Consequently it would be hard not to conclude that the cinema industry will continue to decline and that cable will only add to its problems. Equally, however, American experience would suggest that neither cable nor pay-per-channel film services will be primarily responsible, nor even necessarily very significant. Only when the pay-per-view showing of new films is introduced will the cinema's principal role as a first stage release system be seriously threatened. And that will only happen when the potential pay-per-view cable audience is large enough for it to be worth the film distributors' while. By the time cable becomes an important consideration in the release of a film in Britain, the cinema industry may already be approaching a new equilibrium.

For if there is one certainty it is that the cinema will not disappear altogether. Rather, its use will be confined to a central core of predominantly younger consumers for whom an alternative venue to the home will continue to be important, to enthusiasts and to others who are looking for a special night out. The number of cinemas may be halved, but they will remain very necessary to film distributors as a means of promoting their products in the best conditions. New opportunities will also appear, including public exhibition of pay-per-view sporting events received by satellite for people who do not have access to a pay-per-view television set or cable system. Moreover, until it becomes possible and economic to introduce widescreen high-definition television into the home, probably in the late 1990s, this new and exciting phenomenon could be exploited by cinema entrepreneurs. The cinema will survive as a promotional device and an emotional experience because in these respects the television does not provide a comparable alternative. As the leading British producer, David Puttnam, has argued, 'Once cinemas have undergone the change from being the main source of box-office revenue to being largely promotional vehicles, we could, to our amazement, find ourselves packing people in because it will have become comparatively cheap to see the films on show. The pay-off for the enthusiast who still attends will be the truly cinematic experience of seeing a film on a large screen, in darkness, with the best possible sound; and the pay-off for the industry will be a promotional fulcrum around which word of mouth will feed the interest of a mass audience of cable and satellite viewers. The return for the cinema owner will no longer be box-office receipts but his stake in the home broadcasting industry' (D. Puttnam, 'Film-Maker in Wonderland', in B. Wenham (ed.), *The Third Age of Broadcasting*, London 1982, pp. 65-6).

It is hardly surprising that producers and others in the film industry should be enthusiastic about what must be a new source of revenue and stimulus to production. Using the estimates made earlier for pay subscription and assuming a £4 wholesale price, the various film networks together could be grossing some £123-154 million at 1983 prices (excluding DBS revenue) by 1990, and as much as £307 million by 1994 in the most favourable circumstances. If 40 per cent of this were spent on programming then this would amount to £49-61 million in 1990 and up to £123 million in 1994, with DBS subscriptions possibly increasing these figures by 50 per cent or more. This compares with the £106.8 million gross cinema box-office revenue in 1982 and bare £30.4 million actually paid by exhibitors for film rental.

348

But, although pay film services may eventually be a major source of revenue, they will initially have very little indeed to contribute. Licence payments will be small and, according to Nicholas Mellersh, Chief Executive of United Cable Programmes, could be as low as £2-5,000 for a standard feature film. As he admits, this is a drop in the ocean for a producer trying to put together a film financing package: 'Instead, the producer, after going about raising the money in the normal way, must look to recoup the investment and make a profit by selling the film to broadcast TV here and cable in the States and then exploitation worldwide, with theatrical releases where appropriate. You then can get a small additional amount of money at no extra cost by selling it to us' (N. Mellersh, quoted in *Broadcast*, 2 September 1983, p. 22). Similarly none of the film services will be investing significant amounts in production at the start, although their parent companies may do so. Consequently their promise to encourage popular British productions by screening them will, for the time being, stop short of major production finance.

Nevertheless, and despite the declining film registration figures mentioned earlier, the British film industry is already enjoying something of a revival. The reasons have less to do with the prospects for cable in Britain than with a combination of Channel Four's arrival, the growing need of broadcasting organisations worldwide to cut costs by co-producing and buying in relatively inexpensive films, the opportunities presented by the American cable market and the current technical and financial advantages of making films in Britain. As the number of British feature films registered for cinema release has fallen, so there has been a gradual increase in those made by or for the BBC and ITV, either as single features or as filmed series. For both a primary objective has been to obtain new material, but for the ITV companies an additional incentive has been that profits not invested in this way, in films intended for television release, would otherwise only have gone into the Exchequer levy. Some companies have even established their own wholly-owned film-making subsidiaries, including Thames Television's Euston Films, ATV's Black Lion and former ITV franchisee Southern TV's Southern Pictures. Many television-financed films have actually been intended for a cinema release, as in the TV spin-offs *Porridge* and *George and Mildred* and others such as *The Long Good Friday* and *Gregory's Girl*, which was partly financed by Scottish TV.

The role of television in financing low-budget film production has become increasingly important. Now, however, this trend has been put on an altogether firmer footing by the decision of Channel Four to co-finance about twenty new low-budget films a year at a cost to it of some £6 million. Through co-financing with organisations such as Goldcrest, Rediffusion Films and the British Film Institute Production Board, 27 films have been produced in its first year for a total budget of about £12.5 million, including the critically acclaimed and successful *The Draughtsman's Contract, Moonlighting* and *The Ploughman's Lunch*. Meanwhile the BBC has become heavily involved in co-financing of features, drama serials, documentaries and other types of programming. *Tinker, Tailor, Soldier, Spy* and *Smiley's People* were co-financed by Paramount, the Shakespeare cycle by PBS and Time Life, and *The Barchester Chronicles* and *The Woman in White* by the now defunct Entertainment Channel. Over half of the output of the Corporation's music and arts department is co-financed with such companies as Arts International, ZDF (the German broadcasting organisation), PBS stations and Time Life. In 1983 the BBC entered into one of the most significant deals it has yet made, by committing some £4 million a year to a series of feature films in conjunction with HBO. In doing so it is both cashing in on the new opportunities for reducing costs through co-financing and laying in a stock of valuable product for its DBS services when they appear.

American and European film, cable and television companies are now looking to Britain as a source of co-finance. At the same time the UK is able to offer both a high level of technical expertise in film production and significant financial advantages in making films and programmes here. A favourable exchange rate, comparatively low labour costs and the ability to offset production costs against overall company profits, make major savings possible and encourage production in Britain, in films which qualify as British. As a result the production facilities of Elstree, Twickenham and Pinewood have been responsible for such popular, if mostly American financed, successes as the *Star Wars* and *Superman* trilogies, James Bond's various adventures and *Raiders of the Lost Ark*. Whereas 1981 saw only 24 major films produced in the UK or by British crews, this nearly doubled in 1982 to 51. In what is essentially a separate development, films which might be regarded as recognisably British and initiated in Britain have also scored notable successes and helped to boost the morale of the film-making community. *Gregory's Girl, Chariots of Fire* (largely Middle East financed), *Gandhi* and *Local Hero* have all done well in the most important market of all, the United States.

Leading the way for the UK film industry is Goldcrest, whose projects have included virtually all the most successful of recent British releases – *Chariots of Fire, Gandhi, Local Hero* – as well as several of Channel Four's made-for-TV films, such as the *First Love* series and *Red Monarch*. Central to its success has been its ability to use co-financing and tax advantages to minimise the investment risk. Equally important has been its determination to secure pre-release sales, particularly in the United States, and its readiness to take American partners. Thus it has joined with Orion for *Another Country*, Columbia for *The Dresser*, and Warner for *The Killing Fields*. The financial success of *Local Hero* was guaranteed through pre-release sales even before its first showing. Most important

350

has been Goldcrest's partnership with HBO and Showtime in a number of ventures such as *The Far Pavilions* and *Robin Hood* (the latter also co-produced with HTV), making financing easier and greatly reducing the risk by pre-selling the American cable rights. According to Bill Gavin, Goldcrest's head of sales, 'everything has changed in the space of 18 months, simply because American cable is now devouring everything we can supply, and paying larger sums than we ever imagined in the process (*The Times*, 14 April 1983).

Others such as Rediffusion and Thorn-EMI are now also recognising the opportunities and, most importantly, several major investors are becoming interested. Goldcrest's £22 million capital base comes from bodies such as the National Coal Board, merchant bankers Noble Grossart and a number of investment trusts. Other banks involved in film financing include Guinness Mahon and Samuel Montagu. The Prudential Assurance and Post Office Superannuation Fund have put money into United Media Finance, which joined with Showtime to co-produce *Prisoners of the Lost Universe*. Fleet Holdings put money into *The Far Pavilions* with Goldcrest and HBO, as well as investing in Britannic Films, which is co-financing Tom Stoppard's *Squaring the Circle* with TV South and the American Metromedia Corporation. Investors are using co-financing to put a toe in the water and are discovering that, with cable rights and foreign television sales, a modestly budgeted feature can be a sensible and profitable investment.

The prospects for the British film and production industries look brighter, therefore, than they have for many years. Yet for the time being at least any revival will owe little to the creation of new cable and satellite outlets in Britain itself. Indeed the opportunities abroad and relative unimportance of a British showing is demonstrated by TV South's decision to go into production with *Squaring the Circle* even before getting any agreement to an airing on the ITV network. Encouraging as this may be in some respects, it has also given cause for concern. For what characterises all such co-production deals – whether drama, arts or documentary – is their international rather than purely domestic appeal, raising doubts in the minds of many as to what effect such developments will have on the types of programme made. As Anthony Smith, the Director of the British Film Institute, has suggested, British television is 'an indigenous broadcasting industry which has captured the national market. Now the presence of US money, in the form of underwriter, benevolent as it may be, threatens to drive out that indigenous image.' Indeed, 'for a culturally dependent country, selling programmes and programme ideas could be as insidious as buying them' (quoted in the *Listener*, 3 March 1983, p. 34).

Those who believe that co-production will inevitably influence the character of films or programmes made by British companies point to the popularity in America of the historical or costume drama, such as

Poldark or *Jamaica Inn*, and argue that even essentially British programming will be turned toward the international market, with fewer resources being given to more socially relevant items of purely domestic interest. Others comment that such considerations clearly did not weigh with Central TV in its decision to co-finance the harrowing dramas *Walter* and *Walter and June* with Channel Four, and that films of particular social relevance to Britain, such as *The Ploughman's Lunch*, can nevertheless be commercial. In each case, however, it was Channel Four's support which made them possible and its 'alternative television' brief which determined their character. Certainly Thorn-EMI's re-entry into feature film production has been marked by a conscious recognition of the need for international appeal. According to Verity Lambert, 'We're going to be making films in Britain, but they've got to have themes and subjects which are international' (quoted in *Screen International*, 26 February 1983).

Co-production could therefore both influence the type of film or programme which gets made and lead to editorial/directorial compromises to meet the demands of each of the backers. The BBC insists that it retains complete editorial control over its co-productions, but others are more amenable and have to be in order to find finance. Goldcrest had to give the role of an Indian princess in *The Far Pavilions* to a white American actress in order to increase its interest for HBO's audience; it also had to add a French element to its 26-part series *The Body Machine*, to satisfy co-financer Antenne II, the French television service.

As cable makes international co-production an ever more significant feature of the films and programmes we receive, therefore, it may be that ways will have to be found to preserve an essentially domestic perspective where possible. Co-production will allow programmes of great excellence to be made, such as *Life on Earth, The Making of a Continent, Tinker, Tailor,* and even *Nicholas Nickleby,* but it is very much less certain that it will provide finance for *Boys from the Blackstuff* and *The Nation's Health.* Canada is already facing these problems and the solutions it has adopted may turn out to be very similar to those needed in Britain. Certainly a major requirement of the British industry is script development money to enable good ideas to be developed into a prepared package for presenting to potential backers. *Chariots of Fire* and *Local Hero* have already demonstrated that good British ideas can be commercially successful abroad if they are sufficiently thought out. Consequently there have been numerous proposals for a variety of film finance funds, through an extension of the Eady levy on cinema admissions to films on television and video, the imposition of a levy on blank video-cassettes and even a tax on cable subscription, as in Canada. The funds raised in this way could be channelled through the National Film Finance Corporation, the British Film Institute or other agencies into worthwhile and essentially indigenous projects, with eligibility being defined more strictly than hitherto. In addition it has been suggested that the Government should take up a proposal made in several reports, including ITAP, and develop a coherent policy for the film, television and video industries under the aegis of a single minister. Already, following the 1983 General Election, the Minister for Information Technology, Kenneth Baker, has taken over responsibility for film policy from the Trade Minister and has addressed the question of reforming or replacing the Eady levy. Finally much will depend on how seriously the new Cable Authority takes the Government's injunction to promote British production, and on the definitions it applies as to what is British.

For companies which see international co-financing of quality programmes for pay-TV as the way ahead, there should undoubtedly be real opportunities, although the competition will become ever more intense. The signs for companies looking to the bottom end of the market, however, to serving the basic cable channels, are rather more mixed. Many of the services currently proposed are promising some 4-11 hours each of programming every day, of which between 20-50 per cent will be British produced. Any live news channel will necessarily carry even more, with the greatest demand for original programming after this coming from the sports services. But others will rely heavily on off-the-shelf programming – general entertainment, education, hobbies/leisure and arts in particular – while all will have to use multiple repeats to reduce costs.

Moreover all the signs are that their programme budgets will be pitifully small to keep early losses down to acceptable proportions. Typical figures quoted are in the £5-10,000 an hour range for original material, with the average hourly cost below this and a mere fraction of any of the broadcast services' budgets. Consequently independent producers who wish to make programmes for this market will either have to develop entirely new ways of working to keep costs down, or to discover a guaranteed additional market for their product, such as overseas sales. But, when even the BBC and the ITV companies have extreme difficulty in selling any but the pick of their programmes abroad, the American and European prospects for independent and more cheaply budgeted material must be very limited, with perhaps the main opportunities being for pop promotional videos and arts programming. Some producers see videotape sale and rental of leisure/hobby and educational programmes as an additional possibility, and companies such as Michael Barratt Ltd. are already tapping this market. Nevertheless interest in such material has so far been small, so that costs will have to be kept down and profitability be calculated on the expectation of a slow return. The types of programme which get made will tend to have a long shelf life and to be less transitory than most television – hence hobbies and education. Perhaps the best prospects in Britain, as in the

353

United States, are for companies who specialise in sponsored and industrial material. This sector of the business seems almost certain to grow as sports services, educational and 'infomercial' channels increase the opportunities for companies to get their names on television and even to present programmes in which they have been editorially involved.

In the last two years the appearance of Channel Four has transformed the independent production industry in Britain, with a plethora of new, mainly small companies being created to make programmes for the new services. Most impressive has been the construction of several large and sophisticated facilities houses and studios to provide production and editing services to these independents. Now cable and satellite are seen as new markets to support and confirm this growth and there seems little doubt that they must do so. But the importance and character of that stimulus will depend on a number of factors. Firstly it will depend on the cable industry's recognition that British programmes are still preferred by viewers to all but a very few imports, and that to attract subscribers it must meet their tastes. Secondly it may be shaped in part by the production industry's ability to reduce costs to a minimum, both to compete with foreign material and to come within basic cable services' very small budgets. In the last resort it could depend on the determination and strength of the Cable Authority in requiring cable operators and service providers to pump money back into production. But above all, and for many years to come, the character of cable's stimulus to production will be determined more by new media markets abroad than by those in Britain, by the ever increasing importance of international co-production and by the British production industry's continued ability to produce for that international market. The much lower levels of British programming on cable than on broadcast television, the very much lower budgets and the even greater reliance on co-production all seem destined to make the new services very, very different from the old.

Conclusion:
Into the Cable Age

The public's enthusiasm for new technology would probably be greater now if technology had not been oversold in the past, as something amazing, a cure-all, a cornucopia; if it had not been associated with prestigious, expensive, but commercially doubtful projects. Greater care needs to be taken to present new technology in the same undramatic terms in which consumers typically assess new technology (Versailles Working Group on Technology, Growth and employment, 'Public acceptance of New Technology', March 1983, para.33).

It is very easy to be futuristic about cable; almost as easy to be pessimistic. This book has tried to keep the argument on the ground and not to speculate too much about what may be the state of affairs in thirty years' time. After all, for the immediately foreseeable future changes will probably be less dramatic than many expect. In the United States, with so much going for it, cable has encountered enormous difficulties, and it would be arrogant to believe that Britain will be very different. Whatever the eventual shape of the industry, cable in its formative years will not mean thirty channels, twenty-four-hour services, truly narrowcast programming, well-funded and extensive community and access facilities or widely available interactive services. To many it will mean nothing at all since it will not be available; to others it will be another call upon their disposable income, having to prove itself in the competitive marketplace. Like Prestel, teletext, Channel Four and breakfast television, cable will for some time to come be a case of trial and error, technical problems, programming experiments, marketing mistakes and rapid change in response to economic pressures.

Nevertheless in due course cable will surely prove itself to be every bit as central and valuable to ur society as the telephone and broadcasting services have been. Almost certainly its role will be as much as a gateway to information exchange, service provision and commercial transaction as to entertainment. It will have become an electronic highway enabling all who use it – banks, libraries, emergency and social services, schools and colleges, local government, businesses, retailers of goods and information, public utility operators and telecommunications carriers, as well as providers of entertainment – to offer a much enhanced service.

This bringing together of a variety of communications needs, on to an integrated and all-embracing system of transmission, should be one of cable's major benefits. The second, conversely, could lie in its ability, while serving such needs and enabling them to interrelate, nevertheless to keep them separate and distinct. In this way the national and the local, the specialist and the general, the mass and the personal, and the business and the domestic communication needs of modern democratic socitey could come closer to being met in a coherent but pluralistic manner than at any time since the advent of the mass media.

Perhaps this is too far-fetched a claim and at best only a remote possibility. Yet today the validity of a modern democracy rests crucially on the flexibility and effectiveness of its means of communication in supplying the needs and reflecting the views and aspirations of its citizens – just as, on the other side of the coin, the various totalitarian regimes of the age have found control of the dissemination of information to be as necessary to support themselves as control of the armed forces and means of repression. During the late Victorian period and for at least the first half of the twentieth century the economics of information distribution led to the development of systems of communication which reflected the character of society as man in the mass. First the newspaper, then the cinema and finally radio and television broadcasting all adopted the economic logic of mass, simultaneous distribution of information in all its forms – news, entertainment and advertising.

Many people saw for the first time in broadcasting's universality the opportunity to perfect the democratic system of government by binding the nation together with a common stock of information and culture. To Lord Reith, the great, paternalistic founding father of the BBC, broadcasting could become 'the nervous system of the body politic' and 'an integrator for democracy'. Certainly the attractiveness of such a view of broadcasting as an all-embracing and uniting system of communication and culture is evident. Indeed it has its counterpart in the logic of a national cable network, supplying in one package all the information, entertainment and communication needs of every household. But it is exactly the elegant simplicity of the idea which makes one automatically suspicious. For today neither the concepts of mass society nor of mass communication are considered adequate representations of the immense complexity of human interaction. In the 1960s and 1970s it became steadily more apparent that there were serious inadequacies and inefficiencies in a system which, despite the diversity both of Fleet Street and of the output of the broadcasting organisations, was still to a large extent geared to the logic of the mass. Naturally there remained and remains a huge common ground of interest which can be served by a common mass of information supplied in bulk to all. Yet increasingly the multitude of layers, of tastes and of minority opinion which surround that common ground have sought both to be served and to develop their own means of expression. Nowhere is this more evident than in the remarkable proliferation of specialist journals in the past ten to fifteen years, and of magazines directed to particular sub-cultures.

Television has responded very much more gradually to these new demands. The principal channels have done something, but they are necessarily geared to supplying the common ground. Most recently Channel Four has been directed specifically to address itself to alternative audiences and has done so with determination. But not even four channels can hope to meet all needs and tastes, nor to give adequate opportunities either for the expression of minority and local opinion or for independent producers to place their wares before the wider television audience.

Now, however, we are entering an age where the technical limitations upon the extension of choice in audio-visual media have been removed. Direct satellite broadcasting can double the number of channels available, cable can increase them many times further still and, together with video, help to remove the tyranny of the broadcasting schedule. If they do nothing else, the new media will necessarily increase choice in the sense of giving consumers greater opportunity to decide when they wish to see items which appeal to them, for repeat scheduling will be at the heart of the cable services. How far they will increase choice in the sense of extending the range of programmes and subjects covered, of course, is rather less clear. Certainly in the early years cable will provide little money for new production, except in so far as it has international appeal and attracts co-production money. Nor is there much chance that for a long time it will even attempt many of the types of high quality but limited appeal programmes at which the BBC and ITV have been pre-eminently successful.

Nevertheless the different structure, regulations, finances and objectives of cable to those of broadcasting should ensure that the new services are themselves very different from and in many cases complementary to those which already exist. Cable operators will do all they can to introduce new diversity and to find services which attract subscribers. This will mean providing programmes of which there is currently an inadequate supply (films, sport, music, news), services which are totally absent at present (community and ethnic minority channels), material which is interesting but cheap (sponsored and educational programmes, televised parliamentary proceedings) and informational and interactive services which are of interest and value to our ever more technocratic society. Whether or not cable leads to better or worse programmes, it will almost certainly increase the range of services of all kinds which are available.

Meanwhile, for many years to come the rate of cable's development and the form in which it seems likely to evolve should leave the broadcasting services as necessary as ever to the vast bulk of the television audience, cable or uncabled. Audience fragmentation will be slow and, other than in its effect upon broadcasters' morale, relatively insignificant. Indeed it will be more the anticipation of a threat from cable than the reality of its growth which will lead to the earliest changes in the present broadcasting services.

The coming of the cable age is characteristically seen in two stages, with the eventual, mature cabled society which enjoys the benefits for the new systems being preceded by a period of great uncertainty, upheaval and risk, when all our existing media institutions and methods will be overthrown and new ones, not necessarily better than or even as good as the old, put in their place. Even the Hunt Report described cable as a leap into the dark. Yet to admit that it is neither possible at this stage to foresee how cable will grow nor to prepare for every eventuality is not simply to surrender broadcasting as a hostage to fortune. Rather it is to acknowledge the intrinsically organic and evolutionary character of such instruments of social communication as broadcasting and cable. The signs at present are that cable will develop at a sufficiently gradual pace for us to be able to respond to problems – economic and regulatory – as they arise. Even if it makes its mark rapidly its success will necessarily bring increasing obligations, particularly given the various positive responsibilities placed upon the Cable Authority.

Certainly there is a danger that cable may attract a sufficient audience to affect the amount of original production on broadcast television but insufficient to contribute much itself. Yet Channel Four has demonstrated that lower budgets do not always mean lower standards or more anodyne programmes. Moreover, the likelihood of this happening may be minimised precisely by the determination of the BBC and the ITV companies themselves to respond to the new opportunities and to expand into new areas, seeking to confirm their position at the heart of the ever-widening television environment. If the real value of the broadcasting services is to continue to be recognised, they must seek to retain their distinctive character, by refusing to surrender or abandon any aspect of their programming and, instead, by doing all they can to maintain, improve and increase both the diversity of their output and its high quality.

358

No one would dispute that, sooner or later, cable and the other new technologies must alter radically the character of our broadcasting services and the ways in which we use them. If cable is to earn adequate revenue as an entertainment medium it must and will fragment and reduce the broadcasting audience. People will spend more of their viewing time as members of minorities (albeit still large ones) rather than of majorities. In due course the structure of ITV may have to be changed, with the number of independent television contractors being reduced. Both BBC and ITV will look for additional sources of income and increase the amount of co-production they undertake. Once sponsored programmes appear on cable there will be mounting pressure to introduce then on ITV. Cable may hasten the move to 24-hour broadcast channels. Long-form programmes and mini-series may increase in number but theatrical films on broadcast TV may be reduced. More time may well be given to programmes for the teenage audience. Broadcast television in twenty-five years time will be as different from what we have today as the latter is from what was put out in 1959.

Nevertheless the changes which occur over the coming years will be very much more in the evolutionary tradition of broadcasting's development than the enormous increase in the number of channels and the two-stage revolution view of cable seem to imply. This is recognised implicitly in the current legislation, both in the obligations which have been imposed upon the Cable Authority and in the flexibility of approach which it has been allowed. The structures of television must be organic and flexible if they are to respond adequately to the changing character, demands, aesthetic judgements and moral values of society. Even in the last few years, before the arrival of multi-channel cable, there have been notable changes in the character of our television services. BBC2 and Channel Four have widened the range of programmes, the number of different audiences addressed has increased, news gathering has become faster, production techniques have been transformed and programmes of great interest and value have been made possible through co-production. At the same time international co-production has added new demands and constraints upon what is produced. American made-for-TV films and mini-series have become staples of broadcast television and the ratings war has intensified. Competition in scheduling is increasingly leading to programmes which appeal to the same audience being put out at exactly the same time in a head-to-head contest from which the viewer is the loser. The nature of television is constantly changing and it would be naive to believe that we can ensure it is always for the better. Indeed as an instrument of society if is hardly surprising that TV will seek both to serve society's aspirations and to pander to its imperfections.

Now cable creates the opportunity for, if not the certainty of, even greater responsiveness and flexibility in the future. Better even than broadcast television it has the remarkable ability to unite and serve individuals with a common interest for a brief period, then to separate them and to unite a different set of common interests. It can bring a nation together at a particular moment, but also divide it into its constituent parts far more fully than any previous audio-visual medium. This process of uniting and separating, of recognising the immense diversity within the whole, is surely what democracy and pluralism are all about.

In this respect, therefore, and perhaps more than its critics would care to admit, cable is a natural response to social trends, just as the BBC in the 1920s and 1930s saw itself as an instrument of democratic integration and just as ITV in the 1950s was one manifestation of the new-found affluence and increasing materialism of society. Television has frequently been described as a mirror on society. But the image it has thrown back at us has always been curiously distorted in its very coherence. Now cable promises to splinter the mirror and, in doing so, could mutilate that image still further. Yet it may just be that the fragments in their turn will reflect an altogether truer picture of our complex and pluralistic society than we have ever known.

ADDENDUM, 1 MARCH 1984

A book is like a photograph, always in danger of freezing the action while the subject moves on. Even in the short time since this book went to press the cable industry has taken several more steps, not all of them forward. The broad picture remains the same, but in all countries discussed here the shake-out of unprofitable or potentially unprofitable services continues apace. In Canada another of the regional pay-cable services has closed down and First Choice remains in considerable difficulties. In the United States Spotlight, the smallest of the satellite-distributed pay film services has gone under, as predicted. More worrying are the many system operators who are trying to renege on their franchise promises, either by building smaller-capacity system than initially proposed or by introducing fewer community channels and interactive services. Warner Amex, in the face of the huge losses mentioned above, has taken the drastic step of suspending its Qube. Cable in the United States is still growing rapidly and is now taken by over 40 per cent of all households. But it is widely recognised that single cable 54-channel systems are more than adequate for most people's entertainment needs. Finally developments in Britain are already confirming the forecast made in Chapter 18, that 'the economics are extremely dubious for anything more than one of each type [of cable entertainment service] to survive . . . Certainly several of those [planned] will not even get off the drawing board'. In the last week Thorn EMI and Capital Entertainment Group have agreed to merge their film channels into one to be called Premiere. The two rival sport services have also agreed to combine, and the merger of the two remaining pop-music channels seems equally certain.

Appendices

In 1979 the Mayor of Boston created a committee to consider whether Boston should be cabled at that time and how. This recommended going ahead and suggested the establishment of a non-profitmaking access foundation to manage up to 20 per cent of the subscriber channels for community and leased access programming. This foundation and the recommendation that two leased access channels be provided were intended to resolve the potential problem of a franchise monopoly in which the operator could determine what programmes were excluded.

In September 1980, therefore, a city cable office was set up and initial bids invited, although the city had not yet determined what were its minimum requirements. Nine applicants made bids, including six multiple system operators, two local groups of investors and another which was deemed ineligible because of local newspaper interests. Having seen what was being offered, therefore, the city in February 1981 issued its formal Request for Proposals (RFP), setting out its minimum requirements. These included the giving of 20 per cent of cable capacity to the access foundation, a 3 per cent gross annual revenue franchise fee and a further 5 per cent grant to the access foundation. Also required were an institutional loop for traffic between business and public buildings (schools, offices, etc.) and immediate interactive capability.

The high requirements of the RFP were too much for all but two of the initial applicants, Warner Amex and Cablevision, and even Warner Amex was not keen on the access foundation idea. Unlike Cablevision, however, it did already have experience of building a large urban system.

In June 1981 public hearings were held, and in August the city chose Cablevision. However the provisional licence was not negotiated until March 1982, by which time Cablevision had to demonstrate its financial capability to build such a system involving a capital outlay of $120 million, its banking arrangements, technical competence and also to provide complete street maps of its system layout. Decisions also had to be made on the exact order and speed of cabling, whilst it was required to introduce a public element into the company by the sale of $5 million worth of shares, with a maximum individual holding of $50,000. After further negotiations, during which Cablevision had to provide details of its expected costings, the final licence was agreed in December 1982, with the first cabling starting at the same time.

The franchise area is 45 square miles, with a total population of 550-600,000. There are about 250,000 households in 728 street miles, giving a high average density of over 300 homes per mile. The franchise requires the entire city to be cabled within five years, with about 28 per cent of cabling to be underground. In fact Cablevision initially promised to complete cabling within three and a half years and as of December 1982 believed it could do it in two and a half.

The system consists of a headend and three local hubs, each serving four districts, the entire city being divided into sixteen districts. Three of the community channels will probably therefore carry different programming to different districts, particularly since the city consists of several closely defined communities, including large ethnic sections. For example 75-80 per cent of the East Boston population is Italian (about 32,000 in all) whilst about 80 per cent of the Charlestown area is Irish (116,000 in all). Plans are therefore being made to import RAI, the main national channel, from Italy as well as some Chinese programming for Chinatown.

There are four cables in all, two for subscriber services, one for public institutional use and one for commercial services – data transfer, videoconferencing etc. The two institutional 'loops', each of 55-channel capacity and split evenly between 'downstream' and 'upstream' for full interactivity, are to pass all the principal public buildings and through the major commercial centres of the city, but not the residential areas. The domestic subscriber cables each have 52 channels and all the services on one, including the access foundation channels, all broadcast relay services and some satellite-delivered cable channels will be available without a converter and for a basic rate of only $2 a month. One pay service, HBO, will also be on this cable for an extra $7 a month, and will be 'trapped' at each house taking it. It will cost a further $5.95 a month to receive an addressable decoder and access to further pay services and to pay-per-view and other enhanced services. The latter will include emergency alarm services from the start.

The franchise is for 15 years. Cablevision will need to recoup the equivalent of $35 a month per subscriber at 40 per cent penetration if it is to break even and is expected to do so by year nine, at least by the banks supporting it. To others it is clear that the very low basic rate leaves Cablevision requiring each subscriber to take several pay services and to watch pay-per-view events regularly. They question whether this level of use will be realised. The following table indicates the various sources of revenue and the proportion of total revenue which Cablevision expects to derive from each in the first, fifth and tenth years of operation (1983, 1987 and 1992):

Revenue	1983	1987	1992
Basic and subscriptions	67.8%	77.2%	80.3%
Installation charges	27.5	2.6	2.0
Pay-per-view	1.0	2.4	1.8
Security services	3.5	3.4	3.9
Advertising revenue	0.1	9.1	7.0
Local loop revenue	–	3.8	3.6
Uplink to satellite revenue	–	1.4	1.4

(Source: City of Boston Cable Office, December 1982)

Finally some impression of the complexity of the franchising process and the range of issues which need to be considered can be gained from the following table of contents from the Provisional Licence granted to Cablevision in March 1982:

Provisional Cable Television Licence to Cablevision Systems Boston Corporation 25 March 1982.

TABLE OF CONTENTS

Section 1
Definitions   2

Section 2: Grant of License
Section 2.1   Grant of provisional license   6
Section 2.2   Limitations upon grant of provisional license   7
Section 2.3   Term of provisional license   7
Section 2.4   Transfer and assignment of provisional license   7
Section 2.5   Grant of final license   7
Section 2.6   Term of final license   8
Section 2.7   Transfer and assignment of final license   9
Section 2.8   Non-exclusivity of grant   9
Section 2.9   Police and regulatory powers reserved   9
Section 2.10 Right of condemnation reserved   10
Section 2.11 Removal or abandonment   10
Section 2.12 Governing requirement   10

Section 3: Construction and Installation
Section 3.1   General   11
Section 3.2   Construction schedule   11
Section 3.3   Completion of construction   13
Section 3.4   New construction   13
Section 3.5   Equipment   13

Section 3.6   Extension of time   14
Section 3.7   Safety standards   14
Section 3.8   Location of cable television system   14
Section 3.9   Disconnection and relocation   14
Section 3.10 City property   15
Section 3.11 Notice of city construction   15
Section 3.12 Private property   15
Section 3.13 Pole attachment   16
Section 3.14 Underground facilities   16
Section 3.15 Repairs and restoration   16
Section 3.16 Tree trimming   16
Section 3.17 Temporary relocation   17
Section 3.18 Right to inspection of construction   17
Section 3.19 Limitation on construction obligations   17

Section 4: Maintenance
Section 4.1   General   17
Section 4.2   Maintenance log   18
Section 4.3   Service interruption   18

Section 5: System Design and Configuration
Section 5.1   Hub distribution centers   18
Section 5.2   Capacity for institutional services   19
Section 5.3   Narrowcasting capability   19
Section 5.4   Channel capacity   20
Section 5.5   Satellite earth stations   20
Section 5.6   Satellite uplink   20
Section 5.7   Capacity for interactive residential services   21
Section 5.8   Cablecasting facilities   21
Section 5.9   Standby power   22
Section 5.10 Emergency alert   22
Section 5.11 Interconnection   22
Section 5.12 Parental control capability   22
Section 5.13 Identification of potentially offensive programming   23
Section 5.14 Technical performance   23

Section 6: Service and Programming
Section 6.1   Initial service and programming   27
Section 6.2   Universal basic service   27
Section 6.3   Pay-cable or pay-per-view services   28
Section 6.4   Interactive service   28
Section 6.5   Channel designation transposition   28
Section 6.6   Program guide   28
Section 6.7   Senior citizens' services   29
Section 6.8   Children's services   29
Section 6.9   Municipal services   29
Section 6.10 Access channels   29
Section 6.11 Local origination programming   30
Section 6.12 Leased channels   30
366

Section 6.13 Commercial institutional network   30
Section 6.14 Public institutional network   31
Section 6.15 Development of further services   31
Section 6.16 Continuity of service   31
Section 6.17 New developments   31

Section 7: Rates and Charges
Section 7.1   Monthly rates and installation charges   32
Section 7.2   Notification of change   32
Section 7.3   Free connections to the universal basic service   32
Section 7.4   Boston Housing Authority buildings   32
Section 7.5   Public institutional network connections   33
Section 7.6   Location of connection   33
Section 7.7   Preliminary designations   33
Section 7.8   Custom installation   34
Section 7.9   Service beyond drop cable   34
Section 7.10 Special equipment   34
Section 7.11 Publication and non-discrimination   34
Section 7.12 Credit for service interruption   35

Section 8: License Fee
Section 8.1   License fee entitlement   35
Section 8.2   Payment   35
Section 8.3   Return of fee   36
Section 8.4   Credits   36
Section 8.5   Affiliates' use of system   37
Section 8.6   Late payment   37
Section 8.7   Recomputation   37
Section 8.8   Taxes   37
Section 8.9   Reimbursement for license expense   38

Section 9: Insurance, Bonds and Indemnification
Section 9.1   General   38
Section 9.2   Indemnification   40
Section 9.3   No limitation on liability   41
Section 9.4   Notice of cancellation or reduction of coverage   41

Section 10: Financing
General   42

Section 11
Support for foundation   44

Section 12: Subscriber and User Rights
Section 12.1 Subscriber solicitation   44
Section 12.2 Sales information   44
Section 12.3 Billing practices information   44
Section 12.4 Notice of installation   45
Section 12.5 Business office   45
Section 12.6 Notice of complaint procedure   45

Section 12.7   Response to service complaint   46
Section 12.8   Unresolved complaints   46
Section 12.9   Notice of public meetings   46
Section 12.10   Subscriber privacy information   47
Section 12.11   Monitoring   47
Section 12.12   Polling by cable   47
Section 12.13   Distribution of subscriber information   48
Section 12.14   Information with respect to viewing habits and
                subscription decisions   48
Section 12.15   Privacy Ombudsman   49
Section 12.16   Subscriber and user contracts   49

Section 13: Employment Training and Procurement
Section 13.1   Equal Employment Opportunity and Affirmative
                Action Programs   50
Section 13.2   Employment policy   50
Section 13.3   Employment training program   52
Section 13.4   Employment advertisement   52
Section 13.5   Procurement   52

Section 14: Administration and Regulation
Section 14.1   Performance evaluation sessions   53
Section 14.2   Equal time   53
Section 14.3   Nondiscrimination   53
Section 14.4   Subscriber and user correspondence   54
Section 14.5   Response to inquiries   54
Section 14.6   Emergency removal of plant   54
Section 14.7   Removal and relocation   54
Section 14.8   Inspection   54
Section 14.9   Obscenity   54
Section 14.10   Initial performance test   55
Section 14.11   Monthly performance test   55
Section 14.12   Annual performance test   55
Section 14.13   Quality of service   55
Section 14.14   Liquidated damages   56
Section 14.15   Revocation of license   57
Section 14.16   Determination of breach   57
Section 14.17   Non-exclusivity of remedy   58
Section 14.18   Arbitration   58
Section 14.19   Jurisdiction   58
Section 14.20   Right to repurchase   58

Section 15: Reports
Section 15.1   Construction reports   59
Section 15.2   Financial reports   59
Section 15.3   Records pertinent to value   60
Section 15.4   Number of subscribers   60
Section 15.5   Subscriber complaint report   60
Section 15.6   Significant service interruption report   60

368

Section 15.7   Performance tests reports   60
Section 15.8   Specific complaint report   61
Section 15.9   Dual filings   61
Section 15.10   Contacts with lessees   61
Section 15.11   Status report   61
Section 15.12   Additional information   61

Section 16: Miscellaneous Provisions
Section 16.1   License as contract under seal   62
Section 16.2   Entire agreement   62
Section 16.3   Captions   62
Section 16.4   Separability   62
Section 16.5   Grandfather rights   63
Section 16.6   Impairment   63
Section 16.7   Notice   63
Section 16.8   Force majeure   63
Section 16.9   Subscriber television sets   64
Section 16.10   Garaging of vehicles   64

II. CABLE EMERGENCY ALARM INCIDENTS, SYRACUSE CABLE-SYSTEMS

1. On May 12, 1981, at 2347 hours, Ms Mattie Davis heard glass breaking. She looked out her upstairs window and saw a man standing outside her side door. Ms Davis immediately pushed her emergency panic button, after which she received a call from the police dispatcher. Ms Davis said that she was so shaken up that she was unable to convey any vital information to the dispatcher via the telephone. A car was dispatched to the scene and, according to Ms Davis, the police arrived at her house within a minute from when she pushed the medical/police button. The quick dispatching of a car to the scene was made possible by our computer read-out with all vital information at the police department and resulted in the apprehension and arrest of the suspect on the premises. Ms Davis was very pleased with the operation of her alarm system, and the quick response of the Syracuse Police Department.

2. On December 15, 1981, at 9.07a.m., a fire alarm was reported at 257 Stafford Ave. When the fire department received no answer with the auto-dial call, they immediately dispatched a vehicle to that address. No one was home at the time. The fire department gained access through an unlocked door and discovered smoke in the house. Upon further investigation, a malfunctioning furnace motor was found to be the source of the smoke. The fire department de-activated the furnace, ventilated the house, locked it up and left a note with the subscriber's neighbor explaining what had happened. When Mrs Pelletier arrived home, the odor of smoke hung in the air. She discovered that the furnace had had a problem and that some-

one had removed the cover to the motor. Shortly after her arrival home, Mrs. Pelletier's neighbor arrived with the note from the fireman explaining what happened and what they did. Mrs. Pelletier called them as well. A service man was called to repair the malfunctioning motor. Mrs. Pelletier, needless to say, is very grateful that she had the cable alarm system.

(Taken from Syracuse Cablesystems reports).

Index

ABC, *see* American Broadcasting Company
ABC Video Enterprises, 268
Aberdeen Cable, 305
access channels, 79; in Britain, 283-4, 325-8; in Canada, 91-2; in US, 117, 127, 130, 140, 147, 198, 201, 208-14
Adams, W.C., 202
addictive programming, 183
addressable systems, 15, 192-7, 216
adult films, 29, 75, 77, 183, 185, 186-7, 194, 195, 284-5, 318; *see also* Playboy Channel; pornography
The Adventures of Black Beauty, 153
advertising: access channels, 209; advertiser-supported services in Britain, 318-25; on British broadcast networks, 10, 58-9, 72, 74; on British cable, 56, 69, 72, 286-7, 290, 327; in Canada, 86, 87-8, 108; channel hopping during, 159, 245; children's services, 153; commercial deletion, 88; Hunt Report on, 74-5; ITAP report and, 56, 58-9; on ITV, 337; local advertising, 173-6, 204, 207, 306, 324; and pay services, 188; per-subscriber services, 154-8; revenue available for programming, 69; sponsored programmes, 253-4, 320, 321, 323, 327; on US broadcast networks, 59, 80, 266-7; on US cable, 69, 158-76
Advertising Association, 324, 327
Advisory Council for Applied Research and Development (ACARD), 35, 51
aerials, prohibition of outside, 42; TVROs, 123, 124, 136, 146
Aerospatiale, 26
Aetna life, 27, 234
Alameda, 126
alarm services, 56, 215, 217-21, 309
Aldrich, Michael, 54, 55
All in the Family, 266
All the Rivers Run, 257
Allstate Life Insurance, 234
American Broadcasting Company (ABC): and locations in television, 115; losses before profitability, 168; news programmes, 268; pay-per-view films, 191; programmes for summer months, 269; and SNC, 155; sports coverage, 157, 191, 196, 266; *Taxi*, 184
American Express, 28, 126

American Telegraph and Telephone (AT & T): computer and information services, 27; monopoly, 23, 24, 231; opposition to cable television, 27; teleconferencing, 236; use of satellites, 25; videotex, 222-3, 229
American Television and Communications (ATC), 27, 127, 129, 235, 305
AML multi-channel microwaves, 126
Anik satellites, 25, 26
Annan Report (1977), 46-7, 59, 335, 336
Annie, 181
Another Country, 350
Antenne II, 105, 352
Appelbaum-Hebert Report (1982), 30
Area Cablevision, 207
Argus, 44
artistic freedom, 183
ARTS: advertising, 158, 160, 164, 165, 166, 173; and broadcast network services, 264, 268; local programming, 201; and PBS services, 264; piggy-backing with other services, 145, 169; programme sponsorship, 253-4; programming costs, 159, 164, 172, 252
Arts International, 350
Asian Cine-vision, 210
Associated Film Distributors, 256
Associated Press, 229
AT & T, *see* American Telegraph and Telephone
Atari, 128, 221, 222, 225
audiences: advertising and, 159-76; BBC share, 336, 338-43, 344; in Britain, 293-4; British cinema, 294, 346-7; broadcast networks' share, 261-4, 266-7; effect of cable on life of, 246-8; ITV's share, 337, 338-43; monitoring, 40; preference for five cable channels, 137; special interest groups, 59, 61; US cinema, 249; viewing habits, 243-5; viewing preferences, 61; *et passim*; *see also* subscribers
Audits of Great Britain (AGB), 305
Audubon, 201
Avco, 121

Baker, Kenneth, 51, 52, 277, 352
Baldwin, T.F., 190
bandwidth, 12
Bank of Scotland, 330-1

banking services (telebanking), 17, 19; in Britain, 308-9, 328, 329, 330-1, 333; in US, 215, 223-31

The Barchester Chronicles, 350

Barrett, Michael, 328, 352

Bartleville, 121

Barwise, T., 68, 69

Bay Area Cable Interconnect, 174, 194

BBC, *see* British Broadcasting Corporation

BBC Enterprises, 49, 343

Belgium, 83

Bell, 27, 231

Berks Community TV, 214

Bethel Park, 203

BICC, 297, 305

Birt, John, 77, 338

Bizarre, 183

black community, 210

Black Entertainment Television (BET), 156, 170, 172

Black Lion, 349

Board of Broadcast Governors (BBG), 85, 89

The Body Machine, 352

Boston: access channels, 130, 208, 211, 212; basic tier, 127, 134; business services, 238; cable security, 220; channels in, 125, 130; enhanced services, 225; first tier costs, 134; interactive system, 196; local authority and, 130, 131; local services, 211, 212

Boys from the Blackstuff, 352

BP, 28

Bravo, 187

breakfast television, 338

Bristol, 45, 46

Bristol Myers, 161

Britannic Films, 351

British Aerospace, 26

British Board of Film Censors (BBFC), 285, 318

British Broadcasting Corporation (BBC): audience share, 336, 338-43, 344; broadcasting monopoly, 37; co-finance programming, 343, 350; competition with the IBA, 3; co-production, 317, 352; and DBS, 343, 344; effect of cable on, 335-45; films made by or for, 349; films on, 338, 339; foreign material quotas, 288; and Hunt Inquiry, 70, 71, 72, 74-5; ITAP report and, 58; licence fee, 336-7, 339, 344; licence-fee dodgers, 10; material shown in the US, 187; public service concept, 3; and relay exchanges, 37-8, 39-40; sports coverage, 320; strong position of,

343-4; teletext, 21

British Electric Traction, 28, 44, 71

British Film Institute (BFI), 352; Production Board, 349

British Linen Bank, 305

British Printing and Communications Corporation (BPCC), 49

British Relay, 42, 44, 45

British Telecom (BT): business services, 332; cable systems compatibility with, 280; and cable TV, 40, 43, 48, 49, 66, 280, 300; fibre optic research, 14; financing systems, 305; increased demands and, 22; Interactive Services, 332; ITAP report and, 60; monopoly broken, 24; Prestel, 21, 67, 215, 222, 229, 231, 329-31; privatisation, 24, 53; relations with cable operators, 288-9; satellites, 26; submission to Hunt Committee, 66; system development, 297; use of optic-fibre cables, 53

British Telecommunications Act (1981), 24

Brittan, Leon, 29

broadband telecommunication networks, 13, 25, 53

broadcast networks: affiliate system, 267; cable and, 261-70; audiences in Britain, 293-4; audience share in US, 261-4, 266-7; effect of cable on in Britain, 59, 69, 286, 335-45; films, 264; new techniques, 268; programme costs, 265; as a public service, 39; summer broadcasts, 262, 268-9

Broadcasting Act, 1958 (Canadian), 85

Broadcasting Act, 1978 (Canadian), 109

Broadcasting Research Unit, Working Party on New Technologies, 71

Brookline, 138

Brooklyn, 225

Browne, Bortz and Coddington, 137

burglar alarm systems, 56, 215, 217-21, 309

business services: in Britain, 318, 328-34; in US, 231-8

Business Times, 157, 166

Butler, Adam, 52

'c' band, 25

C-Channel, 99, 100, 101, 311

C-Span, 152-3, 172, 264

Cable and Broadcasting Bill, 276

Cable and Wireless, 53

Cable Authority (proposed), 278-91; and advertising, 287; and British programme production, 288, 353, 354; and community services, 284, 325, 326; and film restrictions,

285, 318; franchise awards, 279-82, 283, 284; and programme exclusivity, 285, 286; and quality of service, 283, 284; and range of services, 284; regulation of service, 282-91; role, 289-91
Cable Bill, 1983 (US), 120, 131
Cable Health Network (CHN), 145, 160, 163, 170-1, 173, 252
Cable Interactive Services, 331
Cable Music, 319
Cable News Network (CNN), 154, 155, 156, 158; advertising, 158, 159, 160, 161, 162, 168, 170; CNN2, 145-6, 155
Cable Satellite Public Affairs Network (C-Span), 152-3, 172, 264
cable services: advantages of, 11; and cultural influences, 30-1; in Britain, 296-300, 308-34; and broadcast networks in Britain, 59, 69, 286, 335-45; and broadcast networks in US, 261-70; business uses, 215-38, 318, 328-34; competition from other distribution systems, 135-8, 140-1; DBS and future growth of, 28-9; economic effect of, 300-2; economic influence, 29, 30; effect on film industry, 60, 180-3, 253-9, 270-2, 346-54; effect on viewers, 246-8; enhanced uses, 215-38, 308-9, 328-34; experiments in, 44-50; 'free', 152; growth in Britain, 302-7; importation of distant services, 18, 42; and the individual, 32, 62; influence of growth in US, 29; ITAP report, 54-60; local character of, 59, 61; as a luxury item, 59, 61; origins, 41-4; ownership, 70-1, 72-3, 116-17, 127-8, 132; physical restraints, 9-10; political factors, 29, 51-80; in poor reception areas, 18, 41-4, 114; and programme production, 44-50, 251-60; provision of new services, 18; reaction to the ITAP Report, 64-73; regulation in Britain, 61-2, 66, 69, 70-1, 73-4, 275-91; regulations in Canada, 30, 85-6, 87-8, 90, 93; regulations in US, 115-20, 237-8; as a socially divisive force, 70; and telecommunications, 27
Cable Sports and Leisure (CSL), 319
cable technology, 12-18; bandwidth, 12; British hardware, 296-300; capacity, 13; copper co-axial, 13-14, 17, 27, 58, 66; mini-star systems, 298; multi-pair copper, 12-13; optic fibre, 13-14, 17, 27, 53, 66, 96-7, 126, 296; relay exchanges, 36-41; switched-star systems, 15, 17, 18, 58, 280, 281, 298, 300; technical standards, 58, 68; terminology, 12-18; tree and branch systems, 15, 17, 18, 58, 281, 297, 298

Cable Television Association (CTA), 46-7, 50, 285
Cablecasting Ltd, 50
Cableshare, 96
Cablesystems, 194, 196, 227, 231
Cablesystem Pacific, 198
Cabletime, 298
Cablevision: alarm services, 220; Boston franchise, 127, 134, 175, 196, 363-9; business services, 235, 238; finance, 139; and Spotlight, 179; subscriber income, 127, 134, 196, 197
Cablevision (Wellingborough) Ltd, 45, 48, 49
Cablevision Scotland, 299, 305
Calgary, 86
Callaghan, James, 51
Calliope, 156, 200
Canada: accelerated growth of cable in, 86-7; access TV, 91-2, 213; advertising, 86, 87-8, 108; availability of US stations in, 84-5, 93; cable in, 83-110; cable revenue, 95; Canadian content in programmes, 99, 101, 103-5, 106, 107, 110; community channels, 45-6, 91-2, 95-6; converter services, 95-6; early cable TV, 83-5; experiences in cable, 79-80; pay-TV, 97-111; programme exports, 104; programming finance, 102-6, 107; programming from France by satellite, 97; promotion of production industry in, 88-9; reception from US satellites, 95, 98; regulations imposed, 85-6, 87-8, 90, 93; satellites, 26, 96; specialist channels, 97; and the UK market, 50; US cultural influence, 30, 83; and US programming material, 86, 88, 89-90, 93
Canadian Broadcasting Corporation (CBC), 86, 97, 100, 108, 109
Canadian Cable Television Association, 96
Canadian Cablesystems, 87, 96
Canadian Creative Development Board, 103
Canadian Radio-Television Commission (CRTC), 86-93, 97-109, 213
Cannon, 256
Capital Cost Allowance Program, 103
capital costs: in Britain, 305-6; enhanced services, 216-17; local facilities in Britain, 325-6; in US, 129-30
Capital Radio, 44
Captain, 222
cartoons, 153
Casablanca, 180
CBFT, 84
CBMT, 84

CBS, *see* Columbia Broadcasting System
CBS Cable, 101, 145, 160, 164, 169, 258, 268, 311
CBS Publications, 252
Ceefax, 309, 329
cellular radio, 21
Central Policy Review Staff (CPRS), 51
Central TV, 49, 342, 352
'Challenge for Change', 91
Channel Four: advertisers and, 322-3, 324;
  audience share, 322, 336, 340, 341;
  co-productions, 352; film financing, 349-50;
  government regulations and, 69; and
  independent production, 63, 292, 353;
  minority interest programmes, 338;
  programming costs, 164; sports coverage, 321;
  see also Independent Broadcasting Authority;
  Independent Television
channel hopping, 159, 245
channels: electronically lockable, 75, 77, 194,
  284; benefits of increased availability, 61;
  viewers preference for number of, 137; *see also*
  individual types, e.g. business channels; pay-per-
  view
Chaplin, Charlie, 186
Chariots of Fire, 350, 352
Charterhouse Japhet, 72
Chataway, Christopher, 45, 51
Chicago, 126, 127, 129, 130, 132
childproof channels, 75, 77, 194, 284
children's services, 97, 153, 308, 311
Chinese-Americans, 210
Christian Broadcast Network (CBN), 152, 168,
  253
churn: and addictive programming, 183; and
  addressable systems, 142; local channels, 200;
  pay-per view, 195; in US, 134-5, 139-40, 177
Cincinnati, 126, 129, 195
cinema: British audiences, 294, 346-7; US
  audiences, 249; *see also* film industry; films
Cinematel, 49
Cinematograph Exhibitors' Association, 347
Cinemax, 128, 178, 179, 181, 185, 189, 266
Citicorp, 22
Cleveland, Ohio, 84
Club 403, 330, 331
CO-AX Cable Communications, 45
coaxial cables, 13-14, 17, 27, 58, 66
co-financed productions, 104, 105, 185, 252,
  257, 258, 259, 343, 349-52
Cohen, I.H., 54, 55
Colony Communications, 199, 203
Columbia Broadcasting System (CBS): in

Canada, 84; early experiments in pay-cable,
  121; film production, 182, 256, 257; invests in
  cable, 117; and localism, 115; videotex, 223
Columbia Pictures, 181, 182, 256, 257, 350
Columbus, Ohio: audience shares, 167, 194,
  204-6; alarm systems, 218, 219; broadcast
  network audience, 261; local government
  broadcasts, 210; pay-per-view channels, 199;
  Qube system, 126; subscribers, 244, 246;
  videotex service, 224-5
commercials, *see* advertising; infomercials
communal viewing, 194
communications satellites: American, 25,
  123-4, 144, 145, 146; broadcast networks, 267;
  Canadian, 96; domestic satellites, 25;
  ownership, 25-6; telecommunications and,
  24-5; *see also* direct broadcasting by satellites
  (DBS)
community antennae television (CATV), 12,
  302
community channels, 19; in Britain, 45-6, 69,
  76, 283-4, 325-8; in Canada, 86, 91-2, 95-6;
  in US, 79, 117, 140, 147, 174, 198, 201-8
CompuServe, 223, 224, 229, 230
computers, home, 230, 294, 329-30;
  transmission systems, 22-3
Comsat, 136
Comstar, 25
conferences, teleconferencing, 231, 232, 234-5,
  236
consolidated narrowcasting, 144
converters, 15, 129, 130, 297, 298
Cooney, Jerry, 192, 193, 195
co-productions, 103, 104, 351-3; *see also*
  co-financed productions
Coral Gables, 222
Coronation Street, 156
Courtney, Roger, 53
Cowan, Edgar, 101
Cox Cable: business services, 235, 236; and the
  New Orleans franchise, 130; pay-per-view,
  191, 192, 196, 268; signal theft, 135; and
  Spotlight, 146, 179; videotex service, 225, 231
Cox Communications, investment in cable, 27,
  116, 128
cross-ownership, 127-8
crosstalk, 14
Croydon, 305
CSS Promotions, 319
CTV, 86, 99, 109

Dale City, 117

374

Dallas, 126, 129, 140
Dallas, 269
Daniel and Associates, 175
Daniels, 235
The Dark Crystal, 181
data communication terminals, 22-3
data transmission: in Britain, 289, 332; in US, 231-8
Davies, C.A., 54
Davies & Co., 129
Daytime; ABC and, 268; advertising on, 158, 160; annual expenditure, 159; and magazine publishers, 252; merger with CHN, 145, 160; programme saleability, 252; sponsorship, 253; in Syracuse, 201; women-orientated programmes, 160, 171, 172
Dearborn, 235
decoders, 15, 129, 130, 297, 298
dedicated access channels, 209-10, 213; *see also* access channels
Deloitte, Haskins and Sells, 305
Denver, 129
Department of Industry (UK), 52, 53-4
Department of Trade and Industry (UK), 54, 279
Department of Transport (Canadian), 85
deregulation, *see* regulation
descramblers, 15
Detroit, 127, 132
Development of Cable Systems and Services (Cmnd 8866), 4, 276-91, 296, 300-1, 318, 335-6, 347
digital signal transmission, 12
Digital Termination Service (DTS), 237
direct broadcasting by satellites (DBS): in Britain, 53, 283, 313; and cable systems, 141; Canadian, 96; and future cable growth, 28-9; interstate 'footprint' of, 30; in US, 123, 136-7, 144, 145, 146
disconnections (churn): and addictive programming, 183; and addressable systems, 142; local channels, 200; pay-per-view, 195; in US, 134-5, 139-40, 177
Disney, Walt, 265
Disney Channel: in Britain, 309-10; competition for Nickelodeon, 153; description of, 186; exclusive programming, 180, 181, 188; and low capacity systems, 189; and moral attitudes, 186, 189; and programme production, 254, 258
disposable traps, 192
domestic satellites (domsats): United States, 25

Donaldson, Lufkin and Jenrette, 142, 190
Dow Jones, 128, 223, 225, 227
Doyle Dane Bernbach, 161, 226
The Draughtsman's Contract, 350
The Dresser, 350
Dunn, R., 328
duplication of programmes, 145-6; *see also* repeats

Eady levy, 351-2
East Lansing, 213
East Midlands Allied Press, 330
Echo 1, 24
Eckersley, Peter, 38, 40
economic growth: cable and, 29; information technology and, 68
Economist Intelligence Unit, 292
Edgbaston, 330
Edinburgh Television Festival, 339
Edmonton, 86
education programming: in Britain, 283, 308, 311, 318; dedicated access, 209, 210, 213
Ehrenberg, A., 68, 69
elderly people: access channels, 210; and local originated channels, 202; medical alert buttons, 220; as subscribers, 242, 243; videoconferencing, 232
electronic funds transfer (EFT), 225, 226
Electronic Funds Transfer Institute, 226
electronic mail, 231
Electronic Rentals Group (ERG), 44, 71
electronics industry, 29, 30
Electrophone Company, 35
Elie and St Eustache, 96
ELRA Group, 140
Elstree, 350
emergency services, 215, 217-21
EMI, 256; *see also* Thorn-EMI
employment, cable industry and, 57, 68, 300-1
'English Channel', 156, 265
enhanced services: in Britain, 294, 308-9, 328-34; in US, 215-38
Entertainment and Sports Programming Network (ESPN): ABC and, 191, 268; advertising, 157, 158, 159, 160, 161, 163-4, 165, 166, 170-1; finance, 154, 156, 157-8; ownership, 28; programme saleability, 252
The Entertainment Channel: BBC and, 187, 343; co-financed productions, 350; description, 187; failure, 101, 145, 187; and PBS, 264; pilots of series on, 181; use of filmed stage plays, 187, 258

equipment, British, 296-300
Eros, 186
Escapade, 187
ethnic programming, 187-8, 195, 310
European Music Satellite, 343-4
European Space Agency, 26
European Telecommunications Satellite Organisation (Eutelsat), 26
Euston Films, 349
evangelical services, 152
exhibitionism, 211
export opportunities, 57, 68
Exxon, 28

Falcon's Gold, 183
Falls River, 203
false alarms, security systems, 218, 220
Falwell, Jerry, 152
The Far Pavilions, 257, 351, 352
FBI, 217
Federal Communications Commission (FCC), 24, 25, 56, 114-23, 128, 131, 132, 136, 208, 237, 270
Federal Cultural Policy Review Committee, 93-4, 98, 100, 109
Ferranti, 297
film channels: in Britain, 183; in Canada, 101-2; experiments in, 17-19; in US, 80, 122, 133, 146, 178-87
film industry: cable TV and, 60; in Canada, 102-6; cinema attendance in Britain, 294, 346-7; cinema attendance in US, 249; concentration of power, 73; effect of cable on in US, 270-2; effect of cable on in Britain, 60, 346-54; HBO and, 179-82; and pay-TV, 180-3, 253-9; and pay-per-view, 191; revenue, 348-9
films: audience ratings, 262-3; on British cable, 308, 310, 311-16, 317-18; and broadcast networks in Britain, 338; and broadcast networks in US, 265; and Canadian programming, 99, 101-2; co-finance, 349-50; duplication between services, 180; exclusive rights, 180, 181, 256; made-for-pay, 181, 183, 184, 185; made-for-TV, 269; pay-per-view, 191, 192-3, 194, 347-8; pay services and, 179-83, 184-5, 187; 'R'-rated, 183, 186-7, 194; repeats, 180; on US cable TV, 118, 119, 123, 178-87; video recorders and, 295, 308; viewing habits, 243; 'X' rated, 47, 75, 77, 284-5, 318
Filmways, 256
finance: access channels, 212-13; advertising, 10, 158-76; and cable growth in Britain, 305-7;

cabled videograms, 221; Canadian pay-TV, 100-6; capital costs in Britain, 129-30, 305-6; co-financed productions, 104, 105, 185, 252, 257, 258, 259, 343, 349-52; competition for sources of, 3, 58-9; film production, 255, 256-8; 'free' services, 154; industry's debt in US, 134; initial, 32, 57; investment in Britain, 57-8, 66-7, 70, 278; investment in US, 121, 129; licence fees, 10, 336-7, 339, 344; local programming, 207, 208; pay-per-view, 192-5; pay service, 177-90; per-subscriber/ advertiser-supported service, 124, 154-8; on programming, 57, 68-9, 102-6, 107, 251-2; rate of return in Canada, 87; rate regulation, 131; regulatory and franchise expenditure, 135; subscriber expenditure, 248-50; subscriber-related costs, 130; US franchise fees, 120, 127, 130; US revenue growth, 121, 125, 133; videotex, 227-8
'financial interest' rule, 270
fire-alarm systems, 215-20
firemen, training films, 210, 233
First Choice Canadian Communications, 98, 99-106, 186, 257
First Love, 350
Fleet Holdings, 351
Fogo Island, 91
Ford, Gerald, 126
Ford Motors, 235
foreign DBS channels, 30-1
foreign-language minorities, 188, 203, 210, 310
Fox, Francis, 83
Fraggle Rock, 183, 184, 258
France: control over television signals, 30; electronics industry, 29; broadband cable TV development, 32
Frances, 181
franchise: in Britain, 74, 76, 278-82, 292, 300, 303; in US, 125-33
'free' services, 152

Galavision, 187-8
Galaxie, 97, 200
The Games Network, 221, 222, 332
Gandhi, 350
Gaumont Films, 168
Gavin, Bill, 351
GEC, 296, 297, 329
GEC-Jerrold, 297, 298
GEC McMichael, 297, 298, 332
GEC-Marconi, 26
General Electric Corporation, 27

General Instrument, 221
George and Mildred, 349
Germany: broadband cable TV development, 32; control over television signals, 30
Getty/ABC, 166
Getty Oil, 28
Gill, Barrie, 319
Gill Cable, 174, 200
Glovertown, 90
Goldcrest, 26, 257, 313, 317, 339, 349, 350, 351, 352
Goldwater, Barry, 135
GPO: and relay exchanges, 36, 38, 40
Grampian TV, 303, 305
Granada, 342
Greater London Council, 301, 326
Greenwich Cablevision, 45-6, 48, 49
Gregory's Girl, 349, 350
Greif, Frank, 140
Group W Cable, 128, 142, 199, 200, 235
Guildford, 303
Guinness Mahon, 351

Harrow, 305
Hartford, Conn., 121
Hartley, D.F., 54
Hattersley, Roy, 65, 276, 278
headend, 12
Hearst Group, 28, 223, 252
Hearst/ABC, 158, 160, 166
Hearst Cable Communications, 166
Heaven's Gate, 255
Hemmings, Tony, 319
Henson, Jim, 183
Hirsch, Michael, 107
Hitler, Adolf, 30
Hodgson, Sir Maurice, 65
Holiday Inn Video Network (HI-NET), 235
Holmes, Larry, 192, 193, 195
home banking, *see* telebanking
Home Box Office (HBO): audience rating, 262; and Canadian productions, 104, 105; children's services, 153; co-financed productions, 104, 105, 343, 350, 351, 352; description of, 122-4; direct reception in Canada, 108; and the FCC's restrictions, 119; on local services, 200; ownership, 127; pay-per-view, 191; pay services, 27, 178, 179, 180-2, 183, 184, 185; and programme production, 254, 256-7, 259; satellite distribution, 123, 144, 145, 146; sporting events, 262; Thibodaux franchise, 125

home computers, 230, 294, 329-30; telesoftware, 330, 332
Home Office (UK), 52, 53-4, 65, 279
Home Theater Network, 128
Home Theater Network Plus, 185, 189, 190
Homelink, 330-1
hotels, teleconferences, 235
Horizon, 51
housing density, and cable installation, 128-30
Houston, 126, 131, 133, 135, 195
HTV, 77, 351
Hughes Communications, 25
Humbard, Rex, 152
Hunt Committee: Report, 73-8; submissions to, 65-73; White Paper and, 276-90

IBM, 27, 296, 329
ICL, 51
ILR, 286, 287
Indax, 192, 225, 228
Independent Broadcasting Authority (IBA); and advertising on cable, 287, 290; competition with BBC, 3; foreign programme quotas, 337; and Hunt Inquiry, 69, 71, 74; programme codes, 69
independent production: in Canada, 103; Channel Four and, 63; effect of cable on in Britain, 61, 346-54
Independent Television (ITV): and advertising on cable, 286-7; audience share, 337, 338-43; effect of cable on, 335-45; films on, 338; films made for and by, 349; foreign material quotas, 288, 337-8; and growth of cable TV, 42; Hunt Report and, 74-5, 77; income, 337, 342; material used in US, 153, 156; sports coverage, 320; teletext, 21
Independent Television Companies Association (ITCA), 287, 290
infomercials, 161
information industry, workforce, 23
information services: in Britain, 328, 329-30; in US, 215-16, 223-31
information technology: investment in, 67; ITAP report, 54-60; political policy, 51-4
Information Technology Advisory Panel (ITAP); Report, 32, 52, 54-60; reaction to Report of, 60, 64-73
Information Technology Unit, 52, 53
Information Technology Year, 52
information transmission, 21, 67
Inspirational Network, 152
Institute of Practitioners in Advertising (IPA),

72, 323
institutional loops, 125, 127, 231-8
Intelsat, 26, 316
integrated business systems, 26-7
Interactive Services, 332
interactive systems: in Britain, 280, 308-9;
  definition, 15; local services, 206; in US, 126,
  127, 144, 192-6, 198, 216
Inter-American Satellite Television, 136
interconnects, 174-5
International Racing Bureau, 319
International Satellite Telecommunications
  Organisation (Intelsat), 26
interpersonal communication, 9
Intimate Strangers, 257
investment: in Britain, 57-8, 60, 66-7, 70, 278;
  in US, 121, 129
ITV, *see* Independent Television

Jacksonville, 207
Jamaica Inn, 352
Japan, broadband cable TV development, 32
Jay, Peter, 78
Jerrold, 297, 299
Joslin, Raymond, 166

'Ka' band, 25
Kagan, Paul, 181, 192, 219
Kansas City, 203
Key Channel, 318
The Killing Fields, 350
King, Don, 191
Kirk, Stephen, 296
Knight Ridder, 128, 223, 229
Koplovitz, Kay, 156-7
KTVU Oakland, 145
'Ku' band, 25

Lambert, Verity, 352
Lansford, 114
The Learning Channel, 152
leased-access channels, 198, 209; *see also* access
  channels
Le Duc, D.R., 86
Lee, James, 339
leisure time, allocation, 246-7
Lemieux, P.H., 162
Lewis, Drew, 216
Lexis, 223
licence fees, 10, 336-7, 339, 344; dodgers, 10
Life on Earth, 352
Link Sound and Vision Ltd, 42

Littlechild, Stephen, 26
Littlewoods, 305
Live and Learn, 194-5
Lively Arts Market Builders, 98-9
Liverpool Post, 305
local advertising, 173-6
local government: British, 282; dedicated
  access, 209-10, 213; local origination
  channels, 211; *see also* franchise
Local Hero, 350, 352
local newspapers, 72, 204, 282
local origination channels (LO), 201-8, 211
local radio, and local advertising, 174-5
local services: in Britain, 283-4, 325-8; in
  Canada, 91-2, 95-6; in US, 117, 140, 144, 198-
  214; standalone channels, 199-200; *see also*
  access channels; community channels
lockable channels, 75, 77, 194, 284
London, 301, 310, 332
London, Ontario, 84
London Dockland Development Corporation,
  296
London Hydraulic Power Company, 296
London Transport, 296
London Weekend Television, 77, 257, 337, 338,
  341
The Long Good Friday, 349
Lorimar, 256

McCombs, M.E., 248-9
McCormack, Mark, 319
McKeesport, 203
McWilliam, John, 297
made-for-pay, 183, 185, 254, 257, 258
made-for-TV films, 269
Madison Square Garden Sports, 156
magazines, promotion, 252
'The Magic Touch', 206
mail order, 225
The Making of a Continent, 352
The Maltese Falcon, 180
Manhattan, 117, 199, 209, 210, 233
Manhattan Cable, 142, 145, 146, 173, 175, 201,
  233, 234, 236
Marlowe Private-Eye, 257
*M*A*S*H*, 266
master antennae television (MATV), 12, 302
Maton, A.W., 36
Mattel, 221
MCI Communications, 24, 236, 237
Mead Data Central, 223
medical alert system, 215, 218

Mellersh, Nicholas, 349
Mercury: all cable systems to be compatible with, 280; backing, 24, 28; business services, 332-3; formed, 24; Goldcrest and, 26; optic trunk lines, 53; relations with cable operators, 288-9
Meredith Corporation, 253
Merriman Report (1982), 9
Merseyside Cablevision, 305
Metromedia, 257, 351
MGM, 256
MGM/UA, 181
Miami, 126
microcomputers, 230, 294, 329-30; telesoftware, 330, 332
Micronet 800, 329-30
Milne, Alasdair, 77
Milton Keynes, 45, 46, 331, 332
mini-series, 269
mini-star system, 298
Minneapolis, 237
minority interests, 11, 69; *see also* special interest groups, *and individual groups*
Mobil, 28
modems, 230, 329
Modern Satellite Network (MSN), 145, 161, 201, 253
Modern Talking Picture Service, 253
monitoring, audience, 40
monopolies, 71, 76, 132; local, 61
Montagu, Samuel, 351
Montreal, 83, 85
Moonlighting, 350
moral standards, 62; *see also* adult films
Motion Picture Exporters Association of America, 49
The Movie Channel (TMC), 122, 146, 154, 178-9, 181, 182, 185, 200
multi-pay services, 142, 177, 185
multiple system operators (MSO), concentration of major, 132; and cross-media ownership, 127-8; financial base, 139; and programme service interests, 132; rise of, 116-17; *see also* individual operators
multi-point distribution services (MDS), 136-7, 141
Murdoch, Rupert, 28, 136
Music Box, 319
Music Channel, 319, 342
music channels, 318-19, 321, 343
Music Corporation of America (MCA), 157, 179, 181, 182, 191

Music Television (MTV), 154, 159, 169-70, 172
Music Vision, 318
'must carry' rule, 40, 283

Nally, West, 319
Naples, Florida, 203
narrowcast channels: advertising, 162-3, 171-3; pay services, 185-9; revenue from, 69
The Nashville Network, 128
National Broadcasting Company (NBC), 115, 266, 267, 269
National Cable Television Association (NCTA), 29, 117, 135, 137
National Coal Board, 351
National Collegiate Athletics Association, 154
National Economic Research Associates (NERA), 129
National Electronics Council Working Party on Technological Opportunities in Broadcasting, 68
National Film Board of Canada, 91
National Film Finance Corporation, 352
National League of Cities, 134
The Nation's Health, 352
Neave, Airey, 51
Netherlands, 36, 37
New Bedford, 203
New Orleans, 130, 225
new towns, 42
New World Pictures, 256
New York, 116, 126, 136, 211, 225, 233
New York Times Cable, 201
New York Times Company, 128
Newhouse, 128
News International, 28
news programming, 145-6, 155, 264, 268; local, 203, 204
News Retrieval, 223, 225
newspapers: local, 72, 204, 282; local advertising, 175
Nickelodeon, 145, 153-4, 172, 200, 201, 251, 252
Nicholas Nickleby, 253, 352
Nielsen, A.C., 161, 167, 203
1941, 255
Noble Grossart, 351
Not the Nine O'Clock News, 183
Nottingham Building Society, 330-1

Oak Industries, 192, 297, 299
off-air subscription television (STV), 135, 136-7, 141
Office of Telecommunications (OFTEL), 279

Olympic Games, 196, 266
Omaha, 225
On Golden Pond, 181, 256
'On the Cable: the Television of Abundance',
  121
Ontario, 97, 106
ONTV, 266
optic-fibre cables, 13-14, 17, 27, 53, 66, 96-7,
  126, 296
Optical Systems Corp, 123
Oracle, 309, 329, 331
Orion, 256, 350
Orion and International Satellites, 26
Orion Pictures, 181, 182
Orlando, 228
ownership: cross-media ownership, 127-8; and
  operators, 72-3; and operating
  responsibilities, 70-1; restrictions in Britain,
  282; restrictions in US, 118

packaging services, 139-40
PAL patents, 28
Palace Video, 319
Palmer Cablevision, 203
The Paper Chase, 183, 184, 257, 258, 266
Paramount; backs USA Network, 156, 191;
  co-financed films, 350; entertainment
  specials, 266; experimental pay-cable, 121;
  and HBO exclusive rights, 181; prohibited
  from backing showtime, 179, 182
Park Cities, 225
pay-per-view: in Britain, 75, 76, 77, 285, 347-8;
  in US, 190-7, 266, 271
pay-TV; and advertising, 188: in Britain, 47-9,
  311-18; in Canada, 97-111; experiments in,
  47-9; and film production, 253-9; films on,
  179-83, 184-5, 187, 270; multi-point
  distribution services, 136; off air subscription
  television, 135, 136; ownership, 178-9;
  programme production, 253-9; prohibition in
  Canada, 86, 87; rate regulation, 131; revenue
  from, 29, 142, 266; signal theft, 134, 135;
  specialist channels, 185-9; sports events, 77,
  188-9; in US, 120-4, 125, 133, 142, 177-90;
  viewing preference and programming policy,
  61
Pay Television Ltd, 44
Peabody, 161
Pearson Longman, 72-3, 305
penalty clauses, franchise agreements, 130
Penthouse, 186
per-subscriber services, 124, 152-4; advertiser-

supported services, 154-8
Philadelphia, 132
Philips, 297, 298
Philips Cablevision, 48, 49
Philips Electronics, 28
piggy-backing, 144, 145, 171, 201
Pilkington Bros, 305
Pilkington Committee, 44
Pinewood, 350
The Pirates of Penzance, 192, 193
Pittsburgh, 126, 138, 195, 202, 216
Playboy Channel, 105, 107, 186, 188, 189, 253,
  258
Playcable, 221, 222
Plessey, 296, 297, 298, 299, 300, 305
The Ploughman's Lunch, 350, 352
Poldark, 352
political affairs programming, 152-3
political factors; cable and, 29, 51-80
polling, electronic, 206
Polygram, 256
pop-music services, 311, 343
pop-videos, 169, 170, 319
pornography, 75, 186-7, 209, 211; in Britain,
  285; *see also* adult films *and individual channels*
Porridge, 349
Portland, Oregon, 194, 198, 200, 201, 210, 227,
  228
Portsmouth and Sunderland Newspapers, 303
Portuguese immigrants, 203
Post Office Engineering Union (POEU), 67
Post Office Superannuation Fund, 351
Premier, 182
Premier Company, 87
pre-financing deals, 257, 259
Press Construction, 305
Prestel, 21, 67, 215, 222, 229, 231, 329-31
Prisoners of the Lost Universe, 351
programming: addictive, 183; American in
  Canada, 86, 88, 89-90, 93; and audience
  preference, 61; in Britain, 292, 310, 311; British
  competitiveness in, 75, 77; British
  regulations, 283; Canadian expenditure on,
  102-6; choice, 62-3; co-financed, 104, 105, 185,
  252, 257, 258, 259, 343, 349-52; duplication,
  145-6; early cable experiments, and, 44, 47,
  49; effect on film and production industries in
  Britain, 292, 346-54; exclusivity, 286; finance,
  57, 68-9, 102-6, 167, 251-2; from US, 60, 75,
  77, 86, 88, 89-90, 93, 287-8, 337-8; increased
  channel availability and, 61; and multi-
  programme choice, 69; New York compared

380

with London, 62-3;production in US, 251-60; quality on pay services, 184; repeats, 145-6, 180, 187, 188, 208, 251, 262; sponsored, 253-4, 320, 321, 323, 327; statutory minimum in Canada, 89; use of foreign material on British cable, 287-8, 337-8; video promotions, 252, 253
Prudential Assurance, 351
Prudential Life Assurance Company, 22
public access channels, *see* access channels
public affairs, 152-3
Public Broadcasting Service, 183, 184, 258, 264-5, 267, 350
Puttnam, David, 348

Qube system, 126, 138, 192, 194-6, 206, 225, 227
Quebec, 97, 106

'R' rated films, 183, 186-7, 194; *see also* 'X' rated films
Racal, 297
Racal-Oak, 297, 305
radio, relay exchanges, 36-41
Radio Corporation of America (RCA) 25, 27, 145, 167, 187
Radio Luxembourg, 38
Radio Monte Carlo, 168
Radio Normandie, 38
Radio Rentals, 42, 48, 49, 316; teletext, 331, 332
Radio Rentals-EMI, 45
Raiders of the Lost Ark, 350
rate regulation, 131
RCA, 25, 27, 145, 167, 187
Read, Charles, 53, 54
Readers Digest, 223
Readers Digest, 252, 253
Reading, Penn., 214, 232
Reaves Cable productions, 251
reception, control over, 31
Red Monarch, 350
Rediffusion: in Canada, 84; community channels, 45; first pay channel offered, 47-9; hardware and systems manufacture, 297, 299, 303; new systems prepared, 302, 303; other services, 43-4; overseas expansion, 42; patnerships, 316; relay services, 37, 38, 42; teletext, 331
Rediffusion Computers, 43, 329
Rediffusion Films, 349, 351
regional interest channels, 145
regulations: in Britain, 61-2, 66, 69, 70-1, 73-4, 275-91; broadcasting services, 69; in Canada,

30, 85-6, 87-8, 90, 93; deregulation in US, 118-20; US, 115-20, 237-8
Reith, Sir John, 38
relay exchanges, 36-41
Relay Services Association, 39, 40
religious channels, 152, 253, 327
religious groups, in Britain, 282
religious programming, 253
remote controlled TV, 159, 245, 293, 322
repeats, 145-6, 251; broadcast networks, 262; films, 180; foreign language minorities, and, 187, 188; local services, 208; pay services, 184; serious material, 264; summer, 268-9
revenue, *see* finance
Rhode Island, 199
Ridgewood, N.J., 223
Right of Way, 257
Ring, James, 65
RKO, 121
Robin Hood, 351
Rockefeller Inc., 187
Rogers Cablesystems; in Britain, 150; business services, 235; children's channels, 97; commercial deletion, 88; community programming, 201, 204; security systems, 96; share of Canadian market, 87
Rolling Stones, 192
Romance, 183
Roots, 269
Royal Shakespeare Company, 253
Ruffell, D., 332

Sacramento, 126
St Louis, 126
San Diego, 116, 126, 135, 225, 228-9
San Francisco, 174, 200, 236
San Jose, California, 167, 174
Sandles, Arthur, 77
Sapper, Alan, 77
Saskatchewan Telecommunications Co., 96
Satcom I, 25, 123, 145
Satcom II, 25
Satcom IIIR, 146
Satcom IV, 187
Satellite Business Systems (SBS), 25, 236, 237
Satellite Master Antenna TV (SMATV), 136, 137, 140-1
Satellite News Channel (SNC), 155, 156, 268
Satellite Program Network (SPN), 162, 168-9, 170, 171, 252
Satellite Television (SATV), 28
Satellite Television Corporation, 136

satellites, *see* communications satellites; direct broadcasting by satellite (DBS)
Saturday Night Fever, 262
Schacht, M., 328
Scientific Atlanta, 297, 298, 299, 300
Scottish TV, 349
Screen Sport, 319
Scripps, C.E., 248
SCTV Network, 266
SECAM, 300
security systems: in Britain, 309, 328, 329; false alarms, 218, 220; in US, 126, 215, 217-21
Select TV, 48, 49
Selkirk Communications, 45
Selsdon, Lord, 39, 40
senior citizens: access channels, 210; and local originated channels, 202; medical alert buttons, 220; as subscribers, 242, 243; videoconferencing, 232
series, 183; programme loyalty, 245
serious programmes, 264
'La Sette', 97
ShareCom, 237
Sheffield, 45, 46
Sheinberg, S.J., 255
Shelmerdine, Mark, 49
shopping services (teleshopping), 17, 19; in Britain, 55, 309, 328, 330; in US, 215, 216, 223-31
Showtime: 'adult' content, 186; anti-competitive laws and ownership of, 178-9, 182; audience appeal, 185; co-finance, 104, 351; as a film service, 178-9, 181, 182, 183, 185, 263; on local channels, 200; non-theatrical film, 183; pay-per-view, 191; programme production, 184, 253, 257-8; productions in Canada, 104; series, 183, 184, 266; subscribers switched to Spotlight, 146
signal enhancement, cable services, 18, 41-4, 114-15
signal theft, 134, 135, 139
signals, digital, 12
Silver Screen Partners, 257
Singer, Aubrey, 344
Six Weeks, 181
Sky Channel, 321, 324
Slan, Jon, 105
Sloan Commission, 121
Smiley's People, 350
Smith, Anthony, 20, 351
Smith, Ralph Lee, 121
Smith, W.H., 330, 332

Smith Cable Security, 218
Snow White, 186
Soap, 266
'Soap Scoop', 206
Sofirad, 168
software, telesoftware, 330, 332
Solent Cablevision, 296
Solihull, 330
Sophie's Choice, 181, 256
Sophisticated Ladies, 193
The Source, 223, 225, 227
Southern Pictures, 349
Southern Satellite Systems, 168
Southgate, C.G., 54
Southgate, Calif., 121
Spanish International Network (SIN), 161, 168-9
Spanish language services, 187-8, 189
spare time allocation, 246-7
special interest services, 56, 59, 172-3; advertising on, 163; pay services, 185-9; *see also* narrowcasting *and individual interests, e.g.* religious channels; sport
sponsored programmes: in Britain, 320, 321, 323, 327; in US, 253-4
sports events: in Britain, 47, 59, 77, 285-6, 319-21; in Canada, 89; local coverage, 192, 204, 327; minority sports events, 321; pay-per-view, 191, 348; pay services, 178; regional, 145; on US cable, 118, 119, 157, 171, 178, 183, 188, 266
Spotlight, 146, 179, 183
Squaring the Circle, 351
stage shows, filmed, 187, 258
Stagecoach, 180
standalone channels, 145, 199-200
standards, technical, 58, 68
Star Wars, 192, 262, 338, 350
Starr, Ringo, 305, 319
Stoppard, Tom, 351
Storer, 27, 117, 126, 128, 133, 135, 138, 146, 179, 235
subscribers: in Britain, 295-6; churn, 134-5, 139-40, 142, 177, 183, 195, 200; expenditure by, 246-50; freedom of choice, 146; growth rate in US, 133; and local services, 202, 206-7; use of time, 246-8; in USA, 133, 239-50; viewing habits, 243-5; *et passim; see also* audiences
summer audiences, 262, 268
Superchannel, 105, 106
Superman, 350
supply and demand, 11

Sutherland, Muir, 338
Sutton Coldfield, 330
Swindon, 47, 327, 332
switched star systems, 15, 17, 18, 58, 280, 281, 298, 300
switching points, 17
Syncom II, 24
Syracuse: churn, 134, 135; community programming, 201, 204, 305; security systems, 217, 218, 219-20; subscribers in, 242
Syracuse Cablesystems, 175, 218, 305, 369-70
System Eight, 299

Table for Five, 268
target-casting, 171
Tarlton, R.J., 114
Taxi, 184, 258, 266
Taylor, Arthur, 187
TDF, 97
technical standards, 58, 68
technology, 12-18; bandwidth, 12; British hardware, 296-300; capacity, 13; co-axial cables, 13-14, 17, 27, 58, 66; mini-star system, 298; multi-pair copper cables, 12-13; optic-fibre cables, 13-14, 17, 27, 53, 66, 96-7, 126, 296; relay exchanges, 36-41; standards, 58, 68; switched-star system, 15, 17, 18, 58, 280, 281, 298, 300; terminology, 12-18; tree and branch system, 15, 17, 18, 58, 281, 297, 298
telebanking, 17, 19; in Britain, 308-9, 328, 329, 330-1, 333; in US, 215, 223-31
Telecable Videotron, 97
teleconferencing, 231, 232, 234-5, 236
telecommunications, 20-32; communications satellites, 24-5; growth, 21-2; and information transfer, 21-3; lines, 12, 13; monopolies broken, 23-4, 53; political parity, 51-4; privatisation, 23-4, 53
Telecommunications Inc (TCI), 132, 146, 179
TeleFirst Entertainment Recording Services, 268, 333
TeleFrance USA, 168
Telefusion, 42, 43, 302, 305
Teleprompter, 27, 121
teleshopping, 17, 19; in Britain, 55, 309, 328, 330; in United States, 215, 216, 223-31
telesoftware, 330, 332
Teletel, 222
Television Entertainment Group (TEG), 311, 316, 322
television receive only (TVRO), 123, 124, 136, 146

teletext services, 56; in Britain, 21, 309, 329-30, 331, 332, 333; business, 231-8; in US, 199, 215, 222-38; *see also individual services, e.g.* Prestel
Telidon, 96, 199, 222, 227
TEN, 311, 316, 322
terminology, cable, 12-18
The Terry Fox Story, 257
Tesler, Brian, 339
Texas Instruments, 22
Thames TV, 44, 338, 342
Thatcher, Margaret, 51, 52
theatre, productions, filmed, 187, 258
TheatreVision, 123
theft, signal, 134, 135, 139
Thibodaux, 125
33 Brompton Place, 183
The Thorn Birds, 269
Thorn-EMI, 296; and British cable, 28, 71; data transfer, 332; film production, 351, 352; local services, 327; music channels, 319; system development, 280, 297, 298; video games channel, 332; videotex services, 329
Thompson, J. Walter, 161, 171
Thomson, Lord, 77
Thomson, D.C. & Co., 303, 305
Time Inc.; and ATC, 27, 127; creates first pay network, 27; electronic publishing, 227; and HBO, 122, 123; and Manhattan Cable, 142; pay services, 122, 178, 179; teletext services, 228-9; and USA Network, 156, 191
Time Life, 350
Time-Life Films, 256
Time Teletext, 228-9
Time-Shared Telidon, 228
Time Video Information Services, 228-9
Times-Fiber, 126, 297, 298, 299
Times-Mirror: and Brookline system, 138; business services, 235-6; cable interests, 27, 128; enhanced services, 223, 225, 228; and Spotlight, 146, 179
Tinker, Tailor, Soldier, Spy, 350, 352
Tocom, 218
Tootsie, 181
Top of the Pops, 343
Toronto, 85, 213
training programmes, 210, 232-3
trans-border television, 30-1
Transworld International, 319
tree and branch systems, 15, 17, 18, 58, 281, 297, 298
Tribune Corporation, 128
Tri-Star, 257

383

Trinity, 152
Tucson, 225
Turner, Ted, 123-4, 145, 154, 155, 267, 268
Turner Broadcasting System (TBS), 169
TV Eye, 337
TV South, 303, 342, 351
TV-AM, 322-3, 324
TVEC, 106
20th Century-Fox, 181, 182, 193, 257, 258
twenty-four hour services: advertising, 157; in
   Britain, 309; pay-per-view, 194; pay services,
   180; piggy-backing, 145-6; repeat material,
   157, 171, 172
two-way interactive services, 126, 127, 151,
   192-6, 216
Twickenham, 350
Tymnet, 237

UEI, 297, 298
'Ugly George', 209
UHF stations, in US, 115-16
Ulster TV, 303
underground cables, cost of, 129
Unisat, 26, 53
United Artists, 256
United Cable Programme (UCP), 311
United Media Finance, 351
United Satellite Communications Inc., 136
United States of America, 113-272; advertising
   in, 50, 69, 80, 158-76, 266-7; ban on cable's
   entry into major market, 116-18; business
   services, 231-8; Canadian programming in,
   104; Canadian reception of stations from,
   84-5, 93; capital costs, 129-30; community
   channels, 79, 117, 140, 147, 174, 198, 201-8;
   competition from other distribution systems,
   135-8, 140-1; cross ownership, 127-8;
   deregulation of cables, 115-20; distant signal
   limitations, 118; early cable development,
   114-15; effect of cable on broadcast networks,
   261-70; effect of cable on film industry, 270-2;
   enhanced services, 215-38; experience in
   cable, 79-80; franchising issues, 125-6, 127,
   129-33; growth of cable, 50, 67; increase in
   advertising, 59; industry's debt in, 134;
   influence on Canada, 83; investment in cable,
   129; local advertising, 173-6; local services,
   117, 140, 144, 198-214; pay-per-view, 190-7,
   266, 271; pay-TV, 120-4, 125, 133, 142, 177-90;
   present mood in, 138-43; programming from,
   60, 75, 77, 86, 88, 89-90, 93, 287-8, 337-8;
   regulation of cable, 115-20; restrictions on

cable ownership, 118; revenue growth, 125,
   133; satellite services, 123-4; subscribers in,
   133, 239-50; technology in Britain, 297-8, 299-
   300; telecommunications monopolies broken,
   24; UHF policy, 115-16
Universal, 193
universality of service, 3, 4
USA Network; advertising, 156, 158, 161, 168,
   170-1; cross media ownership and, 128;
   finance, 154; per-subscriber finance, 154,156;
   programming costs, 251, 252
utility companies, 215

Vancouver, 85, 225
Viacom, 117, 123, 128, 178, 181, 191, 235, 236
'Video Blue', 209
video promotions, 252, 253
video recorders (VCRs), 28, 31; and
   advertisements, 159; in Britain, 57, 67, 80,
   293-5; and consumer demand for
   programming, 29, 57; early development, 68;
   and films, 80, 294-5, 308, 338; time-shift
   viewing, 67, 293, 294; in US, 136, 141
videogames, 159, 216, 221-2, 249, 309, 332
videophiles, 239, 243
videophone services, 17, 19
videotex services, 56; in Britain, 21, 309, 329-
   30, 331, 332, 333; business, 231-8; in US, 199,
   215, 222-38; *see also individual services, e.g.* Prestel
Videotex Industry Association, 230
viewdata, *see* videotex
viewers, *see* audience; subscribers
Viewtel 202, 330
Viewtron, 229
violence, 75, 285; *see also* adult films
Virgin Records, 305, 319
Visionhire, 42, 43, 44, 48, 298, 302, 316, 343
Visnews, 321

Walter, 352
Walter and June, 352
Warner Amex: advertising, 159, 170; business
   services, 235; Dallas franchise, 129, 140;
   enhanced services, 216, 218, 219; investment,
   129; local services, 204-6; losses, 138;
   Nickelodeon, 153-4; no videogames channel,
   222; ownership, 28, 128; pay-per-view
   services, 190, 194-6; pay services, 178, 179, 181;
   Qube system, 126, 138; videotex services,
   224-5
Warner Amex Satellite Entertainment, 156
Warner Amex Security Systems, 218

Warner Bros., 180, 181, 182, 350
Warner Cable, 122
Warner Communications, 28
Washington, DC, 132
Weather Channel, 158, 159, 169, 253
Wellingborough, 45, 46
Wenham, Brian, 348
Westar I, 25
Westar II, 25
Western Union, 25, 296
Westinghouse, 27, 128, 155, 185-6, 188
Westminster, 331
Westminster Cable, 305, 331
WGN Chicago, 154, 155
Whitbread, 305
White Paper, *see Development of Cable Systems and Services*
Whitelaw, Lord, 1, 4, 46, 47, 64, 276
The Who, 192, 193
Wichita, 203
Wilkes Barre, 122, 261
The Winds of War, 269
Wirth, M.O., 190

Wolsey, 297
The Woman in White, 350
women-orientated programmes, 160, 170-1
The Woodlands, 218, 225
WOR New York, 154, 155
Wordley, R.W., 77
World Cable, 365
World in Action, 337
WTBS Atlanta, 123-4, 144, 145, 146, 154-5, 169, 170, 262, 267
Wyvern Television, 318

'X' rated films, 47, 75, 77, 284-5, 318; *see also* 'R' rated films
Xerox, 27

Yorkshire Television, 303, 342
Young and Rubicam, 322

Z Channel, 200
ZDF, 350
Zenaty, J.W., 190
Zenith, 121

DATE DUE

OCT 0 1 1998		
MAR 0 2 1999		